Mystics

Mystics

WILLIAM HARMLESS, S.J.

OXFORD
UNIVERSITY PRESS

2008

OXFORD
UNIVERSITY PRESS

Oxford University Press, Inc., publishes works that further
Oxford University's objective of excellence
in research, scholarship, and education.

Oxford New York
Auckland   Cape Town   Dar es Salaam   Hong Kong   Karachi
Kuala Lumpur   Madrid   Melbourne   Mexico City   Nairobi
New Delhi   Shanghai   Taipei   Toronto

With offices in
Argentina   Austria   Brazil   Chile   Czech Republic   France   Greece
Guatemala   Hungary   Italy   Japan   Poland   Portugal   Singapore
South Korea   Switzerland   Thailand   Turkey   Ukraine   Vietnam

Published by Oxford University Press, Inc.
198 Madison Avenue, New York, New York 10016

www.oup.com

Oxford is a registered trademark of Oxford University Press

Library of Congress Cataloging-in-Publication Data
Harmless, William, 1953–
Mystics / William Harmless.
    p. cm.
Includes bibliographical references and index.
ISBN 978-0-19-530038-3
ISBN 978-0-19-530039-0 (pbk.)   1. Mysticism.   2. Mystics.   I. Title.
BV5082.3.H37 2007
204'.22—dc22   2007014786

Printed in the United States of America
on acid-free paper

For my sister Jane

Acknowledgments

I wish to acknowledge the following publishers for their kind permission to use copyrighted material.

OneWorld Press for excerpts from:
Rumi: Past and Present, East and West: The Life, Teachings and Poetry of Jalāl al-Din Rumi by Franklin Lewis. © 2000, OneWorld Press.

Oxford University Press for excerpts from:
Evagrius of Pontus: The Greek Ascetic Corpus by Robert E. Sinkewicz (trans.) (2005). By permission of Oxford University Press.
The Letters of Hildegard of Bingen (2005) by Joseph L. Baird and Radd K. Ehrman (trans.). By permission of Oxford University Press, Inc.
Rumi: The Masnavi: Book One (2004) by Jawid Majaddedi (trans.). By permission of Oxford University Press.

Paulist Press for excerpts from:
Bernard of Clairvaux: Selected Writings, Classics of Western Spirituality, by G. R. Evans (trans.), copyright © 1987, Paulist Press, Inc., New York/Mahwah, N.J. Used with permission of Paulist Press. www.paulistpress.com
Bonaventure: The Soul's Journey into God, The Tree of Life, The Life of St. Francis, Classics of Western Spirituality, by Ewert Cousins

(trans.) © 1978, Paulist Press, Inc., New York/Mahwah, N.J. Used with permission of Paulist Press. www.paulistpress.com

Meister Eckhart: The Essential Sermons, Commentaries, Treatises, and Defense, Classics of Western Spirituality, by Edmund Colledge and Bernard McGinn (trans.) © 1981, Paulist Press, Inc., New York/Mahwah, N.J. Used with permission of Paulist Press. www.paulistpress.com

Random House for excerpts from:

Conjectures of a Guilty Bystander by Thomas Merton, copyright © 1966 by The Abbey of Gethsemani. Used by permission of Doubleday, a division of Random House, Inc.

State University of New York Press for excerpts reprinted by permission from:

The Heart of Dōgen's Shōbōgenzō, translated by Norman Waddell and Masao Abe, the State University of New York Press © 2002, State University of New York. All rights reserved.

University of Chicago Press for excerpts from:

Mystical Poems of Rūmī, First Selection, Poems 1–200, translated by A. J. Arberry. © 1968, University of Chicago Press.

Preface

We teachers are privileged witnesses. Every now and then, in the swirl of this enterprise called education, we stumble upon these fragile, fleeting moments when the world suddenly stops in its tracks. It can happen during a lecture, as we struggle to pass on old things to new hearers. More often it happens when a student of ours speaks, eloquently on occasion, but more often haltingly, struggling to give voice to the newly glimpsed. Suddenly there is this silent, shared lightning flash of insight. Suddenly we see, and our students see—see things we thought we knew but see them now as if for the first time. If we could bottle such moments, if we could package them, we would. But there is no way to bottle or package epiphanies. In such moments, the classroom becomes sacred ground.

A moment like this happened several years ago when I was teaching a new undergraduate course on mysticism. We had been going along for a few weeks, reading a mystic a day. We began with a modern, Thomas Merton. From there we moved backward in time, back to two classic (and in many ways, opposite) figures: Teresa of Ávila and John of the Cross. We then began rummaging around the Middle Ages, with Bernard of Clairvaux and Aelred of Rievaulx, Francis of Assisi and Bonaventure. It was at this juncture in the semester when one of my students raised her hand. Class had just begun, and the other students were still settling into their seats. I called on her. She said, "I don't want to sound arrogant or anything. But you know—when I read these people, I think that I've experienced something like that. I am beginning to think that I'm a mystic—maybe, not the same way these people are, maybe not as intensely. But I know what they're talking about." There was a pause, then hand after hand began to rise. Each who spoke repeated something similar. These mystics were talking about things that they themselves had tasted, that they too had felt. I put aside the day's lecture. We had something urgent to talk about. We talked about the culture we live in, the way our world ignores—even silences—the mystical, the way it has deprived us of words, stopped us from speaking about the mystery that runs under and through our lives. We talked about the way the mystics give us a language, a vocabulary, to begin to articulate what we all taste and feel. We talked a little about Karl Rahner, about the way he suggests that being a mystic is a constituent element of the human person, that most of us are, in fact, repressed mystics.

This book takes its cues from what my students said on that remarkable day and on the many quieter, but no less remarkable, days since then. My students find that the mystics speak to them with an unexpected and uncanny immediacy—despite the historical gulfs and cultural chasms that divide the mystics' worlds from our own. They were struck—rightly, I believe—by what mystics said on three topics: who God is; how one meets God in prayer; and why the human heart is at once so deep, so beautiful, so selfish, and so hard to sort out. Our investigation here will hover around these three themes.

A book is not a classroom, of course, but I hope to give readers some taste of the dynamic that we used, one that helped the mystics and their message come alive in the classroom's ebb and flow. Most authors who write about mysticism do so in one of two ways. Many use the historical approach, using chronology to organize their survey of mystics and mystical movements; others use a systematic approach, arguing for a particular definition of what genuine mysticism is and then tracing out its dimensions, permutations, and implications. I tap on both approaches but adopt neither. Instead, I use a case-study method, focusing on individual mystics and their best-known writings. This case-study method attempts to balance depth and breadth. I realize that for most readers the great mystics are, at best, names they have heard. So it is crucial to begin with a biographical sketch. I also try, within the limits of this brief study, to situate individual mystics in their wider world, both historically and intellectually. I am concerned that too often mysticism gets presented as a network of psychological or theological abstractions, divorced from the life stories of those who have shaped it—as though it somehow takes place outside the bounds of time and space. Mysticism needs to stay embedded in the thicket of the history that created it.

Another matter: We meet mystics mostly through texts—those that history has chosen to preserve. That means that we need to respect mystical texts as texts, as literary artifacts. However much we may be tantalized to plunge in and dissect mystical experiences, our only access to a mystic's experiences is via texts. And each mystical text *as text* presumes certain things: it presumes a particular audience; it works within the confines and traditions of an inherited genre; it draws on favorite metaphors, quotes favorite scriptural texts, and sets itself within the tradition of (or over against) earlier mystical texts. There is nothing simple about interpreting any text, let alone a mystical one. As Bernard McGinn has insisted, "Mystical masterpieces, which are often close to poetry in ways in which they concentrate and alter language to achieve their ends, have all too often been treated like phone books or airline schedules: handy sources for confirming what we already expect."[1] We need to understand and respect mystical literature as literature, whether texts be autobiographies or biblical commentaries, poetry or sermons.

In a typical semester, I and my students study thirty or more mystics, one a day on average. Here I treat far fewer, only eight. Choosing whom to examine has not been easy, and one can easily argue about the inclusion or exclusion of this or that author. I have chosen not to study the two most famous Christian mystics, Teresa of Ávila and John of the Cross. The choice is deliberate. I fear that Teresa and John have become—perhaps despite themselves—paradigms against which all others are measured. That is unfortunate, and unfair both to the two Carmelites and to the wider Christian tradition. I have tried to choose mystics who as personalities are interesting in and of themselves and whose writings illustrate the pungent diversity of mystical voices.

I begin with two theorists of mysticism, Jean Gerson (1363–1429) and William James (1842–1910). Gerson, the great fifteenth-century churchman and theologian, provides a way to begin to think through the initial issue—and near-impossible task—of defining mysticism, what it is and what it is not. I pair him with William James, the father of American pragmatist philosophy and a pioneer in the modern field of psychology. James's *Varieties of Religious Experience* offered a pathbreaking psychological approach to mystical experience, one that, for better or worse, has set the terms for many modern investigations.

Chapter 2 looks at a recent mystic, the American monk Thomas Merton (1915–1968). He was arguably the most popular spiritual writer of the twentieth century and is best known for his autobiography, *The Seven Storey Mountain*. Merton wedded a passion for contemplation with a sharp-edged social conscience and an openness to the world's great spiritual traditions, especially Zen Buddhism. In many ways, Merton is an emblem for this whole book. The case studies that follow explore figures and trends that interested Merton and shaped his spirituality (e.g., the early Cistercians, the apophatic tradition, the desert fathers, and interreligious dialogue).

From there, we move backward in time, from the modern to the medieval, and look at four mystics: Bernard of Clairvaux (chapter 3), Hildegard of Bingen (chapter 4), Bonaventure (chapter 5), and Meister Eckhart (chapter 6). Bernard (1090–1153), an early Cistercian and the best-known preacher of his day, brought a passionate and poetic eloquence to his exegesis of the biblical Song of Songs and in the process expanded the many-splendored language of love.

Although men have dominated the making of Christian theology, women have been key players in the making of the Christian mystical tradition. And so in chapter 4, we will look at Hildegard of Bingen (1098–1179), one of the most brilliant and original women of the Middle Ages. She was a polymath: an abbess, a visionary, a poet and playwright, one of the earliest known composers in the history of Western music, and the first medieval woman given official papal approval to preach publicly.

The next chapters explore two theologian-mystics, Bonaventure (1217–1274) and Meister Eckhart (c. 1260–1327). Bonaventure was superior general of the Franciscans, a superb scholastic theologian, and a mystical writer of the first order. His treatise, *The Mind's Journey into God*, sets out a classic map of the mystic's pilgrimage. Meister Eckhart, a German Dominican, remains one of the most controversial mystics of the Christian tradition. He joined brilliant paradoxes, striking imagery, and provocative claims with all the subtleties of medieval scholasticism. Both men taught at the University of Paris, and both were recognized as leading theologians of their day. They illustrate the power—and the perils—of joining theology and mystical vision.

Chapter 7 steps back even further in time and explores the pioneers of Christian mysticism, the fourth-century desert fathers of Egypt. These early monks forged techniques of prayer and asceticism, of discipleship and spiritual direction, that have remained central to Christianity ever since. Intellectuals helped record and systematize this early mystical spirituality. The most important—but still little known or appreciated—is Evagrius Ponticus (345–399). He sought to map out the soul's journey to God and is best known for his formulation and analysis of the seven deadly sins. His disciple, John Cassian (c. 360–c. 435), ended up settling in southern France after long experience in monasteries of Egypt. Writing in Latin, he introduced the spirituality of Evagrius and the desert fathers to Western Christianity.

The next two chapters step out of the Christian experience and look at the issue of mysticism in the world religions. A common claim is the "common core" hypothesis, namely, that peak mystical experiences are ultimately the same the world over but are simply expressed differently by different individuals in different religions. To explore this claim—both its grain of truth and its severe limits—we will look (all too briefly) at mystical elements in Islam and Buddhism. Chapter 8 examines Rumi (1207–1273), a leading mystic of Islam and perhaps its finest poet, and chapter 9 examines Dōgen (1200–1253), the founder of Sōtō Zen and Japan's finest spiritual writer. These two men—exact contemporaries of one another and of Bonaventure and Thomas Aquinas—offer intriguing parallels to and striking contrasts with the Christian mystical tradition.

Chapter 10 shifts from looking at individual mystics to the broader question of the nature and varieties of mysticism. Here we take up theoretical issues and examine key threads in the century-long scholarly conversation on mysticism. I bring all this together under three broad headings: mystical texts, mystical communities, and mystical experiences. This three-sided optic provides, I believe, a way of mapping and defining the mystical. We close with a brief look at Karl Rahner, one of the finest theologians of the twentieth century, exploring his bold claim that being a mystic is not only normal, but, in fact, is constitutive of our very nature as human beings.

I intend this book as an introduction. There are already many big books on mysticism, and I hope this much briefer treatment may serve as an entry into those larger ones. I think particularly of Bernard McGinn's excellent, massive, multivolume (though still incomplete) study, *The Presence of God: A History of Western Christian Mysticism*. I also hope that my work will draw readers to explore mystical texts firsthand. Over the last generation, scholars have steadily translated most of the great Christian mystical texts into English. At the forefront of this effort has been the extraordinary 100-plus-volume series *Classics of Western Spirituality*, overseen by McGinn and published by the Paulist Press. The mystics need to be read, savored, and grappled with on their own terms and in their own words, and these recent translations do much to put individual mystics within the grasp of average readers. As I have written this book, I have again and again felt qualms about my brevity, what I have left out and what I have shortchanged by simplifying the profundity of individual mystics, the richness of their world, and the nuances of the scholarly research on them. My hope, in the end, is that the case studies that comprise this book will provide openings into more profound scholarly venues. I have tried to glean a few insights and attractive tidbits from that specialized scholarship. But I hope that others will use my gleanings as prompts to enter further and take up scholarly works that give individual mystics their due. So at the end of the book, I have appended annotated bibliographies to encourage readers to move into greater depths. Although much within each case study will be familiar to specialists, there are original threads, visible in the chapter titles and teased out in each chapter's conclusion, where I highlight a core insight that each case study brings to illuminating the broader phenomenon of mysticism.

This book, though introductory, does break new ground on several fronts. One original element is pedagogical. At first sight, the reverse chronology may look odd, but there is a logic to it: it moves from the more familiar to the less familiar. As we move along, the case studies focus on figures who, for many readers, will be increasingly remote in terms of context and, to some extent, increasingly difficult in terms of content. These case studies will (hopefully) train readers how to read these particular mystics. But I am equally concerned about method. I hope to help readers see how to read mystics and mystical literature in a broader sense, to provide them tools to read mystics and mystical literature beyond those few we touch upon here. The closing chapter makes that method explicit. It certainly brings together what we have studied, but it also provides lenses and analytical tools that may be applied beyond the scope of this book.

A second original element is analytical. Older theorists of mysticism tended to focus on the psychological—on mystical experiences. More recent theorists have tended to focus on the textual—on mystical literature. There is a third equally important element: mystical communities. Mystics typically belong to broader religious communities that have radically committed themselves to seeking God within the here and now—within the depths of their consciousness, within the fabric of their lives, and within the beauties of the natural world. These communities provide their members a rigorous and many-sided spiritual apprenticeship. Within these communities, instruction is often oral and, in many cases, takes place within ritual settings. Scholars, in focusing so much on the psychological or the textual, have tended to miss this. We need to recover the communal, oral, liturgical, and performative dimensions of the mystical. We also need to be alert to dynamics between spiritual masters and the disciples who surround them. In the closing chapter, I coin the term "calligraphers of the ineffable." Mystics themselves often use speech to point to realities that defy speech, to realities that are ineffable. Sometimes they do their own writing and so are themselves calligraphers of the ineffable. But in many cases, mystics attract disciples who transcribe their spoken words and create the written texts that have come down to us. Beyond that are the generations upon generations of scribes who have copied mystical texts and thereby preserved them over the centuries. If we want to understand mysticism, we need to be alert not simply to the mystics themselves, but also to their audiences within those mystical communities, to their transcribers and their copyists. Calligraphy has been a treasured art form among Muslims and

Buddhists, much as it was among medieval Christians. As we will see, this calligraphy of the ineffable is equally a fine art.

Although this book began in the classroom, its current organization came about through a lecture series given at John Carroll University in the fall of 2003, where I was privileged to hold the Walter and Mary Tuohy Chair of Interreligious Studies. I am very grateful to Joseph E. Kelly, chair of the religious studies department, who invited me to serve as the Tuohy Chair and did so much to make me feel at home. So many others at John Carroll were great sources of encouragement and support, especially David Mason, Paul Lauritzen, Sheila McGinn, Nick Baumgartner, and David LaGuardia. I must also mention my Jesuit brothers at John Carroll, who made my stay a joyful occasion, especially Edward Glynn, Howard Gray, Michael Nusbaum, and Thomas Schubeck. In the later stages of research and writing, in which this project was thoroughly revised, I received valuable support from Creighton University's Graduate School, especially Barbara Braden, and from Creighton's Jesuit community, especially Richard Hauser. In the summer of 2006, I received a Faculty Research Fellowship grant from Creighton that enabled me bring this work to completion.

Much of this work steps outside my usual expertise, namely, the history and theology of early Christianity. It has meant venturing not only into the less familiar landscape of medieval studies, but also much further afield into the domain of comparative religion. A number of scholars have kindly read drafts of chapters and have saved me from errors and off-the-mark interpretations. I would like to thank Lawrence Cunningham, Rozanne Elder, Donald Gelpi, Jeffrey Hause, Richard Hauser, Steven Heine, John Peter Kenney, Taigen Dan Leighton, Franklin Lewis, John Markey, Bernard McGinn, Richard Miller, Joan Mueller, Barbara Newman, John O'Keefe, Frank Oppenheim, Kenan Osborne, John Renard, Russell Reno, Brian Sholl, Eileen Burke Sullivan, and Wendy Wright, who kindly read drafts of chapters at various stages of the writing. Also a special thanks to Cynthia Read and the staff at Oxford University Press.

I wish to dedicate this work to my students, past and present, graduates and undergraduates, who for the past seventeen years have enriched my life immeasurably. They have given me not only much insight, but good friendship and unexpected depths of joy. And in this fragile and much-broken world, joy is a very precious thing.

Contents

Mystics

I

A Theology Called Mystical: Jean Gerson and William James

The word "mysticism" is not only widely used, but also widely abused. So let me begin by defining, in a rough, preliminary way, what it is and what it is not. First, the negative side: The mystic is often—and mistakenly—portrayed as an otherworldly, dreamy-eyed figure who lapses into ecstatic trances or levitates during prayer, who beholds strange visions or hears heavenly voices, who works miracles, foretells the future, or communes with the dead. I grant that one finds reports of such things—and stranger—in some mystical texts. Such oddities are perhaps what draw some readers to the subject. But that is not what mysticism is about. As we will see, mystics themselves often regard such phenomena as peripheral to the deeper spiritual quest. They may simply be distractions. They can become barriers to real spiritual progress and, in some cases, be judged demonic. According to commonplace mystical wisdom, such experiences should not be sought after, encouraged, or cultivated; if they come, they come, but one is not to chase after them.

If you wander into your local Barnes & Noble or Border's, you soon discover whole shelves devoted to what booksellers catalog as "mysticism." There you usually find legitimate books on mysticism mixed in with stuff on the occult and witchcraft, fortune-telling, mind reading, and alien abductions. Mysticism, of course, has nothing to do with such matters, but the confusion on the shelves illustrates how in popular parlance "mysticism" can become a catch-all for religious weirdness. In the 1960s it became fashionable to suggest that mystics experienced altered states of consciousness and that such states could be reproduced with drugs or other mind-altering techniques. Much earlier, in the eighteenth and nineteenth centuries, philosophers tended to write off mystics as either gullible cranks or deluded neurotics. I grant that not all mystics have been paradigms of psychological integration, but they are not crazy. Many have not even been otherworldly. More than a few have been hard-nosed practical thinkers, respectful of intellect and education. Many have possessed a healthy, down-to-earth sense of people and politics and have often been movers and shakers in the world of their day.

So if mysticism has little to do with the stereotypes some readers associate with the term, then what is it? To begin to answer that question, I want to begin with brief case studies of two thinkers who pioneered the study of what we call mysticism: the late medieval theologian and churchman Jean Gerson and the twentieth-century philosopher and psychologist William James. These two forged classic definitions. Their definitions will give us a first, not the final, word on mysticism. They provide us points of entry into the discussion, and even if we end up disagreeing with facets of their work, they will prove to be thoughtful debating partners.

MYSTICISM AS EXPERIENTIAL THEOLOGY

Jean Gerson (1363–1429) was a man of wide-ranging talents. In 1395—only one year after receiving his doctorate in theology—he was appointed chancellor of the University of Paris. His was a meteoric rise, and it meant that he held the most prestigious academic post at the most influential educational institution in Europe. But Gerson was more than a talented academic. In the years that followed, he made his name as one of those fearless churchmen who helped end the scandal of the Great Schism. For over a generation, Christendom had been divided between two, and eventually three, rival popes. Gerson threw his lot in with the conciliarists, arguing that supreme authority in the Church lay not in the papacy, but in ecumenical councils. He further insisted that if the warring popes refused to recognize the authority of a council that truly represented the breadth of Christendom, they could legitimately be deposed, imprisoned, and, if need be, executed. Gerson's formidable skills, both as a theologian and a diplomat, came into full display at the Council of Constance (1414–1418), where he and his colleagues engineered the deposition of the three rival claimants to the papal throne and oversaw the election of a new pope, Martin V, which marked the formal end of the schism.

On Mystical Theology

This practical side of Gerson's career is what shows up in the history books. But he had many sides, and one was a long-standing interest in mystics and mysticism. In the early 1400s he authored a two-volume treatise entitled *On Mystical Theology* (*De mystica theologia*).[1] Through this work he sprinkled various definitions of mysticism. One would become classic: "Mystical theology is an experiential knowledge of God that comes through the embrace of unitive love" (*theologia mystica est cognitio experimentalis habita de Deo per amoris unitivi complexum*).[2]

To appreciate Gerson's cogent definition, we need to spend a little time taking it apart. Note first that Gerson speaks not of "mysticism," as we do today. The term "mysticism" is of more recent vintage, dating from the seventeenth century.[3] Instead he speaks of "mystical *theology*." And he means "theology" in the literal sense, "a speaking of God"—as opposed to the looser ways we use the term today when we speak of a "theology of Church" or a "theology of sacrament." For Gerson, theology is God-talk, and as he saw it, the God-talk of the mystics offers us some genuine insight into God. What makes the mystics' knowledge of God unique is its roots: it is *experiential*. Gerson, in his prologue, lists forms of experience that he was familiar with:

> The saints use various names to describe these interior forms of experiential knowledge of God . . . They speak of contemplation, ecstasy, rapture, liquefaction, transformation, union, exultation. They talk of a jubilation beyond the spirit, of being taken into a divine darkness, of tasting God, of embracing the bridegroom, of kissing him, of being born of God, of obeying his word, of being brought into the divine cellars, of being drunk in a torrent of delight, of running into an odor of his perfumes, of hearing his voice, and entering into the bedroom, and of finding sleep and rest in peace in him.[4]

Scholastic Theology

Gerson contrasts this experiential mystical theology with the theology he knew best: scholastic theology. Scholastic theology is, quite literally, a theology done in schools. And it has all the elements and methods of an academic discipline: it is done by professors who lecture and by students who take notes and tests; it takes place in classrooms; it has textbooks; it uses literary methods to analyze texts and scientific methods to discover and weigh evidence and philosophic methods to assess arguments; it employs a sophisticated technical terminology; and it relies on erudite debate between experts to sort out contested issues. This way of doing theology is still with us today and is so firmly entrenched that we may not realize that it is neither the only nor was it the earliest way to do theology. School-centered theology is a medieval creation, forged and refined by Gerson's predecessors there at the University of Paris.

In the early Christian centuries, theology was done, above all, by bishops, whether in the daily routine of preaching or, more rarely but more decisively, in the doctrine-shaping debates of ecumenical councils, from Nicaea to Chalcedon. In the first half of the Middle Ages, theology as a discipline moved from the cathedral to the monastery. Leading theologians tended to be monks rather than bishops, and theology served and expressed monastic concerns about prayer and spirituality and community life. In the twelfth century, theology moved again, from the monasteries to the newly emerging schools in and around Paris. There in Paris, Gerson's thirteenth-century predecessors— Thomas Aquinas, Bonaventure, Duns Scotus—created encyclopedic textbooks, or summae. These cathedrals of the mind welded together biblical texts and patristic snippets, definition and disputation, into intricately detailed and philosophically coherent systems.

A Theology of the Heart

Gerson did not deny the value of scholastic theology and of the whole scholastic enterprise. He was an expert scholastic theologian himself and practiced it well. But he thought that mystical theology, this other theology, had gotten neglected along the way. Where scholastic theology was public and exterior, mystical theology was personal and interior. Where scholastic theology focused on the mind, mystical theology sprang primarily from the heart, the *affectus*.

Note his definition again, the way he says that mystical theology offers a knowledge of God that comes from love. Think about the knowledge that married people have of one another. They have not read books about one another. They have not studied each other academically. They know one another through the union of their lives, an intimacy that touches heart and mind and body. There is certainly a cognitive element in their knowledge of each other, but it is not what we would call an intellectual knowledge. It is certainly not theoretical. Instead, it is a love-wrought knowledge. It is knowledge of this sort that Gerson is referring to when he speaks of the mystic's knowledge of God coming about "through the embrace of unitive love." Gerson is playing on a dictum from the seventh-century pope, Gregory the Great, that "love itself is a knowledge of sorts."[5] The mystic possesses his or her knowledge of God not from books or academic study, but from experience, from the experience of being loved intimately, intensely, by God. The implications of this are breathtaking. Why? Because Gerson believed that the mystic's love-wrought knowledge of God gave him or her a measure of theological authority comparable in certain ways to the academic theologian's. The mystic—or, in Gerson's terminology, the mystical theologian—had a knowledge of God that belonged not simply to himself or herself. The mystic's voice was needed in the theological marketplace.

Gerson recognized what has become obvious to us: that scholastic theology, in its efforts to be scientific, unwittingly severed the intimate link between theology and spirituality, between theologians' public thinking about what the Church believes and believers' personal encounters with God in prayer and worship. Scholastic theology seemed abstract, devoid of devotion, cut off from the heart and from the personal. As Gerson argued, "It is better to have the knowledge of God through a repentant affectivity than through an investigative intellect."[6] That judgment may be unfair to scholastics such as Thomas Aquinas, who were personally moved by great devotion and whose devotion subtly but profoundly shaped their theology. But when scholastics did their theology, they used an objective voice and spoke with professional detachment. In proposing this project called "mystical theology," Gerson sought to repair the split. The split he sensed has, of course, not gone away.[7]

A World of Mystics

Gerson's interest in mystical theology came from his reading of the signs of the times. He knew that he lived in an era of great mystical movements. A century earlier, Meister Eckhart had taught a striking and controversial brand of mystical theology. (We will look at it later.) Certain of Eckhart's teachings were declared by Pope John XXII to be tainted by the "stain of heresy" or at least "evil-sounding and very rash and suspect of heresy."[8] Despite condemnation, Eckhart's works would be much copied and read and spread by circles in Cologne and Strasbourg, by clusters of the mystically minded such as Margaret Ebner's Friends of God. Some of them were perfectly orthodox, such as Eckhart's disciples Johannes Tauler and Heinrich Suso, but they had to work hard to defend their legitimacy. Gerson was attuned to such movements. He appreciated but was also openly critical of one influenced by Eckhart, Jan van Ruusbroec (d. 1381). Gerson thought Ruusbroec's way of speaking about mystical union risked erasing any distinction between God and the soul. He knew of extremists of the recent past, such as the Beguine Marguerite Porete, who was burned at the stake in 1310 for her mystical views. At the same time, he defended the visionary Joan of Arc and thought highly of new movements such as the Brethren of the Common Life.

Gerson knew that, for better or worse, he moved in an age brimming with mystics. And he hoped that such movements and their formidable energies could be re-engaged with theology and with the Church at large. He worried that theology as a discipline had become too elitist. He noted that whereas scholastic theology was practiced by only a handful, mystical theology was much more widespread. Mystical theology could be and in fact was done by the unlearned as well as the learned, by laypeople as well as by clerics, by women as well as by men.[9] Gerson himself was one of the pioneers of writing about mysticism in the vernacular. His early work *The Mountain of Contemplation* (*Montaigne de contemplation*) was written not in Latin, but in French—composed ostensibly for his two sisters, but intended for a wide lay audience.

Recovering Ancient Voices

Gerson did not see himself proposing something new. Quite the opposite: He was convinced that mystical theology was as old as the Church itself. It could be traced, he believed, back to the time of the apostles, back to Dionysius, whom St. Paul had met and converted at the Aeropagus in Athens (Acts 17:34). This Dionysius the Areopagite was believed by Gerson and his medieval colleagues to have authored an extraordinary collection of treatises, including *On Mystical Theology*, the treatise from which Gerson took the title of his own work. This ancient collection, originally written in Greek, had passed to the Latin West in the eighth century. It touched theologians, such as Bonaventure and Aquinas, as well as mystical writers, such as the anonymous English author of *The Cloud of Unknowing*. Gerson and his contemporaries did not realize these writings came *not* from Paul's first-century convert, but from a sixth-century Syrian who had adopted Dionysius as a pen name. In other words, Dionysius the Areopagite was actually Pseudo-Dionysius the Areopagite. This masterful forgery would not be uncovered for another fifty years, not until the remarkable philological researches of early Renaissance scholar Lorenzo Valla (d. 1457). I should add that the fact of the pen name did not (and does not) diminish the power of these extraordinary writings.

But Dionysius was hardly Gerson's only, or even his primary, influence. Gerson saw himself as one in a long list of Christian theologians concerned about mystical theology. At the end of the treatise, he appended what we would call a bibliography, listing "some who have spoken of contemplation":

Augustine, John Cassian, John Climacus, Gregory the Great, Bernard of Clairvaux, Hugh and Richard of St. Victor, and Bonaventure.[10]

Issues

Gerson's definition of mystical theology—this "experiential knowledge that comes from God through the embrace of unitive love"—offers us a point of entry. It also alerts us to a knot of issues that underlies any exploration of mysticism:

- What precisely is religious experience? What does it mean to say that one has experienced God?
- How does such an experience—whatever its form—give one knowledge of God?
- What is the link between love of God and knowledge of God? Which is prior or more important? Or are they one and the same?
- Does mystical union happen all at once or in stages?
- Does the person seeking God do something to make union possible, or is it solely God's initiative?
- Is union required for a person to be called a mystic? How long does union last? Briefly? Constantly?
- Is union even the best way to describe mystical experience? How does one unite with God? That is, how does a finite human being unite with the Infinity that God is?

And then there are the thorny issues of false mysticism that so concerned Gerson and should concern us:

- How do we discern a genuine experience of God from the delusional?
- How does one assess claimants? How do we know that those who claim to have had an experience did so?
- And even if a person has had a genuine experience, how do we discern the conclusions that he or she draws from it? Can one distinguish between the experience itself and the interpretation of that experience?
- What happens when mystics contradict one another? What happens when they contradict religious authorities?
- What authority does mystical experience have as theology? Is it on par with the theology of professional scholars, whether medieval or modern? Do mystics—however unschooled in the public discourse of theology—teach a legitimate theology?

All these issues mattered to Gerson. Their poignancy has not lessened.

MYSTICISM AS RELIGIOUS EXPERIENCE

Let us turn now from a medieval theorist to a modern one, the American psychologist and philosopher William James (1842–1910). My choice is not arbitrary. James's classic study, *The Varieties of Religious Experience* (1902), has in many ways set the terms and trajectory of the modern study of mysticism.

Career

William James came from an illustrious, if eccentric, American family. His brother, the novelist Henry James, is its most renowned member. James's grandfather, an Irish immigrant, was a self-made millionaire; his father, a gentleman of means and no job, was a self-proclaimed spiritual seeker and devotee of Emanuel Swedenborg, the eighteenth-century Swedish mystic. James's father pursued and befriended leading intellectuals of the day, including Ralph Waldo Emerson, Henry David Thoreau, Horace Greeley, Alfred Lord Tennyson, and John Stuart Mill. James grew up in a heady intellectual atmosphere, first in New York, later in England, France, and finally Boston.

William James showed aptitude as a painter and for a time considered a career in art. In the end, he decided to focus on science. He studied medicine and graduated from Harvard in 1869 with an M.D. Three years later he began his academic career, teaching anatomy and physiology at Harvard. His research focus soon shifted from medicine to the newly emerging discipline of psychology. James is now numbered as one of its great pioneers. In 1875 he established the world's first laboratory devoted to psychological research, and in 1890 he published his pathbreaking and magisterial *Principles of Psychology*. It is now considered "the single greatest work in American psychology"; in terms of its foundational importance to psychology, "its only rival is Freud's *The Interpretation of Dreams.*"[11]

The same year he established his psychology lab, James began teaching courses in philosophy. His first articles appeared a few years later, in 1878, and these would be collected and published in 1898 as *The Will to Believe and Other Essays in Popular Philosophy*. James was an American original and stood at the center of a self-consciously American circle of philosophers that included friends—and friendly rivals—Josiah Royce and Charles Sanders Peirce. James helped formulate that most American of philosophic outlooks, pragmatism. The term, coined originally by Peirce, became popular thanks in large part to James's essays.

James owed his popularity, in part, to his gifts as a writer. In 1916 the novelist Rebecca West remarked that James's brother Henry "grew up to write fiction as though it were philosophy," while William wrote "philosophy as though it were fiction."[12] Unlike most academics, William James had an uncanny ability to address both academic peers and the wider literate public. James's popularity stemmed not merely from his luminous prose and quotable turns of phrase. As a student of his once remarked, James "felt with all sorts of men. He understood their demand for immediate answers to the great speculative questions of life. God, freedom, immortality, nature as moral or non-moral—these were for him not matters of idle scientific wonder, but of urgent need."[13]

The Varieties of Religious Experience

In 1901–1902 James delivered the prestigious Gifford Lectures on Natural Religion at the University of Edinburgh and published them under the title *The Varieties of Religious Experience*. It was a groundbreaking work. James stated his bias at the outset: that he approached the topic not as a theologian nor as a historian of religion, but as a psychologist, and "to the psychologist the religious propensities of man must be at least as interesting as any other of the facts pertaining to his mental constitution."[14] James was convinced that "religious feelings" were more than "interesting"; they were, in fact, central to human existence. It is no accident that he subtitled his work *A Study in Human Nature*.

James took religious experience seriously and knew that such an opinion went against the intellectual grain of many in his Edinburgh audience. Science and religion were then bitter antagonists. And so in his opening lecture, he took pains to justify his study of religious experience against scientific detractors, whom he labeled "medical materialists." He knew that many dismissed religious experiences as either undiagnosed medical pathology or psychosexual obsession:

> Medical materialism seems indeed a good appellation for the too simple-minded system of thought which we are considering. Medical materialism finishes up Saint Paul by calling his vision on the road to Damascus a discharging lesion of the occipital cortex, he being an epileptic. It snuffs our Saint Teresa as a hysteric, Saint Francis of Assisi as a hereditary degenerate . . . All such mental overtensions, it says, are, when you come to the bottom of the matter, mere affairs of diathesis (auto-intoxications most probably), due to the perverted actions of various glands which physiology will yet discover.[15]

James did not deny that pathologies, whether physical or psychological, might play a role. But reductionism—discarding religious experiences "by calling them 'nothing but' expressions of our organic disposition"—suffers a logical fallacy.[16] Truth, James argued, is measured not by origin, but by outcome. As James puts it, "Saint Teresa might have had the nervous system of the placidest cow, and it would not now save her theology"; on the other hand, "if her theology can stand" certain pragmatic tests, "it will make no difference how hysterical or nervously off her balance Saint Teresa may have been when she was with us here below."[17] James the empiricist argued that one needed to measure truth claims by pragmatic outcomes. Pragmatic standards, he believed, got rid of "the bugaboo of morbid origin."[18]

James the psychologist was interested in individuals, not institutions. He stated his bias and his method at the outset: "I must confine myself to those more developed subjective phenomena recorded in literature produced by articulate and fully self-conscious men, in works of piety and autobiography."[19] Note his emphasis on the subjective and the autobiographical. What makes *Varieties* so engaging, in part, is the way James weaves a many-threaded tapestry of testimonial and analysis. He draws his first-person testimonials—what he calls *documents humains*—both from spiritual classics and from (often unnamed) contemporary witnesses. Note also James's emphasis on "articulate and fully self-conscious men." Ordinary believers concerned him less than "geniuses," those "pattern-setters ... for whom religion exists not as a dull habit, but as an acute fever."[20] This focus sprang from his estimate of institutional religion. He was convinced that behind or beneath the vast artifice of religion—its institutions, its rituals, its dogmas—were mystical roots: "Churches, when once established, live at second-hand upon tradition; but the *founders* of every church owed their power originally to the fact of their direct personal communion with the divine. Not only the superhuman founders, the Christ, the Buddha, Mahomet, but all the originators of Christian sects have been in this case."[21] It is a point James makes again and again. In a letter to a friend, written midway through the Gifford Lectures, James remarked: "The mother sea and fountain-head of all religions lie in the mystical experiences of the individual."[22]

Defining the Mystical Experience

James's enormously influential discussion of mysticism appears near the end of *Varieties* and is arguably the climax of his study. James denied that he himself experienced mystical states: "My constitution shuts me out from their enjoyment almost entirely, and I can speak of them only at second hand."[23] He felt the terms "mysticism" and "mystical" were too loosely used in his day, too "vague and vast and sentimental." To give them precision, he suggested four qualities that pragmatically define and delimit the mystical experience:

1. *Ineffability.* According to James, the mystical experience "defies expression, that no adequate report of its content can be given in words"—that mystical experience is, in a word, "ineffable."[24] James compared the mystic's experience to the lover's and the musician's: "One must have musical ears to know the value of a symphony; one must have been in love one's self to understand a lover's state of mind. Lacking the heart or ear, we cannot interpret the musician or the lover justly."[25]

2. *Noetic quality.* Mystics stress that their experiences give them "insight into depths of truth unplumbed by the discursive intellect." James referred to this as the "noetic" (or intellectual) "quality" of the mystical. There is a built-in paradox here: although mystics lay claim to illuminations and revelations, these experiences both reveal and hide, both speak and remain inarticulate. Even so, the mystic is convinced and guided by their "curious sense of authority."[26]

3. *Transiency.* James noted in most cases mystical experiences are brief, lasting no longer than an hour, usually less. They are, in other words, "transient." Although "they fade into the light of common day," their effect persists; but should they recur, they are "susceptible of continuous development in what is felt as inner richness and importance."[27]

4. *Passivity.* James stressed that mystics come to their peak experiences not as active seekers, but as passive recipients. In the thrall of such mystical moments, the mystic "feels as if his own will were in abeyance, and indeed sometimes as if he were grasped and held by a superior power."[28]

James knew that mystics had constructed complex typologies to map the variety of mystical states. But he was suspicious of tidy schemes and, following his usual methodological bent, stressed the pluralism of phenomena, observing that "the range of mystical experience is very wide."[29] For James, there is a *"more"* to human experience in general, something that defies intellectual categories and verbal analysis, and that *"more"* is equally, indeed especially, true with mystical experiences.[30] He saw a broad continuum, beginning with epiphanic experiences with "no special religious significance," when "single words, and conjunctions of words, effects of light on land and sea, odors and musical sounds" coalescence into world-shifting insights.[31] He cited a chain of first-person accounts from contemporaries, some describing poignant responses to natural beauty, others describing religious breakthroughs; some he leaves anonymous, others he draws from well-known figures of his day, such as the poet Walt Whitman and the physician Richard Bucke, author of *Cosmic Consciousness*. James also included reports of experiments with drugs and intoxicants, such as chloroform and nitrous oxide. He even mentioned his personal experiments, which convinced him that "our normal waking consciousness, rational consciousness as we call it, is but one special type of consciousness, whilst all about it, parted from it by the filmiest of screens, there lie potential forms of consciousness entirely different."[32]

After this, James shifts his focus from "sporadic mysticism" to its "methodical cultivation," surveying examples from Hinduism, Buddhism, and the Sufis of Islam. He then quotes autobiographical accounts from Christian mystics, such as Ignatius of Loyola, Teresa of Ávila, and John of the Cross, as well as mystical teachings from Pseudo-Dionysius and Meister Eckhart. James was of two minds. On the one hand, he recognized the wide-ranging mystical schools and conflicting mystical doctrines both within and between religions. But he also shared with thinkers of his era the conviction that beneath the variety could be carved out a certain mystical unanimity, that mystics shared certain common perceptions of the divine, however different their religion or historical epoch:

> In mystic states we both become one with the Absolute and we become aware of our oneness. This is the everlasting and triumphant mystical tradition, hardly altered by differences of clime or creed. In Hinduism, in Neoplatonism, in Sufism, in Christian mysticism, in Whitmanism, we find the same recurring note, so that there is about mystical utterances an eternal unanimity which ought to make a critic stop and think, and which bring it about that the mystical classics have, as has been said, neither birthday nor native land.[33]

An Underlying Philosophy of Religion

James's *Varieties of Religious Experience* was an instant classic. It helped put mysticism on the academic map, sparking a spate of scholarly studies in psychology and physiology, sociology and history, literature and philosophy. Not all agreed with James's analysis of this or that question, but his study set a clear trajectory in the modern study of mysticism. It is important for us to be alert to that trajectory.

First, James defined mysticism as "experience"—something subjective, best seen in psychological terms. James's vantage point led him to focus on first-person testimonials. It also led him—and the many who followed his lead—to concentrate on peak experiences, often to the neglect of a mystic's overall biography. We saw that Gerson too stressed personal experience, but with a difference. Gerson saw the mystical as a form of theology—theology with experiential roots. For Gerson, "experience" is the adjective; for James, it is the noun. And that difference is decisive. For James, there was nothing inherently theological in or about mystical experience. On the contrary, he felt it legitimate to shear off the mystic's experience from the theological claims that the mystic—or anyone else—might attribute to it. The experientialist bias that James set in motion raises questions for our investigation:

- Is mysticism best seen in terms of "experiences," as something best studied as psychological phenomena?
- Are first-person narratives or autobiographies the best genre or even the sole genre to study? What about others, such as poems or sermons, aphorisms or biblical commentaries, literature without obvious auto-biographical content?
- Does the mystical report make the mystic? What happens if writers do not report their mystical experiences in first-person narratives? Are they disqualified as mystics? If first-person reports make the mystic, then many writers classified as "mystics" would be disqualified—including some cited by James himself.
- How do mystical experiences link to the mystic's life as a whole? How does the mystical experience fit in with the larger question of holiness—or simply with human integrity?
- What if the subject of a mystical experience suffers some pathology, whether physiological or psychological? Does that invalidate the experience? Is James's appeal to results (and not origin) sufficient?

Second, James defined mystical experiences as "religious" experiences. That, in itself, is not a problem. However, James worked from a quite precise but quite unusual definition of religion. When James thought of religion, he did not think in terms of the great world religions—Christianity, Islam, Buddhism, and so on. Nor did he approach religion in either historical, institutional, or social terms. Early in *Varieties*, he defined "religion" as "the feelings, acts, and experiences of individual men in their solitude, so far as they apprehend themselves to stand in relation to whatever they may consider the divine."[34]

religion = solitude

What is missing here? Lots of things, important things. First, James limits religion to the "experiences of individual men" and to what they experience "in their solitude." In a single stroke, James has set aside, indeed denied, one of the most central facts of religion: that religion is practiced by people in groups and that it is often and sometimes best practiced in public. For a pragmatist and empiricist like James, this is a breathtaking denial. His bias leads to other silences. James ignored the fact of ritual; he has nothing to say about corporate worship. He likewise ignored the fact of scriptures, writings that most religions and most religious regard as sacred, even as God-given, writings to be prayed over, meditated on, sung, analyzed and argued over, preached and lived. He also ignored the fact of history—that religions have histories, and history, for those who practice religion, survives in the form of "tradition," that vast and often hard-to-define web of practices and beliefs, of venerable institutions and venerated texts. James treats history as though it were a stream to be stepped over instead of an ocean we swim in. To ignore history, with its many-layered depths and hidden eddies, means missing what mystics do when they dive deep into their traditions and bring to the surface hidden or lost treasures.

Finally, James's definition ignores theology. This is not simply because he was interested in a purely psychological analysis. It was because he doubted, indeed denied, the intellectual claims of theology. For James, religion is about "feelings." Later in *Varieties*, he spells out his perspective: "I do believe that feeling is the deeper source of religion, and that philosophic and theological formulas are secondary products, like translations of a text into another tongue."[35] He admitted that of itself "feeling is private and dumb" and thus needs reason "to redeem religion from unwholesome privacy, and to give public status and universal right of way to its deliverances."[36] Even so, he did not give truth value to religious claims. James tended to be suspicious of verbal formulas as a clear and distinct guide to truth. He sensed that we do not reason our way to significant things. Rather, we intuit them with an immediacy of feeling, grasping the whole in a way that defies any final verbal formula. James held this view not only about religion, but also about much else, including philosophy. But James held a particular animus against systematic theologians. He compared them to weekend naturalists who neatly collect and pedantically classify dead skins and bleached skeletons. Theologians, in his opinion, lack the courage to venture deep into the great and terrifying wilderness of the human spirit.[37]

Although there is much provocative and stimulating in James's philosophy of religion, his approach as it applies to mysticism is at once too vague and too dismissive of important matters. But it does raise important questions:

- Can mysticism be interpreted rightly if one ignores rituals and scriptures?
- Is mysticism a purely private affair, or is it, like other elements of religion, public in crucial ways? What is one to make of mystical "schools," of organized communities that consciously cultivate ascetic practices and mystical doctrines?
- How do mystics manage history, both the wider traditions of the religion to which they belong and the more specific mystical traditions they inherit? How do they take that religious or mystical inheritance and make it their own?
- Is there an intellectual content to mysticism? Do mystics' theological claims have any merits, any truth value? Or are they purely "secondary products," reason's halting efforts to give voice to "dumb" but powerful feelings?

One last matter: James gave voice to the not uncommon claim that all religions are the same at the top—that mystics speak with a certain unanimity, that one can glide easily from Christian mystics to Islamic mystics to Buddhist mystics, and that, once one prunes off that extraneous overgrowth called theology, one uncovers an irreducible common core. That notion—popular even today—cannot be presumed. It must be tested. In the meantime, we need to bear in mind an obvious but little appreciated fact—one aptly articulated by Bernard McGinn: that "no mystic (at least before the present century) believed in or practiced 'mysticism.' They believed in and practiced Christianity (or Judaism, or Islam, or Hinduism), that is, religions that contained mystical elements as parts of a wider historical whole."[38]

Readers may feel that this first attempt to define mysticism, drawing on Gerson and James, has been a little abstract. That feeling is understandable. It is difficult to look at mysticism before one looks at mystics. But it was important, I believe, to set out key issues, at least in a preliminary way. We can now begin to flesh things out by looking at individual mystics, at their lives and their mystical theologies. What follows will be, in a sense, a Jamesian investigation, a series of case studies. But it will be broader. I do not think it sufficient to limit oneself to autobiography and to reports of peak experiences. It is Jamesian in another sense as well: I did not want to impose a definition of mysticism, but hope to draw one out from empirical studies of individual cases. We will look at figures commonly classified as mystics, and from these cases, taken as a whole, we will be in a better position to address some of the questions raised here. Let me close with one final snippet from James. In a poetic turn of phrase, he noted the way mystics' experiences and insights, though they often "stir chords within" us, escape any easy definition or classification: "There is a verge of the mind which these things haunt; and whispers therefrom mingle with the operations of our understanding, even as the waters of the infinite ocean send their waves to break among the pebbles that lie upon our shores."[39]

2

Mystic as Fire Watcher:
Thomas Merton

Thomas Merton had a knack for getting the mystical to speak to the modern. In 1968, the year of his death, Merton wrote an essay at the request of a student literary magazine at nearby University of Louisville. In it he addressed—in the parlance of the 1960s—the "relevance" of monastic life. The title of the essay, "Contemplation in a World of Action," names both his perspective and dilemma. He begins by posing tough questions for himself: "What does the contemplative life or the life of prayer, solitude, silence, meditation, mean to man in the atomic age? What can it mean? Has it lost all meaning whatever?"[1] Merton was temperamentally impatient with run-of-the-mill pieties and warned that "real Christian living is stunted and frustrated if it remains content with the bare externals of worship, with 'saying prayers' and 'going to church,' with fulfilling one's external duties and merely being respectable."[2] He insisted not on saying prayers, but on *prayer*, and prayer meant "the awareness of God . . . even if sometimes this awareness may amount to a negative factor, a seeming 'absence.'" He was aware of fads among college students, their dabblings in Oriental meditation, and argued that "the real purpose of meditation . . . is the exploration and discovery of new dimensions of freedom, illumination and love, in deepening our awareness of our life in Christ." He then returned to his central question:

> What is the relation of this to action? Simply this. He who attempts to act and do things for others or for the world

without deepening his own self-understanding, freedom and integrity and capacity to love, will not have anything to give others. He will communicate to them nothing but the contagion of his own obsessions, his aggressiveness, his ego-centeredness, his delusions about ends and means, his doctrinaire prejudices and ideas.[3]

The year 1968 was one of extraordinary political ferment. Activism was sweeping college campuses, and Merton himself was an activist of long standing, an outspoken critic of nuclear war, racism, consumerism, and mass culture. He called on his youthful readers to stop—to understand how activism, despite lofty intentions, can do real harm because it is so oblivious to its own subtle egotism. He warned of these matters because he knew he himself could be equally guilty of them.

In this chapter we will explore mystical elements in Thomas Merton's life and writings. I begin with an extended biographical sketch and follow with an analysis of a few elements of Merton's mystical theology. This two-part pattern—biography first, mystical theology second—will serve as a template for subsequent case studies.

KNOWING THE CHRIST OF BURNT MEN

Family and Education

Merton was born in France in 1915. As he notes in the opening page of his acclaimed autobiography, *The Seven Storey Mountain*, it was "the year of a war"—World War I, that most bloody of modern wars—and "not many hundreds of miles away from the house where I was born, they were picking up the men who rotted in the rainy ditches among the dead horses."[4] Merton, a lifelong pacifist, savored the brutal irony of his own coming to life so near the terrible trenches of World War I. Merton's father, Owen, a painter, was from New Zealand; his mother, Ruth, was an American. Merton's mother died of cancer when he was only six, leaving him and his younger brother, John Paul, devastated. His early education took place in boarding schools, first in France and later in England. Not long after beginning high school, his father was diagnosed with a brain tumor; he died a few years later. So by age sixteen, Merton found himself an orphan. A couple of years later, he graduated and received a scholarship to attend Cambridge University. There, not unlike some freshmen before and after, he frittered away his first year drinking and partying. He also got a young girl pregnant. Merton's American guardian stepped in, a legal settlement of some sort was apparently made, and the young Merton was yanked back to the United States. One sometimes comes across the report that the young woman, together with her and Merton's child, died during World War II in the firebombing of London; however, this often-repeated report has been recently challenged.[5]

In 1935 Merton enrolled at Columbia University in New York. There he studied literature and came under the spell of Mark Van Doren, an accomplished poet and nationally renowned poetry critic. Van Doren helped Merton appreciate a range of authors, including John Donne, William Blake, Ezra Pound, T. S. Eliot, and Franz Kafka. Also at Columbia Merton met a circle of friends with whom he remained close the rest of his life. They were a talented group. Robert Giroux, for instance, would later become one of the top editors in the United States (of Farrar, Straus, and Giroux), while Adolph Reinhardt would become a well-known painter, a member of the New York school of abstract expressionism.

In his autobiography, Merton recounts a spiritual turning point during his college years. He and his college roommates befriended and ended up housing a wandering Hindu monk named Bramachari. Merton, who always had an eye for the humorous, delights in telling of his first meeting with Bramachari, who combined traditional and modern dress: a yellow turban and sneakers. Merton and Bramachari hit it off and talked at length. Merton had been reading Aldous Huxley's *Ends and Means*, which sparked an interest in mysticism, East and West, and asked Bramachari about Hindu mysticism. Bramachari sagely advised Merton to begin with the Western tradition, with Augustine's *Confessions* and Thomas à Kempis's *Imitation of Christ*.

Conversion to Catholicism

In 1938 Merton completed his bachelor's degree at Columbia. He immediately began work on a master's in literature. It was during this period that he converted to Catholicism. Merton had been under the sway of Catholic thinkers such as Jacques Maritain and Étienne Gilson for a while and had occasionally attended Mass at a parish not far from Columbia. The turnabout took place in September 1938 on a dreary Sunday afternoon. Merton was in his room reading a book on the Jesuit poet Gerald Manley Hopkins (d. 1889). What grabbed his attention was way that Hopkins (an Anglican at the time) had written to John Henry Newman (d. 1890), the onetime leader of the Oxford Movement and a recent Catholic convert, seeking his advice on the Catholic Church. Then, as Merton recounts it: "All of a sudden, something began to stir within me, something began to push me, to prompt me. It was a movement that spoke like a voice. 'What are you waiting for?' it said. 'Why are you sitting here? Why do you still hesitate? You know what you ought to do? Why don't you do it?' "[6] He got up, walked nine rainy blocks to a local parish, and there chanced upon the priest and professed his desire to become Catholic. Merton was baptized not long after, in November.

Merton's spiritual quest was just beginning. He thought of becoming a priest and applied to the Franciscans. After he confessed his past—presumably his Cambridge misadventures—he was asked to withdraw his application. The rejection left him disoriented, adrift. In the meantime, he was busy as a teacher. He also worked as a volunteer with the poor in Harlem, at a center run by a Russian émigré and recent Catholic convert, Baroness Catherine de Hueck. This period was crucial, for it attuned Merton to the plight of the poor. He would later write eloquently on race matters well before the civil rights movement became popular.

The Cistercians

During Holy Week of 1941 Merton made a retreat at the Abbey of Gethsemani in Kentucky. The monastery was run by the Cistercians of the Strict Observance, better known as Trappists. The Trappists were a seventeenth-century French reform of the Cistercians, who were in turn a twelfth-century reform of the Benedictines. Merton, in *The Sign of Jonas*, offers a capsule description of Cistercian life:

> The average Cistercian monastery is a quiet, out-of-the-way place— usually somewhere in France—occupied by a community of seventy or eighty men who lead a silent energetic life consecrated entirely to God. It is a life of prayer and penance, of liturgy, study, and manual labor. The monks are supposed to exercise no exterior ministry—no preaching, teaching, or the rest . . . The life is physically hard, but compensation for this hardship is interior peace. In any case, one soon becomes used to the hardships and finds that they are not hard after all. Seven hours of sleep are normally enough. The monks' diet is extremely plain, but is ordinarily enough to keep a man healthy for long years, and monks traditionally die of old age. One soon gets used to sleeping on straw and boards . . . The life is quiet. There is no conversation. The monks talk to their superiors or spiritual directors when necessary. In the average monastery, Cistercian silence is an all-pervading thing that seeps into the very stones of the place and saturates the men who live there. Farm labor is the monks' support, and the ordinary thing is for all the monks to

work outdoors for five or six hours a day. When they are not work-ing, or praying in choir, the monks devote their time to reading, meditation, contemplative prayer.[7]

The monks at Gethsemani, their demeanor, and their way of life deeply im-pressed Merton. In his retreat journal, he recorded his first fervor: "This is the center of America. I had wondered what was holding the country together, what has been keeping the universe from cracking and falling apart. It is this monastery if only this one... This is the only real city in America—in a des-ert."[8] The retreat moved Merton in a new direction and toward a new decision: to become a monk. Merton formally entered the Monastery of Gethsemani nine months later, on December 10, 1941, three days after the Japanese attack on Pearl Harbor. He followed the normal course of formation, officially be-coming a novice in early 1942 and taking simple vows in 1944. During this time, he endured one more family tragedy when his brother John Paul, a pilot in the Canadian Air Force, died in a plane crash in the English Channel.

In the years before his ordination and with the encouragement of the abbot, Merton began writing an autobiography. He entitled it *The Seven Storey Mountain*, alluding to Dante's image of the seven-tiered mountain of purga-tory. Merton's autobiography, published in 1948, became a best seller, selling 600,000 hardback copies. Merton found himself a celebrity almost overnight. The book touched something deep in America's shattered postwar psyche. One early reviewer described it as "a hymn of positive faith sung in the midst of a purposeless world searching for purpose, a book that can be read by men of any faith or none at all."[9] For all its narrative power and rich human textures, it offered a vision of monastic life and of the wider world that Merton would later reject. Toward the end of his life, Merton looked back and satirized his youthful self-righteousness, describing himself as one "who spurned New York, spat on Chicago, and tromped on Louisville, heading for the woods with Thoreau in one pocket, John of the Cross in another, and holding the Bible open to the Apocalypse."[10]

The Seven Storey Mountain was the first of many books that poured from Merton's pen. Others quickly followed: *What Is Contemplation?* (1948), *Seeds of Contemplation* (1949), *The Ascent to Truth* (1951), *The Sign of Jonas* (1953), *No Man Is an Island* (1955). Alongside these ran a parallel stream of poems and essays. Merton knew he was a born writer: "It is possible to doubt whether I have become a monk (a doubt I have to live with) but it is not possible to doubt that I am a writer, that I was born one and will most probably die as one. Disconcerting, disedifying as it is, this seems to be my lot and my vocation. It is what God has given to me that I might give it back to him."[11] Writing clashed in certain ways with his Cistercian vocation. As he once remarked, "An author in a Trappist monastery is like a duck in a chicken coop."[12] Yet over the years Merton's superiors made accommodations, allowing their suddenly famous monk the space and time he needed to write. Merton was also given key roles within the monastery. He had taken final vows in 1947 and was ordained to the priesthood in 1949. In 1951 he was appointed master of scholastics, which meant that he oversaw the theological and spiritual education of the young monks; and in 1955 Merton was appointed master of novices, a position he held for the next ten years.

Pacifist and Social Critic

In the mid-1950s Merton's outlook began shifting, at first subtly, then profoundly. He began to make his peace with the world he left behind. A new vision would crystallize in what some scholars see as a mystical experience. It took place in March 1958 in Louisville as Merton stood on the corner of Fourth Street and Walnut. (More on this incident in a moment.) Merton's turn to the world—a turn at once compassionate and critical—shaped what he wrote about and how he wrote about it. Merton took on social issues—writing, for example, on civil rights and against racism—long before such things were fashionable. His outlook struck a chord. Eldridge Cleaver, the former Black Panther leader and author of *Soul on Ice*, noted that no white man wrote with such a sympathetic eye on the plight and poignancy of Harlem as Merton did.[13] During this time Merton befriended Dorothy Day, the New York–based social justice activist, and contributed regular columns to her publication, *Catholic Worker*.

Merton was a committed pacifist. In October 1961 he published in *Catholic Worker* an article entitled "The Root of War Is Fear," giving public voice to what had long been his private stance. He became increasingly vocal about matters of war and peace and harshly critical of the American nuclear arsenal and the whole cold-war culture. This heightened long-standing tensions with censors in the Cistercian order, who had earlier marred *The Seven Storey Mountain* by chopping out any mention of Merton's fathering a child. Things came to a head in 1961–1962 when the abbot general of the order personally intervened, ordering Merton to stop publishing on war and peace. While Merton officially obeyed, he also adopted an underground publication tactic. He put antiwar reflections into private correspondence, which were then collected under the title *The Cold War Letters* and circulated in mimeograph. A vindication for his outspoken anti-nuclear views came when Pope John XXIII issued the encyclical *Peace on Earth* (*Pacem in Terris*, 1963). After this, Merton was allowed to publish openly. Works he had written earlier but left on the shelf, such as *Seeds of Destruction*, were published. As the 1960s progressed, Merton came to correspond with and befriend antiwar activists such as Daniel and Philip Berrigan. Mahatma Gandhi, the twentieth century's patron saint of nonviolence, had been Merton's hero since his high school days. In 1965 he put together an anthology of Gandhi's writings under the title *Gandhi on Non-Violence* (1965), prefacing it with an essay on the spirituality of nonviolence.

While Merton remained physically within the confines of his Kentucky monastery, his correspondence embraced the globe. The sheer volume of his correspondence—over 4,000 letters—and the range and fame of his correspondents are astonishing. He exchanged views with leading theologians and religious scholars, including Jacques Maritain, Jean Leclerq, Martin Marty, John Tracy Ellis, Jean Danielou, Bernard Häring, Paul Tillich, and Rosemary Radford Reuther. Merton also kept in close touch with leading literary figures around the world, from the Russian novelist Boris Pasternak to the Polish poet Czesław Miłosz to the Nicaraguan poet Nicanor Parra. He befriended writers in the United States as well, including the novelists Henry Miller and Walker Percy and the poets William Carlos Williams and Lawrence Ferlinghetti. Merton also wrote letters to and received letters from two popes, John XXIII and Paul VI.

Merton's turn to the larger world included a strong commitment to ecumenism. As he noted in his *Conjectures of a Guilty Bystander*:

> If I can unite in myself the thought and the devotion of Eastern
> and Western Christendom, the Greek and the Latin Fathers, the
> Russians with the Spanish mystics, I can prepare in myself the re-
> union of divided Christians. From that secret and unspoken unity in
> myself can eventually come a visible and manifest unity of all
> Christians ... We must contain all divided worlds in ourselves and
> transcend them in Christ.[14]

Merton's turn went beyond Christianity to a dialogue with the world religions, especially their monastic and mystical traditions. This turn is evident in his wide-ranging correspondence: for instance, with the great Jewish theologian Abraham Heschel; with a leading Islamic scholar, Louis Massignon, and a Pakistani Sufi, Abdul Aziz; with Thich Nhat Hanh, the Vietnamese Buddhist monk, and D. T. Suzuki, the famous Japanese expert on Zen. Merton was a pioneer in what we now call interreligious dialogue. He became deeply conversant in and published essays on the most varied spiritual traditions: on the Jewish Hasidim, on the Sufis of Islam, on Protestant Shakers and Russian Orthodox startsy, on Chinese Taoists and Japanese Buddhists. Zen especially fascinated Merton, and his essays on it appear in two late works, *Mystics and Zen Masters* (1967) and *Zen and the Birds of Appetite* (1968). Merton had learned much from Suzuki's works. The two not only corresponded; in 1964, Merton was given permission to make his first long trip away from the monastery to go to New York City, where he and the elderly Suzuki were able to meet face to face.

Solitude

Merton's outward turn to the world was matched, paradoxically, by an inward quest for solitude. Contrary to what many would suspect, Cistercian lifestyle, at least in the 1940s and 1950s, allowed little time or leeway for solitude. This had long been a problem for Merton. Merton's research into the early history of the Cistercian order alerted him to forgotten traditions of hermitage. Making his case with these historical precedents, he began pleading for greater opportunities to be alone and in 1953 was granted permission to use a small building, "nothing more than a toolshed." In 1960 Merton and his novices built a cabin that was to be used as an occasional hermitage and also a center for ecumenical discussions. In August 1965 Merton officially began his life as a hermit. A Latin American journal asked Merton to describe his experience in solitude, and he replied with an eloquent essay, "Day of a Stranger." He first described the physical layout and how he shared his wooded confines with birds:

> I exist under trees. I walk in the woods out of necessity. I am both a prisoner and an escaped prisoner. I cannot tell you why, born in France, my journey ended here in Kentucky . . . Do I have a "day"? Do I spend my "day" in a "place"? I know there are trees here. I know there are birds here. I know the birds in fact very well, for there are precise pairs of birds (two each of fifteen or twenty species) living in the immediate area of my cabin. I share this particular place with them: we form an ecological balance. This harmony gives the idea of "place" a new configuration. As to the crows, they form part of a different pattern. They are vociferous and self-justifying, like humans. They are not two, they are many. They fight each other and the other birds, in a constant state of war.[15]

This passage lets one see the various threads of Merton's inner life: his eye for nature, his taste for contemporary literature, his thoughts on prayer and contemplation, even his social protest. At one point he mentions seeing American bombers flying overhead:

I have seen the SAC plane, with the bomb in it, fly low over me and I have looked up out of the woods directly at the closed bay of the metal bird with a scientific egg in its breast! A womb easily and mechanically opened! I do not consider this technological mother to be the friend of anything I believe in. However, like everyone else, I live in the shadow of the apocalyptic cherub.[16]

Just as Merton was settling into a hermit's life, he fell deeply, madly in love. Around Easter 1966 Merton had to undergo back surgery in a Louisville hospital. There he met a young nurse nearly thirty years his junior. They began an intense relationship, exchanging love letters, calling surreptitiously on the phone, meeting secretly. Throughout the affair, Merton recorded his intense, almost overwhelming feelings in his private journals, which have only recently been published. It lasted roughly six months. Merton and "M"—as she is called in the journals—may not have had sexual intercourse, but the temptation was certainly there. Merton discovered both the fragility of his own integrity and the depths of his sexual yearnings. He also rediscovered how deeply committed he was to his vocation as a monk and a contemplative. It proved, in the end, a momentous and difficult voyage of self-discovery, both disconcerting and healing.[17]

Late in life Merton took up photography, and with encouragement from friends who were professional photographers, such John Howard Griffin, the camera became for Merton a contemplative discipline. It offered him a new medium for "natural contemplation," that "intuition of divine things in and through the reflection of God in nature."[18] Merton's surviving photos, done during these years, explore the play of light and dark on objects both ordinary and ignored.

Pilgrimage to Asia

In 1968 Merton received an invitation to attend a conference of Western and Eastern monks in Bangkok. It offered him a chance to see Asia and its monasticism at first hand for the first time. It was also his longest extended departure from the monastery in twenty-six years. On his way to Asia, he meandered, stopping first in New Mexico, California, and Alaska, scouting possible sites for a future hermitage. He also used the opportunity to visit friends, staying with the Beat poet and founder of City Lights Lawrence Ferlinghetti in San Francisco. Once in Asia, Merton spent almost two months traveling in and around India. In a talk delivered in Calcutta in October, he described his outlook and hopes:

I have left my monastery to come here not just as a research scholar or even as an author (which I also happen to be). I come as a pilgrim who is anxious to obtain not just information, not just "facts" about other monastic traditions, but to drink from ancient sources of monastic vision and experience. I seek not only to learn more (quantitively) about religion and about monastic life, but to become a better and more enlightened monk (qualitatively) myself.[19]

One pivotal meeting was with the young Dalai Lama in Dharamsala near the Himalayas in northern India. Another key moment was a visit to Sri Lanka, to the ancient ruins of Polonnaruwa, famous for its great reclining Buddha and other magnificent Buddhist sculptures. The site provoked a powerful spiritual and aesthetic experience:

Looking at these figures I was suddenly, almost forcibly, jerked clean out of the habitual, half-tied vision of things, and an inner cleanness, as if exploding from the rocks themselves, became evident and obvious . . . The thing about all this is that there is no puzzle, no problem, and really no "mystery." All problems are resolved and everything is clear, simply because what matters is clear. The rock, all matter, all life is charged with *dharmakaya* . . . everything is emptiness and everything is compassion. I don't know when in my life I have ever had such a sense of beauty and spiritual validity running together in one aesthetic illumination. Surely, with Mahabalipuram and Polonnaruwa my Asian pilgrimage has become clear and purified itself. I mean, I know and have seen what I was obscurely looking for. I don't know what else remains but I have now seen and have pierced through the surface and have got beyond the shadow and the disguise.[20]

Merton arrived for the conference in Bangkok on December 7. On the morning of December 10 Merton delivered his paper "Marxism and Monastic Perspectives" to the gathered monks and scholars. A question-and-answer session was scheduled after lunch, but Merton did not appear. Several people went searching for him and discovered him dead in his room. It appears that he had taken a shower after lunch and was fatally electrocuted when he turned on the electric fan—which, it turns out, had a short. His body was flown back to the United States aboard a military aircraft, together with the bodies of American soldiers killed in Vietnam. The irony of this final flight, given Merton's outspoken antiwar stance, has not been lost on later observers.

At his funeral, the final pages of *The Seven Storey Mountain* were read aloud. In these pages, the "I" who speaks is not Merton, but Christ, who speaks prophetically to young Merton about his future and his death:

> I will give you what you desire. I will lead you into solitude. I will lead you by the way that you cannot possibly understand, because I want it to be the quickest way... Everything that touches you shall burn you, and you will draw your hand away in pain, until you have withdrawn yourself from all things. Then you will be all alone... Do not ask when it will be or where it will be or how it will be: On a mountain or in a prison, in a desert or in a concentration camp or in a hospital or at Gethsemani. It does not matter. So do not ask me, because I am not going to tell you. You will not know until you are in it. But you shall taste the true solitude of my anguish and my poverty and I shall lead you into the high places of my joy and you shall die in Me and find all things in My Mercy which has created you for this end... That you may become the brother of God and learn to know the Christ of the burnt men.[21]

MYSTICISM OF A GUILTY BYSTANDER

This biographical sketch should forewarn us that there was nothing simple about Merton. He was at once a monk and a spiritual director, a social critic and an ecumenist. But above all, he was a writer: a prolific—even obsessive—essayist, poet, letter writer, and journal keeper. And for one who spent the bulk of his adult life in one place, in an isolated monastery in the hills of Kentucky, his intellectual and imaginative world was vast. It moved backward in time, to studies on the early desert fathers and medieval Cistercian hermits; it moved outward to newspaper headlines, to burning social issues such as nuclear weapons, the Vietnam War, and the civil rights movement; and it moved across the globe, to a religious landscape that included Sufi mystics and Taoist solitaries, Hasidic rabbis and Zen masters. All of this fed into and shaped his mystical theology. His mystical theology is a remarkable synthesis—made all the more remarkable by the fact that his work remains so immensely readable.

Merton's synthesis could only have appeared in the modern world. He encapsulated his unique vantage point in the title of one of his finest works, *Conjectures of a Guilty Bystander*. As a monk, he had consciously chosen to stand on the world's sidelines. Yet as one born in a bloodstained age, he shared humanity's collective guilt. What he offered were not answers, but conjectures—questions and queries, perspectives from a sidelined but deeply committed watcher. I will not try and summarize Merton's mystical spirituality here. Others have done that better and in a depth appropriate to the scale of his corpus. I will focus, rather, on a few of his most famous passages to draw out what he says about God, about prayer, and about our hard-to-read hearts.

Fourth and Walnut

Merton does not seem the stereotypical mystic. He reports no visions or voices and, in fact, was openly skeptical of such things. But in his journals he records both extraordinary experiences and remarkable reflections on them. These detail his profound sense of God's presence in—and absence from—the world around him. Merton experts have singled out several accounts that could be designated "mystical." I mentioned one earlier, his experience at Polonnaruwa. But the most famous is an incident that took place on March 18, 1958, while he happened to be in Louisville running an errand. Standing at the intersection of Fourth and Walnut, he had a sudden, extraordinary epiphany. Merton's account of it, which appears in his *Conjectures of a Guilty Bystander*, is memorable and needs to be quoted at length:

> In Louisville, at the corner of Fourth and Walnut, in the center of the shopping district, I was suddenly overwhelmed with the realization that I loved all those people, that they were mine and I theirs, that we could not be alien to one another even though we were total strangers. It was like waking from a dream of separateness, of spurious self-isolation in a special world, the world of renunciation and supposed holiness. The whole illusion of a separate holy existence is a dream. Not that I question the reality of my vocation, or of my monastic life; but the conception of "separation from the world" that we have in the monastery too easily presents itself as a complete illusion: the illusion that by making vows we become a different species of being, pseudo-angels, "spiritual men," men of interior life, what have you . . . This sense of liberation from an illusory difference was such a relief and such a joy to me that I almost laughed out loud. And I suppose my happiness could have taken form in the words: "Thank God, thank God that I *am* like other men, that I am only a man among others." To think that for sixteen or seventeen years I have been taking seriously this pure illusion that is implicit in so much of our monastic thinking. It is a glorious destiny to be a

member of the human race, though it is a race dedicated to many absurdities and one which makes many terrible mistakes; yet, with all that, God Himself gloried in becoming a member of the human race. A member of the human race! To think that such a commonplace realization should suddenly seem like news that one holds the winning ticket in a cosmic sweepstake. I have the immense joy of being *man*, a member of a race in which God Himself became incarnate . . . My solitude, however, is not my own, for I see now how much it belongs to them—and that I have a responsibility for it in their regard, not just in my own. It is because I am one with them that I owe it to them to be alone, and when I am alone they are not "they" but my own self. There are no strangers! Then it was as if I suddenly saw the secret beauty of their hearts, the depths of their hearts where neither sin nor desire nor self-knowledge can reach, the core of their reality, the person that each one is in God's eyes. If only they could all see themselves as they really *are*. If only we could see each other that way all the time. There would be no more war, no more hatred, no more cruelty, no more greed . . . Again, that expression, *le point vierge* (I cannot translate it), comes in here. At the center of our being is a point of nothingness which is untouched by sin and by illusion, a point of pure truth, a point or spark which belongs entirely to God, which is never at our disposal, from which God disposes of our lives, which is inaccessible to the fantasies of our own mind or the brutalities of our own will. This little point of nothingness and of *absolute poverty* is the pure glory of God in us. It is so to speak His name written in us, as our poverty, as our indigence, as our dependence, as our sonship. It is like a pure diamond, blazing with the invisible light of heaven. It is in everybody, and if we could see it we would see these billions of points of light coming together in the face and blaze of a sun that would make all the darkness and cruelty of life vanish completely . . . I have no program for this seeing. It is only given. But the gate of heaven is everywhere.[22]

This famous passage can be read psychologically, as a breakthrough. It is important to remember Merton's background. The young Merton, the Merton of *The Seven Storey Mountain*, had been a world-denier. To use the rhetoric of old-school monasticism, he had fled the world to save his soul. Yet here in this midlife moment, he recognized that all that was an illusion, that for sixteen or seventeen years he had lived a lie of sorts, that he had fashioned his religious identity around a "dream of separateness," as he now called it. He celebrated now not his separateness, but his solidarity, his "immense joy of being *man*." That meant that he had to recenter his identity. He now had to live his solitude not over against, but for the sake of, others. But there is something more at play here. This is not simply an intellectual insight, but something deeper—intuitive, instantaneous. He sees, knows, feels, all at once, his solidarity with others, that "they are not 'they' but my own self."

But the passage describes something more than a psychological breakthrough. It voices a profound and fundamental religious insight: one should see in each person a God-given dignity. In many mouths, that insight might be no more than a well-worn truism. But Merton speaks of it here as an experience pungently savored. The very force of the telling seems to point to the unexpected depths, indeed, to a mystical source for this realization. He speaks of seeing "the secret beauty of their hearts, the core of their reality, the person that each one is in God's eyes." Notice that Merton makes no mention here of a "vision" in imaginative terms. He is not seeing something inside his head. It is not an innerworldly nor an otherworldly experience. There is no mention of ecstasy, no trance or out-of-body experience. There is nothing dreamlike about it. On the contrary, it is a seeing that makes ordinary seeing seem dreamlike. He sees people with his senses fully operative. At the same time, he sees them in a way that breaks through the surface of things, seeing them not simply with his senses, but seeing them as they are in their truest identities, as images of God who walk around the streets oblivious to their God-given beauty. That is the mystical here. Note the way he says that if others could see what he was seeing, there would be no more war, no more hatred. The seeing is the breakthrough. The mystical here is not about visions; it is not seeing another world or an inner world. The mystical is seeing this world in a God-given light. And in this seeing, as he says at the end, "the gate of heaven is everywhere."

Was this a mystical experience? In the preface, I noted that we cannot be naive in the way we understand mystics, that we meet mystics and their experiences via texts that have come down to us and that we need to be alert to mystical texts, first of all, as texts. This passage is a good example. The publication a few years ago of Merton's private journals enabled scholars to compare this famous version in *Conjectures* with the original journal entry, written eight years earlier on the very day of the event. The private journal version is much simpler, much shorter, with little mystical language.[23] This raises a key question: Do we presume that the early, simpler version records the real event and therefore interpret the mystical language of the *Conjectures* version as a later overlay? Or, on the other hand, do we read the later version as the more authentic—that Merton's own mystical insight has awakened and deepened over time? This is a key question, and one that occurs with other famous mystics such as Julian of Norwich.[24]

Merton was a longtime reader of mystical authors, and his language in this passage owes much to earlier mystical texts. But Merton does not parade his sources. They lie beneath the surface, within his seemingly spontaneous word choice and imagery. But one instance leaps out, his phrase *le point vierge* (virginal point). Merton says, "I cannot translate it," not because he cannot produce a literal translation, but because the phrase held such a rich cluster of meanings. It came from Louis Massignon, a French specialist in the mystical thought of Islam. Massignon wrote extensively on the tenth-century Sufi mystic and martyr al-Hallāj and regularly quoted one of al-Hallāj's sayings: "our hearts are a virgin that God's truth alone opens." [25] The "virginal point" refers to the mystic's inner depths where, according to al-Hallāj, "no dreamer's dream penetrates, . . . where the presence of the Lord alone penetrates." Massignon, in an essay on medieval Christian and Muslim mystics, remarked that "introspection must guide us to tear through the concentric 'veils' which ensheathe the heart, and hid from the virginal point (*le point vierge*), the secret wherein God manifests Himself."[26] This passage shaped Merton's language here. Merton and Massignon began corresponding in 1959, one year after Merton's Fourth-and-Walnut experience. They became friends, and Merton—who was fluent in French—read Massignon's works extensively. He found Massignon's terminology (and, behind it, the Muslim mystic's terminology) a cogent way to express his earlier experience.

What does one make of all of this—the two accounts of the event, the borrowed phraseology? Does all this disqualify it as a "mystical experience"? Some might think so. I would argue, rather, that hindsight, combined with reading, taught Merton how to speak more precisely about the mystical element in his own experience. His readings of Massignon and Sufi mysticism had increased his vocabulary, so to speak, enabling him to better articulate his experience. Even if one grants this, was the incident at Fourth and Walnut "mystical" in the sense of being an experience of God? We saw how Gerson spoke of the mystical as an experiential knowledge of God that came through "unitive love." Was this an experience of "unitive love"? It was certainly an experience of Merton's unitive love with his fellow human beings. He experienced the people he saw around him as sacred, as bearers of the divine stamp. Some might argue that the incident is not, per se, a *direct* experience of God. This, of course, presumes that God can be experienced *directly*, without any mediation whatsoever. The incident at Fourth and Walnut was clearly an epiphany, and on reflection, Merton saw it as a profound experience of God's presence. Does this answer the question? Perhaps not. But it does show how tricky it is to single out this experience—and possibly any experience—as unequivocally "mystical."

Contemplation

William Shannon, one of Merton's finest interpreters, has remarked out that "contemplation was not one of many topics in Merton's field of vision, it was the focal point...the center from which his reflections on the human condition came forth and the goal to which they returned. It is no exaggeration to say that contemplation was the explicit theme, or at least the implied background, of everything that Merton wrote."[27] Merton addressed the issue of contemplation over the breadth of his career, from one of his first books (*What Is Contemplation?*, 1948) to one of his last (*Contemplation in a World of Action*, 1971).

Merton gives a cogent exposition in what many consider his best book, *New Seeds of Contemplation* (1962). In its opening chapters, Merton spells out what contemplation is and what it isn't. Contemplation, he argues, "is not trance or ecstasy, nor the hearing of sudden unutterable words, nor the imagination of lights"; it is not "emotional fire" nor the "sweetness" of religious exultation; nor is it the gift of prophecy; a contemplative is not a thinker per se, "still less one who sits around with a vacant stare."[28] Contemplation—defined positively—"is the highest expression of man's intellectual and spiritual life"; it is "that life itself, fully awake, fully active, fully aware that it is alive"; it is "a vivid realization of the fact that life and being in us proceed from an invisible, transcendent and infinitely abundant Source"; it "*knows* the Source, obscurely, inexplicably, but with a certitude that goes beyond both reason and beyond simple faith."[29] These may sound like definitions, but the way that Merton piles one definition upon another makes it clear that he is trying not to define contemplation but to point to it as a lived reality, as an experience that defies definition. He often resorts to paradox, even oxymoron. He admits, for instance, that contemplation is a "kind of spiritual vision," but then he retracts the claim, arguing that contemplation is "not vision because it sees 'without seeing' and knows 'without knowing.'" He says that it offers knowledge, but "a knowledge too deep to be grasped in images, in words, or even in clear concepts."[30]

Merton admits that poets, musicians, and artists taste something like the contemplative experience. But Merton is a theist and a Christian, and for him, contemplation involves a this-worldly encounter with God: "Contemplation reaches out to the knowledge and even to the experience of the transcendent and inexpressible God. It knows God by seeming to touch Him. Or rather it

knows Him as if it had been invisibly touched by Him . . . Hence contemplation is a sudden gift of awareness, an awakening to the Real within all that is
real. A vivid awareness of infinite Being at the roots of our own limited being."[31] Merton here captures the paradox. The God whom the contemplative
seeks is both experienced and beyond experience, is both knowable and un-
knowable. Merton makes this point more precisely in a late essay: "The heart of
the Christian mystical experience is that it experiences the ineffable reality of
what is beyond experience. It 'knows' the presence of God, not in clear vision
but 'as unknown.'"[32] Note also that Merton says that in contemplation one
knows "as if . . . invisibly touched by Him." Merton the Christian insists that we
do not touch God; God touches us. William James had spoken of mystical
experience as "passive." For Merton, contemplative experience is not passive,
but graced, "a sudden gift of awareness." In Christian mysticism, the initiative
always comes from God. Merton makes this point later, shifting metaphors
from touch to hearing: "Contemplation is also the response to a call: a call from
Him who has no voice, and yet Who speaks in everything that is, and Who,
most of all, speaks in the depths of our own being: for we ourselves are words
of His."[33] Again Merton resorts to paradox. Contemplation is a "call" from
One-with-No-Voice. How does one hear God? Here he points to two places:
outward to creation, where God "speaks in everything that is," and inward to
our own heart, where we discover that "we ourselves are words of His." Merton
draws on here—yet leaves unnamed—two distinct Christian mystical traditions, the Franciscan (finding God in creation) and the Augustinian (finding
God within).

What does contemplation feel like? What is the experience? Merton offered many descriptions over the course of his career, but in *New Seeds* he gives
his most striking. He begins by contrasting ordinary seeing with contemplative
seeing, noting that "the sharpest of natural experiences is like sleep, compared
with the awakening which is contemplation." He then points out that the way
upward to God is really inward, and that at one's deepest center one discovers a
sort of trapdoor:

A door swings open in the center of our being and we seem to fall
through it into immense depths which, although they are infinite,
are all accessible to us; all eternity seems to have become ours in this
one placid and breathless contact. God touches us with a touch that
is emptiness and empties us. He moves us with a simplicity that
simplifies us. All variety, all complexity, all paradox, all multiplicity
cease. Our mind swims in the air of understanding, a reality that
is dark and serene and includes in itself everything. Nothing more is

desired. Nothing more is wanting. Our only sorrow, if sorrow be possible at all, is the awareness that we ourselves still live outside of God.[34]

Toward the end of *New Seeds*, Merton offers still another definition of contemplation: "The union of the simple light of God with the simple light of man's spirit, in love, is contemplation."[35] Note the stress on "union," on "love." This echoes Gerson's definition, but where Gerson spoke of "mystical theology" Merton speaks of "contemplation." The difference in terminology is conscious. Merton preferred to speak the language of contemplation. The word "mysticism" simply carried too much baggage. It also tended to be limited to "peak experiences." Merton thought of contemplative experience not simply as "peak experiences" (such as the Fourth-and-Walnut episode)—it was broader, more routine, finding God's presence in the ordinary and the everyday. There are other convergences between Gerson and Merton. Like Gerson, Merton pleads for a reunion of theology and the mystical:

> Contemplation, far from being opposed to theology, is in fact the normal perfection of theology. We must not separate intellectual study of divinely revealed truth and contemplative experience of that truth as if they could never have anything to do with one another. On the contrary, they are simply two aspects of the same thing. Dogmatic and mystical theology, or theology and "spirituality," are not to be set apart in mutually exclusive categories, as if mysticism were for saintly women and theological study were for practical but, alas, unsaintly men. This fallacious division perhaps explains much that is actually lacking both in theology and spirituality. But the two belong together. Unless they are united there is no fervour, no life and no spiritual value in theology, no substance, no meaning and no sure orientation in the contemplative life.[36]

In Merton's day, as in Gerson's, scholastic theology (what Merton calls here "dogmatic theology") still held the field. And like Gerson, he was critical of its lack of fervour and appalled that theology and holiness would somehow seem like contrary vocations.

Seeking One's True Face

One of Merton's most poignant themes concerns the notion of the "false self." For Merton, sin is not so much doing bad things as it is living an illusion. In *New Seeds*, Merton argues that "for me to be a saint means to be myself.

Therefore the problem of sanctity and salvation is in fact the problem of finding out who I am and of discovering my true self."[37] Merton makes his meaning clear by contrasting human beings with the rest of creation. He notes that trees and animals are saints because they are what God made them to be. We, on the other hand, are free, free to be ourselves or free to be something else, true or false, real or unreal. But, as Merton notes: "We may wear now one mask and now another, and never, if we so desire, appear with our own true face. But we cannot make these choices with impunity. Causes have effects, and if we lie to ourselves and to others, then we cannot expect to find truth and reality whenever we happen to want them."[38] Merton is redefining original sin here. As he notes: "To say I was born in sin is to say I came into the world with a false self. I was born in a mask"; we are living contradictions in terms and "came into existence and nonexistence at the same time because from the very start I was something that I was not."[39] Merton thus frames the quest for holiness as the quest for one's true face.

Practice of Presence

Merton wrote much on prayer. How then did he himself pray? That, interestingly, is not easy to discover. As Lawrence Cunningham has noted, "For all of Merton's use of the 'I' in his writing he was notoriously reticent about his own life of prayer and his own contemplative experiences. Merton was both self-revealing and self-concealing."[40] Merton broke his silence in a fascinating January 1966 letter with Abdul Aziz, a Pakistani Sufi with whom Merton corresponded from 1960 until his death. Aziz asked Merton to speak about his daily life and his own practice of prayer. Merton replied that he did "not ordinarily write about such things" and asked that Aziz be "discreet about it." He added that such self-revelation was "a testimony of confidence and friendship." In the letter, Merton first outlined his daily routine and then offered the following account:

> Now you ask about my method of meditation. Strictly speaking I have
> a very simple way of prayer. It is centered entirely on attention to
> the presence of God and to His will and His love. That is to say that it
> is centered on *faith* by which alone we can know the presence of
> God. One might say this gives my meditation the character described
> by the Prophet as "being before God as if you saw Him." Yet it
> does not mean imagining anything or conceiving a precise image of
> God, for to my mind this would be a kind of idolatry. On the con
> trary, it is a matter of adoring Him as invisible and infinitely beyond

our comprehension, and realizing Him as all. My prayer tends very much to what you call *fana*. There is in my heart this great thirst to recognize totally the nothingness of all that is not God. My prayer is then a kind of praise rising up out of the center of Nothing and Silence. If I am still present "myself" this I recognize as an obstacle about which I can do nothing unless He Himself removes the obstacle. If He wills He can then make the Nothingness into a total clarity. If He does not will, then the Nothingness seems to itself to be an object and remains an obstacle. Such is my ordinary way of prayer, or meditation. It is not "thinking about" anything, but a direct seeking of the Face of the Invisible. Which cannot be found unless we become lost in Him who is Invisible.[41]

Merton speaks here with a Muslim accent. He quotes a prophetic saying (*hadīth*) and speaks of his prayer as *fanā'*, "annihilation," a term used by Sufis to describe union with God. Merton is sensitive to Aziz's perspective and is conversant with Sufi terminology. Even so, one can get a glimpse of Merton's way of prayer. What is striking is what he excludes. Note that he does not use the imagination. He does not picture God—in fact, he sees such a practice as "idolatry." Nor does he speak. There is no mention of words, of saying prayers (though he, of course, prayed the Psalms and the Eucharist in his daily routine). Nor he does "think about" God or anything else. Instead, his prayer centers on "presence"; it presumes and builds on faith; it praises without words and adores without gesture. It comes up out of the "center"—which presumes, of course, that one has found that interior center amid the swirl of one's inner consciousness. Merton resorts to paradox. He speaks of seeking the face of One who has no face, of finding God by becoming lost in Him. Merton does not mention it here, but this method of imageless, wordless, thought-free prayer is an ancient Christian practice, one cultivated for centuries among Christian monks. Merton was familiar with it from his study of the desert fathers, especially Evagrius Ponticus and John Cassian. The language of "Nothing" and "Silence" is found both in Sufism and in the Christian mystical tradition. For Merton, we must come before God as we are, and compared to the Reality that God is, we are nothings.

THE FIRE WATCHER

One of Merton's early works, *The Sign of Jonas*, ends with a twelve-page epilogue entitled "The Fire Watch, July 4, 1952," describing his experience as a night watchman in the monastery. Many consider it Merton's finest prose. The abbey of Gethsemani suffered from a history of devastating fires, and superiors worried about fire hazards: the tinderbox buildings, the old wiring, the crowded dormitories. And so it became customary for one monk each night to stay awake all night, keeping watch and making the rounds, keeping an eye out for possible signs of fire.

Merton tells how he spent such nights, moving through the monastery's dark corridors and catacombs. The prose is dense, at once description and metaphor: "At eight-fifteen I sit in darkness. I sit in human silence. Then I begin to hear the eloquent night, the night of wet trees, with moonlight sliding over the shoulder of the church in a haze of dampness and subsiding heat."[42] He traces his journey not only through places, but through time, moving backward, for example, as he revisits the dark novitiate and is "suddenly haunted by my first days in religion, the freezing tough winter . . . the smell of frozen straw in the dormitory under the chapel, the deep unexpected ecstasy of Christmas—that first Christmas when you have nothing left in the world but God!"[43] At the end, he describes his ascent up to the bell tower in an account shimmering with symbolic resonances:

> Now the business [of making the rounds] is done. Now I shall ascend
> to the top of this religious city, leaving its modern history behind.
> These stairs climb back beyond the civil war . . . And now my whole
> being breathes the wind which blows through the belfry and my hand
> is on the door through which I see the heavens. The door swings
> out upon a vast sea of darkness and of prayer. Will it come like this,
> the moment of my death? Will You open a door upon the great
> forest and set my feet upon a ladder under the moon, and take me out
> among the stars?[44]

Narrative and symbol join here. For Merton, the journey up to the bell tower is the soul's upward journey to God; the night sky, a glimpse of God's dark infinitude.

This fire-watcher image is an apt summary of Merton's whole mystical vision. For Merton, the journey to God is a journey through an ordinary, everyday landscape, but changed somehow, charged with the presence of God. It is also a journey that offers no easy answers. It is a journey through darkness. The mystic, Merton implies, is to be a watchman, to alert us to the fires, to the dangers in our world, helping us see things we do not see because we are consumed by sleep. Merton made no distinction between his writings on contemplation and his writings on social issues. The two sets of books were simply two sides of the same vigilance. Both came from Merton the fire watcher. He wrote on racism and nuclear war because he looked out from a monastery's belfry to a wider world. From this belfry-turned-fire tower, he could see the massive dangers of our world, its playing with the genocidal fire of nuclear weapons. He also peered down and saw the darkness of the human heart where such fire making is first devised and rationalized by those who know themselves only as the masks of the false self.

The mystic as fire watcher has another function: to help us recover our night vision, to see the beauty of our God-charged world. In the closing words of his epilogue, Merton describes the inbreaking dawn: "There are drops of dew that show like sapphires in the grass as soon as the great sun appears, and leaves stir behind the hushed flight of an escaping dove."[45] The image here is iconic: The mystic who flies at first light like a dove is the same mystic who gives us eyes to see the fragile ephemeral beauty of our God-charged world, where drops of dew glisten like sapphires for a few fleeting moments in a dawnlight through which most of us routinely sleep.

3

Mystic as Experienced Exegete: Bernard of Clairvaux

Bernard of Clairvaux had friends in high places. One was Haimeric, a cardinal and chancellor of the Church of Rome. He once asked Bernard to address some tough theological questions. Bernard thought the task daunting: "You usually ask me for prayers, not answers to questions."[1] But one question did intrigue him: Why love God? This, Bernard noted, "tasted sweeter" than the rest. And so he answered Haimeric with a remarkable treatise, *On Loving God* (*De diligendo Deo*). Its opening words confront the issue directly, tersely:

Vultis ergo a me audire	So you wish to hear from me
quare et quo modo	why and in what way God
diligendus sit Deus.	should be loved.
Et ego:	Here's my answer:
Causa diligendo Deum,	The cause of loving God—
Deus est;	it's God himself.
modus, sine modo diligere.	And the measure—it's to love [him] without measure.[2]

In the pages that followed, Bernard teased out this epigrammatic reply. That we love God springs naturally from gratitude: that God loved us first, that God has bestowed on us every imaginable gift—the air we breath, the sights we see, the food we eat, the very dignity we possess as human beings.[3] Bernard noted how we are creatures of limitless desire. Nothing really satisfies us: the well-dressed always want better clothes; the wealthy always want more money; men with beautiful wives always have a wandering eye for other beauties.[4] These cravings—these loves that scatter us in a thousand wrong directions—reveal something about our very constitution as human beings: that we are made to love, that nothing less than the infinite and infinitely desirable God can satisfy our inborn and insatiable yearnings. God has loved us first, and secretly, within the very fabric of our humanity and within the winding road of our lives, he woos us to love him:

> God causes you to desire and he himself satisfies your desire. I said before that God is the cause of loving God. I spoke the truth... He himself provides the occasion. He himself creates the longing. He himself fulfills the desire. He himself causes himself to be (or rather be made) such that he should be loved. He hopes to be so happily loved that no one will love him in vain. His love both prepares and rewards ours.[5]

The paradox of this fascinated Bernard. This inborn desire to love God comes from God and ends in God. God is the one who first causes us to love God; and God is the end toward which all our love is drawn. Bernard knew that love is often messy, and its motives, mixed. There are degrees of love, and we begin loving God for rather selfish reasons. But in time, we learn to love God for God's own sake. But that is not the end. Bernard suggests that at the pinnacle of spiritual ascent there is a pure self-emptying mystical love—one that can be tasted, if only briefly, in this life:

> When will flesh-and-blood experience such depths of feeling that our very being, drunk with divine love, forgetful of self,... throw us wholly upon God and, clinging to God, become one spirit with him and say, "My flesh and my heart have fainted, O God of my heart, O God, my share in eternity" (Ps. 72:26)? I would say this: a person is blessed and holy if he or she is gifted to taste this most rare experience in the course of mortal life—even if it be but once and last but a moment. To lose yourself as if you no longer existed, to sense yourself no more, to be emptied, virtually annihilated—that comes not from human feelings, but a heaven-sent conversion.[6]

This should give a good first taste of Bernard of Clairvaux (1090–1153), the most influential mystic of the Middle Ages—and arguably the most eloquent. He was a monk, an abbot, but hardly a retiring figure. Through much of his career, he moved on the world stage, and he was perhaps the best-known figure in Europe in the first half of the twelfth century. Bernard had a way with words and conjured up a new language for the Western mystical tradition, the language of mystical marriage. In this chapter, we will look first at Bernard's life and then at his mystical theology.

A MONASTIC CHIMERA

It is difficult to find entirely trustworthy sources for a biography of Bernard. The earliest biography, the *First Life* (*Vita Prima*), was the work not of a single author, but of a team of authors. One was William of St. Thierry (d. 1148), a Benedictine abbot and one of Bernard's closest friends (and, I should add, a gifted mystical writer in his own right). Another was Geoffrey of Auxerre, Bernard's longtime personal secretary. Given their long acquaintance with Bernard—not to mention their literary talents—one would expect both accuracy and poignant stories. But the *First Life* is disappointing. Medievals were rarely objective biographers. They wrote not for history's sake, but to convince readers that their subject was holy and deserved imitation and canonization. The *First Life*, like other medieval hagiographies, relies on stock motifs: childhood scenes that quaintly foreshadow later holiness, demonic temptations brilliantly thwarted, and so on. This makes reconstructing Bernard's life, especially his early years, difficult.[7] But critically used and combined with Bernard's own writings, the main lines of his career can be charted out.

Cîteaux and the Cistercians

Bernard was born of a noble family in Burgundy, in Fontaines-les-Dijon. He had a good literary education and would become one of the age's finest Latin stylists. In 1113, around the age of twenty-three, he entered the monastery of Cîteaux. There was nothing commonplace about Bernard's entrance nor about the place he entered. According to William, Bernard did not knock on Cîteaux's door alone. He had convinced some thirty others (including two brothers and an uncle) to accompany him. Equally striking was the monastery he joined. Cîteaux was a new foundation. Early documents call it just that: the *novum monasterium*, the "new monastery."[8] Its newness was not simply its age. Cîteaux marked a new approach to medieval monasticism. Its founders saw themselves embarking on a noble and a radical experiment of restoring Christian monasticism to its pristine origins. Cîteaux would become the fountainhead for a new European-wide order, the Cistercians. Cistercians would dominate the twelfth century, much as the Benedictines of Cluny had dominated the tenth and eleventh and as the Franciscans and Dominicans would later dominate the thirteenth. Cîteaux had been founded a generation earlier, in 1098, by a charismatic reformer, Robert of Molesme. Robert was succeeded by his disciple, Alberic, and then by a gifted Englishman, Stephen Harding. Under Harding's leadership, the experiment began to take off. A second major foundation, La Ferté, was in the works just as Bernard and his band of brothers arrived. Bernard's leadership skills were recognized almost immediately. At the young age of twenty-five, he was elected abbot of another new foundation, Clairvaux.

The early Cistercians, like other religious revolutionaries, joined slogan and symbol to carve out a distinctive identity. Their slogan was "back to the Rule," by which they meant getting back to the sixth-century *Rule of Benedict*. Most Western monasteries already adhered to it, and the most admired representative of the Benedictine vision had been the monastery of Cluny, with its vast network of affiliated monasteries sprawled across Europe. Benedict's *Rule* had its ambiguities, and every monastic house had, over time, filled in the gaps with local practices and local interpretations. The Cistercians came at the *Rule* with a rigorist eye and argued against what they saw as unwarranted mitigations of the *Rule*'s primitive rigor. The Cistercians noted Benedict's accent on simplicity and extended that principle to everything: food, dress, housing, even church architecture. They therefore denied themselves the "extravagance" of dyeing their robes black, and their plain white lambswool habit thus became their highly visible trademark. Bernard had a wicked sense of humor, and in his famous *Apology* to William of St. Thierry, delighted readers in the way he skewered his rivals at Cluny for their gourmet meals and their taste for fine wines, their stylish monastic garb and their costly church decor.[9]

The Cistercians backed up symbol and slogan with other differences. According to Benedict's *Rule*, a monk's daily life balances three elements: prayer (*opus Dei*, literally, the work of God), spiritual reading (*lectio divina*), and manual labor (*opus manuum*). Over the years, Cluny had altered that balance, throwing priority onto the *opus Dei*, the communal chanting of the Psalms. Cluny had become a sort of prayer factory, a spiritual energy plant where monks spent their days in near-continuous prayer for the welfare of the wider world. The Cistercians reacted against this and argued for a return to the *Rule*'s balance, which included restoring manual labor. When Cistercians sought land from their noble patrons, they asked not for prime real estate. They preferred to live in the wilderness, on land that was remote and undesirable. They thus began the twelfth century as pioneers, felling forests, clearing rocky ground, and draining swamps. Of course, today's pioneer quickly becomes tomorrow's landed gentry. But in Bernard's time, the Cistercians were genuine frontiersmen and seen as such.

On Conversion

Bernard was a born recruiter. We get a glimpse of his talent and methods in an incident that took place in Paris. Paris was then emerging as the center of one of the twelfth century's greatest creations, the university. Although the founding date of the University of Paris was 1200, when it received its official papal charter, the city had become a thriving educational center decades earlier. There, in 1140, Bernard delivered before a large assembly of faculty and students a breathtaking sermon that has come down to us as *On Conversion* (*De conversione*). When Bernard spoke of "conversion," he did not mean what we mean. He was not referring to changing religions or to converting to Christianity. He meant it in a quite specific and thoroughly medieval sense: becoming a monk. *On Conversion* is a recruiting talk. He opens by calling his hearers to listen not just to his words, but to turn within and listen to an inner voice, a "voice of magnificence and power, rolling through the desert, revealing secrets... The difficulty is to shut your ears to it. The voice speaks up; it makes itself heard; it does not cease to knock on everybody's door... Listen to the inner voice; use the eyes of the heart, and you will learn by experience."[10] Here Bernard plays on the Augustinian idea of Christ the inner teacher, who whispers to each person from the core of the human heart. Note also Bernard's appeal to experience. His audience included both theology students and master theologians. They were all readers, and central to medieval pedagogy was book learning, appealing to venerable, ancient authorities found within the pages of books. Bernard knew this and argued that, if his hearers simply joined the monastic life, they would learn of God not from books, but from personal experience.

Bernard then described monastic life in glowing terms: that it opened one to vast interior realms "where a man may eat the bread of angels,... a paradise of pleasure planted by the Lord,... a garden of sweet flowers... a cool resting place."[11] He promised that the mystical awaited them, that monastic life offered a first taste of heaven:

> These [mystical pleasures] are not among the rewards of eternal life. They should be thought of as wages of the soldiering of this life. They do not belong to what is promised to the Church in the future, but rather to what she is promised now. For this is the hundredfold reward which is set before those who despise the world. You do not need any speech of mine to commend this to you. The Spirit reveals it himself. You do not need to look it up in the pages of a book. Look to experience instead.[12]

This appeal to experience over books turned out to be remarkably successful. By sermon's end, twenty had committed themselves, and by the next morning three others had come around.

On the World Stage

The schools of Paris occupied Bernard in other ways. The city became the birthplace not only of Western higher education, but also of scholastic theology. Bernard was not a fan. He opposed the most famous Parisian professor of the day, Peter Abelard (d. 1142), and played a key role at the Council of Sens in Abelard's ouster and downfall. He later opposed one of Abelard's gifted students, Gilbert of Poitiers, though with less success. One sometimes reads in textbooks a contrast between Bernard's more traditional monastic theology and the new emerging scholastic theology, with its rationalist tone, its methods of doubt and logical rigor. The contrast, while not without merit, is sometimes overdrawn. Bernard had friends, such as William of Champeaux and Peter Lombard, trained in scholastic methods. And his writings show that from time to time he even adopted scholastic style: tight definition, rigorous syllogism, philosophic jargon. Bernard was not opposed to scholasticism as such, but to a scholasticism that, he believed, undermined the contemplative search for God.

Bernard held the title of abbot, but he hardly spent his days retired behind cloister walls. For much of his career, he moved on the world stage, a formidable figure knee-deep in the politics of both Church and state. In 1130 the papacy was rent by schism, resulting in rival popes, Anacletus II and Innocent II. Bernard threw in his lot with Innocent and traveled for several years as part of Innocent's entourage. In 1146 one of Bernard's own disciples, Eugenius III, was elected pope, the first Cistercian to become so. It would occasion one of Bernard's most eloquent works, *On Consideration* (*De consideratione*). In it he mixed admonition with satire, contrasting the poverty of St. Peter's papacy with Eugenius's pomps: "Peter is not ever known to have gone in procession adorned in jewels and silks, nor crowned with gold, nor mounted on a white horse, nor surrounded by knights, nor encircled by clamoring servants . . . In these respects you are the heir not of Peter, but of Constantine."[13] Bernard once complained in a letter to Eugenius that he was treated as the unofficial pope: "People are saying that it is not you but I who am the Pope and from all sides they flock to me with their lawsuits."[14] Eugenius, in turn, enlisted Bernard and his eloquence to recruit kings and armies for the Second Crusade. Bernard's recruiting succeeded, but the Crusade did not. It was a military disaster, and the blame rebounded, in part, on Bernard, tarnishing his reputation.

After all his wanderings, his preaching tours and recruiting efforts, his plunges into papal politics and ecclesiastical squabbles, Bernard knew himself to be no model contemplative. At his life's end, he admitted how the contradictions had worn him down. In one letter, he remarks: "May my monstrous life, my bitter conscience move you to pity. I am a sort of modern chimera, neither cleric nor layman. I have kept the habit of a monk, but I have long ago abandoned the life."[15] Bernard died a few years later in 1153, the cloud of failure still hanging over him. But opinion soon shifted. He would be canonized in 1174 and declared a Doctor of the Church in 1830.

THE SOUL'S BRIDEGROOM

Bernard's collected works now fill eight large volumes and include sermons, theological tracts, and some 547 letters. Étienne Gilson, one of Bernard's finest interpreters, once remarked that Cistercians give up everything for God except the art of good writing.[16] We saw that to be true for a modern Cistercian, Thomas Merton. It is even truer of Bernard, one of the finest Latin stylists of the Middle Ages. His prose is often dazzling, full of intricate wordplay: puns, alliterations, rhymes, even subtle cryptograms. Jean Leclerq, editor of Bernard's Latin works, once noted that "whole paragraphs can be arranged in the form of free verse, with couplets, refrains, and repetitions."[17] In reading Bernard, we need to remember that he was a monk and spent some hours each day practicing the monastic discipline of *lectio divina*, or sacred reading, that slow, meditative chewing over sacred words, whether from the Bible or from Church Fathers. The careful reader can hear a hundred voices behind Bernard's, the way he subtly absorbed phrases from Augustine or Gregory the Great, from the Psalms or the Gospels or St. Paul. But Bernard's works are neither pastiche nor patchwork. The voice is always his own, yet within it or under it there are haunting echoes of more ancient voices. It is no accident that later centuries dubbed him *doctor mellifluus*, the "honey-tongued teacher."

Sermons on the Song of Songs

Bernard's mystical masterpiece is the *Sermons on the Song of Songs* (*Sermones super Cantica canticorum*).[18] It comprises eighty-six sermons composed between 1135 and 1153 (the year of his death) and offers a verse-by-verse commentary— though Bernard only reaches the Song's third chapter. These sermons often sound spontaneous, but their final written form should not be mistaken for extemporaneous performances. Bernard apparently dictated them to scribes,

then worked and reworked them into highly polished literary artifacts. Even
after their initial publication, he continued to revise and polish them for years,
leaving the manuscript tradition with competing versions of the same texts.[19]

When Bernard chose to write on the Song of Songs (also called "Song of
Solomon" or, in older literature, "Canticle of Canticles"), he singled out one of
the most unusual books in the Bible. The Song of Songs itself is a love poem
(or poems), a marriage song, full of imagery both exotic and erotic. Its literary
merits are obvious to even the casual reader, but it hardly seems religious. How
then did it come to be included in the Old Testament? Not without some
dispute. The rabbis who shaped the canon of the Hebrew scriptures came to
see it not as a lusty nuptial, but as the Covenant's love song, a duet sung
between God as bridegroom and the Jewish people as his bride. In Christian
hands, it received new interpretations. It came to be read as an allegory of
Christ's love for his bride, the Church. Here "bride" was taken in the collective
sense, as a symbol for the *whole* Church. But Origen, the third-century Alex-
andrian biblical scholar, added a new layer. He treated it (at least sometimes) as
a love song between God and the *individual* soul. Origen's *Commentary on the
Song of Songs* (only a portion of which survives) was translated into Latin, and
its themes were picked up and repeated by the later Latin Fathers Ambrose and
Gregory the Great.[20]

Bernard knew and drew on this earlier tradition. But the Song became, in
his hands, something new. Certain mystics—and Bernard is among them—
have the uncanny ability to conjure up new languages to express the ineffable.
In these sermons, we see Bernard the wordsmith. He forged a new language
for the Western mystical tradition, creating a whole repertoire of images and
themes. Bernard was convinced that the Song of Songs' central theme—the
passions and love play of the wedding night—provides the best analogy for describing the human encounter with the divine. The claim is breathtaking. We
today use the term "mystical marriage" without thinking about how astonishing it is to claim that God and a human being can so unite as to be "married."

Mystical Union

In his inaugural sermon, Bernard noted that the Song of Songs, on the surface,
records passionate exchanges between a man and his wife on their wedding
night. But, he argued, the Song, beneath its exotic and erotic imagery, really
"celebrates the praises of Christ and his Church, the gift of holy love, the sacrament of endless union with God" and "expresses the mounting desires of the
soul, its marriage song, an exultation of spirit poured forth in figurative lan-

guage pregnant with delight."[21] This means that when the Song speaks of the "bridegroom" it refers (usually) to Christ and when it speaks of the "bride" it refers (usually) to the "soul."[22] In other words, Bernard (usually) interprets the "bride" to refer not just to women, but to men as well. It does help that the Latin word for "soul" is *anima*, a feminine noun. Even so, Bernard's language is strange. Bernard speaks of himself (and his fellow monks) in feminine terms, as "bride." Odd perhaps, but Bernard's portrayal of Christ as "bridegroom of the soul" would become a mainstay of the Western mystical tradition, much repeated and expanded over the centuries by mystic after mystic, most famously by the sixteenth-century Carmelites Teresa of Ávila and John of the Cross.

In these sermons, Bernard explores the union of God and the soul, its nature, its movements, and its joys. For Bernard, no word expresses that union better than "marriage": "When she loves perfectly, the soul is wedded to the Word . . . Truly this is a spiritual contract, a holy marriage. It is more than a contract, it is an embrace: an embrace where identity of will makes of two one spirit."[23] Note Bernard's terminology here: mystical marriage is an *identity of will*; Christ and the soul become *one spirit*. Bernard consciously echoes Paul's Letter to the Corinthians: "he who is united to the Lord becomes one spirit with him" (1 Cor. 6:17).[24] This text provides Bernard terminology to make a fundamental distinction. He did not take mystical union to mean the annihilation of the human, the swallowing up of the finite human into the divine infinity. Nor is this union of the human and the divine the same as the union of Christ and the Father. Following the traditional language of Christian doctrine, Bernard insisted that Christ and the Father "have and are one substance." With human beings, this union is different: "On the contrary, since God and man do not share the same nature or substance, they cannot be a unity, yet they are with complete truth and accuracy said to be one spirit, if they cohere with the bond of love. But that unity is caused not so much by the identity of essences as by the concurrence of wills."[25] Note Bernard's final phrase, "concurrence of wills" (as well as the earlier-cited "identity of will"). There are many ways to be united, many ways to be one. A person can be united with his or her body, a "oneness of person." That is not the unity Bernard is speaking of. On the other hand, a group of people can work together, the way that a football team or a musical chorus or an army work together, united in will, united in a common task. That is closer to what Bernard means. In this "concurrence of wills," God remains God and we remain ourselves, united but distinct. But for Bernard, mystical union is more than teamwork, much deeper, much more intimate. Bernard insists that this is a genuine marriage; however, "there is no betrothal or union of equals here."[26] God initiates everything; the soul "surrenders

wholly to grace, attributing to him both the beginning and the ending," real-
izing that "he was her lover before he was her beloved."[27]

Erotics of the Mystical

Bernard did not shy away from the Song of Songs' most erotic images: of
kissing, of breasts, of bridal chambers and marriage beds. Consider one example. Bernard spends no fewer than eight sermons explaining a single verse:
"Let him kiss me with the kiss of his mouth." This, to Bernard's ear, is a very
peculiar turn of phrase, this "kiss . . . with the kiss." How can a kiss kiss? The
phrase suggested to him a key theological distinction: Christ is the "kiss" who
alone receives the Father's "kiss"; we, by contrast, are "kissed by the kiss," that
is, by Christ.[28] This being "kissed by the kiss" is the "kiss of participation" in
the life of God:

> Felicitous . . . is this kiss of participation that enables us not only to
> know God but to love the Father, who is never fully known until he is
> perfectly loved . . . For if marriage according to the flesh constitutes
> two in one body, why should not a spiritual union be even more
> efficacious in joining two in one spirit? And hence anyone who is
> joined to the Lord is one spirit with him.[29]

Bernard spiritualizes things here and at every turn. A kiss is spiritualized
into a "participation" in which Christ becomes "one spirit" with us. The erotic
is thus deflected, turned inward, abstracted. Though he again and again takes
the greatest pains to deny the Song's literal meaning, such disavowals are only
half of the story. I believe that it is precisely the high tension between the literal
erotic imagery of the Song and its decoded mystical meaning that gives Bernard's language much of its pungent emotional force. Think of electricity, the
way sparks leap across gaps. The gap that arcs between the Song's eroticism
and the mystical decoding charges the air and gives Bernard's words their jolt,
their flash of luminosity.

THE BOOK OF EXPERIENCE

Traditional medieval theology spoke of God's giving two books to humankind,
books that allow us to read and know who God is. The first is the "book of
creation"; the second, the Bible. Bernard suggested that there is a third book: as
he says in sermon 3, "Today the text we are to study is the book of our own
experience."[30] This idea is one of Bernard's favorites. We got a glimpse of this

earlier when we saw how he stressed to the students of Paris that it is through experience, not books, that the monk comes to know God. Bernard deserves credit for bringing the word "experience" into the vocabulary of the Western mystical tradition.[31] But we need to be alert here. Although Bernard speaks of the mystical in experiential terms, he is no modern, and we must not conflate his understanding of experience with our own.

Bernard insisted that in "things divine" the experienced are the experts, that such matters remain "totally unknown except to those who have experienced them."[32] But even the experienced struggle to bring their experience into speech. Near the end of his life Bernard remarked: "Do you suppose, if I were granted that [mystical] experience, that I could describe to you what is beyond description?"[33] Bernard's remarks here presage William James's stress on the ineffability of the mystical experience. The views of the two men coincide in other ways. Bernard too emphasized the transiency of the mystical encounter. He once had a profound experience, entering the Word's "bedroom," but lamented (in a famous rhyme): "How rare a day, how short the stay!" (rara hora et parva mora).[34] Bernard appealed not only to his own experience, but also to that of his hearers and readers, asking them to compare his words against their own experience.

Experience of the Word

In sermon 74, Bernard speaks at length of his own experience of God. Harvey Egan has called this sermon "one of the most stunning attempts in the entire mystical tradition to describe the mystical experience."[35] Bernard opens the sermon by meditating on Song of Songs 2:17, on the word "return." Bernard reads this as the voice of the bride who pines for her absent beloved and calls him to "return." This prompts Bernard to speak of his own experience of God's comings and goings, the alternating ebb and flow of presence and absence: "Now bear with my foolishness for a little while. I want to tell you of my own experience, as I promised . . . I admit that the Word has also come to me— I speak as a fool—and has come many times."[36] "Many times"—that is the key phrase. Bernard claims to be much experienced. At the same time, we see the paradox of Bernard the writer: he speaks in his own voice, but the phraseology is St. Paul's (2 Cor. 11:1, 17). Bernard knew his monastic audience would hear the Pauline undercurrent and would remember that Paul too experienced a mystical transport; they would grasp that Bernard, like Paul, was boasting in his foolishness to celebrate the wisdom of God.

Bernard tries then to describe the experience of God's coming into the soul:

Yet however often he has come, I have never been aware of the moment of his coming. I have known he was there; I have remembered his presence afterward; sometimes I had an inkling that he was coming. But I never felt it, nor his leaving me. And where he comes from when he enters my soul, or where he goes when he leaves it, and how he enters and leaves, I frankly do not know. As it says, "You do not know where he comes from, nor where he goes" (John 3:8). That is not surprising, for of him was it said, "Your footsteps will not be known" (Ps. 76:20). He did not enter by the eyes, for he has no color; nor by the ears, for he made no sound; nor by the nostrils, for he is not mingled with the air, but the mind. He did not blend into the air; he created it. His coming was not tasted by the mouth, for he was not eaten or drunk; nor could he be touched, for he is impalpable. So by what route did he enter? Or perhaps he did not enter at all, because he did not come from outside? For he is not one of those who are without. Yet he does not come from within me, for he is good, and I know that there is no good in me.[37]

Note how often Bernard invokes negatives: God is *not* sensed, *not* seen, *not* heard, *not* touched, *not* tasted. Here Bernard describes by negating—a standard tactic of mystical discourse—insisting later that "none of my senses showed me that he had flooded the depths of my being." Earlier, he echoed Paul; here he quotes two biblical texts (John 3:8 and Ps. 76:20), both with negatives to underline his negative theology.

Bernard then anticipates the reader's obvious question: "You ask then how I knew he was present." After further negatives—"there was no sound of his voice, no glimpse of his face, no footfall"—Bernard finally affirms: "only by the warmth of my heart . . . did I know that he was there."[38] Bernard experienced a profound interior revolution "when the Bridegroom, the Word, came" to "root up and destroy, build and plant, water dry places and light the dark corners, make crooked straight and the rough places smooth," a "remaking and renewing of the spirit of my mind."[39] He speaks here of his interior experience of God, but again his wording is drawn from scripture. It is a conflation of two prophetic texts: first, the call of the prophet Jeremiah, who is told that God has appointed him "over nations and over kingdoms to pluck up and to pull down . . . to build and to plant" (Jer. 1:10); second, the prophecy of (Second) Isaiah who proclaimed the liberation of the exiles in Babylon by saying that God will "make straight in the desert a highway for our God," that "every mountain and hill be made low, the uneven ground shall become level" (Isa. 40:3–4).

In one crescendo, Bernard speaks of this experience as both an experience of God and an experience of his own vastness, of inner peaks and inner depths:

> I have climbed up to the highest that is in me, and see! The Word is far, far above. A curious explorer, I have plumbed my own depths, and he was far deeper than that. If I looked outward, I saw him far beyond. If I looked inward, he was further in still. And I knew that what I had read was true, that in him we live and move and have our being (Acts 17:38). But blessed is he in whom he has his being, who lives for him and is moved by him.[40]

For Bernard, this was an experience of God's omnipresence—that "in him we live and move and have our being." But we should not miss what Bernard is saying here. This was neither an unmediated nor an uninterpreted experience. It was an experience whose meaning only came clear from reading: *"that what I read was true."* Reading—in this case, reading Acts 17:38—gave him words to name an otherwise ineffable experience.

Bernard insisted that he discovered God's presence by the experience of God's absence: "when the Word left me," everything became "dim and weak and cold"; it was as though "you had taken the fire from under a boiling pot." For Bernard, the Song of Songs' pungency, its force, comes from the way it so precisely names this experience of absence: "With such an experience of the Word, is it surprising if I speak the words of the Bride and call him back when he absents himself, when even if I do not burn with an equal desire, I burn with a desire like hers? It will be natural to me as long as I live to speak 'Return,' the word of recall, to call back the Word."[41]

Sermon 74 is telling in important ways. Bernard strives to articulate something he has experienced, he says, "many times." These experiences were interior, perhaps ecstatic. There is nothing in Bernard's report of voices or visions, nothing of the sort of stereotyped mystical paraphernalia that contemporary readers might expect. Bernard's report is simpler, more austere. He recounts an experience of presence and of love—of loving God and being loved by God. That, interestingly, is Bernard's very definition of divine presence.[42]

The Biblical and the Autobiographical

Sermon 74, I should add, is easy to misinterpret. On the surface, it sounds like autobiography, pure and simple. Bernard, after all, speaks in the first person and says explicitly that he is recounting his own experience. But such a reading is off the mark. For medievals, truth lies not in personal experience, but in the Bible. The biblical quotations that lace this passage are not mere rhetoric. They indicate what Bernard sees himself doing: using the Bible to sift through, discern, and articulate his experience. Michael Casey, in a recent study, has stressed how Bernard sees things differently from moderns:

> Neither Bernard nor his contemporaries would have considered it appropriate to parade their inner experience nakedly before their readers as a means of instruction. There is a reluctance to take personal experience as normative for others, and a reticence in speaking about the intimacies of spiritual encounter . . . For the medieval mind, experience was not automatically self-authenticating; its truth was demonstrated *a posteriori* by its conformity with revelation. Just as it is only by experience that we discover the full import of what we read, so the authentic meaning of experience is unveiled through its correspondence with divine revelation.[43]

Casey is not denying that sermon 74 reflects Bernard's experience. But he is aware of the peculiarly modern bias that locates truth in the subjective. That is not how Bernard understood "experience." For him and his medieval colleagues, we human beings are, because of sin, out of touch with the real world. Our world, however beautiful, is not the real world. God is the real world, heaven is the real world. We, on the other hand, move in a shadow realm, what Bernard liked to call the "land of unlikeness" (*regio dissimilitudinis*).[44] On the far side of Adam's Fall, we no longer see God, no longer know God amid the shadows of flesh and world. We do have an inner compass, at least the remnants of one, but cannot read it right without grace. That is why we need the Bible (and not just the biblical text itself, but the Bible interpreted over the centuries by the Church). The Bible provides the only sure guide. It is not an accident that Bernard describes his experience of the mystical in a biblical commentary. Nor is it an accident that when Bernard speaks, he "speaks Bible," making the Bible's vocabulary his own, weaving an intricate web of quotation and allusion. For Bernard, the Bible is a lexicon, a word book for naming experience. It also provides him the measure of that experience. The significance of this is not to be underestimated.

IMAGE AND LIKENESS

In sermons 80–83—among the very last he composed—Bernard asked a key question: What is "the affinity of the soul to the Word"?[45] Let me put this in more contemporary phrasing: What is it about human beings—about our constitution as human beings—that makes union with God even a possibility? This question probes the foundations of mysticism, its philosophic basis. To address the question, Bernard focused his reflections on Genesis 1:26, which says that human beings were made in God's "image and likeness." This pivotal text already had had a long history in Christian theological reflection. Bernard meditated upon it again and again in the *Sermons on the Song of Songs*, playing upon it as a melodic theme within the larger polyphony of his work.[46]

Bernard distinguished "image" from "likeness." We human beings, he insisted, possess an inherent nobility, a sacred dignity. This is God's image in us. It is impossible to lose, impossible to erase. Bernard often linked it to certain indelible human qualities, notably our freedom of choice.[47] I should add one theological wrinkle to this: For Bernard and the wider medieval theological tradition, Christ alone is the Image of God, while we are the image of the Image. Christ is the prototype, the true and original Image; we have been made "according to the image" (*ad imaginem*). This means that while Christ is God and we are not, we nonetheless bear a deep "kinship" (*cognitio*) with God. We have a natural "affinity" (*affinitas*) for God; we are drawn to God by a hidden force, by the deep-down core of our identity as human beings.[48]

Although our dignity as images of God remains, our likeness to God does not, at least not on the far side of Adam's fall. Adam's sin—and our own sins— have made us *unlike* God and, in a sense, have unmade our very humanity. Adam originally had the ability not to sin; we now are unable to avoid sinning. Our likeness to God has become blurred, faded, covered with sin's crass graffiti. In the beginning, God made human beings to be like himself in the moral sense, that is, "righteous," "upright" (*rectitudo*). Bernard notes while other animals walk about on all fours, humans walk upright. Our bodies are symbols of what we should be: we walk upright, we should be upright in heart and spirit. But sin has changed all that. We suffer a curvature (*curva*) of the spirit; we are bent souls in upright bodies. We are, quite literally, walking contradictions.[49] In our bentness, in our unlikeness, we have wandered off into this land of unlikeness. We now know neither God nor ourselves—at least not clearly. There is a profound irony in this, as Bernard notes: "Inasmuch as the soul becomes unlike God, so it becomes unlike itself."[50] Sin means we lose not only God, but our very selves. Sin quite literally goes against the grain of our nature.

Bernard was never one to downplay the depths of human evil. But he remained, in certain ways, an optimist about human nature. Early in sermon 83, he crafts a single twisting vinelike sentence that encapsulates the paradox of the human condition:

We have learned that every soul—
even though sin-burdened, vice-entangled, pleasure-enticed;
even though in exile, a prisoner-of-war, incarcerated in body,
     mud-stuck and mire-deep, limb-fastened and care-fixated;
even though strung-out over business wranglings,
     fear-knotted and sadness-crushed;
even though errant in wrong-headed wanderings,
     in anxious uneasinesses,
     in restless suspicions,
even though a foreigner in a foreign land, among enemies,
     and—as the Prophet says—one polluted by death with the dead
     and numbered among those going down to hell—
even so, we have learned, I believe, that every soul
     (however condemned, however hopeless)
can turn around, can turn back, and breathe once more
not only the hope of mercy, the hope of pardon,
but can even dare breathe aspirations of wedding-nights
     with the Word.[51]

This, for Bernard, names the human condition: no matter how anguished our current plight, the nobility of our nature offers hope. As Bernard adds, "Why should (the soul) not venture with confidence into the presence of him by whose image it sees itself honored, and in whose likeness it knows itself made glorious? Why should it fear a majesty when its very origin gives it ground for confidence?"[52] The long, winding road back to God is about recovering our "likeness" to God. In this journey, as the soul turns back to God, it at the same time turns back to itself and back into its true self. This gradual recovery of its original "likeness" is, according to Bernard, what "marries the soul to the Word." And, he adds: "It is like him in nature, but it shows that it wants to be like him by loving as it is loved."[53]

    The secret of mystical marriage is the discovery that to be oneself is to be in love with Love. In sermon 83 and throughout his writings, Bernard repeats the classic text from 1 John 4:16, that "God is love."[54] For Bernard, this meant that God is love in the absolute sense—that love is God's being, God's substance. And because God is Love itself and because we as creatures are made in God's image and likeness, we are by nature lovers. There is nothing more natural to us than loving. And so in one of the great crescendos of the *Sermons on the Song of Songs*, Bernard returns to a theme he had addressed decades earlier in *On Loving God*: "Love is its own merit and its own reward. Love needs no cause, no fruit besides itself; its enjoyment is its use. I love because I love; I love that

I may love. Love is a great thing; as long as it returns to its beginning, goes back to its origin, turns again to its source, it will always draw afresh from it and flow freely."[55] We love because we are lovers; we do what we are. That is Bernard's answer to the question he first raised in sermon 80, the question of "affinity of the soul to the Word." The key, as he sees it, is how we love and to what we turn our love. Love, to be pure, loves love. Pure love returns us to God, the original lover. God is the wellspring from which love flows and to which love flows back. This is the centerpiece of his teaching.

EXPERIENCE AND EXEGESIS

Jean Gerson deeply admired Bernard. On August 20, probably in 1402, Gerson delivered a sermon at the Cistercian College in Paris, celebrating Bernard as a man "most loving and most beloved by God."[56] Following Gerson, one could say that Bernard embodies one essential type of mystic: the mystic as beloved lover. There is no doubt that this two-sided experience of love—of loving God and being beloved by God—is the heart of his mysticism.

But I think that Bernard offers us another more urgent lesson as we probe this thing called mysticism. In chapter 1, we saw that William James did much to set the terms of the way mysticism is studied. James understood mysticism, above all, as experience. Bernard, at first sight, seems to confirm that bias. As I noted, Bernard can be credited with introducing the category of experience into the vocabulary of the Western mystical tradition. Repeatedly Bernard spoke of his own experience, and repeatedly he asked that his readers compare his words with their experience. However much Bernard appealed to the "book of experience," I think we misunderstand him if we detach his mysticism from that other book, the Bible. In the very first *Sermon on the Song of Songs*, Bernard says: "Only the touch of the Spirit can inspire a song like this [Song of Songs], and only personal experience can unfold its meaning. Let those who are versed in the mystery revel in it; let all others burn with desire to attain this experience rather than merely learn about it."[57] Bernard believed that reading moves back and forth, between the Bible and the book of experience. One book illuminates the other. They are not equal reading. As Bernard makes clear, the Bible is the superior, and if something is found in the Bible that is missing in one's experience, then one needs to "burn with desire" to experience that something.

William James tried to understand mysticism stripped of the accoutrements of institutional religions, stripped of theologies, of rituals, of scriptures. This, I believe, is wrongheaded. Frankly, without them, Bernard's mysticism is unimaginable and unintelligible. Without his theology of image and likeness, his mysticism loses its philosophic intelligibility. Without the rituals of monasticism—chanting Psalms, preaching, *lectio divina*—the wellsprings that fed his mystical articulations are lost from view. And without the Bible, his mysticism descends into rootless poetics. For Bernard, mysticism is about more than experience. Bernard insists that the mystic must be an exegete, an interpreter. But in the end—and this is what is surprising—it is not so much the mystic who interprets the Bible; it is, instead, the Bible that interprets the mystic.

4

Mystic as Multimedia Artist: Hildegard of Bingen

In 1146 Bernard of Clairvaux was on the road, preaching and recruiting troops for the Second Crusade. He was also in the thick of a rancorous campaign against one of Abelard's disciples, Gilbert of Poitiers, trying (unsuccessfully) to get Gilbert's theology condemned as heresy. About this time he received an unusual letter from an unknown German abbess. She spoke in self-deprecating terms, calling herself "wretched, and indeed more than wretched in my womanly condition." Why had she written? "I am greatly disturbed by a vision which has appeared to me through divine revelation." She added that she had seen such "great marvels" ever since childhood. She claimed that the Holy Spirit had taught her to interpret the scriptures through a vision that touched her heart "like a burning flame." She did know how to read, but "only at the most elementary level," and she was untrained in "deep analysis." Her visionary gifts sometimes caused her great grief and left her bedridden. She had revealed her secrets to only one monk, but was now writing Bernard because a vision had prompted her to contact him to get his advice "about how much I should say of what I have seen and heard." In the vision, she had seen Bernard himself, "a man looking straight into the sun, bold and unafraid." At the letter's close, she waxed poetic, and in a closing prayer she gave hints of a fresh, original theological outlook: "May the Father, who sent the Word with sweet greenness (*viriditate*) into the womb of the Virgin, from which He soaked up flesh, just as honey is surrounded by the honeycomb, . . . lift up your spirit so that you may respond expeditiously to these words of mine."[1]

The writer of this letter was Hildegard of Bingen (1098–1179), one of the most remarkable women of the Middle Ages. The letter marked the beginning of her public career and the public recognition of her considerable gifts. Despite Bernard's sometime combative temperament, he responded favorably to her pleas, and his warm reception helped launch Hildegard's long and successful career of writing, preaching, and artistic achievement.

In this chapter, we are going to explore the life, artistry, and mystical writings of Hildegard. I focus on her for several reasons. First, this case study helps highlight a basic fact about Christian mysticism: that although men have dominated the history of Christian theology, women have been key players in the history of Christian mysticism. There are other, better-known women mystics, such as Teresa of Ávila or Julian of Norwich. But in the last forty years, scholars have been busy rediscovering, translating, and analyzing the writings of a host of lesser-known but no less remarkable women mystics: Birgitta of Sweden, Elisabeth of Schönau, Gertrude of Helfta, Mechthild of Magdeburg, Hadewijch, Margaret Ebner, and of course Hildegard.

But of all these, why Hildegard? Simply because she is interesting. She was a woman of wide-ranging talents: an abbess and a visionary, a musician and a composer, a dramatist and a poet, a medical writer and an herbalist, a preacher and a reformer. She was also, as Barbara Newman has noted, a woman of many "firsts."[2] She was the only medieval woman permitted by the pope to write books on theology and the only medieval woman permitted to preach publicly before both clergy and laity. She was the first known writer of a morality play and the only twelfth-century playwright known by name. She was a musician and composer of exceptional merit, and one of very few twelfth-century composers whose name is even known to us. Finally, Hildegard was a prolific writer of theological works and has been called "the first great woman theologian in Christian history."[3]

THE FEATHER OF GOD

The earliest biography of Bernard came from a circle of friends who wrote to promote his canonization. The same is true of Hildegard. The *Life of St. Hildegard* (*Vita Sanctae Hildegardis*) does not attempt to be objective, but sees the supernatural at every turn. Hildegard's first biographer was Godfrey of Disibodenberg, a monk who knew Hildegard only in her later years. Godfrey died even before Hildegard, leaving the project incomplete. So Hildegard's friends hired another monk, Theodoric of Echternach, to finish the work. Although Theodoric had a local reputation as a Latin stylist, he was not well equipped for the job. He had not even met Hildegard and knew little of her writings. Fortunately, he made an interesting editorial decision. Rather than composing a new biography, he published a collection of reminiscences Hildegard had once dictated to Godfrey, into which he interspersed his own less-than-helpful comments. He thus helped preserve precious firsthand accounts. A few other sources allow us to cross-check things: Hildegard's own writings are prefaced with autobiographical remarks, and she left behind a large body of letters.

Hildegard was born in 1098, the tenth and youngest child of a noble family in Bermersheim. Her parents "set aside their daughter for the service of the Church,"[4] and at the tender age of eight, she was assigned to serve Jutta of Sponheim, an anchoress who had set up a cell next to the monastery of St. Disibod in the diocese of Mainz. Jutta, like Hildegard, was a daughter of a noble family, and in those early years Hildegard worked as her handmaid. Jutta, in turn, acted as Hildegard's schoolmistress. Under her supervision, Hildegard learned Latin—vital to a religious life that required reading the Vulgate Bible and chanting the Psalms in Latin. Although Hildegard had little choice about her status as a child oblate, her decision to take lifelong religious vows was her own—something she did as a teenager. Jutta attracted a following, and before long, other noble women joined to form a fledgling Benedictine community.

When Jutta died in 1136, Hildegard was elected abbess. In an age teeming with new experiments in religious life, Hildegard was a bit old-fashioned, upholding traditional Benedictine values. She admired Benedict's *Rule*, in particular the way it stressed moderation in all things. In a letter to a fellow abbess, she spoke of the *Rule* as a ship's pilot, wise enough and skilled enough to steer those on board to harbor.[5] In another letter, she spoke of Benedictine abbots as gardeners who have "a garden of people" which, with God's grace, can "grow green through the dew and the rain of the fountain of living water."[6] Hildegard was old-fashioned in another way: her monastery had only women of noble birth in it, and she adamantly refused to admit nonnobles. This was not uncommon at the time, but in 1140s, it was beginning to seem out of step. A reform-minded canoness, Tengwich of Andernach, challenged the nobles-only policy in a letter to Hildegard that mixed pleasantries and venom. Hildegard snapped back: "Who would gather all his livestock indiscriminately into one barn—the cattle, the asses, the sheep, the kids?"[7] Hildegard was convinced that God had layered both creation and human society into well-ordered hierarchies; mixing noble and nonnoble could only lead to tawdry vices in both groups.

Not all was traditional in Hildegard's monastery. Tengswich cites rumors of odd, even scandalous behavior among Hildegard's nuns:

> We have, however, also heard about certain strange and irregular practices that you countenance. They say that on feast days your virgins stand in the church with unbound hair when singing the psalms and that as part of their dress they wear white, silk veils, so long that they touch the floor. Moreover, it is said that they wear crowns of gold filigree, into which are inserted crosses on both sides and the back, with a figure of the Lamb on the front, and that they adorn their fingers with golden rings.[8]

Hildegard answered at length, defending the ceremonial with a carefully crafted theology of virginity. Although married women must be subject to their husbands, preserve modesty, and not indulge in "prideful adornment of hair," and although they should not wear crowns or gold ornaments without their husband's permission, virgins need suffer no such restrictions. They stand in "the unsullied purity of paradise, lovely and unwithering." Virgins could celebrate their beauty, leaving their hair flowing, unbound and uncovered. They "are married with holiness in the Holy Spirit" and have the right to wear white bridal garb as "lucent symbol of betrothal to Christ." Crowns stamped with the seal of the Lamb of God symbolize both present reality and future hope as they come before "the great High Priest as an oblation presented to God." She adds that such ceremonial was inspired by "the revelation of the mystic inspiration of the finger of God" and that her defense comes not "from a human being but from the Living Light."[9] Hildegard does not say so here, but the hymns they sang likely included compositions by Hildegard herself.

In 1141, at the age of forty-two years and seven months—she dates it quite precisely— Hildegard experienced a sudden and powerful calling as a prophet: "Heaven was opened and a fiery light of exceeding brilliance came and permeated my whole brain, and inflamed my whole heart and my whole breast."[10] She claimed it gave her a miraculous ability to interpret the Bible. While she had had visionary experiences since childhood, this was different. The "Living Light" (*lux vivens*) had called her to put her visionary experiences into print and to promulgate their meanings. She received confirmation and encouragement from Volmar, a monk from the adjoining monastery of Disibodenberg who served for over thirty years as her secretary. This writing became her mystical masterpiece, the *Scivias*, a work we will examine in a moment.

Hildegard's career took its public turn, as we saw earlier, after her 1146 letter to Bernard of Clairvaux. Bernard intervened on her behalf with Pope Eugenius III, an ex-Cistercian and a disciple. Hildegard's own archbishop,

Heinrich of Mainz, also sent a delegation to Eugenius alerting him to her remarkable gifts. And so, in the winter of 1147–1148, Eugenius presided at a synod of bishops in nearby Trier. He procured a copy of the still unfinished version of the *Scivias* and read it aloud to the gathered bishops, commending it publicly. This papal commendation gave her the green light to continue writing the *Scivias*.

In a letter to Eugenius written about this time, Hildegard spoke of herself as a feather blown about by the breath of God.[11] It would become a favorite image, an emblematic self-portrait, appearing again and again in her letters. She may have thought of herself as powerless, as a plaything of God, but mere mortals had to reckon with her iron will. Soon after receiving Eugenius's approval, Hildegard announced another career-altering vision. She claims that a vision instructed her to leave the monastery of Disibodenberg, to which she and her nuns were attached, and found a new one some thirty miles away on the ruins of an old Carolingian monastery in Bingen. Hildegard cast all this as divine inspiration, but she clearly had a vested interest in such a move. Moving to Bingen meant she would enjoy both financial and jurisdictional independence from Kuno, then abbot of St. Disibod—just at a moment when Hildegard's reputation as a seer was attracting women of noble standing who were bringing along sizable dowries. Such a move also meant starting from scratch, or as Hildegard put it, "to go from a lushness of fields and vineyards and from the beauty of that place to an arid place with no conveniences."[12] She faced strong opposition both from within and without. There were even whisperings of demonic delusion. The abbot strongly opposed the move, as did a number of her own nuns. But Hildegard was tenacious and won the abbot's grudging permission, and she and twenty nuns moved on. In 1152 her new monastic community, named after and dedicated to St. Rupert, was formally consecrated. The move, in the end, cost her dearly. Her closest friend within the community, Richardis von Stade was elected abbess of a prestigious monastery. Despite Hildegard's protests and prophetic warnings, her appeals to Richardis's family, to archbishops, even to Pope Eugenius, Richardis departed, leaving Hildegard devastated.

When Hildegard had first written Bernard, she was little-known. After his commendation and Eugenius's official approval, though, she became an international celebrity, renowned for her prophetic abilities. Nicknamed "the Sibyl of the Rhine," she was consulted far and wide, as her letters give ample testimony. She corresponded with popes (Eugenius, of course, but also Anastasius IV and Hadrian IV) and with royalty (Emperors Conrad III and Frederick Barbarossa of the Holy Roman Empire; King Henry II of England and his wife, Eleanor of Aquitaine; and the Byzantine Empress Irene—to name only the most famous).

Her career took an even more public turn in 1158 when she embarked on a series of public preaching tours. The first took her to Mainz and Würzburg; the second, in 1160, to Trier and Metz; the third, from 1161 to 1163, up the Rhine to Cologne; and the fourth, in 1170 and 1171, to Swabia. We get a glimpse of her firebrand preaching from copies of sermons that she preserved in various letters.[13] She focused on reform themes typical of the Gregorian revolution of the century before, for example, the need for clerical celibacy, and the need for clergy to serve the Church instead of pursuing political favors. She also took up a defense of orthodoxy against the Cathar heresy that was making inroads into Germany from its base in southern France.

In the 1150s she was summoned to the imperial palace in Ingelheim and gave a private prophetic oracle to the Emperor Frederick I (better known as Frederick Barbarossa). Frederick had initially been supportive of Hildegard, bestowing on her an imperial charter in 1163 awarding privileges and protections for her new foundation at Rupertsberg. But for many years he was ensnarled in a complex political duel with the papacy, and he threw his support to the antipope Victor IV against the widely recognized Alexander III. When Victor died, Frederick refused to make peace and instead orchestrated the election of two more antipopes, one in 1164 and another in 1168. Hildegard turned against Frederick in 1164 and used her prophetic persona to denounce Frederick in dire apocalyptic terms.

Hildegard faced an unusual crisis in the year before her death. An excommunicated nobleman had been buried in the cemetery at Hildegard's monastery at Rupertsberg. The prelates of Mainz ordered her to have the body exhumed. When she refused, she and her nuns were placed under interdict, forbidden to celebrate the sacraments or the daily Liturgies of the Hours. This event occasioned one of Hildegard's most eloquent letters, in which she protested the interdict and used the opportunity to set out her distinctive theology of music. (More on this later.) The squabble was finally resolved, and the interdict was lifted months before her death.

When Hildegard died in 1179, her friends and the nuns at Rupertsberg worked for her canonization. They prepared not only the *Life of St. Hildegard*, but also a deluxe and lavishly illustrated edition of her theological writings and musical compositions. There was good hope for success, given Hildegard's papal contacts, but in Rome, then as now, things move leisurely. The canonization proceedings only began some fifty years after her death, in 1227. By then, virtually all witnesses were dead. The pope at the time, Gregory IX, admitted the bureaucratic bungling. In 1940 the Vatican approved the celebration of her feast for dioceses in Germany. Not only in Germany, but also among Benedictines, she is spoken of as "St. Hildegard."

THE VOICE OF THE LIVING LIGHT

Guibert of Gembloux, a Flemish monk, became Hildegard's final secretary in 1177, when she was seventy-nine years old. Two years earlier Guibert had introduced himself to Hildegard in a letter bubbling with enthusiasm. Concerning her reputed mystical powers, he had many, many questions:

> We—my friends and I—wish to know whether it is true, as is commonly said, that you completely forget what you have spoken in a vision once it has been taken down by your amanuenses at your bidding... We also desire to know whether you dictate those visions in Latin, or whether, after you have uttered them in German, someone else translates into Latin. We wish to know too whether you have mastered letters or the Holy Scriptures through study, or whether you have learned through divine anointing alone, which chooses those it would inspire.[14]

Hildegard delayed answering. So Guibert wrote again, this time with new questions: "Do you, for example, receive your visions in a dream while asleep, or do they come to you in an ecstatic state while awake?"[15]

When Hildegard finally answered, her lengthy reply was both striking and precise. It offers us a fascinating window into her experience:

> The words I speak are not my own, nor any human being's. I merely report those things I received in a supernal vision... I am now more than seventy years old. But even in my infancy, before my bones, muscles, and veins had reached their full strength, I was possessed of this visionary gift in my soul, and it abides with me still up to the present day. In these visions my spirit rises, as God wills, to the heights of heaven and into the shifting winds, and it ranges among various peoples, even those very far away. And since I see in such a fashion, my perception of things depends on the shifting of the clouds and other elements of creation. Still, I do not hear these things with bodily ears, nor do I perceive them with the cogitations of my heart or the evidence of my five senses. I see them only in my spirit, with my eyes wide open, and thus I never suffer the defect of ecstasy in these visions. And, fully awake, I continue to see them day and night... The light that I see is not local and confined. It is far brighter than a lucent cloud through which the sun shines. And I can discern neither its height nor its length nor its breadth. This light

I have named "the shadow of the Living Light," and just as the sun and moon and stars are reflected in water, so too are writings, words, virtues, and deeds of men reflected back to me from it. Whatever I see or learn in this vision I retain for a long period of time, and store it away in my memory. And my seeing, hearing, and knowing are simultaneous, so that I learn and know at the same instant. But I have no knowledge of anything that I do not see there, because I am unlearned. Thus the things I write are those that I see and hear in my vision, with no words of my own added. And these are expressed in unpolished Latin, for that is the way I hear them in my vision, since I am not taught in the vision to write the way philosophers do. Moreover, the words I see and hear in the vision are not like the words of human speech, but are like a blazing flame and a cloud that moves through clear air. I can by no means grasp the form of this light, any more than I can stare fully into the sun. And sometime, though not often, I see another light in that light, and this I have called "the Living Light." But I am even less able to explain how I see this light than I am the other one. Suffice it to say that when I do see it, all my sorrow and pain vanish from my memory and I become more like a young girl than an old woman.[16]

Hildegard offers similar accounts elsewhere: in the preface to the *Scivias*, in her 1148 letter to Pope Eugenius III, and in autobiographical reminiscences dictated to her first biographer Godfrey. But this late account to Guibert is the fullest and most precise. Both here and elsewhere, she remarks that she enjoyed (or suffered) visions since childhood. Note how strongly she insists that her experience comes neither from dreams (like those of her contemporary Rupert of Deutz) nor from ecstasy (like those of her contemporary Elisabeth of Schönau). Instead she saw things with "eyes open." These were not ephemeral out-of-body experiences, but a permanent waking vision.

What she saw was light, like a cloud illumined by the sun, but brighter and without borders ("I can discern neither its height nor its length nor its breadth"). This bright light served as a sort of interior movie screen onto which were projected "writings, words, virtues, and deeds of men." In other words, her visionary experience was a bit like watching a foreign movie, with both images and subtitles projected up on a white surface. She often spoke of seeing things shimmering, and so her metaphor here of seeing the sun and moon and stars reflected in water is an apt one. Note also how she stresses here, as throughout her writings, that she was "unlearned." She heard things in "unpolished Latin" and did not "write the way philosophers do." This was part of her prophetic persona, the contrast between the self-negating, unlearned, unpolished "poor female" and the commanding and confident voice of the "Living Light."

Charles Singer, an early-twentieth-century historian of medicine, was fascinated by Hildegard's reports. He noted how often she reported seeing flashing lights and having visions of concentric circles and fortress figures, and how sensitive she was to weather changes, to storms and wind. He concluded that Hildegard must have suffered from migraines, ones whose symptoms included visual auras, or "scintillating scotomata." The contemporary neurologist and popular science writer Oliver Sacks agreed and has done much to popularize Singer's diagnosis.[17] Such a condition may have been a factor in Hildegard's experience, though her descriptions, unlike modern accounts of the disease, stress the permanent character of the light she experienced. Even if one argues that some physiological condition influenced her visionary experiences—impossible to diagnose with any confidence, given the 800-year gap between her and us—Hildegard transformed this "disability" into a fount of enormous creativity.[18]

Hildegard's experiences, which she routinely described as "mystical," as offering "mystical knowledge" or "mystical secrets," led her more outward than inward. They prompted her to create a vast body of work: theological texts, illuminations, music, drama, and much else. To that we need to turn.

A VISIONARY THEOLOGY

A famous manuscript illumination shows Hildegard seated within her cell, holding a wax tablet on her knee and writing with a stylus; from the ceiling a five-tongued fire reaches down and covers her head; meanwhile her monastic secretary, Volmar, peers in through a window, looking down at what she writes. (See figure 4.1). This illumination captures in a nutshell how Hildegard saw her work as a mystic and theologian. She saw herself not as a religious author, but as an amanuensis of the divine. She reports that in her dramatic prophetic call of 1141 she heard: "O human, speak these things that you see and hear. And write them."[19] It was a common command, one she heard often: she was to "cry out and preach and write down my mysteries—what you see and hear in mystical vision."[20] That year she began writing her first text, a massive visionary theological summa—nearly 500 pages in its modern edition and nearly ten years in the making. She entitled it *Scivias*, a shortened form of the Latin phrase *Scito vias Domini*, "Know the Ways of the Lord," and divided it into three long books, each focused on a theological topic: book 1 deals with creation; book 2, redemption; and book 3, salvation history. Each book follows the same format. First, she narrates a vision she has witnessed. She then follows this narrative with an (often lengthy) exegesis of the vision's meaning, opening her commentary with stereotyped phrases; for example: "again I heard the voice from Heaven, saying to me . . . ."[21] She thus attributes neither the vision's imagery nor the commentary to herself, but insists she is a medium, simply writing whatever she sees or hears. Book 1 of the *Scivias* is organized around six visions; book 2, seven; and book 3, thirteen.

Hildegard's *Scivias* is more than a text. It is a multimedia work and seems to have been envisioned as such from an early date. Around 1165, in Hildegard's later years, a deluxe edition was prepared at her monastery in Rupertsberg. It included thirty-five magnificent illustrations, visual counterparts to the visions that she describes in the text. Tragically, this Rupertsberg manuscript disappeared during World War II, during the time of the bombing of Dresden. Fortunately, black-and-white photos of the original had been made back in 1925, and between 1927 and 1933 the nuns of Eibingen made a fresh copy by hand, with illustrations redrawn according to their original color scheme. Thus we can see with extraordinary accuracy what the original manuscript looked like.

There is no evidence that Hildegard was herself a painter. The illuminations were likely the work of a monk from St. Disibod. But they are unlike other manuscript illuminations of the time. As Madeleine Caviness has noted:

> Whereas clarity and orderliness are period features, the pictures in the *Scivias* have irregular frames, with immense figures too large to fit juxtaposed with clusters of tiny ones, some turned sideways or even upside down along with their architectural settings. Jagged, flamelike areas of brilliant gold or silver light, or of torrid darkness, irregular stars, clouds, and mountains all contribute to the kinetic effect . . . I regard these pictorial expressions as counterpoints of Hildegard's idiosyncratic writing style, forming the perfect complement to her texts.[22]

Caviness goes on note that "gaps in the text are audaciously filled in by the pictures, in a way one could hardly expect of anyone restrained to making literal illustrations."[23] Some illuminations portray elements found not in Hildegard's vision, but in the accompanying commentary. For these reasons, Caviness has argued that we need to see Hildegard as sort of "art director" who did not execute the work herself, but who carefully oversaw its production—much as a modern film director might take great care overseeing the visual

ad exponendum. ⁊ indocta ad scriben
dum ea dic ⁊ scribe illa nñ sedm os homi
nis. nec sedm intellectum humane ad
inuentionis nec sedm uoluntate huma
ne compositionis. ꝰs sedm id quod ea in
celestib; desup in mirabilib; di uides ⁊ au
dis. ea sic edisserendo pferens. quemadmo
dum ⁊ auditor uerba pceptoris sui pcipi
ens. ea sedm tenorē locutionis illi. ipso uo
lente. ostendente. ⁊ pcipiente ppalat. Sic
⁊ tu ó homo. dic ea q̃ uides ⁊ audis. ⁊ sc
be ea non sedm te. nec sedm aliuꝰ homi
nem ꝰs secundū uoluntate scientis uiden
tis ⁊ disponentis omnia in secretis miste
riorum suorum. Et iterū audiui uocē
de celo michi dicente. Dic q̃ mirabilia
hec. ⁊ scribe ea. hoc modo edocta ⁊ dic.

actum ē in millesimo centesimo
quadragesimo pmo filii di ihu x̃i
incarnationis anno. cū q̃draginta duoꝝ
annoꝝ septē q; insuum eem maxime coruisca
tionis igneū lum apto celo ueniens totū
cerebrū meū trñsfudit. ⁊ totū cor totūq;
pectus meū uelut flamma nñ tam ar
dens ꝰs calens ita inflammauit. ut sol
rem aliquam calefacit. sup quam radi
os suos ponit. Et repente intellectum
expositionis libroꝝ uidelicet. psalterii
euangelii ⁊ alioꝝ catholicoꝝ tam ue
teris quam noui testamenti uolumi
num sapiebam. nñ aute inpretatio
nem uerboꝝ textus eoꝝ nec diuisioē

Et ecce quadra
gesimo tercio
temporalis cur
sus mei anno
cum celesti uisi
oni magno ti
more ⁊ tremu
la intentione inhererem uidi maxi
mū splendorē. in quo facta ē uox
de celo ad me dicens. O homo fragi
lis ⁊ cinis cineris ⁊ putredo putredi
nis. dic ⁊ scribe q̃ uides ⁊ audis. Sed
quia timida es ad loquendū ⁊ simplex

FIGURE 4.1. Hildegard's Mystical Inspiration. From Hildegard of Bingen, "Inspired by Heavenly Fire," *Scivias*; Codex Rupertsberg (1165) (reproduction; original disappeared during World War II). Used with permission: Erich Lessing/Art Resource, NY.

presentation of a scene even if he or she did not do the actual carpentry or painting or costumes.

I want to look only at a single example: Hildegard's vision of the Trinity, the second vision in book 2 of the *Scivias*. Here is her account of what she saw:

> Then I saw a bright light, and in this light the figure of a man the color of a sapphire, which was all blazing with a gentle glowing fire. And that bright light bathed the whole of the glowing fire, and the glowing fire bathed the bright light; and the bright light and the glowing fire poured over the whole human figure, so that the three were one light in one power of potential.[24]

The illustration from the Rupertsberg manuscript brings out the technicolor grandeur of what she witnessed. (See figure 4.2) A sapphire-colored figure stands at the center, hands held up slightly, palms outward. He is ringed by two concentric bands, the inner one gold, the outer one white. The whole vision is placed within a deep blue backdrop and is surrounded by an intricate latticework border.

Hildegard reports that she hears from the "Living Light" an explanation of the vision. The bright light (white in the illustration) represents God the Father; the sapphire figure in the center represents God the Son, the Incarnate One, while the glowing fire (gold in the illustration) represents the Holy Spirit. After decoding the three elements within the vision, she offers a quite traditional medieval exposition of the doctrine of the Trinity. She stresses the inseparability of the three divine Persons: that "the Father is not without the Son, nor the Son without the Father, nor the Father and the Son without the Holy Spirit, nor the Holy Spirit without Them"; that they are "inseparable in Divine Majesty"; that they are "inviolable without change."[25] She goes on to expound the Trinity using three analogies. She first compares the Trinity to three qualities of a stone (cool dampness, solidity, sparkling fire); then to three qualities of a flame (brilliant light, red power, fiery heat); and finally to three aspects of human words (sound, meaning, breath).[26] Such analogies, Hildegard recognizes, risk overplaying distinctions between the divine persons, and so she carefully balances her exposition by stressing the Trinity's "unity of essence."

While Hildegard's exposition is conventional, the iconography is not. In her vision, only Christ is imaged as a human being; the Father and the Spirit are portrayed in non-figural, non-imagistic ways. Hildegard recognizes a fundamental theological insight that was sometimes muddled in medieval thought and art: God the Son *alone* became incarnate. And that is what Hildegard is stressing. Christ is portrayed as luminous but fully human. As Peter Dronke has noted, this vision captures a fundamental theological insight: that

FIGURE 4.2. Hildegard's Vision of the Trinity. From Hildegard of Bingen, "The Holy Trinity," *Scivias*, Codex Rupertsberg (1165) (reproduction; original disappeared during World War II). Used with permission: Erich Lessing/Art Resource, NY.

"the human is inseparable from the divine—that in truth [the human] is at the center of the divine."[27] It was common in her time—and even more dramatically in the Renaissance—to speak of human beings as a "microcosm" of the "macrocosm," as a mini-cosmos of the larger natural world. For Hildegard, the cosmos of the human person and the cosmos of the natural world were linked by an intricate web of correspondences. This theme appears repeatedly in her writings, notably in a vision she experienced toward the end of her life. In the manuscript illumination that accompanies her account, she is portrayed seeing a human being standing at the center of a circle, not unlike the more famous version later done by Leonardo da Vinci. For Hildegard, the human and the cosmos were linked because they were made by God and mirror the divine prototype.

Here I have touched only on a single vision in the *Scivias* and noted the way Hildegard combines written text and manuscript illumination to communicate her message. But written text and manuscript illumination are only two of the media Hildegard used. At the end of the *Scivias*, she integrates two others: song lyrics and drama. The closing vision of book 3 is the "symphony of the blessed." Here she gives a set of eight poems, or more precisely song lyrics. She says that she heard "the voice of a multitude, making music in harmony."[28] Hildegard was a composer, and these poems were among the many compositions that she put to music, ones that she and her nuns performed there at the Rupertsberg. She then follows this cluster of songs with the text of a brief drama, an "exhortation of the virtues and the fight against the Devil."[29] She would develop this as well into a full-scale dramatic production, *Play of the Virtues (Ordo virtutum)*, a morality play set to music.

The three books of *Scivias* made up the first volume of a massive theological trilogy. Hildegard composed the second, *The Book of Life's Merits (Liber vitae meritorum)*, between 1158 and 1163. This work focuses on the moral life, particularly on the vices, their types and pathologies, and the remedies to heal them. This work also gives one of the earliest descriptions in Western literature of purgatory. The third work in her theological trilogy, *The Book of Divine Works (Liber divinorum operum)*, was composed between 1163 and 1173. It explores the human person as a microcosm. These two later compositions follow the same format as the *Scivias*: accounts of visions, followed by theological exegesis.

THE MUSIC OF GREENNESS

Over the centuries, mystics have drawn on many literary genres—letters, essays, autobiographies, sermons, biblical exegeses, lyric poems—to describe their experiences and to set out their teachings. Hildegard was a multimedia artist, and the medium perhaps dearest to her heart was music. Musical compositions form one of the most original and distinctive features of her mystical project. She was not only an accomplished composer herself, but also sketched out an original and provocative theology of music. Even before her first literary projects were published, she was already receiving acclaim for her music. In 1148 Odo of Soissons, a theologian teaching at Paris, wrote to her, remarking that she had a fine reputation among the intellectuals there in France not simply for her visions, but also for her ability to "bring forth the melody of a new song, although you have studied nothing of such things."[30]

Symphony of the Harmony of the Celestial Revelations

Hildegard's major musical work is an anthology she called the *Symphony of the Harmony of the Celestial Revelations* (*Symphonia armonie celestium revelationum*). It is a cycle of seventy-seven poems scored to monophonic melodies. Most are liturgical pieces—antiphons, responsories, sequences—and would have been sung either at Liturgies of the Hours or at Mass. It is unclear whether the song lyrics that conclude the *Scivias* were a first draft of the *Symphonia* or whether Hildegard appended excerpts from the *Symphonia* to the *Scivias*. In any case, most of the *Symphonia* was composed between 1150 and 1160. Just as the illustrations in the Rupertsberg manuscript were unusual by standards of the day, so was Hildegard's music. As one musicologist has noted, Hildegard drew on the traditional repertoire of Gregorian chant, but she imbued her melodies "with extraordinary intensity and individual inflection. The neumatic ornamentation is rich and heavy, the [vocal] ranges great, the melodic motion active."[31] For Hildegard, melody, like text, flowed from vision.

To truly appreciate her work, one needs not just to read about her music, but to hear it. Early music groups such as Sequentia have performed and recorded nearly all of Hildegard's work. I strongly encourage readers to pause here and to go and listen to a sampling of her compositions.

Hildegard composed not only the melodies, but also the lyrics. To get a glimpse of this side of her mystical project, let us explore what many consider her musical masterpiece, "O viridissima virga" (O greenest branch), a hymn celebrating the Virgin Mary and the Incarnation. Here is the text, with the Latin and English in parallel columns:

O viridissima virga, ave	Hail, O greenest branch,
que in ventoso flabro sciscitationis	who, in the swirling windgust
sanctorum prodisti.	of sainted questing, have come forth.

Cum venit tempus	When that once-upon-a-time came
quod tu floruisti in ramis tuis,	that you bloomed in your tree-boughs—
ave, ave fuit tibi	hail, hail be to you!
quia calor solis in te sudavit	For sun's heat distilled in you
sicut odor balsami.	like balsam scent.
Nam in te floruit pulcher flos	Thus in you a fair flower flowered,
qui odorem dedit omnibus	gave its scent to once-spiced things,
aromatibus que arida erant.	all withered, gone dry.
Et illa apparuerunt omnia	And then there appeared,
in viriditate plena.	in greennesses full, all things.
Unde celi dederunt rorem	Heaven's dew dropped down
super gramen	over the grass
et omnis terra leta facta est,	and all the earth grew glad:
quoniam viscera ipsius	for from its womb
frumentum protulerunt	sprouted wheat-grain
et quoniam volucres celi	and the birds of the sky
nidos in ipsa habuerunt	set their nests in it.
Deinde facta est esca hominibus	Hence humanity's food was made,
et gaudium magnum epulantium.	and for those who feasted, great joy.
Unde, o suavis Virgo,	Henceforth, O sweet virgin,
in te non deficit ullum gaudium.	in you no joy, no gladness, is lacking.
Hec omnia Eva contempsit.	All things, all of these, Eve once scorned.
Nunc autem laus sit Altissimo.	But now let the Most High be praised.[32]

This poem tosses us headlong into the intricate and subtle world of medieval symbolism, a complex code woven from biblical allusions and natural symbols. The theology that underlies Hildegard's poetry here is both deeply traditional and deeply original. Hildegard's central theme here is *viriditas*, greenness. It is one of her favorite and most idiosyncratic theological concepts.[33] She may have encountered the term in the writings of Pope Gregory the Great, where it meant not simply greenness as a color, but also, by extension, vigor, vibrancy, and health (both physically and spiritually).[34] For Hildegard, *viriditas* is visible in the greenness of the earth in general and of plants in particular. But beneath this visible greenness is a deeper greenness, an inner life force. Anything life-giving has its *viriditas*, its greenness. Thus Hildegard speaks even of the air living "in greenness"; she can speak of human beings' physical and emotional maturing as a "greenness"; she can apply it, by extension, to the moral life, that one "greens" in virtue.[35] She also can apply it, as she does in this poem, to the history of salvation. In the *Scivias*, she speaks of the "greening" power of the Holy Spirit active in the Incarnation: "before any creatures were made the

Infinite Word was indivisibly in the Father; Which in the course of time was to become incarnate in the ardor of charity, miraculously and without the stain or weight of sin, through the Holy Spirit's sweet greenness (*per uiriditatem*) in the dawn of blessed virginity."[36] In "O viridissima virga," "greenness" is applied not to the Holy Spirit, but to the Virgin Mary. Mary is the "greenest branch" because she gives birth to the Savior; Christ is thus the "fair flower" who "flowered" from Mary the branch.[37] Before the coming of Christ, the fallen, sinful world had "withered, gone dry," losing its fragrance. But with Christ's coming, the world has again grown green and grassy, fragrant once more with balsam scent. And from the verdant earth springs wheat. For Hildegard, Christ is the wheat, the grain which makes the bread of life; on the far side of the Incarnation, Christ present in the eucharistic bread has become "humanity's food."

Hildegard's poetry, like her music and her theology, has its idiosyncrasies. Her nineteenth-century editors did not know what to make of it, dismissing it as "mere sketches, the rough drafts of hymns and sequences."[38] She did not use meter or standard poetic forms, but her language has both richness of image and a dense musicality. Today we would call it free verse. But Hildegard was not so much anticipating modern poetic practice as playing off the liturgical tradition, with its unmetered hymns and its chanting of biblical prose.

A Theology of Music

When Hildegard first wrote Bernard of Clairvaux, she alluded in passing to her theology of "greenness." She also hinted at her theology of music. In her closing prayer, she invoked the Trinity and spoke of "the Sound, the power of the Father," a cosmic music with "which all creation echoes."[39] In a letter written not long before her death, Hildegard set out a fuller account of her theology of music. She and her nuns had been placed under interdict for allowing an excommunicated nobleman to be buried in the monastery's cemetery. She protested strongly in a letter to the clergy of Mainz that has come down to us as letter 23. She claimed to speak not on her own authority, but as a reporter of the "voice coming from the Living Light." She pointed out that music making was no secular matter, but a central thread in the history of salvation. The angels, of course, sing their praises before God. Adam shared that angelic vocation and, with a voice of extraordinary power, spent his days singing in the garden. But when he sinned,

> Adam lost that angelic voice which he had in paradise, for he fell asleep to that knowledge which he possessed before his sin, just as a

person on waking up only dimly remembers what he had seen in his dreams ... For, before he sinned, his voice had the sweetness of all musical harmony. Indeed, if he had remained in his original state, the weakness of mortal man would not have been able to endure the power and the resonance of his voice.[40]

For Hildegard, Adam's Fall marked music's fall. She went on to note that the prophets not only composed hymns of praise, but even constructed musical instruments "to enhance these songs of praise with melodic strains." These outward words and material instruments are dignified by the way they awaken in us inward things. But Hildegard went further. She argued that music enabled the prophets—and even people today—to "get beyond the music of this [present] exile and recall to mind that divine melody of praise which Adam, in company with the angels, enjoyed in God before his fall."[41] In other words, music is a vehicle of grace that helps undo the Fall. It awakens ancient memories and ancient voices.

Hildegard's theology of music also touches on the devil and his role. She suggested that when the devil heard Adam singing the songs of heaven—"mankind's homeland"—he was filled with anguish. It was precisely Adam's singing that led the devil to try and bring about Adam's Fall.[42] I should add that in her morality play, the *Ordo Virtutum*, the devil is the only character who does not sing his lines; he simply shouts them out. (Scholars suspect that in the play's inaugural performance the monk Volmar, the one male in Hildegard's monastery, would have played the devil's role). For Hildegard, the devil is out of harmony with God and the God-given universe and is thus inherently antimusical. She argues, by implication, that the prelates of Mainz who put her monastery under interdict are, in effect, doing the work of the devil—by robbing God of praises and by undermining music's saving power of restoring the singers to paradise.

For Hildegard, to be human is to be musical. As she says in letter 23: "The body is the vestment of the spirit, which has a living voice, and so it is proper to the body, in harmony with the soul, to use its voice to sing praises to God."[43] To sing reflects the celestial harmony. Here Hildegard touches on her theology of creation, which holds that there is a link between microcosm and macrocosm, between the harmonic unity of the human person's body and soul and the larger cosmic harmonies visible in creation. But she does not stop there. She stresses that the very act of singing recalls the Incarnation of Christ: "Consider, too, that just as the body of Jesus Christ was born of the purity of the Virgin Mary through the operation of the Holy Spirit so, too, the canticle of praise, reflecting celestial harmony, is rooted in the Church through the Holy Spirit."[44] In other words, music making echoes the Incarnation. To make music is to join spirit with body, inner word with outer voice. Music making is an incarnate act of praise that undoes sin's tragic atonality.

MYSTIC OR PROPHET?

We have looked briefly at Hildegard's mystical output. It took shape in many ways, in letters and theological texts, in poetry, melody, and manuscript illumination. As rich as her work was in all these, she also threw her energies into other unusual projects. She was much interested in medicine and in science and worked extensively on what we would call natural healing. Two of her works have survived, *Physics* (*Physica*) and *Causes and Cures* (*Causa et curae*). She also tinkered with a very unusual project, what she called *Unknown Language* (*Lingua ignota*). It is a glossary of terms that sets terms in Latin side by side with this odd "unknown language." She once composed a hymn, "O orzchis Ecclesia," that mixes words from both languages.

Hildegard is no longer the obscure medieval figure that she was even forty years ago. Not only scholars, but also a wide range of readers and music lovers, have come to appreciate Hildegard's extraordinary—and extraordinarily varied—achievements. Her multimedia genius is not in question. But was she a mystic? This question can be asked legitimately of each of the figures we are studying. But with Hildegard it has a special poignancy. Even scholars deeply sympathetic to her many projects and well attuned to the contours of her world have raised the question. They question whether "mystic" is the best category to describe her. One of the finest Hildegard scholars, Barbara Newman, has suggested that Hildegard is seen better as a visionary and a prophet.[45] Why? Because Hildegard does not seem concerned with mysticism in the usual sense—even the sense in which her contemporaries, such as Bernard of Clairvaux or William of St. Thierry, thought of it. She does not describe mystical union, nor does she chart a mystical pathway to it. She says little about asceticism, except in the most traditional ways, and makes no mention of mystical prayer.

Obviously she was a visionary. But are all visionaries mystics? The medieval scholar Caroline Walker Bynum has remarked that Hildegard "took her revelations as a text for exegesis, not an experience for re-living"; "she wrote not about union, but doctrine."[46] It is true that Hildegard's message directed readers outward, not inward. She cited and expounded visions either to explain Christian doctrine or to pronounce prophetic judgment on evildoers. Her visionary style owes much to biblical sources, to Old Testament prophets such as

Isaiah and Ezekiel and to New Testament visionaries such as John of the book of Revelation. In light of all this, McGinn has concluded that though Hildegard may be regarded as a mystic, she was not a mystical author; she herself may well have had mystical experiences of God, but her writings do not constitute a mystical theology.[47] Her visionary experiences were her own; her pathway was her own. She did not encourage others to become visionaries.

These points are all well-taken. But I do not think we should ignore the obvious: Hildegard's visionary experiences—which she claimed as experiences of God and which her contemporaries accepted as divinely inspired—energized her career as a political and ecclesial reformer. And they were, by her own account, the fountainhead from which both her theological works and her artistic achievements sprang. I agree that visions do not make the mystic. But as I have tried to show, aspects of her theological vision are both striking and original. We have looked at two: her concept of "greenness" and her theories on divine and human music. These two themes flow from and undergird how she saw God's presence in the world: as a "greenness," an underlying life force that imbues creation and salvation, cosmos and history; as a cosmic "music," a harmony just beyond our hearing that knits all things together in a polychoral symphony. So where does that leave us? Hildegard may not have written about union or the journey to God as other mystical writers did then and later. But she did write, preach, expound, and even sing and dramatize a mystical vision of a God-imbued universe and a God-imbued history. I really see no reason to question her mystical credentials.

5

Mystic as Cartographer: Bonaventure

Explorers have for centuries embarked on epic journeys, traversing oceans, scaling mountains, navigating the poles' icy wastes. However much they yearn for uncharted realms, they do not like to leave them uncharted. For explorers, mapmaking is an essential skill. They often bring along old maps, but they also bring cartographers' tools—compasses, surveyors' scopes, and so on—to turn what was terra incognita into well-charted terrain. Mystics too are explorers, and they too have a zest for mapmaking. From an early date, Christian mystics have marked out the milestones—and road hazards—in the journey to God. In the third century, Origen probed the narratives of Exodus and Numbers and argued that the desert wanderings and oasis stops recorded there offer a treasure map of sorts, cryptic but decipherable, to guide the soul's return to God. A seventh-century monk from Sinai, John Climacus, noted Jesus's thirty "hidden" years and plotted out thirty rungs in his *Ladder of Divine Ascent*. Better known to modern readers is Teresa of Ávila's *Interior Castle*, which traces a progressively inward journey through seven "dwelling places" of a diamond castle called the human soul.

Here we will examine one of the most brilliant cartographers of the mystical, Bonaventure (c. 1217–1274). His classic treatise, *The Mind's Journey into God* (*Itinerarium mentis in Deum*), offers one of the best-known and most carefully crafted itineraries. That text will be our focus. I have chosen Bonaventure not only for his skills as a cartographer of the spirit, but also because his career helps correct certain misconceptions about mystics. First, Bonaventure was among the finest theologians of the Middle Ages. His witness offers a counterweight to the idea that mystics are purveyors of the irrational. Second, Bonaventure spent much of his career as head of the Franciscans, a post that, in the best of times, demanded considerable administrative and diplomatic expertise—and his were not the best of times. Here too Bonaventure undercuts a common prejudice, that mystics are otherworldly and unsuited to the practical business of running things. Mysticism need not be opposed to academic rigor nor to the everyday administrative routine of conflict management.

A LIFE OF DISPUTED QUESTIONS

Mystics such as Bernard and Hildegard attracted a circle of friends and disciples who were passionately convinced of their holiness and who set about gathering stories and composing hagiographic accounts of their lives. Also, they themselves left behind letters that give us spotty but vivid glimpses of their take on things. With Bonaventure, we have no close-in sources. He left behind a formidable body of theological writings and official documents, but they contain few autobiographical tracings. As Étienne Gilson famously remarked, Bonaventure "the man disappears behind the work he did."[1]

We know almost nothing of Bonaventure's early life. He was born sometime between 1217 and 1221—exactly when is disputed—and was named after his father, Giovanni di Fidanza. His hometown, Bagnoregio, is a small but scenic locale, perched atop a steep hill in the rugged countryside north of Viterbo, not far from Rome.

Joining the Franciscans

Like many bright young men of his day, Bonaventure traveled to far-off Paris, drawn by the allure of its prestigious university. There he came under the sway of Alexander of Hales (d. 1245), an Englishman and one of the leading theologians of the day. At mid-career, Alexander had dramatically cast his lot in with the new and controversial Franciscan Order. When he joined, he brought his academic chair—with all its prestige and privileges—with him, enabling the Franciscans to establish their own school within the orbit of the wider University. Alexander's combination of profound learning and Franciscan simplicity deeply impressed the young Bonaventure, who entered the Franciscans around 1243. In a rare personal reminiscence, he mentions what first drew him to the order:

For I confess before God that what made me love Saint Francis's way of life so much was that it is exactly like the origin and the perfection of the Church itself, which began first with simple fishermen and afterward developed to include the most illustrious and learned doctors. You find the same thing in the Order of Saint Francis; in this way God reveals that it did not come about through human calculations but through Christ.[2]

Bonaventure completed a master of arts degree around the time he entered and immediately embarked on advanced theological studies under Alexander and other leading Franciscan masters, such as John of LaRochelle, Odo Rigaud, and William of Middleton. Theological study at Paris focused on scripture, of course, and theologians were known as "masters of the sacred page." But in this heyday of scholastic theology, students also mastered Christianity's first theological textbook, the dry, encyclopedic *Sentences* of Peter Lombard (d. 1160). A graduate student in theology in those days was often called a *sententarius*, so central had the Lombard's work become to the enterprise of teaching theology. Bonaventure's earliest work was a massive four-volume *Commentary on the Sentences*, the fruit of his early years as a teacher.

Clash with William of St.-Amour

On the eve of being recognized as a *magister* (the equivalent of the modern doctorate) and appointed to the prestigious Franciscan chair of theology, a huge scuffle broke out in the University of Paris. One other famous figure found himself in much the same academic no-man's-land as Bonaventure: the great Dominican theologian Thomas Aquinas (d. 1274). Tensions had been brewing between the faculty at Paris, the Dominicans, and the Franciscans for some time. A little background: The University of Paris was not like a modern university. It had no campus greens, no ivied buildings. Medieval universities were not even places. They were guilds of faculty and students, what we would call a union. And unions get their power by uniting during crises and going on strike. Whenever the university locked horns with the city fathers of Paris, it simply went on strike. Classes were suspended, and faculty and students left town and set up shop elsewhere, depriving the city of income. Tensions flared between the university and the two mendicant orders because the orders owed their first allegiance not to the university, with its intricate self-governing rules and procedures, but to their religious superiors and to the constitutions of their respective orders. In 1253, when the university went on strike to protest police brutality, neither order joined. They continued taking in students and holding classes. Their secular colleagues viewed them as strikebreakers and for a time expelled them from the university.

Tensions came to a head when William of St.-Amour (d. 1272) launched a ferocious theological attack against the mendicants.[3] The title of his treatise says it all: *Concerning the Antichrist and His Ministers.* Initially William's tirade garnered support not only at the level of the streets, with students composing ribald songs against the mendicants, but also at the highest levels of the Church. Pope Innocent IV was sympathetic to William. But the tide soon turned. Both orders marshaled their finest theologians to answer the charges. Thomas Aquinas defended the mendicants in his *Against Those Making War on the Worship of God*, while Bonaventure did the same with his *Letter to an Unknown Master* and *Disputed Questions on Evangelical Perfection.* In the end, the mendicants were vindicated by the intervention of Pope Alexander IV, who in 1255 declared William's position heretical and in 1257 demanded that the university officially recognize the academic status of both Aquinas and Bonaventure.

Though Bonaventure did not receive formal recognition as the Franciscan chair until 1257, he was its de facto holder. It was a productive time despite the turmoil. Out of it came his *Disputed Questions on Christ's Knowledge* and *Disputed Questions on the Mystery of the Trinity*, both composed in traditional scholastic style. This period also produced his masterfully brief summa of theology, the *Breviloquium.*

The Joachite Controversy

Intertwined with this controversy was a second, even more perilous controversy. A half century earlier, a Calabrian abbot-turned-prophet named Joachim of Fiore (d. 1202) had published controversial treatises on biblical interpretation and on the book of Revelation. He claimed that by looking back on the Bible he could look forward and read the future, much as a hiker crossing a mountain pass "can see backward as well as forward and determine the right direction to take for the remainder of his journey by contemplating the road he has come."[4] Not unlike some modern fundamentalists, Joachim read Revelation's symbols as prophecies of current events and forecast soon-to-come end-of-the-world cataclysms. None of his ideas was more controversial than his view of salvation history. Joachim linked history to Trinity and spoke of three ages: the "Age of the Father," which lasted from Adam to Christ; the "Age of the Son," which lasted from the New Testament up to his era; and the "Age of the Spirit," which, according to Joachim's calculations, would come to pass in the mid-thirteenth century. Joachim's scheme could easily be taken to imply that much of the institutional Church, including hierarchy and papacy, might well fade away with the fading of the Age of the Son. These were dangerous sentiments. Joachim also prophesied that in the new Age of the Spirit, there would be a great clash: the Antichrist would confront two new religious orders, an order of hermits and an order of preachers.

Certain Franciscans saw themselves and their Dominican counterparts reflected in the mirror of Joachim's prophecies. In Paris in 1254, a Franciscan named Gerard of Burgo San Donnino set off a firestorm when he published a commentary on Joachim entitled *Introduction to the Eternal Gospel*. Gerard and other pro-Joachim Franciscans probably thought that reading Francis and the Franciscans into Joachim's prophecies might help stem the tide of criticism at Paris and justify their predestined place in salvation history. It was a fatal miscalculation. One recent study has called the Franciscan appeal to Joachim "one of the most serious blunders in the history of apologetics."[5] Gerard's apocalyptic claims provided ammunition for William of St.-Amour's polemic. In 1257 Gerard's treatise was declared heretical, and Gerard was sentenced to life in prison.

The controversy also cost John of Parma, the much-beloved minister general of the Franciscans, his job. John, a man of genuine learning but also of deep commitment to Francis of Assisi's vision of poverty, was no extremist. But his Joachimite leanings were on record. Pope Alexander IV quietly demanded John's resignation. In the general chapter held in Rome to choose a successor, John himself nominated Bonaventure, who was then in his late thirties. On February 2, 1257, Bonaventure assumed the office of minister general, a position he would hold for the next seventeen years, until just before his death in 1274.

Minister General

Bonaventure inherited an order that, in the wake of the mendicant and Joachimite controversies, had veered dangerously close to formal condemnation. These near-catastrophes were tied, in part, to the booming success story that was the Franciscan order. In 1210, when the order first received Pope Innocent III's approval, there were only twelve Franciscans. By the time Francis died in 1226, there were several thousand. By the time Bonaventure assumed office, there were, by recent estimates, 30,000 Franciscans.[6] As minister general he traveled widely, visiting Franciscan communities in Italy, Germany, France, Spain, and perhaps England. The charismatic fervor of the sprawling, unwieldy Franciscan movement faced both potential divisions internally and continued serious criticisms externally. Bonaventure somehow managed to hold together its creative reform impulses with some semblance of order. Bonaventure oversaw the general chapter of Narbonne in 1260, which collated and codified the order's legislation. Bonaventure's balancing act did not hold. In the generation after him, the order became bitterly divided by competing wings, the so-called Spirituals and Conventuals. These later centrifugal forces led, in the early fourteenth century, to a heavy-handed papal-sponsored persecution of Franciscan Spirituals, resulting, in a few cases, in executions by the Inquisition. While Bonaventure led, the traditional accent on radical poverty was balanced by a commitment to the universities and to pastoral ministry. In the generation after him, some Franciscans branded this a betrayal and cast Bonaventure and his tenure in villainous terms.[7]

One issue that kept resurfacing, both before and after Bonaventure's time, was the interpretation of the life and legacy of Francis of Assisi. Competing biographies of Francis were being written, and these offered, beneath the surface, competing visions of what it meant to be a Franciscan. One of Bonaventure's most famous works was his *Life of Francis* (*Legenda maior*). It was declared to be the order's official biography, but attempts to suppress its many competitors never succeeded.

Despite the rigors of his travels and the rigors of poverty, to which he was committed, he continued to write. Two years after his election, he composed *The Mind's Journey into God*, the mystical treatise that will be our focus. Other mystical and devotional works poured from his pen: *The Triple Way*, *The Tree of Life*, *The Mystical Vine*. He often returned to Paris, where from time to time he offered afternoon lecture series, known as "collations." These included his *Collations on the Ten Commandments*, the *Collations on the Gifts of the Holy Spirit*, and most famous of all, the *Collations on the Six Days of Creation* (*Collationes in Hexaemeron*), a set of nineteen lectures, which, though unfinished, offer a glimpse of a final, brilliant theological synthesis.

Final Days

In 1273 Bonaventure was named cardinal and bishop of Albano by Pope Gregory X, who wanted Bonaventure's expertise for an upcoming ecumenical council scheduled to meet in Lyons in 1274. The main issue on the agenda was reuniting the Greek and Latin churches, divided at that point for more than two centuries. There were high hopes, and leading theologians were called to come and lend their expertise. Thomas Aquinas died en route. Tragically, Bonaventure too died during the council itself, on July 15, 1274. His fame faded over the next century, but after lobbying by Jean Gerson, the Franciscans took up the cause. Bonaventure was canonized by Pope Sixtus IV in 1482 and named a

Doctor of the Church by Pope Sixtus V in 1588. The pope also confirmed the title that Gerson had bestowed on him, *Doctor Seraphicus*, a title drawn, as we will see, from his best-known mystical treatise.

MAPPING THE JOURNEY

Bonaventure's mystical masterpiece is *The Mind's Journey into God*—usually referred to by its original Latin title *Itinerarium mentis in Deum*. The work is astonishingly concise: seven brief chapters, a mere 10,000 words. As McGinn has remarked, "No other treatise of comparable size in the history of Western mysticism packs so much into one seamless whole."[8] Bonaventure himself acknowledged its density and cautioned readers: "You should not run rapidly over the development of these considerations, but should mull them over slowly with the greatest care."[9] We need to remember that this is the work of a systematic theologian. Not only does it have its own carefully crafted integrity; it also alludes to and presupposes theological ideas that Bonaventure develops in greater depth elsewhere. And it is a mid-career work. Themes he introduced here were expanded on later, especially in his final *Collations on the Six Days*.

Itinerarium

Bonaventure chose his title with care. The Latin *itinerarium* is usually translated "journey," but the word had a cluster of associations. It could mean exactly what "itinerary" in English means: a journey's outline, the plotting out of routes and stops. The word also had meanings not evident in contemporary English. It could mean an account of a journey, a travelogue. It often meant a religious journey, a pilgrimage, especially one to the Holy Land. Finally, it could refer to a prayer prayed over those embarking on such journeys. All these meanings are at play in the text.[10]

Other terms in the title are equally significant and precise. Some translators have rendered this title in English *The Soul's Journey to God*. Neither "soul" nor "to" is accurate. Bonaventure speaks of "mind" (*mens*), not "soul" (*anima*). For us, mind implies logic, rationality. Bonaventure's view is different. It is also quite precise and rather complex. Let me say simply that he distinguishes between an "inferior reason," which seeks knowledge, and a "superior reason" which seeks wisdom. For Bonaventure, this higher wisdom-seeking mind is "the image of God, an image which is everlasting, spiritual, and within us."[11] And so this is a journey of the wisdom-seeking mind returning to its divine prototype, to God who is Wisdom itself. Finally, Bonaventure speaks of this as a journey not *to* God (*ad Deum*), but *into* God (*in Deum*). Our destiny is not to stop at God's doorstep, so to speak, but to enter into union, into mystery.

Francis's Vision

In the prologue, Bonaventure recounts what inspired the treatise. In October 1259, around the anniversary of Francis's death, he had gone on retreat to Mount La Verna. For Franciscans, this was sacred ground: it was there that Francis had had his famous vision of a six-winged seraph. Here is Bonaventure's account:

> On a certain morning about the feast of the Exaltation of the Cross, while Francis was praying on the mountainside, he saw a Seraph with six fiery and shining wings descend from the height of heaven. And when in swift flight the Seraph had reached a spot in the air near the man of God, there appeared between the wings the figure of a man crucified, with his hands and feet extended in the form a cross and fastened to a cross ... When Francis saw this, he was overwhelmed and his heart was flooded with a mixture of joy and sorrow ... Eventually he understood by a revelation from the Lord that divine providence had shown him this vision so that, as Christ's lover, he might learn in advance that he was to be totally transformed into the likeness of Christ crucified, not by the martyrdom of the flesh, but by the fire of love consuming his soul. As the vision disappeared, it left in his heart a marvelous ardor and imprinted on his body markings that were no less marvelous. Immediately the marks of nails began to appear in his hands and feet just as he had seen a little before in the figure of the man crucified ... Also his right side, as if pierced with a lance, was marked with a red wound from which his sacred blood often flowed, moistening his tunic and undergarment.[12]

As Bonaventure emphasizes, Francis found himself, in the vision's afterglow, marked physically, permanently, with the stigmata—the first instance of this in the history of Christianity. (See figure 5.1 for Giotto's famous rendition.) By 1259 Bonaventure was a man in his early forties, two years into his tenure as minister general. As he prayed on Mount La Verna, he had a breakthrough, a moment of insight. He became convinced that Francis's vision had not been for Francis alone. It also mapped out a road, a *via*, for the rest of us.[13]

The angel's wings, Bonaventure believed, provided the clue: "The six wings of the Seraph can rightly be taken to symbolize the six levels of illu-

FIGURE 5.1. The Stigmata of St. Francis of Assisi. Giotto di Bondone (1266–1336), "St. Francis receiving the stigmata." Fresco, Upper Church, S. Francesco, Assisi, Italy. Used with permission: Scala/Art Resource, NY.

mination by which, as if by steps or stages, the soul can pass over to peace through ecstatic elevation of Christian wisdom."[14] In other words, the road included seven stages, a six-step ascent plus one final unending stage, heaven's ecstatic peace. The mythic resonances of sixes and sevens echoed in Bonaventure's Bible-saturated mind. It reminded him of creation itself: "Just as God completed the whole world in six days and rested on the seventh, so the smaller world of man is led in a most orderly fashion by six successive stages of illumination to the quiet of contemplation."[15] The cosmic consequences seemed clear: God does things in sevens, both the creation of the world and the re-creation of the mystic. Macrocosm and microcosm, the vast universe and the individual person—both, in Bonaventure's mind, were knit together by a cosmic correspondence because both sprang from a single author and artist, Christ, God's Word.[16]

Six-Fold Architecture

Bonaventure was an architectonic thinker and writer. The seven-stage journey
of mystic ascent is mirrored in the seven-chapter design of the treatise (see
figure 5.2). The *Itinerarium*'s architecture reflects a basic premise: "The universe itself is a ladder by which we can ascend into God."[17] The chapter titles
give a good overview of that ladder:

> Chapter 1: The . . . speculation on God through the vestiges that are in the
> universe.
> Chapter 2: The speculation on God in the vestiges in the world of sense
> realities.
> Chapter 3: The speculation on God through the image imprinted on our
> natural powers.
> Chapter 4: The speculation on God in the image reformed by the gifts of
> grace.
> Chapter 5: The speculation on the divine unity through God's primary
> name, which is Being.
> Chapter 6: The speculation on the most blessed Trinity in its name,
> which is the Good.
> Chapter 7: The mystical transport of the mind in which rest is given
> the intellect and through ecstasy our affection passes over totally to
> God.[18]

Note that the first six chapters form three pairs, and each pair signals a distinct
way of encountering God:

- Stages 1 and 2 involve seeing God's presence in the visible universe—
  what Bonaventure calls God's "vestiges." Here the journey is directed *outward*. "We must pass," according to Bonaventure, "through
  his vestiges, which are material, temporal, and outside us (*extra
  nos*)."[19]
- Stages 3 and 4 involve seeing God's presence within ourselves, within
  the dynamic of our psyche—what Bonaventure calls God's "image."
  Here the journey is directed *inward*. Bonaventure insists here that "we
  must also enter into our mind, which is God's image, everlasting,
  spiritual, and within us (*intra nos*)."[20]
- Stages 5 and 6 involve seeing God as he is in himself. Here the journey is directed *upward*. As Bonaventure puts it, "We must go beyond
  to what is eternal, most spiritual and above us (*supra nos*), by gazing
  upon (God) the First Principle."[21]

Chap./Stage	Tradition	Ways of Encounter	Ways of Speculating on God	Ways of Perceiving	Powers of Soul	Theology	Biblical Image
7			*ecstasy:* rest given to intellect, affection passes into God				Mercy Seat in the Holy of Holies
6	Spirituality of Pseudo-Dionysius	Journey Upward: "The First Principle, eternal, most spiritual, and above us"	*in* God's Name ("Goodness"): God as Trinity	self-transcendence via mind (*mens*)	summit of mind (*apex mentis*)	mystical	
5			*through* God's Name ("Being"): God as Unity		intelligence (*intelligentia*)		
4	Spirituality of Augustine	Journey Inward: "God's image, eternal, spiritual, and within us"	*in* the image reformed by gifts of grace	self-reflection via spirit (*spiritus*)	understanding (*intellectus*)	literal (*propria*)	Temple's Sanctuary
3			*through* the image stamped on natural powers		reason (*ratio*)		
2	Spirituality of Francis of Assisi	Journey Outward: "material, temporal, and outside us"	*in* vestiges in sense world	perceive God's presence in creation via senses (*sensualitas*)	imagination (*imaginatio*)	symbolic	Temple's Outer Court
1			*through* vestiges in the universe		senses (*sensus*)		
Where Noted:		(*Itin.* 1.2)	(*Itin.* Chapter Headings)	(*Itin.* 1.4)	(see *Itin.* 1.6)	(*Itin.* 1.7)	(*Itin.* 3.1, 5.1)

FIGURE 5.2. Bonaventure's Map of the Mind's Journey into God.

The elegance and symmetry of the *Itinerarium*'s plan need to be savored: the journey into God is outward, then inward, then upward. Each pair draws on a distinctive tradition of Christian mysticism. Stages 1 and 2 take their cues from Francis of Assisi; stages 3 and 4, from Augustine of Hippo; and stages 5 and 6, from Pseudo-Dionysius. (More on this in a moment.)

Given these threes, why six stages? Note the chapter headings. Bonaventure distinguishes between seeing God "through his vestiges" and "in his vestiges," and between seeing God "through his image" and "in his image." The prepositions "through" (*per*) and "in" (*in*) clearly signal some difference.[22] That said, the distinction is not obvious, and even a careful reading of the *Itinerarium* does not clear things up. In his earlier *Commentary on the Sentences*, Bonaventure explains the distinction: "It is one thing to know God *in* a creature, another to know Him *through* creatures. To know God *in* a creature is to know his presence flowing into the creature. But to know God through a creature is to be raised up by the knowledge of the creature to the knowledge of God, as by means of a ladder between them."[23]

In the *Itinerarium*'s opening chapter, Bonaventure not only sets out this basic map, but teases out all sorts of links, various threes and sixes and sevens. He ponders our threefold constitution as human beings (at least, how medieval thinkers conceived our constitution). At the lowest level, we are creatures of sense. Our minds know certain things via the senses, what Bonaventure calls *sensualitas*. This matches the first two stages where we encounter God in the visible world via our senses. At the next level, we are creatures with a psychology, with self-consciousness. Our minds can also know via self-reflection, what Bonaventure calls *spiritus*. This matches the next two stages where we encounter God in our very dignity as human beings. But for Bonaventure, what really defines us is our capacity to go beyond ourselves, our self-transcendence, what he calls *mens*. This matches the final two stages where we encounter God as unity and as trinity.

This trio gives a hint of the intricate number play that pervades the work. Bonaventure lists three forms of theology (symbolic, literal, mystical), three types of law (nature, scripture, grace), six powers of the soul (senses, imagination, reason, understanding, intelligence, spark of conscience), and seven properties of creatures (origin, magnitude, multitude, beauty, fullness, activity, order).[24] It is easy to get lost in all this. Bonaventure's architecture—like that of a Gothic cathedral—is not only orderly, but also highly ornamented. Bonaventure and his medieval colleagues loved their numbers and believed that number provided a glimpse into the hidden architecture of the God-crafted universe and, by extension, into the workings of the mind of God.[25]

Speculatio

Bonaventure, in the chapter headings, describes the first six stages as "speculations" on God. This terminology can be misleading. We associate speculation
with breezy or baseless thinking. This is not what Bonaventure means. What
Bonaventure is talking about is different ways of looking upon God. The Latin
speculatio is related to *spectare*, meaning "to look at, to gaze." It thus has a con-
notation not evident in English. It implies looking at things through a mirror,
since the Latin word for "mirror" is *speculum*. Medieval mirrors were polished
metal; once tarnished, the mirror's reflected image dimmed, grew cloudy. For
Bonaventure, all creation is a mirror, a *speculum*, for seeing God refracted
through the myriad beauties of the universe. So too is human consciousness a
mirror of the divine. The problem in both cases is clarity. As Bonaventure notes,
"The mirror presented by the external world is of little or no value unless the
mirror of the soul has been cleaned and polished."[26] The journey thus includes
and presumes purification—of morals, of heart, of mind.

THE JOURNEY OUTWARD

In Paris, around the time Bonaventure composed the *Itinerarium*, two learned
composers, Léonin and Pérotin, were experimenting with a new musical form,
one that came to define Western music itself: polyphony, singing multiple
melodies simultaneously. Bonaventure's *Itinerarium* is a polyphonic work.
Three voices shape its melodic flow: Francis of Assisi, Augustine of Hippo, and
Pseudo-Dionysius. Each contributes motifs to and shapes the *Itinerarium's*
overall architecture. True, here and there Bonaventure taps other voices—
those of Bernard of Clairvaux and Hugh of St. Victor, for instance—but to
appreciate in broad strokes what Bonaventure is doing, we need to listen to the
way he orchestrates these three principals, weaving their melodies into his
own.

Francis's voice takes the early lead. As we saw, Francis's six-winged seraph
provided Bonaventure's core inspiration. But there are other influences. In the
prologue, Bonaventure notes that Francis "at the beginning and end of every
sermon . . . announced peace; in every greeting he wished for peace; in every
contemplation he sighed for ecstatic peace."[27] Francis had worked to halt
bloody feuds in the city-states of medieval Italy. Family rivalries could spiral
into bloody urban battles—brilliantly dramatized in the clash of the Monta-
gues and Capulets in Shakespeare's *Romeo and Juliet*. Francis was known, as

Bonaventure notes, to greet people with a sign of peace. So Bonaventure greets the reader with his own peace prayer, praying that through the intercession of Francis, God would "enlighten the eyes of our soul to guide our feet in the way of that peace which surpasses all understanding."[28]

Francis's spirituality inspired Bonaventure's first two stages: seeing God through and in the visible universe. Francis is fondly remembered for his childlike wonder at the beauties of creation. There are famous legends of his miraculous dealings with wild animals—healing a wolf, preaching to swallows. All these were part of Franciscan lore, famously celebrated in Giotto's magnificent frescoes lining the walls of the Basilica in Assisi. Francis's love of nature comes through in his famous *Canticle of Brother Sun*. Adopting the courtly language of the troubadours, he poured out praises to God as "most high" king and counted as companions "Brother Sun" and "Sister Moon," "Brother Fire" and "Sister Water," those good gifts of God's royal beneficence.[29]

Bonaventure saw this love for the created world as a defining feature of Franciscan spirituality:

> Aroused by all things to the love of God, [Francis] rejoiced in all the works of the Lord's hands and from these joy-producing manifestations he rose to their life-giving principle and cause. In beautiful things he saw Beauty itself and through his vestiges imprinted on creation he followed his Beloved everywhere, making from all things a ladder by which he could climb up and embrace him who is utterly desirable. With a feeling of unprecedented devotion he savored in each and every creature—as in so many rivulets—that Goodness which is their fountain-source.[30]

Bonaventure here draws out the theological implications: that in beautiful things Francis glimpsed God, who is Beauty itself. Bonaventure uses the same metaphor here he repeatedly uses in the *Itinerarium*: creation as a ladder. He also speaks of creation as a great river that leads us back to its "fountain-source." This alludes to Bonaventure's view of God the Father as the *fontalis plenitudo*, a "fountain-like outpouring fullness."[31] Finally, Bonaventure says that Francis "followed his Beloved everywhere" by following God's "vestiges imprinted on creation."

That is how Bonaventure defines the *Itinerarium*'s initial ascent: "From the first two stages in which we are led to behold God in vestiges, like the two wings covering the Seraph's feet, we can gather that all the creatures of the sense world lead the mind of the contemplative and wise man to the eternal God."[32] The key word is "vestiges." The Latin word *vestigium* means "footprint." Footprints are, of course, signs; they point to the presence of living beings. They can also be followed. For Bonaventure, creation is not God, but God's footprints, signs that, if followed, lead back to God.

Bonaventure thought of creation as a sign in another sense. In the *Itinerarium*, he says that creation is a "book" in which one can read "the primacy, sublimity, and dignity of the First Principle and thus the infinity of power."[33] This book metaphor is another of Bonaventure's favorites.[34] At the end of his life, in his *Collations on the Six Days*, he remarks that before Adam's Fall, creation was an open book: its lettering was clear, easily decipherable, so that "through its representations, humankind was carried up to God." To see God, the first couple simply read the book of creation. But with Adam's Fall, "that book, namely the world, now seemed as if it were a dead letter, deleted, scribbled over."[35] With Christ's coming and with a new book, the scriptures, the book of creation became legible again. For Bonaventure, spiritual progress thus begins with reading God's presence through the book of creation, rediscovering its lucid calligraphy.

THE JOURNEY INWARD

Chapter 3 signals the shift from the early stages of the journey to the middle ones:

> The two previous stages, by leading us into God through his vestiges, through which he shines forth in all creatures, have led us to the point of reentering into ourselves, that is, into our mind, where the divine image shines forth. Here it is that, now in the third stage, we enter into our very selves; and, as it were, leaving the outer court, we should strive to see God through a mirror in the sanctuary... Enter into yourself then.[36]

Whereas the first two stages draw inspiration from Francis, the next two draw from Augustine of Hippo (d. 430). Bonaventure's call to "enter into yourself" is one that he—and the entire Latin West—inherited from Augustine.

That call reflects Augustine's unique spiritual journey, recorded in his autobiographical classic, *Confessions*. Unlike modern autobiographies, *Confessions* has few facts and only a handful of stories. It is, instead, a history of Augustine's heart, autobiography told from the inside. As Augustine saw it, if God is Love (as it says in 1 John 4:7) and if we human beings are made in God's "image and likeness" (as it says in Gen. 1:26), then we are, by nature, lovers. Often, as sinners, we love the wrong things, or more precisely, love good things in the wrong way. The *Confessions* records the history of Augustine's often misdirected loves up to and through his midlife conversion and baptism. In one renowned passage, he laments:

> Late have I loved you, beauty so ancient, so new: late have I loved you.
> And see: you were within, inside me, and I was outside, and out there
> I sought you. And I—misshapen—chased the beautiful shapes of
> things you had made. You were with me, but I was not with you.
> Beautiful things kept me far off from you—those things which, if not
> in you, would not be, not be at all. You called and shouted out and
> shattered my deafness; you flashed, you blazed, and my blindness
> fled; you were fragrant, and I drew in my breath, and panted for you;
> I tasted you and hunger and thirst for more; you touched me, and
> I burn for your peace.[37]

In Augustine's view, we often get lost chasing outer beauties. Conversion requires turning inward and discovering the beauty of our own God-imbued interiority. Our very psyches are "images" of God and mirror him in some dim way. Bonaventure follows Augustine's lead here, insisting: "You will be able to see God through yourself as through an image, which is to see 'through a mirror in an obscure manner' (1 Cor. 13:12)."[38]

Bonaventure follows Augustine's lead a step further. Augustine believed that if God is truly Trinity, then human beings, who are made in God's image and likeness, should themselves be Trinitarian in some way. In the *Confessions*, Augustine suggests that in the depths of human consciousness a Trinitarian impress can be uncovered:

> I wish that people would reflect upon the triad within their own
> selves . . . The three aspects I mean are being, knowing, willing. For
> I am and I know and I will. Knowing and willing I am. I know
> that I am and I will. I will to be and to know. In these three, therefore,
> let him who is capable of so doing contemplate how inseparable in
> life they are: one life, one mind, and one essence, yet ultimately
> there is distinction, for they are inseparable, yet distinct. The fact is
> certain to anyone by introspection.[39]

Augustine's intuition here found fuller exposition in another masterpiece, *On the Trinity*, written over the course of the next twenty years. This psychological triad is only one of many Augustine considers in *The Trinity*. In book 10, Augustine suggests a modified version: memory (*memoria*), understanding (*intelligentia*), and will (*voluntas*).[40]

In the *Itinerarium*, Bonaventure takes up Augustine's psychological triad and argues that "if God is a perfect spirit, he has memory, understanding, and will." For Bonaventure (as for Augustine), there was an inner dynamism within the life of the Trinity: from the Father "the Word is generated and Love breathed forth," and thus God is "the blessed Trinity of the Father, the Word and Love, three persons, coeternal and coequal." Bonaventure's point is not to offer a lesson in Trinitarian theology. His concern is to call readers to see their God-imbued identity: "When, therefore, the soul considers itself, it rises through itself as through a mirror to behold the blessed Trinity."[41] By such an inward turn we discover, or rediscover, that the obvious has been overlooked: "It seems amazing when it has shown that God is so close to our souls that so few should be aware of the First Principle within themselves."[42]

Bonaventure also plays on Augustine's views on nature and grace. Although human beings were made in God's image, human nature, on the far side of Adam's Fall, remains damaged; what had once been formed in our nature needs to be re-formed by grace. And so at the fourth stage, Bonaventure traces out what that re-formation involves. He outlines a threefold process of purification, illumination, and perfection. Bonaventure, like Augustine, stressed that we possess not only senses on the outside—eyes, ears, and so on—but also "senses" of a sort on the inside. This interior healing restores our inner sight, our inner hearing, our inner tastes, all our inner senses. In language that echoes that of Bernard of Clairvaux, Bonaventure says that "having recovered these senses, when it sees its Spouse and hears, smells, tastes, and embraces him, the soul can sing like the bride in the Canticles of Canticles" and "see the highest beauty, hear the highest harmony, smell the highest fragrance, taste the highest sweetness, apprehend the highest delight." Thus the soul becomes capable of "passing over into him through ecstatic love."[43] For Bonaventure, as for Augustine, sin is a disordering of the order that God made us to be; grace reorders, or, as Bonaventure puts it, "our spirit is made hierarchical in order to mount upward."[44]

At the end of chapter 4, Bonaventure returns to the image of the Seraph and its six wings: "These two middle stages through which we enter into contemplation of God within us as in mirrors of created images, are like the two middle wings of the Seraph spread out from flight."[45] That flight, as we will see, turns upward.

THE JOURNEY UPWARD

Bonaventure marks the next shift, from the middle stages to the upper ones, with a summary and a forecast: "We can contemplate God not only outside us and within us but also above us: outside through his vestiges, within through his image and above through the light which shines upon our minds, which is the light of Eternal Truth."[46] The journey thus moves to contemplating God in himself. It is a journey into light.

The Mercy Seat

Bonaventure begins with an Old Testament image: the "Mercy Seat." Over the centuries, Christian mystical theologians had mined various Old Testament motifs to articulate the mystical journey. Origen had drawn on the Exodus from Egypt; Gregory of Nyssa had appealed to Moses's ascent of Mount Sinai. Here Bonaventure draws on descriptions of the Jerusalem temple: that the ascent into God corresponds to moving deeper and deeper into the temple precincts. Matching metaphor to scheme, he first compares finding God in creation's vestiges to standing within the temple's outer court; he then compares finding God within the human heart to standing within the temple's sanctuary.[47] Finally he says that seeking God in himself is like entering "with the high priest into the Holy of Holies where the Cherubim of glory stand over the ark overshadowing the Mercy Seat."[48]

The biblical account says that within the Holy of Holies, there were two angelic figures, two cherubim, each standing alongside side of the throne of God, each facing inward, eyes turned toward God (invisibly) seated on the Mercy Seat above the Ark of the Covenant. Bonaventure reads this symbolically: "By these Cherubim we understand two modes or stages of contemplating the invisible and eternal things of God."[49] Thus, stage 5 means gazing in from one angle (like the first cherub), seeking to contemplate God as oneness, God as Being. Stage 6 means gazing in from the opposite angle (like the other cherub), seeking to contemplate God as Trinity, as three-person Goodness. The Mercy Seat metaphor is an apt one. It allows Bonaventure to hold in unity and in tension a double theological truth: that in approaching God we approach a single reality, yet that reality, if true to Christian fundamentals, must be grasped simultaneously from two opposite (and seemingly contradictory) vantage points—God as one and God as three.

Bonaventure packs a lot of theology into these two brief chapters. Readers unfamiliar with Trinitarian basics can find it pretty tough slogging. In meditating on God's oneness, Bonaventure gathers superlatives into tight paradoxes: God as "Being itself is first and last, is eternal and most present presence, is simplest simplicity and greatness, is most real reality and most unchangeable unchangeability, is most perfect perfection and immensity, is, at the very peak, oneness and yet all-embracing."[50] Bonaventure's discussion of God's threeness produces a similar harvest of paradoxes. But these two chapters are not meant as exercises in academic theology. They are exercises in holy awe. Again and again Bonaventure stresses that "you should be amazed."[51]

Pseudo-Dionysius

Although the Mercy Seat metaphor and the Trinitarian paradoxes strike readers first, there is an undercurrent here, a mystical voice subtly shaping the flow. It is the voice of Pseudo-Dionysius. If stages 1 and 2 (God outside us) draw especially from Francis and stages 3 and 4 (God within us) draw especially from Augustine, then stages 5 and 6 (God above us) draw especially from Pseudo-Dionysius. Medieval theologians such as Bonaventure presumed that Dionysius, St. Paul's convert from the Areopagus in Athens, had authored a handful of brief mystical treatises: *The Divine Names*, *The Celestial Hierarchy*, and *The Mystical Theology*. Bonaventure and his colleagues viewed these as "sub-apostolic," writings whose authority veered close to apostolic (and thus biblical) stature. We know what Bonaventure did not: that Dionysius is really *Pseudo*-Dionysius, and that these treatises come not from Paul's first-century convert, but from a sixth-century Syrian. These remarkable texts first became known in the Latin West when the pope sent a copy to the Frankish king Pepin in 785. A second version was sent by the Byzantine Emperor Michael to the Holy Roman Emperor Louis the Pious in 807, and this was translated by John Scotus Erigena into Latin a few years later. Dionysius's works were much esteemed in Paris, partly because a legend traced Christian origins in France to the preaching of a Dionysius. St. Denis, as he was known, was thus celebrated as the French church's founder and patron. To faculty and students at the University of Paris, the writings of Dionysius represented a heady blend, a joining of Athens and Jerusalem, of Greek philosophy and Gospel wisdom.

Suger of St.-Denis

By Bonaventure's time, the Dionysian writings had already shaped Western spirituality in decisive ways. They inspired one of the extraordinary developments in Christian architecture, the Gothic cathedral. A century before Bonaventure, a monk named Suger (d. 1151) had been elected abbot of the monastery where Dionysius was believed buried, the Abbey of St. Denis. It was prestigious, wealthy, and a favorite pilgrimage site. It also served as the royal abbey, the burial place of France's kings. Abbot Suger decided to renovate the abbey church, and as he set about the task, he drew inspiration from the opening words of Dionysius's *Celestial Hierarchy*:

"Every good endowment and every perfect gift is from above, coming down from the Father of lights" (James 1:17). But there is something more. Inspired by the Father, each procession of the Light spreads itself generously toward us, and, in its power to unify, it stirs us by lifting us up. It returns us back to the oneness and deifying simplicity of the Father who gathers us in. For, as the sacred Word says, "from him and to him are all things" (Rom. 11:36). Let us, then, call upon Jesus, the Light of the Father, the "true light enlightening every man coming into the world" (John 1:9), "through whom we have obtained access" (Rom. 5:2) to the Father, the light which is the source of all light... We must lift up the immaterial and steady eyes of our minds to that outpouring of Light which is so primal, indeed much more so, and which comes from that source of divinity, I mean the Father. This is the Light which, by way of representative symbols, makes known to us the most blessed hierarchies among the angels. But we need to rise from this outpouring of illumination so as to come to the simple ray of Light itself.[52]

Note Dionysius's stress on light: God is the "Father of lights," and Jesus is the "Light of the Father" and the light that enlightens us. This outflowing of divine light not only "lifts us up"; it "returns us back to the oneness" and "deifies" us. Dionysius later adds: "Material lights are images of the outpouring of an immaterial gift of light."[53] For Dionysius, the material world was no hindrance to spirituality; on the contrary, it was, if seen rightly, aglow with divine presence, a shimmering gateway back to God.

This outlook inspired Suger and the whole later Middle Ages. Suger embraced the Dionysian view that light is *the* symbol of God's presence, and he sought to fill his new church with light. To do so, he exploited a recent invention, stained glass: where once there had been thick stone, Suger inserted into the church's walls large, stained-glass windows. The once-dark abbey church now became a bastion of light. Suger felt that his renovated church offered a glimpse of heaven, a foretaste of eternal light: "When the enchanting beauty of the house of God has overwhelmed me... then it seems to me that I can see myself, as if in reality, residing in some strange region of the universe which had no previous existence either in the clay of this earth or in the purity of the heavens, and that, by the grace of God, I can be transported mystically from life on this earth to the higher realm."[54] Gothic architecture, with its great outpourings of light, did more than transport one, however briefly, to "some strange region of the universe." It transformed how one saw the whole visible world. Suger had an inscription placed over the doorway into St. Denis: "The dull mind rises to truth through that which is material / And, in seeing this light, is resurrected from its former submission."[55]

This excursus on Pseudo-Dionysius and Suger of St. Denis is not meant as an out-of-the-way stop. It is essential to understanding Bonaventure. The Abbey of St. Denis was not far from medieval Paris (and is now within Paris's suburbs). Suger's invention defined the Gothic style, and his renovations became the template for every cathedral in France. Bonaventure knew it well, having lived for years in the shadow of Nôtre Dame de Paris. Dionysius's mysticism of light shaped Bonaventure's own. So too did Suger's use of stained glass. In his *Collations on the Six Days*, he remarked: "As you notice that a ray of light coming in through a window is colored according to the shades of the different panes, so the divine ray shines differently in each creature."[56] For Bonaventure, the whole created world shimmered like a vast stained-glass window.

Metaphysics of Emanation and Return

Bonaventure thought of Dionysius as Christianity's foremost theologian. Once he remarked that although Augustine deserved acclaim for his doctrine and Gregory the Great for his moral theology, Dionysius was superior because he taught "the ultimate goal of both, . . . the union of the soul with God."[57] Bonaventure took ideas both great and small from Pseudo-Dionysius. He quoted him often. The *Itinerarium*'s opening words echo the opening words of Dionysius's *Celestial Hierarchy*: "In the beginning I call upon the First Beginning from whom all illuminations descend as from the 'Father of lights' from whom comes 'every good and every perfect gift.' "[58] Bonaventure's theology shows Dionysian touches at key points: his angelology; his theory of symbol; his stress on hierarchy, both cosmic and ecclesial; his view that the spiritual life consists of a threefold movement of purgation, illumination, and union.

Deeper still, Bonaventure found in Dionysius a metaphysical vision, a vision of the universe's origin and destiny. Look again at the passage I quoted from the *Celestial Hierarchy*. There Dionysius speaks of God the Father as Primal Light, as a light that pours down from above enlightening all and that, in turn, gathers and draws all back up into a deifying unity. This, in a nutshell, is Dionysius's mystical metaphysics. It is a metaphysics that has its roots in Plotinus, the third-century Neoplatonist philosopher. It is also a metaphysics that appealed deeply to Bonaventure and stands at the heart of his own worldview. Near the end of his life, he articulated his core conviction: "This is the whole of our metaphysics: It is about emanation, exemplarity, and consummation; that is, to be illumined by spiritual rays and to be led back to the Supreme Being. And thus you will be a true metaphysician."[59]

Bonaventure invokes three technical terms here: "emanation," "exemplarity," and "consummation." *Emanation* refers to God's creation of the world. It is the outflow (*egressus*) of created beings from the One Supreme Being, the many lights from the one Light. *Consummation* refers to history's end, the return (*regressus*) of the cosmos into union with God. In the vast in-between, between creation's beginning and history's end, there is *exemplarity*, in which all created things carry, however dimly, "a refulgence of the divine exemplar . . . some kind of opacity combined with light."[60] For Bonaventure, everything exemplifies God, but in different ways: the material world as "vestiges"; human beings as "images"; the morally righteous as "likenesses."[61] But, he insists, there is only one true Exemplar, both within the life of God and within human history: Christ. (More on this in a moment.)

This metaphysics—a vision of a vast cosmic circle, a movement that flows out from God and returns to God—undergirds Bonaventure's whole mystical theology. As Zachary Hayes has noted, "It is within the circle of creation . . . that Bonaventure envisions the movement of the spiritual life. The spiritual journey to which all are called is nothing other than *the personal engagement* in the great movement of created reality out of God and back to God."[62]

Divine Darkness

For Bonaventure, the true metaphysician is not the thinker, not the philosopher, but the mystic "illumined by spiritual rays" and "led back to the Supreme Being."[63] This illumination is pure gift. One can have perfectly good eyes, but if there's no light, one cannot see. So at this fifth stage, when the mind has been raised above itself, it does so "through the light which shines upon our minds, which is the light of Eternal Truth."[64]

Bonaventure thought a lot about vision and light. He notes that we often focus on the things that sunlight lights up, but tend to ignore sunlight itself: "The eye, concentrating on various differences of color, does not see the very light by which it sees other things; and if it does see this light, it does not advert to it."[65] In the same way, we tend to ignore how God lights up our minds, enabling us to understand this or that; we tend not to advert to the Light that God is: "Strange, then, is the blindness of the intellect, which does not consider that which it sees first and without which it can know nothing."[66] Bonaventure was convinced that we already see the light of God simply because we see the world around us, simply because we understand this and that about it.[67] How, then, does one turn one's gaze and contemplate the divine light directly?

This poses a problem. One cannot simply look upon God, any more than one can stare at the sun. The sun, gazed at directly, blinds our eyes. In the same way, God blinds the mind's eye. Bonaventure takes his cues from Dionysius and his famous description of divine darkness. For Dionysius, God is uncreated light, a light beyond our vision. Bonaventure agrees. He compares us to bats, whose night vision is paralyzed by sunlight; in the same way, "our mind, accustomed to the darkness of beings and the images of the things of sense, when it glimpses the light of the Supreme Being, seems to itself to see nothing."[68] This is a paradox: what seems darkness is actually light, albeit a blinding light: the mind "does not realize that this very darkness is the supreme illumination of our mind, just as when the eye sees pure light, it seems to itself to see nothing."[69]

Apophatic Theology

At the peak of the ascent, the mind passes over into ecstasy. As Bonaventure notes in his *Disputed Questions on Christ's Knowledge*: "This ecstasy is that ultimate and most exalted form of knowledge which is praised by Dionysius in all his books, but especially in the book *On Mystical Theology*... This type of knowledge can be understood only with great difficulty, and it cannot be understood at all except by one who has experienced it."[70] Bonaventure, like other mystics, insists that ecstasy defies speech, that here one enters the ineffable. Following Dionysius, he resorts to negations. Dionysius is famous for coining a classic distinction. He speaks of two types of mystical theology: cataphatic and apophatic.[71] Cataphatic theology speaks positively, saying that God is like this or like that; apophatic theology speaks negatively, saying that God is unlike this or unlike that. Bonaventure, following Dionysius, insists that at this mystical pinnacle, one must use apophatic speech: "In trying to explain this (ecstasy), negations are more appropriate than affirmations, and superlatives are more appropriate than positive predications. And if it is to be experienced, interior silence is more helpful than external speech."[72]

In the *Itinerarium*'s final chapter, Bonaventure speaks of a "mystical ecstasy in which rest is given to our intellect when through ecstasy our affection passes over entirely into God."[73] Here he embraces Dionysius at his most paradoxical, quoting one of the densest passages in the *Mystical Theology*: "at the super-unknown, superluminous and most sublime summit of mystical communication" one faces the divine Trinity; there, "new, absolute, and unchangeable mysteries of theology are hidden in the superluminous darkness of a silence teaching secretly in the utmost obscurity which is supermanifest—a darkness which is super-resplendent."[74] Silent teaching, superluminous darkness, supermanifest hiddenness: paradoxical indeed. But Bonaventure does not leave off where Dionysius does. Here, at the pinnacle of the mind's journey into God, he turns back to Christ crucified.

THE CENTER: CHRIST CRUCIFIED

One expects Christian mystics to center on Christ. Not all do, in fact. But it is hard to name a mystical theology more self-consciously Christ-centered than Bonaventure's. He often speaks of Christ as the *medium*, Latin for "middle" or "center." In his *Collations on the Six Days*, he insists: "The beginning is best made from the center (*medium*), that is, from Christ. For he himself is the mediator between God and humankind, holding the central position in all things, as shall be seen. Therefore it is necessary to start from Christ if one wants to reach Christian wisdom."[75]

Francis of Assisi had, by his life and teaching, compelled contemporaries to savor the unvarnished radicalism of the Gospel Jesus. Bonaventure recognized this and slowly thought through the massive theological implications— what it meant to recenter theology on Christ, poor and crucified.[76] Francis had been no theologian, no scholar; he taught "more by example than by word," as Bonaventure himself notes.[77] At the *Itinerarium*'s end, Bonaventure circles back to what inspired him, back to Francis and his vision. Francis had not seen just a six-winged angel, but a cruciform angel, an angel who held within his outstretched wings a crucified man; and when the vision faded, the crucified man remained, so to speak, in Francis's *stigmata*. Bonaventure thus insisted that Francis exemplified the journey into God: "He passed over into God in ecstatic contemplation and became an example of perfect contemplation . . . so that through him . . . God might invite all truly spiritual men to this kind of passing over and spiritual ecstasy."[78] Francis was an exemplar because he exemplified Christ the exemplar. Francis's vision of the seraph meant, according to Bonaventure, that "there is no other path but through the burning love of the Crucified."[79]

That pathway, as we have seen, has steps and stages. The universe is a ladder, but we cannot climb it without help: "Our soul could not rise completely from these things of sense to see itself and the Eternal Truth in itself unless Truth, assuming human nature in Christ, had become a ladder, restoring the first ladder that had been broken in Adam."[80] Christ, then, is the repairer of ladders, both human and cosmic. He also is the one doorway: "No matter how enlightened one may be by the light of natural and acquired knowledge, he cannot enter into himself to delight within himself in the Lord unless his mediator be Christ, who says: 'I am the door.' "[81]

Bonaventure, in his systematic works, speaks of Christ as center in two senses. First, Christ is the center of the Trinity.[82] He is the middle person who originates from the Father and who co-originates the Holy Spirit. Just as sunlight is the visible image of the sun, so the Son is the visible Image of the Father, Light from Light. He is also the Father's outspoken Word, his perfect self-expression.[83] Second, Christ is at creation's center. Christ stands at the center of the great cosmic movement of the going forth from God and the returning back to God:

> Since God is the Beginning and the End of all things, it is neces-
> sary ... to posit an intermediary in the going forth (*in egressu*) and in
> the return (*regressu*) of things: in the going forth, a center (*medi-
> um*) which will be closer to the productive principle [= the Father];
> in the return, a center which will be close to the one returning.
> Therefore, as creatures went forth from God by the Word of God,
> so for a perfect return, it was necessary that the mediator between
> God and humanity be not only God but also human so that this
> mediator might lead humanity back to God.[84]

Christ is at once creation's medium and salvation's mediator. If God is an artist and creation is his artwork, then Christ is the Father's Artistry, the medium through whom all his artistic output is poured out. Christ is thus creation's exemplar—both its prototype and archetype—so that all creation reflects, whether clearly or dimly, the stamp of Christ. Christ is also mediator between God and humanity because he is both fully God and fully human. For Bonaventure, the summit is not so much the Incarnation that joins the infinite divine with finite humanity, but rather the bloody, self-emptying crucifixion.

The crucified Christ is mediator in that he rebridges the human and the divine. He is the "pass-over," the *transitus*, as Bonaventure terms it. This is not just dogma, an item to be believed. It arcs the return path for the journey into God. Bonaventure insists that at the sixth stage, after the mind has risen above itself and contemplated God through and in the light, it must pass over through Christ: "It now remains for our mind by contemplating these things, to transcend and pass over not only this sense world but even itself. In this passing over, Christ is the way and the door; Christ is the ladder and the vehicle, like the Mercy Seat placed above the ark of God and the mystery hidden from eternity."[85] In the *Itinerarium*'s final phrases, Bonaventure embraces Dionysius's language of divine darkness—but with a difference. Whereas Dionysius ends with God's imagelessness, Bonaventure ends with the image of Christ crucified: "Let us, then, die and enter into the darkness; let us impose silence upon our cares, our desires and our imaginings. With Christ crucified let us pass out of this world to the Father so that when the Father is shown to us, we may say with Philip: 'It is enough for us' (John 14:8)."[86]

SPECULATIO PAUPERIS IN DESERTO

I have taken a risky course here. I focused the analytical spotlight not only on Bonaventure, but also on his sources, tracing how he wove together the three very different voices of Francis, Augustine, and Dionysius. My strategy risks leaving Bonaventure in fragments and without his own voice. Readers of the *Itinerarium* come away with the exact opposite impression: that Bonaventure's work is profoundly unified, that it is all of a piece in both content and style. That impression is accurate. Bonaventure was no mere compiler, no eclectic collector of others' ideas. Like the engineers who built the great Gothic cathedrals, Bonaventure constructed something new out of inherited elements, something poised to turn one's gaze upward. As Denys Turner has remarked, "Augustinian and Dionysian emphases are poised in equilibrium, the points of contact between the elements of structure being placed with an exactness and accuracy of an engineer who knows his structural dynamics and of an architect who is confident of his own aesthetic."[87] This engineering brilliance, Bonaventure's near-seamless joining of traditions, has led scholars to speak of the *Itinerarium* as the "*summa* of medieval Christian mysticism."[88]

I highlighted Bonaventure's sources for a reason. It concerns how we need to understand mysticism, or more precisely, mystical speech. The mystic, like anyone else, must communicate via a medium. Accounts of mystical experiences and mystical journeys come to us always (or almost always) through the medium of words. (I say "almost always" because a few, such as Hildegard, used other media, such as painting and music). Like speakers of any language, mystics do not invent the language they speak. They cobble together inherited words and phrase them within an inherited grammar. If they speak well, they join words and phrases that they did not invent in order to express things uniquely their own. Bonaventure is interesting as a mystical speaker because he is so brilliantly and so self-consciously multilingual. He illustrates how mystical writers often negotiate earlier mystical languages. Bonaventure stands out because he negotiates three different mystical languages and makes them his own quite seamlessly.

Between the *Itinerarium*'s prologue and first chapter, Bonaventure inserted a heading: "Here begins the reflection of a poor man in the desert"

(*Incipit speculatio pauperis in deserto*).[89] Bonaventure speaks here of himself, but obliquely. He saw himself as poor, not simply because he was committed to Francis's stern poverty, but also because he wished to come before God as one poor in spirit. Being "in the desert" sounds negative, but it is not. In the *Itinerarium*'s final chapter, he says that the poor man "passes over the Red Sea by the staff of the cross [of Christ], moving from Egypt into the desert—there where he will taste the hidden manna."[90] Did Bonaventure himself "taste the hidden manna"? Was he himself a mystic? Or was he simply a mapmaker who never voyaged to the places he writes about? There is no doubt that he was self-effacing, that we have few autobiographical traces, that as Gilson poignantly noted, Bonaventure "the man disappears behind the work he did." If autobiography makes the mystic, then Bonaventure is no mystic. But that, I believe, is looking at the subject through a modern lens, with Jamesian glasses. Bonaventure does speak, at key junctures, about ecstasy and rapture. He stresses that these give one knowledge of God only understood by those who have experienced them. One could argue that he is simply repeating Bernard of Clairvaux, and it is true that Bonaventure knew Bernard's writings and, on occasion, quotes them. But I think one can fairly accept that when he insists on knowing from experience, he speaks from experience.

Our contemporary fondness for autobiography, for its tease of self-revelation, diverts us from understanding Bonaventure in his own terms. He understood himself as a theologian. Though he was trained in and often spoke in a strictly academic style, his focus, especially in later years, was mystical theology. And he had a quite precise sense of his task. It was not about sharing personal experiences. He says, rather, that "the theologian considers how the world, which was made by God, will be brought back to God."[91] We need to savor Bonaventure's theology as a whole, for at its root it is a mystical vision of a cosmic return to God. Its central thrust is clear: everything is a ladder—the universe, our psyche, and, at the core, Christ. Put simply, there are handholds everywhere.

People who write travelogues tell us what they have experienced. Sometimes they induce us to make similar voyages, but, just as often, they allow us to stay at home and imagine voyages we ourselves never take. A cartographer, by contrast, tells us virtually nothing about himself. The maps he makes, however aesthetically attractive, are not for our entertainment. They are not for stay-at-home imaginings. They are tools for voyagers. I think it is better to understand Bonaventure as a cartographer of the mystical, a mapmaker who wants us to understand not *his* experience, but rather how we and all creation might "be brought back to God."

6

Mystic as Mystagogue:
Meister Eckhart

Mystics try to speak with great precision about realities that defy speech. At times they deliberately use words to upset us, to turn our world on its head, to jolt us into seeing mysteries that surge beneath the crust of our lives. Few mystics have used words with greater precision and with greater shock effect than Meister Eckhart (c. 1260–1328), one of the most brilliant and controversial mystics in the history of Christianity.

We need, I believe, to hear and absorb the shock of Eckhart from the outset. The following comes from sermon 52, one of his most daring, preached in the vernacular before a popular audience:

> When I stood in my first cause, I then had no "God," and then I was my own cause. I wanted nothing, I longed for nothing, for I was an empty being, and the only truth in which I rejoiced was in the knowledge of myself. Then it was myself I wanted and nothing else. What I wanted I was, and what I was I wanted; and so I stood empty of God and everything. But when I went out from my own free will and received my created being, then I had a "God," for before there were any creatures, God was not "God," but he was what he was. But when creatures came to be and received their created being, then God was not "God" in himself, but he was "God" in the creatures . . . For in the same being of God where God is above being and above distinction, there

I myself was, there I willed myself and committed myself to create this man. Therefore I am the cause of myself in the order of my being, which is eternal, and not in the order of my becoming, which is temporal. And therefore I am unborn, and in the manner in which I am unborn I can never die. In my unborn manner I have been eternally, and am now, and shall eternally remain. When I am in the order of having been born, that will die and perish, for it is mortal, and so it must in time suffer corruption. In my birth all things were born and I was the cause of myself and of all things, and if I would have wished it, I would not be nor would all other things be. And if I did not exist, "God" would also not exist. That God is "God," of that I am the cause; if I did not exist, God too would not be "God." There is no need to understand this.[1]

On first reading, this seems bizarre, even mad. Eckhart sounds as though he is saying that he himself is God, or beyond God, or greater than God—that God is somehow dependent on him. But if one reads the passage again, carefully, one realizes that that is not at all what he is saying. This excerpt, one might argue, is not even mystical. It simply expresses quite orthodox theological ideas—though with a rhetorical bravado that is both startling and provocative. I routinely introduce this text to my undergraduate classes, challenging them to try and decode it. One year I had a bright student (well-known on campus for coloring his hair pink or purple or green) who took one glance at the excerpt and announced to the class: "All Eckhart is saying is that before our life here and now, we existed as ideas in God's mind. When we were in God's mind, there was no separation. We *were* God. Only after getting created could we and God be different." Exactly. I cite this because what sometimes sounds deeply mystical in Eckhart may not be, at least not in a conventional sense. It may simply be fundamental theology, boldly framed. The mystical is certainly at the heart of Eckhart's project, but the usual lenses do not easily capture what he is up to.

This passage should give readers a first taste of why people both gravitate to Eckhart and are puzzled by him. He can be subtle. He can certainly be misunderstood. Like Bonaventure, he was both a first-rate theologian and a first-rate mystical writer, and these two vocations came together seamlessly, in Eckhart's case with volatile results. It would be tempting to skip someone as subtle as Eckhart in an introductory work such as this. There are, after all, so many other mystics, so many who are more accessible. But it would be, I believe, unfair to readers and untrue to the task if we sidestepped Eckhart simply because he is difficult. He is too important to sidestep, whatever the difficulties he poses. That said, I will have to simplify things here. Let this chapter be a doorway into a figure who deserves, indeed, requires, further study.

A THREE-PART WORK

We know little of Eckhart's early life. He was born, it seems, around 1260 in Thuringia, what is now central Germany.[2] At a young age, he entered the Dominicans. From the beginning, the order founded by St. Dominic (d. 1221) deeply valued education, which it saw as prerequisite to its core mission of preaching. Gifted students such as Eckhart received the order's finest educational opportunities and resources. Eckhart may have studied the arts at the University of Paris in the late 1270s. If so, he witnessed the condemnation of radical Aristotelians by Stephen Tempier, the bishop of Paris. Included in Tempier's blanket condemnation were propositions drawn from the greatest (and recently deceased) Dominican theologian, Thomas Aquinas. When Eckhart ran into his own difficulties later, he recalled this episode:

> In my own lifetime, the masters of theology at Paris received a command from above to examine the books of those two most distinguished men, Saint Thomas Aquinas and Brother Albert the Bishop, on the grounds that they were suspect and erroneous. Many have often written, declared and even publicly preached that Saint Thomas wrote and taught errors and heresies, but with God's aid his life and teaching alike have been given approval, both at Paris and also by the Roman Pontiff and the Roman curia.[3]

Eckhart admired not only Aquinas, but also Aquinas's illustrious teacher, Albert the Great (the "Brother Albert the Bishop" Eckhart refers to here). Albert had established a *studium generale*—a center for advanced studies—in Cologne in 1248 and was active there until his death in 1280. Eckhart was privileged to have studied there and may have met the elderly Albert.[4] In 1293 and 1294 Eckhart was back in Paris, lecturing on the *Sentences* of Peter Lombard, fulfilling a key step toward the doctorate in theology. Eckhart was eventually awarded the degree and with it the title *magister*, in German *meister*, an epithet ever after attached to his name.

Magister and Superior

Over the next twenty years, Eckhart held a string of high-profile positions, alternating between demanding administrative posts within the order and prestigious academic appointments. In 1294 he was appointed prior of the Dominican house in Erfurt and vicar for Dominicans throughout Thuringia. During this phase, he published his first vernacular work, *The Talks of Instruction* (*Die rede der underscheidunge*), intended for novices under his care. In 1302 he was awarded one of the two Dominican chairs in theology at the University of Paris, the same chair Aquinas had once held. During this time or soon after, he conceived and began outlining a grand academic project, a *summa* to be entitled *The Three-Part Work* (*Opus tripartitum*).[5] The project was never completed. Only the prologues survive, but his later commentaries on Genesis, Exodus, and the Book of Wisdom, as well as his massive *Commentary on the Gospel of John*, were intended to fit into its superstructure. In 1303 he returned to Germany, having been elected to serve as provincial superior for the new province of Saxonia. This meant that Eckhart held one of the order's highest positions. As provincial, he was required to travel hundreds of miles, usually on foot, moving from house to house, caring for the men under his jurisdiction. From 1311 to 1313 he was back at Paris, where he once more held the Dominican chair of theology. To hold the chair once was a great privilege; to hold it twice was a singular honor. In the Middle Ages, only Aquinas and Eckhart did so.

The Beguines

During his second stay in Paris, Eckhart lived with the Dominican inquisitor William Humbert, who in June 1310 oversaw the condemnation and execution of a "relapsed heretic," the Beguine mystic Marguerite Porete, author of the controversial *Mirror of Simple Souls* (*Le mirourer des simples ames*).[6] The Beguines were women who, according to thirteenth-century chronicler Matthew Paris, "call themselves 'religious,' and take a private vow of continence and simplicity of life, though they do not follow the Rule of any saint, nor are they confined within a cloister."[7] The Beguines cultivated a deep, if often self-taught, interior piety. Some claimed visions and mystical revelations; others practiced what they called the *iubilus* (literally, "jubilation"), a form of ecstatic prayer; some claimed the stigmata. A few, such as Hadewijch of Brabant and Mechthild of Magdeburg, authored remarkable mystical treatises. But others, such as Marguerite, ran afoul of the authorities.

In 1311 Pope Clement V summoned an ecumenical council to meet in Vienne, and the Beguines became part of the agenda. The council issued stern condemnations of what it branded the "heresy of the free spirit," denouncing supposed libertines who, it claimed, declared themselves free of moral duties because of their mystical achievements.[8] The council's decrees singled out for condemnation "women commonly known as Beguines . . . who seem be led by a particular insanity; they argue and preach on the holy Trinity and the divine essence, and express opinions contrary to the catholic faith with regard to the articles of faith and the sacraments of the church. These Beguines thus ensnare many simple people, leading them into various errors."[9] The council did acknowledge legitimate lay piety: "Of course we in no way intend . . . to forbid any faithful women, whether they promise chastity or not, from living uprightly in their hospices, wishing to live a life of penance and serving the Lord of hosts in a spirit of humility."[10] Even so, the council's blanket condemnation left the door open to arbitrary persecutions.

These events sparked a seismic shift in Eckhart's career. Recent studies have shown that he had in fact read and in subtle ways drawn inspiration from Beguine writers, including the condemned Porete.[11] After his tenure in Paris, Eckhart was sent to Strasbourg, a volatile center of the Beguine movement. The city had become the epicenter of a debate on mystical matters, partly because its bishop, John of Zurich (bp. 1306–1328), was one of the architects of the Vienne condemnations and was a zealous heresy hunter. For the next decade, from 1313 to 1323, Eckhart devoted some of his best energies to the pastoral care of Dominican nuns and local Beguines in and around Strasbourg. Though Eckhart was not uncritical of Beguine enthusiasms, he remained a sympathetic critic and boldly threw his lot in with their cause.[12]

Vernacular Preaching

Eckhart's career had, to this point, been a "two-part work," defined first by academics and second by administration. In Strasbourg a third came to the fore: preaching. Preaching stood at the heart of his vocation as a Dominican. Aquinas had famously contrasted the Dominican vocation with the monastic: "It is a greater thing to hand on to others what has been contemplated than merely to contemplate."[13] This handing on of matters contemplative moved to the center of Eckhart's self-understanding. In his *Book of Divine Consolation* (*Daz buoch der götlîchen træstunge*), written in his Strasbourg years, Eckhart stressed the legitimacy of mystical evangelizing: "We shall be told that one ought not to talk about or write such teachings to the untaught. But to this I say that if we are not to teach people who have not been taught, no one will ever be taught, and no one will ever be able to teach or write."[14] He pointed to the Gospels, especially the sublimely mystical prologue of John's Gospel: "Saint John narrates his holy gospel for all believers and also for all unbelievers, so that they might believe, and yet he begins his gospel with the most exalted thoughts any man could utter here about God; and both what he says and what our Lord says are constantly misunderstood."[15] Eckhart thought it better to risk misunderstanding than to silence the truth of the mystical. That risky move came back to haunt him.

Eckhart's fame, both among his contemporaries and among moderns, rests on his extraordinary sermons, delivered in the vernacular, that is, in Middle High German. One hundred and fourteen of them survive.[16] Many date from this later phase of his career.[17] It used to be presumed that these surviving texts were *reportationes*, unofficial stenographic transcripts taken down by eager disciples. It was thus presumed that the texts were in all likelihood less-than-dependable records of his actual words. Recent studies have sharply reversed that view.[18] Scholars note not only the consistency of the manuscript traditions, but also clear verbal parallels between Eckhart's unquestioned vernacular writings (like the *Book of Divine Consolation*) and his surviving sermons. They also note that when teachings from his sermons later came under fire from authorities, he did not, as a rule, challenge their authenticity. Scholars thus conclude that Eckhart himself had a careful hand in their production, either writing them out himself or at least checking disciples' transcriptions for accuracy. As we will see, Eckhart's vernacular sermons display a mystical theology of uncanny depth and rhetorical fearlessness.

Trial in Cologne

In 1323 Eckhart was reassigned to Cologne. Cologne was the site of the famed Dominican *studium generale* where Eckhart himself had studied, but we do not know why or for what job he was sent there. Whatever the reason, he came to town as a man in his sixties, a widely respected scholar and a leading figure within the order. In Cologne Eckhart's career took a tragic turn. The city, like Strasbourg, was a major hub of Beguine spirituality. According to Matthew Paris, the Beguines "so multiplied themselves within a short time that two thousand have been reported in Cologne and the neighboring cities."[19] Cologne's archbishop, Henry II of Virneberg (bp. 1304–1332), was a stern critic of the Beguines and, like his colleague in Strasbourg, had had a hand in the Vienne condemnations.

It did not take Eckhart long to get into hot water. Even within Dominican circles his preaching was raising concerns. In 1325 a general chapter meeting in Venice warned about "friars in Teutonia who say things in their sermons that can easily lead simple and uneducated people into error."[20] Authorities within the order apparently sensed trouble. To nip things in the bud, they ordered an internal investigation. A papal-appointed visitor, Nicholas of Strasbourg, sent

Eckhart a list of suspicious passages from his *Book of Divine Consolation* and asked for an explanation. Eckhart replied, and Nicholas pronounced himself satisfied with Eckhart's orthodoxy. This in-house inquiry did not silence critics. Two fellow Dominicans started the ball rolling, drawing up a list of seventy-four controversial passages from the full scope of Eckhart's works, both academic and popular, both Latin and German. These they presented to the Archbishop of Cologne. Other lists were gathered, one with passages from his vernacular sermons, another from his *Commentary on John*.

On September 26, 1326, Eckhart was summoned before the Inquisition.[21] This was unprecedented. Theologians before him had been investigated and, on occasion, censured, but Eckhart was the first medieval theologian to be summoned before the Inquisition on charges of heresy. We have the text of Eckhart's *Defense*. He defused things at the outset, insisting: "If there is something false that I do not see in [the passages under scrutiny] or in my other remarks and writings, I am always ready to yield to a better understanding... I can be in error, but I cannot be a heretic, because the first belongs to the intellect, the second to the will."[22] Compliant in some ways, Eckhart could also lash out. At one point he lambasted accusers for their "ignorance and stupidity," pungently adding that "the first mistake they make is that they think everything they do not understand is an error and that every error is a heresy."[23] He also reminded the court that it lacked proper jurisdiction, for, according to privileges granted to the Dominicans by the papacy, he belonged to an exempt order; he insisted therefore: "I am not held to respond to you and or to anyone except the Pope and the University of Paris."[24] He agreed to appear "from my own generosity, though with a protestation of the exemption of my order," because "I still wanted to write down and present these things to you so that I do not seem to be avoiding what has been falsely brought against me."[25]

Papal Condemnation

Eckhart's defense in Cologne was of no avail. So he issued an official appeal to the pope and in spring 1327 set off for Avignon. The pope at the time, John XXII (1313–1334), was, to put it mildly, controversial. A few years earlier he had revamped papal tax collection, leading critics across Europe to accuse him of merciless greed. In 1318 he dealt with Franciscan dissidents decisively and ruthlessly. When circles of Franciscan Spirituals embraced St. Francis's radical standards of poverty, the pope ordered them to modify their extremes and submit to their superiors—or else. When they refused, he had them arrested and tried before the Inquisition. In the end four were burned at the stake. John did not stop there. In 1323 he declared that "the persistent assertion that our Redeemer and Lord Jesus Christ and his apostles did not possess any goods or other property, either privately or in common, should be designated heretical."[26] This attacked one of the most deeply held Franciscan convictions and succeeded in alienating even moderate Franciscans. It also began whispers of papal heresy.[27]

After Eckhart's arrival in Avignon, the pope appointed two commissions to examine the long lists of disputed passages. At some point, the commissioners whittled them down from 150 to 28. A précis of the proceedings has survived, and one can trace both Eckhart's defense of disputed points and the commissioners' own disagreements and final judgments. The case wore on for months, when, in the thick of things, Eckhart died. He would have been 67 or 68 years old.[28] In April 1328 the pope sent a letter to the archbishop of Cologne, noting that though Eckhart had died, the case against him was proceeding. A year later, in March 1329, John issued the bull *In the Field of the Lord* (*In agro dominico*), announcing his final judgment. It was harsh one. Of the 28 articles, John declared 15 to contain "error or stain of heresy"; 11 others he branded as "quite evil-sounding and very rash and suspect of heresy," adding that "with many explanations and additions, they might take on or possess a Catholic meaning."[29] This comment is both telling and intriguing: Eckhart's careful expositions—those "many explanations and additions"—demonstrated that his views, if put back into proper context, were orthodox in principle. Two other propositions were declared heretical, though the pope accepted Eckhart's claim not to have preached them. The pope pointedly did not condemn Eckhart himself because Eckhart had "professed the Catholic faith at the end of his life" and had publicly renounced any articles that the pope and commissioners might eventually condemn "insofar as they could generate in the minds of the faithful a heretical opinion."[30] The nuance of this final phrase is crucial. Eckhart, in effect, had renounced not his views in and of themselves, but only as they might be wrongly understood.

Remarkably, despite condemnation, Eckhart's writings survived, preserved by disciples and defenders. The next generation of Dominican mystical writers, especially Johannes Tauler and Heinrich Suso, did much to defend Eckhart's views and legacy against heterodox interpretations. They also knew that in some ways Eckhart's own disciples had damaged his cause and fueled the clash with authorities. In one sermon, Tauler gently chided his hearers: "Our loving master taught you and told you about these matters, and you did not understand him. He spoke from eternity, and you took it as referring to time."[31] Eckhart's speaking "from the point of view of eternity" is, as we will see, easy to misunderstand. It is also the key to understanding him.

A GOD WHO BOILS AND SPILLS

Eckhart's vernacular sermons dazzle modern readers just as they did his first hearers. He has a way of speaking of God and of us that is at once inviting and jarring, earthy and strange. He often starts clearly enough, enumerating points, but before long tends to bolt off in strange directions, with unexpected leaps, sudden reversals, striking paradoxes. One walks away a little dizzy, hard-pressed to repeat what exactly he said, but with a sense that his words point to something of breathtaking urgency. Beneath the scatter of themes that dot Eckhart's sermons is a larger architecture, coherent though incomplete, something glimpsed only in bits and snatches, but sketched with nuance in his academic works. Most of us come to Eckhart in ways not unlike his original hearers. Few of us know our way around scholastic theology, with its razor-sharp logic, its love of subtle distinction, its mathematical brevity. Even ordinary scholastic theology was subtle and intricate—and Eckhart was no ordinary scholastic theologian. Thomas Aquinas seems straightforward by comparison. Eckhart admitted to his judges—who did know their way around scholastic theology—that he spoke of "rare and subtle" things.[32] I cannot begin to do justice to his thought in these few pages. Even book-length surveys only begin to do so. Here I will first sketch out a few theological basics, to give readers a taste of their striking formulation and a glimpse of their inner coherence. Then we will focus on two landmarks in the wider mystical landscape that he sketches: the birth of God in the soul and the breakthrough into the ground.

Metaphysics of Flow

Earlier we touched on Bonaventure's metaphysics of emanation and return, how all things flow out from God and are destined to flow back to God. This "metaphysics of flow," as McGinn has called it, is Eckhart's theological frame as well.[33] Eckhart offers quick summaries of it here and there. In sermon 53, he remarks: "The Father speaks the Son always, in unity, and pours out in him all created things. They are all called to return into whence they have flowed out. All their life and their being is a calling and a hastening back to him from whom they have issued."[34] Note Eckhart's phrasing here: "The Father speaks the Son always, in unity." God the Father is, in a sense, always talking; his eternal speech is his eternal offspring, God the Son.

Eckhart plays here on a theological tenet at the heart of Christian orthodoxy. Its classic formulation dates to the fourth century, to the great debate on

Christ's divinity sparked by Arius (d. 336). Arius claimed that Christ was not true God, that he was not eternal, and that he had been made by God before the world's beginning. The Council of Nicaea, held in 325, denounced this as heretical and in its famous creed proclaimed that Christ is "God from God, light from light, true God from true God, begotten not made, one-in-being with the Father." Athanasius (d. 373), the brilliant and much-exiled bishop of Alexandria, defended Nicaea's formulation. He argued that Christ as God must be without beginning and that Christ as Son is begotten from the Father eternally, unceasingly, much as sunlight is constantly, unceasingly, generated by the sun, or as springwater gushes up constantly, unceasingly, from its fountainhead.[35]

Eckhart, in his sermons, returned again and again to this core theological tenet: "the Father gives birth to his Son without ceasing."[36] He sometimes gave it a clever edge: "I was once asked what the Father does in heaven. I answered: He gives birth to his Son and this activity pleases him so much and is such a delight to him that he never does anything else but give birth to his Son."[37] Eckhart also drew out its maternal resonances: God the Father spends eternity "lying in childbed like a woman who has given birth."[38] Eckhart had a knack for putting theological dicta in inflammatory ways. He often remarked, for example, that the Father begets the Son "whether he likes it or not."[39] That is simply an ear-catching way of saying that God the Father does not *will* the begetting of God the Son.[40] The Father as Father begets. It is his identity, not his choice. He does what he is.

God as *Bullitio*, Creation as *Ebullitio*

Eckhart probed what the Son's eternal birth implies about God's inner life. Because the Father begets the Son unceasingly, then within God there must be an unceasing dynamism, an unceasing inner creativity. To express this, Eckhart played on the image of water in a rolling boil. In his *Commentary on Exodus*, he describes God's inner life as "a 'boiling' (*bullitio*), a giving birth to itself—glowing in itself, and melting and boiling in and into itself, light that totally forces its whole being in light and into light and that is everywhere totally turned back and reflected upon itself."[41] A boiling pot of water can, of course, boil over and spill everywhere. This image-logic is exactly where Eckhart goes. The created world is a "boiling over" (*ebullitio*), spilling out from God's inner "boiling" (*bullitio*): " 'Life' expresses a type of 'pushing out' by which something swells up in itself and first breaks out totally in itself, each part into each part, before it pours itself forth and 'boils over' on the outside.

This is why the emanation of the Persons in the Godhead is the prior ground of creation."[42] Note the final sentence. With his terminology of *bullitio* and *ebullitio*, Eckhart links God as Trinity with God as Creator. God is an inner bursting creativity that spills out as joy, as exuberance, as beauty: "God delights in himself. In the delight in which God delights in himself, he delights also in all creatures."[43] Eckhart once noted how an unbridled horse playfully gallops across an open plain: "Such is the horse's nature that it pours itself out with all its might in jumping about the meadow ... So, too, does God find delight and satisfaction where he finds sameness. He finds it a joy to pour his nature and his being completely into the sameness, for he is this sameness itself."[44]

The One

This God who "boils" (as Trinity) and "spills out" (as Creator) is the God we know. But Eckhart also pointed to a less accessible mystery, a "God beyond God." To express it, he invoked a sharp distinction between "God" (*Gott*) and "Godhead" (*Gottheit*): "God acts, while the Godhead does not act. There is nothing for [the Godhead] to do, for there is no action in it. It has never sought to do anything. The difference between God and Godhead is that one acts and the other does not."[45] The two, he adds, are as different as "heaven and earth." What is this Godhead? Initially, it might sound as though Eckhart was calling his hearers to look beyond God as Creator. But his point is much more provocative. He, at times, called hearers to go beyond God as Trinity: "If the soul contemplates God ... as three, the soul lacks something"; it needs to "contemplate only the Simple One ... the naked formless being of the divine unity, where there is a being above being."[46] In Eckhart the two poles of Christian orthodoxy, God as one (essence) and God as three (persons), do not get equal billing—unlike the self-conscious balance we saw in Bonaventure. Eckhart's accent lies squarely on oneness, and he preached it with breathtaking boldness. In sermon 48, he calls hearers to enter into "the simple ground, into the silent desert, into which distinction never gazed, not the Father, nor the Son, nor the Holy Spirit."[47] In sermon 2, he says starkly that God "is not Father or Son or Holy Spirit, and yet he is a something that is neither this nor that."[48] This is provocative. It may sound as though Eckhart has abandoned the basic Christian doctrine of the Trinity. That is how enemies in Cologne heard him when they excerpted sermon 2 for their lists of suspect passages.[49]

Had Eckhart lapsed? No. He wanted hearers to enter into the mystery of God as *unum* ("oneness"). When we hear "one," we think number. Eckhart did not. He insisted that God is utterly transcendent. Eckhart's term for this is "indistinct."[50] Think a moment: when we distinguish things, we are saying, "This is not that." In distinguishing, we number them—even if we don't realize it. "This" and "that" implies there are two things. Eckhart insisted that "in the proper sense God is exempt from all number."[51] He once said—with his usual fondness for exaggeration—even "if there were a thousand Persons (in God), there would still be only unity."[52] He chided priests who "take three in the sense of three cows or three stones."[53] For Eckhart, God *is* Trinity, but God is not a *number-able* Trinity. Rather, God "is one without Unity, three without Trinity."[54] This is not wordplay. God in Godself, Eckhart insisted, is beyond distinction. Yet being-beyond-distinction is precisely what makes God different from everything else, or, as Eckhart paradoxically puts it, God is "distinguished by his indistinction."[55] This means that God's "unity is the distinction, and the distinction is the unity."[56] This did not satisfy Eckhart's critics. The pope listed the claim that "every distinction is foreign to God, both in nature and Persons" as "evil-sounding and very rash and suspect of heresy," though he had to admit that with "many explanations" it could be given a "catholic meaning."[57]

The Nameless

Eckhart played on the terminology of "God" and "Godhead" in other ways: God is nameable, the Godhead is not. Whenever we name God, whether in prayer or preaching, in sermons or lectures, we apply adjectives (or "predicates") to him. We speak of God as good, wise, just, and so on. Scholastic theologians insisted that one predicate only perfections of God: God is perfect goodness, perfect wisdom, perfect justice. Any sense we might have of these qualities—of goodness, of wisdom, of justice—is derivative. We know only faint imitations, faded photocopies. And if we ourselves are good or wise or just, then we are, at best, shadowy mimics of God's perfections. God remains the reality and the standard. Eckhart thus speaks of God as the "omni-nameable name" (*nomen omninominabile*), the name every true perfection names.[58] But this naming of God is God as creation knows him and names him; it is not the Godhead: "God becomes God when all creatures speak God forth: there 'God' is born . . . And why do they not speak of the Godhead? All that is in the Godhead is One, and of this no one can speak."[59] In other words, when God created the world, when he spoke the world into being, the world in turn spoke back. It recognized God as its creator and spoke God's praises. God thus became "God" only when something other than God came into being. So creation, paradoxically, marked God's birth as "God," as nameable. I opened this chapter quoting sermon 52, where Eckhart tinkered with this same idea. Here is the passage again: "When I went out from my own free will and received my created being, then I had a

God, for before there were any creatures, God was not 'God,' but he was what he was. But when creatures came to be and received their created being, then God was not God in himself, but he was 'God' in the creatures."[60]

Eckhart was not crafting paradoxes for their own sake. He was pointing his hearers to a Godhead beyond name, a oneness of which "no one can speak." When asked how we should love God, Eckhart spoke in bold negatives: "You should love him as he is a non-God, a nonspirit, a nonperson, a nonimage, but as he is a pure, unmixed, bright 'One,' separated from all duality; and in that One we should eternally sink down, out of something into nothing."[61] We saw earlier Pseudo-Dionysius's famous distinction between cataphatic and apophatic, between speaking of God affirmatively (God *is* this or that) and speaking of God negatively (God *is not* this or that). Eckhart favored the apophatic. Once he listed four favorite sermon topics; the fourth was "the purity of the divine nature, for the brightness of the divine is beyond words. God is a word, a word unspoken."[62] For Eckhart, the Godhead—God in Godself—is ineffable. Faced with this ultimate reality, silence may seem the truest speech. But Eckhart the preacher sought ways to bring to speech this speech-defying reality. Thus one finds him flaunting in the strongest terms the breakdown of human speech:

> Now pay attention: God is nameless, because no one can say anything
> or understand anything about him . . . So if I say: "God is good,"
> that is not true. I am good, but God is not good . . . And if I say: "God
> is wise," that is not true. I am wiser than he. If I say: "God is being,"
> it is not true; he is a being transcending being and a transcend-
> ing nothingness . . . So be silent, and do not chatter about God; for
> when you chatter about him, you are telling lies and sinning.[63]

This is strong language. It is one thing to say that language breaks down when applied to God; it is another to call it "telling lies and sinning." This sort of flamboyant attack on traditional religious language made its way into the articles of the papal condemnation.[64]

These themes—God as *bullitio*, God as a oneness beyond number, God as a namelessness beyond words—are basic and, at times, controversial threads in Eckhart's intricate theological framework. The liturgy where Eckhart preached these ideas was not a classroom, nor were his sermons part of a lecture course in systematic theology. In worship, the theological task was, as McGinn notes, "not so much to reveal a set of truths about God as it was to frame the appropriate paradoxes that would serve to highlight the inherent limitations of our minds to mark off in some way the boundaries of the unknown territory where God dwells."[65]

THE BIRTH OF GOD IN THE SOUL

One Christmas Day Johannes Tauler, one of Eckhart's talented disciples, preached on a traditional theme. He reminded hearers that Christmas celebrated not only Christ's birth in a manger in Bethlehem. Christ, in fact, has three births: he is begotten unceasingly from the Father in eternity; he was born from the Virgin Mary in time; and he comes to birth in the heart of the just person.[66] Tauler linked the three but inserted careful distinctions. His approach was cautious; Eckhart's was not. Christ's three births, Eckhart argued, are in reality one birth:[67]

> The Father gives birth to his Son in eternity, equal to himself, "The
> Word was with God, and God was the Word" (John 1:1); it was the
> same in the same nature. Yet I say more: He has given birth to him
> in my soul. Not only is the soul with him, and he equal with it,
> but he is in it, and the Father gives his Son birth in the soul in the
> same way as he gives him birth in eternity, and not otherwise. He
> must do it whether he likes it or not. The Father gives birth to his
> Son without ceasing; and I say more: He gives me birth, me, his Son
> and the same Son. I say more: He gives birth not only to me, his
> Son, but he gives birth to me as himself and himself as me and to me
> as his being and nature. In the innermost source, there I spring out
> in the Holy Spirit, where there is one life and one being and one
> work. Everything God performs is one; therefore he gives me, his Son,
> birth without any distinction. My fleshly father is not actually my
> father except in one little portion of his nature, and I am separated
> from him; he may be dead and I alive. Therefore the heavenly
> Father is truly my Father, for I am his Son and have everything that I
> have from him, and I am the same Son and not a different one.[68]

This text comes from sermon 6, one of Eckhart's most controversial. It can be shocking—and he likely meant it to be shocking. On first reading, it sounds bizarre, as though Eckhart is saying that he is Christ, that he is God's Son. Well, in fact, that *is* what he is saying—in a sense. The question is: In what sense? We need to look at what he is saying and how he says it.

One theological tenet shaping Eckhart's thinking here is one we saw earlier: God the Father gives birth to God the Son in eternity without ceasing. Note how Eckhart adds (provocatively) something else: that the Father "must do it whether he likes it or not." A second traditional theological tenet operates beneath the surface of Eckhart's comments: that human beings are (in some sense) made in God's image.[69] Eckhart puts the two tenets together with explosive effect: Because our soul is in God's image, and because God's inner life involves the Father's unceasing giving-birth to the Son, that means that the Father gives birth unceasingly to the Son *within us*. God's bubbling exuberant inner creativity—his *bullitio*—is equally at work within us.

Eckhart gets shocking—and yet theologically precise—when he insists that the Father "gives me birth, me, his Son and the same Son." This sounds, on first hearing, like autotheism—like he is saying he himself is Jesus. Schizophrenics can talk crazy that way. But Eckhart was no schizophrenic, nor did he suffer delusions of grandeur. The trick is to follow how Eckhart uses "I" and "me."[70] Sometimes, when Eckhart says "I," he means it in the obvious sense: he is speaking about himself, for example, when he mentions his "fleshly" father and says that his father may or may not still be alive. Other times Eckhart uses "I" as a way of speaking about every human being. In these cases, Eckhart speaks in the first person not as Eckhart but as Everyman. That shapes his message here: that within Eckhart himself and within us all, God is coming to birth; that he and we are, in our deepest identity, God's Son. Using "I" this way makes theological truths leap to life; it makes them personal—which, of course, they are.

But there is a third facet: Eckhart speaks in the first person as though he is speaking from eternity. The "I" who speaks is his (and our) eternal self, the self as it preexisted in God's mind before creation and as it exists even now in the eternal now of God.[71] Eckhart, speaking in this "first-person eternal," makes startling claims—though he does give hearers fair warning. Three times he announces: "I say more." With each "I say more," the logic leaps, skips steps, makes startling equations. Traditional theological distinctions—divine being versus human beings, Christ's sonship versus ours—go by the boards. In the Godhead, distinctions collapse, for "everything God performs is one" and "there is one life and one being and one work." Speaking in this first-person-eternal, Eckhart can announce: "He gives me, his Son, birth without any distinction"; "the heavenly Father is truly my Father, for I am his Son"; "I am the same Son and not a different one." What makes the leaps legitimate, even necessary, is the Godhead's oneness, its radical "indistinction." In that oneness, a logic of indistinction holds sway.

Sermon 6 shocked Eckhart's inquisitors. John XXII, in the papal bull, singled out this passage as "evil-sounding, rash, and suspect of heresy," but he had to acknowledge that this, like others, could be salvaged by "many explanations."[72] Eckhart, when challenged by inquisitors in Cologne on a similar text, protested and insisted that his point was traditional and orthodox:

Doers [of good] are sons of God by the one Son who is God. He is *the* image; we are made to the image. He is *the* likeness, we are so according to the likeness. He is Son by nature, we by adoption, transformed in that very image that he himself may be the first-born of many brothers. He is heir, we, co-heirs inasmuch as we are sons and members according to which he himself is the one and only savior.[73]

Here Eckhart backs off his radical equations and offers a traditional and face-saving distinction: Christ is Son by nature, we by adoption. This same distinction appeared routinely in his academic works.[74] But in his sermons, he spoke otherwise, flaunting the boldest of equations: "out of the purity he everlastingly bore me, his only-begotten Son, into that same image of his eternal Fatherhood."[75]

This theme of the birth of God in the soul was not original to Eckhart. Versions of it go back to Origen, in the third century (Eckhart knew this and quotes Origen in sermon 41).[76] The theme is one of Eckhart's favorites, appearing in 47 of the 114 German sermons.[77] (It appears also in a scatter of his Latin sermons and commentaries).[78] He once remarked that this birth of God in the soul is the heart of Christianity and the deepest motive for the Incarnation:

If anyone were to ask me: Why do we pray, why do we fast, why do we do all our works, why are we baptized, why (most important of all) did God become man? I would answer: in order that God may be born in the soul and the soul be born in God. For this reason all the scriptures were written, for that reason God created the world and all the angelic natures: so that God may be born in the soul and the soul be born in God.[79]

In some sermons, the birth theme appears only in passing. But here and there, he treats it at length. He once gave a sequence of four sermons devoted to it, what have come down as sermons 101–104.[80] These date from his years as provincial of Saxonia, and the audience, it seems, was made up of fellow Dominicans. He began the sequence, appropriately, on Christmas Day. He sounded his theme at the outset: "We are celebrating the eternal birth which God the Father bore and bears unceasingly in eternity, because this same birth is now born in time, in human nature."[81] He stated that his mystical reading presumed things about his hearers, both morally and religiously: "These words ... are only for good and perfected people," people whose lives show forth the "lofty teachings of our Lord Jesus Christ."[82] This sermon sequence was carefully structured and revolved around pointed questions on this divine birth, its nature and its meaning. These sermons, unlike many of his, have a classroom feel. Eckhart role-plays both professor and student; he poses questions as a student and then answers them as a professor. Let us look at three questions Eckhart himself asks.

First, he asks: where within us does this birth of God take place? He then answers that God enters the soul's "noblest part," the "purest, loftiest, subtlest, part that the soul is capable of." This part of us is deeper than our memory, deeper than our capacity for thinking. It is the part of us that is, quite literally, beyond this world: "No creature ever entered there and no image"; it is "by nature receptive to nothing save only the divine essence."[83] Well, what is that? Eckhart often speaks of it as a "little spark" (vünkelîn). In sermon 37, he says that this is "none other than a tiny spark of the divine nature, a divine light, a ray and imprint of the divine nature."[84] In sermon 48, he explains that "this spark rejects all created things, and wants nothing, but its naked God, as he is in himself," and—Eckhart adds provocatively—this "light" is "uncreated and not capable of creation."[85] To speak of this highest part of the soul as "uncreated and not capable of creation" sounds as though we have some divine fragment in us. That could easily be taken wrong—and, as it turned out, was taken wrong. The pope branded the phrase as heretical.[86] Why? Metaphysically, it could imply that God was divided, his oneness shattered like small glass shards and scattered among human souls. It also could imply a sort of pantheism: that human beings are God in the literal sense that they have the "uncreated" at their core. Eckhart veers quite close to this, but it is not his view. I should add that this metaphor of the "little spark" is only one he uses. Another is a "little castle" (burgelîn).[87] A third—and arguably even more important—is "the ground of the soul" (grunt der sêle). More on this in a moment.

Second, Eckhart asks: what role do we play in this birth? The initiative is God's, he insists; our role is passive, adopting "a wholly God-receptive attitude, such that one's own self is idle, letting God work within one."[88] To appreciate Eckhart here, we need to remember his world. For his hearers, being holy was inseparable from being ascetic. The medieval world had honed a vast, intricate, and carefully calibrated array of ascetic disciplines: fastings, prayer regimens, vigils, a sprawl of popular pieties and devotions clustered about saints and feast days. The trend in Eckhart's world was toward religious hyperactivity. Eckhart never denied these "ways" altogether, but he repeatedly downplayed their value. His asceticism was not a doing but an undoing, a radical interior purgation of mind and heart and will. He referred to it as "detachment" (abgeschiedenheit) or "letting go" (gelassenheit). In these sermons, he spelled out its radicalism. He called his hearers to "shun and free" themselves "from all thoughts, words, and deeds and from all images created by the understanding."[89] Why? Because our whole mental apparatus—our senses, our thinking, our heart, our will—is instinctively outward-directed, geared to drinking in endless images from the created world. Our mental "powers," as Eckhart calls them, leave the soul "scattered abroad," making "her ability to work inwardly...enfeebled." Eckhart called his hearers to move inward, to move against this outward thrust: "How much more then should we withdraw from all things in order to concentrate all our powers on perceiving and knowing the one infinite, uncreated, eternal truth! To this end, then assemble all your powers, all your senses, your entire mind and memory; direct them into the ground where your treasure lies buried."[90] This withdrawal into the soul's deepest depths is "a forgetting and an unknowing." It is also radical receptivity and listening: "There must be a stillness and a silence for this Word to make itself heard."[91] Our coming-to-birth comes from hearing: "Hearing draws in more, but seeing leads outwards... In hearing I am passive, but in seeing I am active."[92] This is important: for Eckhart, this birth is not about seeing God; it is not having a vision.

Third, Eckhart asks whether this birth can be sensed somehow, whether we can actually feel it, or at least, whether there are signs that it has taken place.[93] Here he addresses what we today call mystical experiences. Eckhart's answer has several sides. As a rule, he showed little interest in mystical phenomena, in visions or ecstasies or whatever. Sometimes he was quite critical and saw such things either as superficial or as needless distractions from the real quest. Here and there, however, he discussed extraordinary phenomena more positively. Usually he did so by focusing on biblical "mystics" such as Moses or St. Paul. In sermon 102, he described the birth as an experience of light and cited Paul as an exemplar: "It is a property of this birth that it always comes with fresh light... In this birth God streams into the soul in such abundance of light, so flooding and the essence and ground of the soul that it runs over and floods into the outward man. Thus it befell Paul when on his journey God touched him with His light and spoke to him."[94] On those (rare) occasions when Eckhart described the birth in experiential terms, he emphasized its earth-shattering suddenness. It comes, he said, like a bolt of lightning; and much as lightning (with its electromagnetic force) makes a tree with its thousands of leaves "all turn right side up towards the strike, so it is with all in whom this birth occurs: they are promptly turned towards this birth with all they possess."[95] God, he says, does not tinker with the soul the way a carpenter tinkers on some woodworking project. The birth does not happen in steps and stages. Rather, "when God finds you ready, He *has* to act, to overflow into you." Both nature and God abhor a vacuum: if there is "anything empty under heaven, whatever it might be, great or small, the heavens would either draw it up to themselves or else, bending down, would have to fill it with themselves."[96]

This sermon sequence is unusual both in its detail and in its experiential accent. Eckhart usually speaks of this birth not as an event in time, but as a reality best glimpsed from the vista of God's eternity. In sermon 10, Eckhart stresses: "God's day is where the soul stands in the day of eternity in an essential Now, and the Father gives birth to his only-begotten Son in a perpetual present and the soul is herself born again into God."[97] How, then, does the birth of God in the soul's eternity fit in with our ordinary life, lived in the flow of time and history? Eckhart addresses this in sermon 57. He speaks of the "two faces" of the soul. One face is turned toward the world. Here the soul "works virtue, knowledge, and holy living." The other face, Eckhart says, is "turned directly to God": "There the divine light is without interruption, working within, even though (the soul) does not know it. When the spark of intellect is taken barely in God . . . *then* the birth takes place. This birth does not take place once a year or a month or once a day, but all the time, that is, above time in the expanse where there is no here or now, nor nature nor thought."[98]

Why did Eckhart speak so often and so boldly about God's birth in the soul? Why did he make the equation that Christ's three births are one birth, that we are God's one Son in that one birth? Eckhart knew perfectly well how to make proper distinctions, how to distinguish between Christ as Son by nature and us as sons and daughters by adoption. Why did he risk misleading hearers and risk bringing ecclesiastical wrath down upon his head? Frank Tobin has suggested one answer: "Because the reality of this birth—the fact that we are capable of achieving real union with God—is so overwhelming, so existentially vital, that [for Eckhart] all else pales beside it . . . Our being is God's being, and this is what [Eckhart] the preacher took such pains to impress on his hearers. This was the one insight they simply had to have for true spiritual orientation."[99]

BREAKTHROUGH INTO THE GROUND

When we surveyed Eckhart's theology, we saw two sides. One side was God's ceaseless and joyous creativity, inwardly as Trinity and outwardly as Creator. The other side was God's otherness, a Godhead beyond activity, beyond number, beyond name. Here Eckhart spoke apophatically, in negatives and paradoxes. Eckhart's mystical thought also has two sides, and these closely mirror his theology. One side, the birth of God in the soul, parallels Eckhart's stress on God's creativity. The birth is God's *bullitio*, God's unceasing life-giving, as it takes place within the soul. Now we need to turn to the other side of his mystical thought. This closely parallels his apophatic theology. Eckhart spoke of the Godhead in negative terms, and he spoke of the soul in the same way. The soul, he says, "is free of all names, it is bare of all forms, wholly empty and free, as God himself is empty and free. It is so utterly one and simple, as God is one and simple, that man cannot in any way look into it."[100] Sometimes Eckhart invoked metaphors to speak God's namelessness: the Godhead is a desert, a vast featureless wilderness. Eckhart applied the same metaphors to the soul. The soul, he said, "is a strange land, a wilderness, being more nameless than with name, more unknown than known."[101] Eckhart linked the Godhead's namelessness with its oneness (*unum*). He spoke of the soul in the very same way: It "is like the divine nature; in itself it is one and has nothing in common with anything."[102] All this sounds as though Eckhart thought that the soul is what God is, or even that the soul is God and God is the soul. That, in fact, is what he says: "God's being is my life. If my life is God's being, then God's existence must be my existence and God's self-identity is my self-identity, neither less nor more."[103]

To speak of this union—or better, this identity—of God and the soul, Eckhart turned again and again to a key metaphor: "the ground." Here is the classic text: "Truly you are the hidden God, in the ground of the soul where God's ground and the soul's ground are one ground."[104] Eckhart insisted that God and the soul share common ground, or rather, that they *are* a single ground, a fused identity. This extraordinary claim is extraordinarily easy to misinterpret. When Eckhart spoke of "the ground," he used the Middle High German word *grunt*. At the literal level, *grunt* meant what "ground" means in modern English: the earth, the ground we walk on. It also meant "the lowest," "the bottom"— somewhat like the way we can speak of the "ground floor." It had extended meanings: "origin," "beginning," "cause," "reason"—a bit like the way we speak, in law, of the "grounds for a case," or, in philosophy, of "grounding an argument." It could also mean a thing's innermost identity, its essence. For this, we tend to use the word "core," not "ground," as Eckhart does. Eckhart applied the term "ground" as a way of speaking of both the essence of the soul and the essence of God: "In the ground of divine being where the three Persons are one being, the soul is one according to the ground."[105]

Bernard McGinn has, in his latest studies, advanced the theory that with this language of "the ground," Eckhart created something new in the history of Christian mysticism, a new mystical language.[106] To appreciate McGinn's view, we need to recall Bernard of Clairvaux. Bernard and his Cistercian contemporaries forged what, by Eckhart's time, had became the mystical status quo. Bernard used to speak boldly of a union of God and soul. At the same time, he insisted, despite his poetic flights and extravagances, that the two remain distinct. Why? Because, according to Bernard, "God and man do not share the same nature or substance," because their unity "is caused not so much by the identity of essences as by the concurrence of wills."[107] What guided Bernard's thinking about this union of God and the soul was a master metaphor: marriage.

Eckhart's master metaphor was not marriage, but ground. With it, he forged a subtle network of concepts, connections, and imagery. Josef Quint, the senior editor of Eckhart's German works, speaks of Eckhart's concept of the ground as a "mystical word-field" (*mystiches Wortfeld*).[108] Let me cite one example. Eckhart says: "The soul . . . seeks the ground, continuing to search, and takes God in his oneness and in his solitary wilderness, in his vast wasteland, and in his own ground. Thus it remains satisfied with nothing else, but keeps on searching [to discover] just what it is that God is in his divinity and in the possession of his own nature."[109] We can see the "word-field" assemble itself. On the one hand, Eckhart links the word "ground" with images: "solitary wilderness," "vast wasteland." These images evoke a feeling, a mood. They tap into our experience. We all know what it feels like to gaze out at a desert landscape, at its vast beautiful sameness. At the same time, Eckhart links "ground" with concepts: "God in his oneness," "God in his divinity and . . . his own nature." Eckhart here turns "ground," which had no history as a theological term, into a term with definite theological precision. Here we glimpse Eckhart setting about inventing a new vernacular theology.

One other matter: note how Eckhart speaks of the soul "seeking," "searching." Often when he spoke of a ground where God and the soul are one, he simply treated it as a metaphysical truth. There is no mention of growth or stages, process or progress. But here he speaks of it as a reality as yet unrealized; it must somehow be sought out. The same dynamic terminology appears in sermon 42: "Now know, all our perfection and our holiness rests in this: that a person must penetrate and transcend everything created and temporal and all being and go into the ground that has no ground. We pray our dear Lord God that we may become one and indwelling, and may God help us into the same ground."[110] Here Eckhart defines Christian holiness: it involves "penetrating" the ground, "going into the ground" (which, paradoxically, "has no ground").

This introduces another of Eckhart's central themes: the "breakthrough" (*durchbruch*). Sometimes he explained it by playing on the metaphor of cracking open a shell to extract the seed or kernel:

> I have said before the shell must be *broken through* and what is inside must come out, for if you want to get at the kernel you must break the

shell. And also, if you want to find nature unveiled, all likenesses must be *broken through*, and the further you *penetrate*, the nearer you will get to the essence. When the soul finds the One, where all is one, there she will remain in the Single One.[111]

Eckhart did not make maps or plot itineraries. For him, the journey into God is sudden—a breaking through, cracking open the shell of what we thought about ourselves and about God, discovering within something utterly new, a unity at the heart of everything.

Eckhart's classic account of this breakthrough into the ground appears in sermon 52, the same sermon I quoted at the beginning of the chapter. Here is the key passage:

A great authority says that his breaking through is nobler than his flowing out; and that is true. When I flowed out from God, all things said: "God is." And this cannot make me blessed, for with this I acknowledge that I am a creature. But in the breaking-through, when I come to be free of will of myself and of God's will and of all his works and of God himself, then I am above all created things, and I am neither God nor creature, but I am what I was and what I shall remain, now and eternally. Then I received an impulse that will bring me up above all the angels. Together with this impulse, I receive such riches that God, as he is "God," and as he performs all his divine works, cannot suffice me; for in this breaking-through I receive that God and I are one. Then I am what I was.[112]

Here many threads we have seen come together. In this excerpt, as before, Eckhart speaks in his first-person-eternal voice. He speaks of himself (and us) "flowing out" from God. This alludes to his "metaphysics of flow," that all things flow from God and flow back to God. The flowing out is creation. With creation, God becomes "God" because creation looks back and acknowledges its separateness and thus announces: "God is." For Eckhart, being created is not blessedness. Blessedness is the return to God, the breaking through into the Godhead. That is why he says here that "his breakthrough is nobler than his flowing out." When one "breaks through," one rediscovers one's own oneness in the Godhead. This is freedom beyond imagining, freedom from everything created, freedom from one's own will, freedom from God's will (as a creature knows it), freedom even from God himself (as a creature knows God). In "breakthrough," one rediscovers and recovers one's ancient and eternal identity with God. Here again Eckhart's logic of indistinction kicks in. In "breakthrough," one is above all created things and above "God" as creatures know him; one is neither God nor creature, one simply is what one was before creation. This breakthrough means that "I receive that God and I are one."

This language of breakthrough, of penetrating into the ground where God and the soul are one ground, can be bewildering and easy to misunderstand. In Eckhart's lifetime and after, even his disciples misconstrued his claims. There is an odd work, *The Sister Catherine Treatise* (*Schwester Katrei*), composed in Eckhartian circles. In the story, a woman announces to her confessor, "Father, rejoice with me, I have become God!"[113] Eckhart's disciple Heinrich Suso took pains to challenge such popular misreadings. He once composed a brilliant satirical dialogue called *The Little Book of Truth*. It has two characters, "the Disciple" and "the Nameless Wild One" (*das namelos wilde*). This Nameless Wild One (symbol of Eckhart's wayward and reckless followers) repeatedly cites "the learned teacher who denied all distinctions," who "denied all mere similarity and union" between God and creature, and who "posited us, naked and free from all (mere) similarity, in pure oneness."[114] The Disciple (Suso himself) takes on the Nameless Wild One, correcting his misunderstanding point by point, carefully putting Eckhart's teaching back into its proper theological context.

We today are equally likely to misconstrue Eckhart's language of oneness. It can bewilder us on several levels. One is experiential: What, psychologically speaking, is Eckhart talking about? What does this oneness feel like? It is important to recognize that questions of this sort reflect our concerns, not Eckhart's. Eckhart knew of unusual psychic states, from classics (such as Bernard) and from Beguine writers (such as Mechthild), as well as from pastoral encounters with the Beguines. He acknowledged these psychic states on occasion but did not give them much weight. When we hear Eckhart's talk about breaking through into a oneness with God—especially combined with his talk about detachment from senses, from thinking, from everything creaturely in us—we get the impression that he is talking about putting oneself into some strange, permanent psychological state. We are liable to think that he wanted people to seek a starry-eyed, otherworldly, always-looking-at-God experience. Quite the opposite. Eckhart himself satirized such a pursuit: "Some people want to see God with their own eyes, just as they see a cow; and they want to love God just as they love a cow."[115] People love cows, he added, because they give milk and cheese. Those who chase visions of God are the same. They are not interested in God as God, but only in mystical experiences God may give them.

Eckhart's own mystical outlook was, in practical terms, surprisingly this-worldly. In this, he moved against the grain of his religious milieu. In his world, lifelong world-denying contemplative withdrawal was the mystical status quo.

Advocates of that status quo appealed to the story of Martha and Mary in Luke's Gospel. Martha, who was "busy about many things," exemplified the active life, while Mary, who sat and listened at Jesus's feet, exemplified the contemplative. Medieval exegetes and preachers routinely pointed out that because Jesus commended Mary for having "chosen the better part" (Luke 10:41), the contemplative life was superior to the active. This was often taken to mean that the everyday holiness that came from spending one's day in selfless service was second-rate holiness. Eckhart disagreed. In sermon 86, Eckhart turned the traditional reading on its head. He acknowledged that Jesus had commended Mary, but that was only because she was going through a necessary, but passing, contemplative phase; she needed "to be schooled and to learn about life." Martha, in Eckhart's reading, is the hero of the story. Martha, in her everyday busyness, had "a mature power of reflection which enabled her to accomplish external works with the perfection that love demands."[116]

So let me return to the question: Did Eckhart describe oneness with God as experiential? If one looks hard, one can find passages here and there that touch somewhat obliquely upon it—but its rarity should imply that he might not have thought that *consciously experiencing* that oneness was really all that important. Still he did give a few indications of an experiential quality. In sermon 71, he explored the story of Paul's knock-down encounter with the risen Jesus on the road to Damascus. In Acts 9:8, it says that "Paul rose from the ground and with eyes open he saw nothing." The phrase "rose from the ground" is, for Eckhart, a loaded term. This led him to explore what the word "nothing" might mean here. Eckhart says that it has four meanings. First, he says, when Paul saw "nothing" he saw God as nothing—as *no thing*. Second, when Paul got up, "he saw nothing but God." One might presume Eckhart would discuss ecstatic experience here. But that is not what he does. He presses on to a third meaning, which is the key: "In all things Paul saw nothing but God." Here is the heart of Eckhart's this-worldly mysticism. It is not about visions. It is about seeing God in all things. When one sees God in all things, then one sees all things for what they are: nothings. Thus the fourth meaning is that "when Paul saw God, he viewed all things as nothing."[117] Seeing God puts the world in proper focus. In sermon 103, Eckhart makes similar points in talking of the birth of God in the soul. The birth, he says, is like a lightning strike: "Your face is so fully turned toward this birth that, no matter what you see or hear, you can get nothing but this birth from all things. All things become simply God to you, for in all things you notice only God, just as a man who stares long at the sun sees the sun in whatever he afterwards looks at."[118] Whatever Eckhart is speaking of, breakthrough is not about visions; it is a seeing that sees this world in God, and God in and through this world.

A second way we tend to misconstrue Eckhart is conceptually: Did Eckhart really mean that we are God, as he seems literally to say in so many passages? Yes—but in what sense? We need to grasp how conceptually he made those startling and controversial equations. Let us take one example: "If my life is God's being, then God's existence must be my existence and God's self-identity is my self-identity, neither less nor more."[119] This comes from sermon 6, a sermon we looked at earlier in regard to the birth of God in the soul. The sermon as a whole centers on the theme of justice, on what it is to be a just person, to live rightly. This equation—that "God's self-identity is my self-identity"—was singled out as suspect by the Inquisition. In his *Defense*, Eckhart explained himself: "It must be said that this is false and an error, as it sounds. But it is true, devout, and moral of the just person, *insofar as he is just*, that his entire existence is from God's existence, though analogically."[120] Eckhart's key term here is "insofar as" (*inquantum*). This qualifier "insofar as" is at the core of Eckhart's logic. In his *Defense*, he defined it precisely: "The words 'insofar as,' ... exclude from the term in question everything that is other or foreign to it."[121] What did he mean? Take the issue he cited: a just person. Eckhart was not saying that a person who lives rightly, who acts justly, is God in everything that he or she is. The just person is not, for example, the creator of the universe. The just person does not make the sun, moon, stars, flowers, mountains, and seas. But the just person is God *insofar as* he or she acts justly. When one is just, one bears God about within oneself. God is being born in one's soul and into the wider world. This "insofarness," this *inquantum* principle, is at the root of Eckhart's most startling equations. As Eckhart told the inquisitors, if they did not understand this, they did not understand him.[122]

This *inquantum* principle offers insight into how Eckhart, in terms of logic, made some of the equations he did. But it also gives us a clue about Eckhart himself, about how he saw things. Eckhart had a bias. Where many of us see how unlike one thing is from another, Eckhart was struck by samenesses. Once, in a sermon, he hinted at his worldview: "I wondered—this is many years ago—whether I would be asked how it is that each blade of grass can be so different from the others; and it happened that I was asked how they could be so different. I said: 'What is more surprising is how they are all so alike.'"[123] Eckhart admitted that we differ from God and we differ from one another in ways too numerous to count. That, for him, was not the point. The point was how we are the same and how our sameness comes from God's sameness. Eckhart was concerned that we be just persons, that we mirror God's justice in the way we justly live. Eckhart's mystical vision was about living justice, a justice that mirrored God to everyone else, that united us to God and to one another. That union is not about feelings or ecstasies or mystical flights—even if those happen to occur. What matters is that we live our lives out of that union, whether we feel it or not. What matters is the way we live points everyone and everything back to the source from which all poured forth.

THE ART OF MYSTAGOGY

Many surveys treat Eckhart as the mystic's mystic, the one with unquestioned credentials. But we cannot sidestep the question: Was Eckhart himself a mystic? That depends. If, by "mystic," one means someone who gives auto-biographical reports of mystical experiences, then Eckhart was no mystic. Whatever Eckhart was doing, he was remarkably unconcerned about sharing his own personal experiences of God. For that matter, he showed remarkably little interest in mystical experiences. Some Eckhart experts have argued that he was no mystic, that the designation is simply wrong-headed. They argue that Eckhart was simply a philosopher-theologian, a metaphysician at heart.[124] His ideas can be explained by his (subtle) ontology and his (idiosyncratic) logic, by his theories of predication, analogy, and unicity, a whole host of technical philosophical principles and practices. Any in-depth treatment of Eckhart must come to grips with such things (and I have tried to tread upon these as lightly as possible). They help one trace out subtle threads in his thought. But that interpretation of Eckhart, I believe, misses the big picture. It fails to account for what Eckhart thought he was doing the last fifteen years of his life, why he risked everything—career, reputation, and much else—preaching what he preached and how he preached. When Eckhart moved to Strasbourg and later to Cologne, he was not in the business of teaching Parisian metaphysics to the unschooled masses.

So once again: Was Eckhart a mystic? He was certainly a mystical theo-logian if one looks at the content of his sermons. Not all ideas were mystical, of course. Some, such as God as *bullitio* and creation as *ebullitio*, simply articulate Christian basics on the nature of God and creation. They may be clever or insightful, but they are not, of themselves, mystical. Other ideas do have a mystical texture and focus. We saw two key notions: the birth of God in the soul and the breakthrough into the ground. (Others, such as detachment, I touched upon only in passing). The birth of God in the soul may not have been original to Eckhart, but he gave it a centrality and a radicalism that testify to his own deep-felt concerns. His ideas about breakthrough and the ground were original and testify to ways that Eckhart set about creating a new vernacular mystical theology. So, yes, Eckhart preached a mystical content.

But what caught the ear of his medieval hearers or what catches the eye of his modern readers is not simply Eckhart's mystical *content*. Eckhart was doing something quite original and, I believe, unquestionably mystical—but not as we normally come at the idea. We need to begin with the obvious: Eckhart was a preacher. Yes, he had learned scholastic treatises and commentaries, and yes, these are vital to seeing him in a balanced way and for grasping the under-the-surface dynamic of his sermons. But it was preaching that made him famous. It is also what sparked his troubles (even if propositions from his academic works were, in the end, also singled out for condemnation). As a preacher, his focus was not himself. Preaching was not about his experiences—mystical or otherwise. It was about his hearers, about *their* experience and *their* lives. We are dealing here with preached mysticism.

A second clue comes, I believe, from Johannes Tauler's poignant remark when he chided Eckhart's old audience that "the loving master...spoke from eternity, and you took it as referring to time." Tauler names Eckhart's uniqueness. Eckhart not only *taught about* God's ground as the soul's ground; he tried to *speak from that vantage point*. As performances, Eckhart's sermons are utterly unique. There is nothing in the history of Christianity quite like them. When I opened this chapter, I quoted from sermon 52 and noted that the content of that excerpt was not, of itself, mystical. But I do think sermon 52 is mystical in a different sense. It is mystical in terms of performance. It tries to articulate what our identity looks and sounds like from the vantage point of eternity, of our deepest identity in God.[125]

Karl Ruh has suggested that there is a proper and old-fashioned category to describe what Eckhart was up to: mystagogy.[126] Mystagogy literally means "teaching mysteries." Mystagogical sermons were routine in early Christianity. They were given to the newly baptized during Easter Week, that is, in the days right after their initiation into the then-secret rituals of baptism, chrismation, and eucharist. Baptism was, in the Greek theological tradition, often called "enlightenment," and these sermons shed light on the enlightening mysteries of initiation. Eckhart as mystagogue was initiating his hearers into mystery, into the mystery that God dwells at the core of our identity as human beings. Eckhart certainly talked about that identity. But he did more: he sought to enact it, to awaken it in his hearers. That is what lies behind all his brilliant verbal strategies, his metaphors, his abrupt and startling turns of logic, his first-person-eternal voice. He was convinced his words could, with God's initiative, awaken that identity in his hearers here and now. As he once put it:

I say yet more (do not be afraid, for this joy is close to you and is in you): there is not one of you who is so coarse-grained, so feeble of understanding or so remote but he may find this joy within himself, in truth, as it is, with joy and understanding, before you leave this church today, indeed before I have finished preaching: he can find this as truly within him, live it and possess it, as that God is God and I am a man.[127]

7

Mystic as Desert Calligrapher: Evagrius Ponticus

Here we are going to make a leap further back in time, out of the Middle Ages and back to the early Church, back to the origins of Christian mysticism, to one profound mystical stream that sprang up during Christianity's early years. In the fourth century, the deserts of Egypt became the nerve center of a radical movement we now call monasticism. Clusters of Christians began moving from the populous Nile Valley to the nearby desert wastes. These burgeoning settlements became the outposts for a new frontier in Christian living. In the famous words of Athanasius, "The desert was made a city by monks, who left their own people and registered themselves for citizenship in the heavens."[1] These early monks—the so-called desert fathers—forged techniques of prayer and asceticism, of discipleship and spiritual direction, that became part of the common coinage of Christian spirituality. They were also great storytellers, among Christianity's finest.

So I would like to open with one of their stories. This comes from the *Sayings of the Desert Fathers* (*Apophthegmata Patrum*), a fifth-century collection of aphorisms from and anecdotes about the early monks of Egypt. This, like many stories in the collection, describes an encounter between a younger monk and his *abba*, or spiritual father. One day, a young monk called on Macarius the Egyptian (d. 390) and begged: "Abba, give me a word that I may be saved." Macarius ordered the monk to go to the local cemetery and curse the dead. A strange command perhaps, but the monk did as he was told: he went out to the tombs and cursed the dead, throwing rocks to signal his disgust. When he returned, Macarius asked if the dead said anything back to him. "No," the monk answered. Macarius ordered him to go back and, this time, praise the dead. Again the monk did as he was told. Praises poured from his tongue. He called them "apostles," "saints," "righteous." Again he returned to Macarius, who again asked him what the dead said back. "Nothing," the monk replied. Macarius then gave the young monk a "word": "You know how you insulted them and they did not reply, and how you praised them and they did not speak; so you too, if you wish to be saved, must do the same and become a dead man. Like the dead, take no account of either the scorn of men or their praises, and you can be saved."[2]

We are liable to misinterpret this anecdote. The young monk here was not simply asking for wise advice. He was seeking something more profound, something riskier. He sought to tap into Macarius's charismatic power, a God-given second sight that enabled the old man to read inquirers' hearts. Macarius discerned in this inquirer a deep-seated character flaw, a propensity to have his life shaped by others' praise and blame. It is not an uncommon flaw. We all know how easily and how often our lives can be shaped by others' praise and blame. That this flaw is so widespread—and Macarius's insight into it so acute—is surely why this story was remembered, why it was passed down orally and eventually written down. But Macarius did not intend his "word" for posterity. He intended it for *this* monk at *this* moment. Macarius's fame came from his uncanny ability to read the dusty palimpsest of the human heart, to decipher the deeper signature beneath the varied texts scrawled across its surface.

In this chapter, we are going to look at one of Macarius the Egyptian's very articulate disciples, Evagrius Ponticus (345–399). Evagrius is among the most original and most influential figures in the history of Christian spirituality. Yet he remains little known. Only recently has his name begun to make its way into reference works and basic surveys of Church history. Evagrius may be an obscure name to many, but most know one of his analytical inventions: the "seven deadly sins" (though, as we will see, he has eight, not seven, and calls them "thoughts," not sins). Evagrius was an astute psychologist of the spirit, and his analyses of what ails the soul form but one thread within a subtle and intricate theology of the spiritual life. Evagrius helped pioneer Christian mysticism, advocating unceasing prayer, and was among the first to plot milestones in the soul's journey to God.

BLOWN BY A DESERT WIND

What we know of Evagrius's life comes mainly from his disciple, Palladius of Helenopolis (d. 430s), who, as a young man, was part of Evagrius's inner circle in Egypt.[3] Palladius recounts his experiences in the *Lausiac History*, a collection of some seventy snapshot portraits of holy men and women that he had either met or heard of.[4] Other details can be gleaned from his *Life of Evagrius*, an early essay now preserved only in Coptic.[5] The major fifth-century Church historians (Socrates, Sozomen, and Gennadius) all offer brief notices on Evagrius in their respective narratives.

Evagrius was the son of a Christian bishop and grew up in the province of Pontus, near the Black Sea, in what today is northern Turkey. He moved among a who's who of fourth-century Christianity. He joined the entourage of Basil of Caesarea (d. 379), who ordained him lector. Later Gregory of Nazianzus (d. 389), who served as bishop of Constantinople and authored the magisterial *Theological Orations*, ordained him deacon. Basil and Gregory are now numbered among the great architects of Christian orthodoxy and are best known for their pathbreaking defense of the divinity of the Holy Spirit and for formulating the classic doctrine of the Trinity. As Gregory's archdeacon in Constantinople, Evagrius earned fame for his eloquent defense of the emerging orthodox position. He was on site when the Council of Constantinople of 381 formulated the version of the Nicene Creed that Christians recite today.

Soon after, Evagrius fell in love with a woman married to a high government official. The feelings were mutual, and the risk of scandal was great. One night he had an ominous dream. He saw himself under arrest, standing in chains in an iron collar before an angelic judge. The angel compelled him to swear an oath on the Gospels that he would leave town. Upon waking, he caught the first available ship and sailed off to Jerusalem. There he came under the sway of one of the extraordinary women in early Christianity, Melania the Elder (d. 411). Melania was an aristocrat of the senatorial class and one of the wealthiest women in the Roman Empire. She had established a Latin-speaking monastic community just outside Jerusalem, on the Mount of Olives. This community was beginning to win international fame as a vibrant intellectual center, a sort of monastic think tank. There Rufinus of Aquileia (d. 410) did his influential translations of Greek theological and monastic works for the Latin West. Evagrius remained friends with both Melania and Rufinus the rest of his life. Melania convinced Evagrius to adopt the monastic life and sent him on to her friends in Egypt.

In 383 Evagrius settled at Nitria, a large cenobitic monastery, on the western edge of the Nile delta, some forty miles southeast of the metropolis of Alexandria. We have some vivid descriptions. Palladius, who lived there for a year, claims some 5,000 monks called it home, some living in solitary cells, some in pairs, some in larger houses. Like most Egyptian monks, they wove baskets or rope; they also produced wine and cultivated gardens. Discipline was tough. Palladius reports that near the monastery's church were three date palms; on each hung a whip: one for backsliding monks, one, for marauders, and a third for any robber who happened by. Rufinus had visited Nitria back in the 370s and left a vivid (if romanticized) account of the hospitality he received:

> So as we drew near to that place and they realized that foreign brethren were arriving, they poured out of their cells like a swarm of bees and ran to meet us with delight and alacrity, many of them carrying containers of water and of bread . . . When they had welcomed us, first of all they led us with psalms into the church and washed our feet and one by one dried them with the linen cloth with which they were girded . . . , as if to wash away the fatigue of the journey, but in fact to purge away the hardships of worldly life with this traditional mystery. What can I say that would do justice to their humanity, their courtesy, and their love.[6]

After a two-year apprenticeship in Nitria, Evagrius moved on to the remote anchoritic settlement of Kellia ("The Cells"), located twelve miles farther south.[7] Evagrius has left no description of the place, but his friend Rufinus did. Rufinus says that it lay in the "interior desert, . . . a vast wasteland" where "cells are divided from one another by so great a distance that no one can catch sight of another nor can a voice be heard." Kellia's solitude was reserved for advanced monks, for those who wanted "to live a more remote life, stripped down to bare rudiments." The monks of Kellia gathered on Saturdays and Sundays for liturgies and common meals. Rufinus was touched by what he saw at such gatherings: "They meet in church and, glimpsing this way and that, see one another as the heaven-restored." Rufinus was also struck by Kellia's communal silence. It was palpable, a "prodigious silence and a great stillness."[8]

Evagrius apprenticed in the monastic life under several famed desert fathers. I mentioned one earlier, Macarius the Egyptian, who around 330 founded Scetis, one of the earliest monastic settlements. Located in Wādī al-Natrūn, west of the Nile, it remains to this day a major center of Coptic monasticism. Whenever Evagrius sought out Macarius, he had to embark on a twenty-five-mile cross-desert trek. An anonymous fifth-century travelogue, *History of the Monks in Egypt*, notes that this could be "a very perilous journey for travelers, for if one makes even a small error, one can get lost in the desert and find one's life in danger."[9] From Macarius, Evagrius learned a balanced asceticism: "Our saintly teacher with his great experience in the practical life [of asceticism] used to say: 'The monk must ever hold himself ready as though he were to die to-morrow, and in turn must treat the body as though he would have to live with it for many years.'"[10] The historian Socrates says that Evagrius learned much from Macarius and other desert fathers, "absorbing from them a philosophy of deeds; before this, he only knew a philosophy of words."[11]

While most Egyptian monks made their living weaving rope or baskets or mats, Evagrius made his living as a calligrapher. Palladius reports that his penmanship was excellent and that he had mastered the elegant Oxyrhynchus style (whatever that was). Copying manuscripts became a venerable monastic occupation later, in the Middle Ages, but it was rare, though not unprece-dented, in this era. Evagrius not only copied books; he also wrote them—many, as we will see. He was part of and eventually leader of a circle of intellectual monks. Palladius, in his little-known *Life of Evagrius*, offers a glimpse of the way Evagrius led the circle of disciples around him:

> This was his practice: The brothers would gather around him on Saturday and Sunday, discussing their thoughts with him throughout the night, listening to his words of encouragement until sunrise. And thus they would leave rejoicing and glorifying God, for Eva-grius's teaching was very sweet... Furthermore, he was so hospita-ble that his cell never lacked five or six visitors a day who had come from foreign lands to listen to his teaching, his intellect, and his ascetic practice.[12]

Palladius's comments are revealing. Evagrius and the other monks of Kellia were, for the most part, hermits who spent Monday through Friday alone in their cells praying, practicing asceticism, and doing manual labor. The week-ends were times for community meals and liturgies. Like other *abbas*, Evagrius used these occasions to meet with disciples and offer ongoing spiritual counsel. The author of *History of the Monks* once met Evagrius and reports that he "was a wise and learned man who was skilled in the discernment of thoughts, an ability he had acquired by experience."[13] His leadership skills were such that at one point Theophilus, the patriarch of Alexandria, wanted to recruit Evagrius and ordain him as bishop of the delta town of Thmuis. Eva-grius refused and reportedly fled to avoid being forcibly drafted into the episcopate.

Evagrius tends to be self-effacing in his writings, but here and there one finds passing personal references. In one surviving letter, he speaks poignantly both of his evangelical zeal and of his sense of isolation: "Oh, if only I were the 'river of the Lord' (Ps. 64:10) and could joyfully flow into the sea of the world in order to sweeten the bitterness of the evil of the reasonable souls of men. But instead I am a 'waterless cloud' (Jude 18) which has been blown by the wind into the desert."[14] Evagrius grew up watching the wild rivers of Pontus flow into and "sweeten" the vast expanse of the Black Sea. This image encapsulates his own exuberant desire to "flow into the sea of the world," to "sweeten the bitterness of evil." But by midlife he had been blown, as he saw it, by the Holy Spirit's mysterious wind into Egypt's harsh deserts. He was a foreigner in a foreign land. One senses here his felt sense of the mystery of his calling and, beneath it, a certain discouragement—that he remained a desert's "waterless cloud."

Evagrius died in his mid-fifties, after a brief illness, in 399. Later that year the Patriarch Theophilus turned against Evagrius's friends, denouncing them as heretics and chasing them out of Egypt. He accused them of promoting the boldest speculations of Origen, the third-century biblical scholar. One was Origen's hypothesis that all humankind, together with all other spiritual beings, had once preexisted as minds in union with God but had suffered a pre-Eden Fall into psyches, and that God, in turn, rescued these fallen psyches by creating the material world as we know it. A second was Origen's hypothesis that all humankind will be saved in a final cosmic redemption (*apokatastasis*). A century and half later, in 553, Evagrius would be posthumously condemned, together with Origen, by the Second Council of Constantinople. Like others branded as heretics, Evagrius suffered a *damnatio memoriae*. His name was largely forgotten, and his prolific writings went underground. Remarkably, most survived.

PROVERBIAL MEDICINE

The survival of Evagrius's writings points to one overlooked feature of mysticism: that reading public who preserve mystical texts for centuries. Monk-calligraphers, those monks who, like Evagrius himself, made their living by copying manuscripts, continued to copy his works for centuries, and the corpus of his writings gradually spread across the ancient Christian world, especially in the East, beyond the borders of the Roman Empire. Some Greek originals were lost, but their contents were preserved in a host of ancient translations into Syriac, Armenian, Coptic, Arabic, and Ethiopic. Other texts were preserved through disguise, attributing them to venerable fathers such as Basil of Caesarea or Nilus of Ancyra. Why were they preserved? Because those monk-calligraphers who read them simply found their psychological and mystical insights too penetrating to discard.

Only in the twentieth century did scholars begin to recover Evagrius's works and slowly piece together the magnitude of his achievement. The story of that recovery reads like the twists and turns of a good detective novel.[15] By the mid-twentieth century, French-speaking scholars realized Evagrius had been one of the most influential voices in the history of Christian spirituality— though that influence had been under the surface and often anonymous.[16] The Swiss theologian Hans Urs von Balthasar claimed that Evagrius "is the almost absolute ruler of the entire Syriac and Byzantine mystical theology, and . . . has influenced in a decisive manner Western ascetical and mystical teaching as well."[17] The English-speaking world has been very slow to pick up on these developments. There have been exceptions. Thomas Merton had come across Evagrius in his research on the desert fathers, alerted to discoveries by French scholars.[18] In 1972 Merton's disciple John Eudes Bamberger published the first translation of Evagrius into English.[19] Only in 2003 was a fairly complete translation of Evagrius finally made available to the English-speaking world.[20]

Evagrius's best-known works are collections of terse numbered paragraphs called "chapters" (kephalaia). Many are proverbs; for example: "If you are a theologian, you will pray truly; and if you pray truly, you will be a theologian."[21] Others read like definitions. One would become famous: "Prayer is the ascent of the mind towards God."[22] His best-known work, The Monk (Praktikos), is a collection of 100 chapters that list and diagnose diseases of the soul, what Evagrius calls the eight "thoughts." This is the first known example of this 100-chapter or "century" genre and would be imitated by other Greek mystical writers such as Diodochus of Photice and Maximus Confessor. The Monk is intended, as Evagrius himself notes, as the first volume of a trilogy.[23] The second is The Gnostic (Gnostikos), a 50-chapter treatise that counsels advanced monks how to guide their circle of disciples. The third is his controversial Gnostic Chapters (Kephalaia gnostica), a sprawling 540-chapter treatise on creation and providence. Several works, such Chapters on Prayer (De oratione) and Reflections (Skemmata), stress imageless contemplation and map the mind's journey to God. One variant of Evagrius's numbered proverbs is his Counter-Arguments (Antirrhetikos), a list of 498 temptations, grouped under the eight "thoughts," and followed by apt scriptural quotations. Evagrius drew his inspiration from the example of Jesus, who faced down Satan in the desert and rebutted him with scriptural one-liners. Evagrius also wrote two introductory works, To Eulogius and Foundations of the Monastic Life. These do not use the numbered-proverb format, but are straightforward essays. Less well-known are his biblical commentaries on Psalms, Proverbs, Ecclesiastes, Job, and Luke.

These do not proceed verse by verse but offer terse notes (*scholia*) on problematic passages. Finally, sixty four of Evagrius's letters have been preserved. The most famous is his *Letter to Melania*, in which he sets out a vision of cosmic redemption.

Evagrius is not easy reading. His chapters are dense wisdom sayings that need to be mulled over, even deciphered. His preference for proverbs had precedents both in secular Greek literature and in the Bible itself, but he seems to have chosen this literary vehicle because of his monastic experience in the desert. The heart of desert spirituality was that momentous encounter when a monk begged a mystically gifted *abba* for a "word of salvation." We saw a classic instance of it in the opening story of Macarius and the young monk. Encounters such as this, hundreds of them, were recorded and assembled in the great collections of *Sayings of the Fathers* (*Apophthegmata Patrum*) or *Sayings of the Old Men* (*Verba Seniorum*) that spread about the Christian world over the next century, translated into the many languages of Christian antiquity, not only Greek and Latin, but also Coptic, Syriac, Armenian, and Ethiopic. These collections record stories from monks of Evagrius's generation, but they were only assembled and written down a century later. The *earliest* written collection comes from Evagrius. He appended a small collection to his treatise, *The Monk.* Evagrius saw himself recording a venerable oral tradition, "the upright ways of the monks who have gone before us" and by which "we may correct ourselves";[24] "we should honour our elders like the angels, for it is they who anoint us for the struggles and who heal the wounds inflicted by the wild beasts."[25] Some modern commentators stress Evagrius's originality and speculative gifts. That is certainly not how he understood himself. Evagrius was, by profession, a calligrapher, and he saw himself preserving through transcription a precious wisdom, turning oral word into written text. The wisdom he transcribed marked a pathway for the follower and a corrective for the wayward; it was an anointing that strengthened one for the inevitable struggle and a medicine that healed the inevitable wounds.

DEMON THOUGHTS

Deserts are dangerous places. The hazards are not simply physical. Equally perilous are psychic and spiritual threats. In early monastic literature, there is little romanticism about the desert's stark beauties. Early Christians viewed the desert as devils' land, lifeless and haunted. Demons exerted, it was believed, long-standing squatters' rights. And so when the early monks took up residence in the desert, they had to evict these pesky and ill-tempered neighbors.

Combat with demons is a dominant theme in Athanasius's famous *Life of Antony*, the first great work of monastic literature, a text that became *the* template for all later Western hagiography.

Demons figure prominently in Evagrius's writings. He was an astute psychologist of the spirit, and large chunks of his surviving corpus are devoted to charting the nature and intricate web of demonic temptations that beset those who seek God. According to Evagrius, demons attack monks through psychic obsessions, what he calls "thoughts" (*logismoi*). In various treatises, Evagrius charts out eight deadly ones, ordered hierarchically: (1) gluttony, (2) fornication, (3) avarice, (4) sadness, (5) anger, (6) listlessness (*acēdia*), (7) vainglory; and (8) pride.[26] This list should look familiar. It would become, with some modification, the "seven deadly sins" and would figure prominently in medieval spirituality. In Dante's hands, it came to define the very geography of the afterlife, both the Inferno and the Purgatorio. The one who brought Evagrius's scheme to the Latin West was his disciple John Cassian who discussed its intricacies in his *Institutes* and again in his *Conferences*.

To get a sense of Evagrius's psychological acumen, let us look at his account of one of these eight "thoughts," *acēdia*. The Greek term *acēdia* has no easy equivalent in English. Medievals referred to it as "sloth," but that is not what Evagrius meant. John Cassian translated it into Latin as *taedium cordis*, "weariness of heart."[27] Many modern translators render it as "listlessness." The best solution, I believe, is to look at Evagrius's own description. Here it is:

> The demon of acedia, also called the noonday demon (cf. Ps. 90:6), is the most oppressive of all the demons. He attacks the monk about the fourth hour [10 A.M.] and besieges his soul until the eighth hour [2 P.M.]. First of all, he makes it appear that the sun moves slowly or not at all, and that the day seems to be fifty hours long. Then he compels the monk to look constantly towards the windows, to jump out of the cell, to watch the sun to see how far it is from the ninth hour [3 P.M.], to look this way and that lest one of the brothers . . . And further, he instills in him a dislike for the place and for his state of life itself, for manual labour, and also the idea that love has disappeared from among the brothers and there is no one to console him. And should there be someone during those days who has offended the monk, this too the demon uses to add further to his dislike (of the place). He leads him on to a desire for other places where he can easily find the wherewithal to meet his needs and pursue a trade that is easier and more productive; he adds that pleasing the Lord is not a question of being in a particular place: for scripture says

that the divinity can be worshipped everywhere. He joins to these suggestions the memory of his close relations and of his former life; he depicts for him the long course of his lifetime, while bringing the burdens of asceticism before his eyes; and, as the saying has it, he deploys every device in order to have the monk leave his cell and flee the stadium. No other demon follows immediately after this one: a state of peace and ineffable joy ensues in the soul after this struggle.[28]

Here Evagrius sketches the face of boredom. We all know the feeling, when time moves at a crawl, when "the day seems to be fifty hours long." Notice how Evagrius describes the monk looking out the window, again and again, to see how far it is from 3 P.M. That was the time when monks in Egypt ate their one meal of the day. Evagrius describes *acēdia* as the "noonday de- mon," a phrase lifted from Psalm 60:6. This demon of boredom attacks not under the cover of darkness, the way the demon of fornication does. Instead it attacks in broad daylight, from 10 A.M. to 2 P.M., when the sun is at its peak and the midday heat saps one's best energy and robs one's concentration. This demon induces the monk to stare hard at the drab sameness of his life. Eva- grius masterfully captures here the ebb and flow of the monk's feelings. On the one side, he despises his narrow life, the confines of his cell, the tedium of manual labor, the foibles of his monastic colleagues. On the other side, he bubbles with wistful desires: for family, for his old life, for a life elsewhere, anywhere else. Evagrius had an eye for the way religious people invoke plati- tudes to mask the real issue. Here the monk complains about how community life is going downhill, how it has lost basic Christian charity. The monk in- vokes truisms: God can be worshipped anywhere, of course. But this is self- deception, a ruse to justify his plans to go somewhere else, anywhere else. In another treatise, Evagrius notes how "a monk afflicted with *acēdia* proposes visiting the sick, but is fulfilling his own purpose."[29] Good deeds can mask deeper fears, hidden temptations.

The monk plagued by *acēdia* yearns for escape, for distraction of some sort, of any sort. Note Evagrius's phrase: "that lest one of the brothers. . . ." Evagrius deliberately uses this sentence fragment to capture the breathless restlessness of the monk who keeps looking out the window, hoping upon hope that some visitor will drop by. The monk pines for companionship, to flee this wrestling with boredom. In his treatise *On the Eight Thoughts*, Evagrius highlights this dynamic: "The eye of the person afflicted with *acēdia* stares at the doors con- tinuously, and his intellect imagines people coming to visit. The door creaks and he jumps up; he hears a sound, and he leans out the window and does not leave it until he gets stiff from sitting there."[30] He goes on to paint a portrait of the monk bored by the tedium of spiritual reading:

> When he reads, the one afflicted with *acēdia* yawns a lot and readily drifts off into sleep; he rubs his eyes and stretches his arms turning his eyes away from the book, he stares at the wall and again goes back to reading for awhile; leafing through the pages, he looks curiously for the end of texts, he counts the folios . . . finds fault with the writing and the ornamentation (in the margins). Later, he closes the book and puts it under his head and falls asleep, but not a very deep sleep, for hunger then rouses his soul and has him show concern for its needs.[31]

Here Evagrius teases out this restless boredom: the yawning, the wandering eyes, the petty fault finding, the inability to concentrate on anything, even sleep. Note how the monk critiques both the style of writing and the bookbinding—interesting observations from a professional writer and calligrapher.

We today tend to be uncomfortable with discussions of demonology. Some readers may accept the existence of demons, some may not. That is beside the point here. The issue is how demonology, at least in its ancient form, fits in with the mystical. For Evagrius and his contemporaries, Christianity is about journeying to God. Evagrius sought to plot out not only what moves us along the path to God, but also what diverts us from that path. This is where demons come in. They are roadblocks. They divert us. They send us on winding and potentially deadly detours. They use our own consciousness against us. They know our weaknesses and exploit them to make us undo ourselves. For Evagrius, knowing about demons is essential to knowing ourselves—and vice versa. Demonology is, properly speaking, the underside of mystical theology. Evagrius believed that analyzing the eight demon-inspired "thoughts" is about equipping oneself for the ascent to God. It is a vital part of good medical know-how. David Brakke, in a masterful study entitled *Demons and the Making of the Monk*, argues that for Evagrius and other early monastic theologians, demons—however evil of themselves—were vital to monks' training.[32] Ancient monks were compared to and compared themselves with athletes. Look again at the passage, where Evagrius speaks of succumbing to *acēdia* as "fleeing the stadium"—an act of athletic cowardice. Monks were ascetics, and the Greek word *ascesis* was a sports term before it was a spiritual one. It meant "training," and athletic training, then as now, required that one renounce many things to pursue athletic excellence and that one discipline one's body in a variety of ways. Ancient monks had unique training methods. Some were renunciations, some, disciplines. They renounced property, family, and marriage. Some, like

Evagrius, chose harsh isolated landscapes such as deserts to live in. To this environmental challenge they added disciplines (fasting, all-night vigils, simplicity of life). For Evagrius, demons were an essential part of the *making* of the monk. They were one's sparring partners. Wrestling with one's psychic demons, while risky, was a necessary part of becoming a well-trained athlete. Demons, of course, did not intend to make monks better fitted to journey to God. But, as Evagrius saw it, demons were God's unwilling servants; they were the unwilling and unwitting instruments of grace because they helped purify the monk, awakening himself to who he was and forcing himself to take stock of his impurities.

MAPPING THE JOURNEY

Evagrius was a pioneer in mystical mapmaking. He divided the spiritual life into two phases or stages, the life of ascetic practice (*praktikē*) and the life of mystical knowing (*gnostikē*) (for a chart outlining what follows, see figure 7.1)

Ascetic Practice

This first stage of ascetic practice Evagrius defined quite precisely: "Ascetic practice is the spiritual method for purifying the passionate part of the soul."[33] Evagrius taught that the human psyche has three parts: the rational, the concupiscible, and the irascible.[34] The two lower parts, the concupiscible and the irascible, together form this "passionate part of the soul." The ascetic life requires purifying these two. Purifying the concupiscible means coming to grips with hungers, with sexual urges and fantasies, with our relentless acquisitiveness—all those desires and yearnings that sully purity of heart. Purifying the irascible means coming to grips with anger, fears, unspoken resentments—all those violent energies that lurk in the depths of the human heart. Purification must touch the deepest levels of one's psyche.

To speak of purification frames the spiritual task negatively. But Evagrius also describes asceticism positively: as seeking virtue. In a key chapter in *The Monk*, Evagrius says that as one progresses, different parts of the psyche give birth to different virtues. From the rational part emerge prudence, understanding, and wisdom; from the irascible part, courage and patience; and from the concupiscible part, continence, charity, and temperance. Finally, there is justice, a virtue that saturates the psyche as a whole and cultivates an inner "concord and harmony between the parts of the soul."[35] For Evagrius, as one

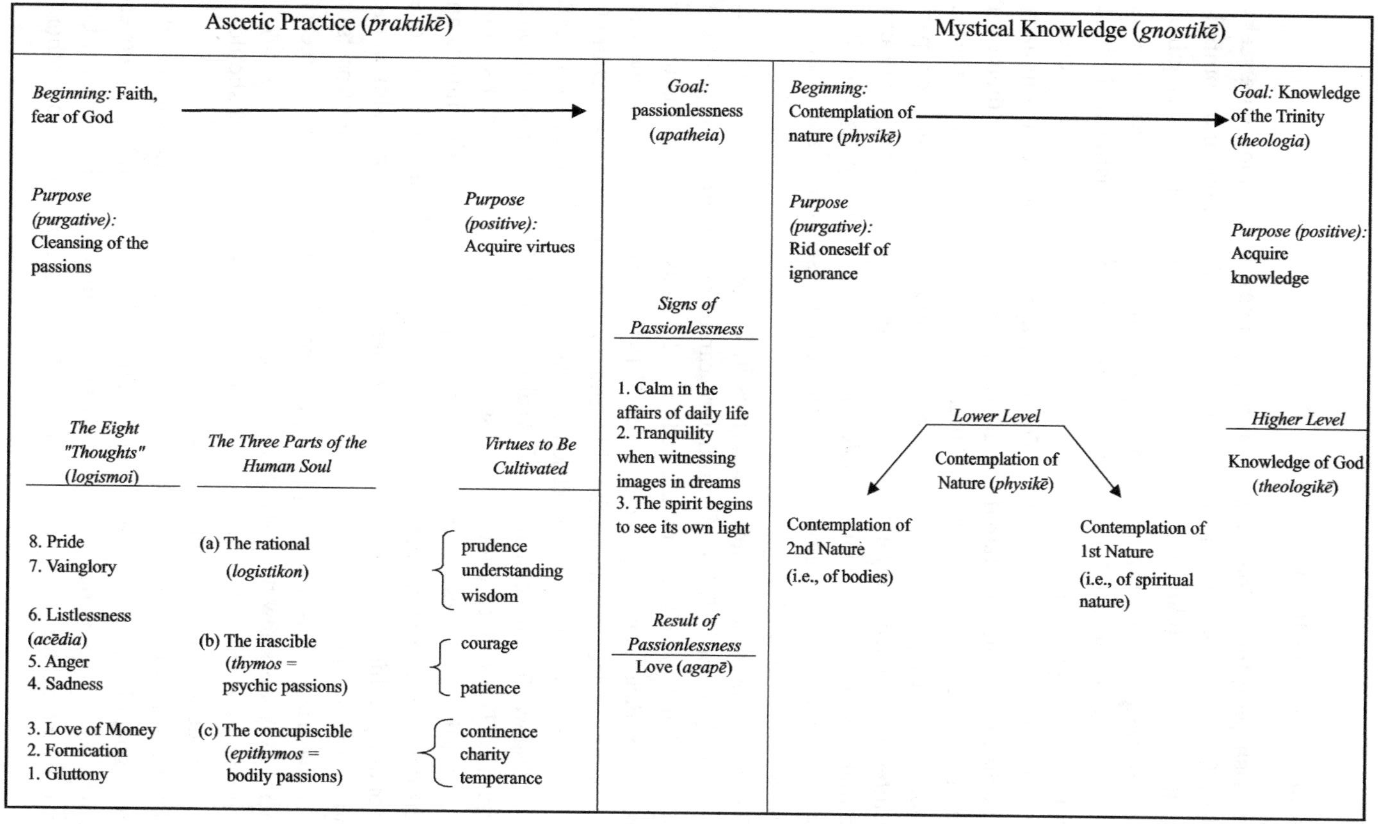

Ascetic Practice (praktikē)

Beginning: Faith, fear of God

Purpose (purgative): Cleansing of the passions

Purpose (positive): Acquire virtues

Goal: passionlessness (apatheia)

The Eight "Thoughts" (logismoi) — The Three Parts of the Human Soul — Virtues to Be Cultivated

The Eight "Thoughts" (logismoi)	The Three Parts of the Human Soul	Virtues to Be Cultivated
8. Pride 7. Vainglory	(a) The rational (logisikon)	prudence understanding wisdom
6. Listlessness (acēdia) 5. Anger 4. Sadness	(b) The irascible (thymos = psychic passions)	courage patience
3. Love of Money 2. Fornication 1. Gluttony	(c) The concupiscible (epithymos = bodily passions)	continence charity temperance

Signs of Passionlessness
1. Calm in the affairs of daily life
2. Tranquility when witnessing images in dreams
3. The spirit begins to see its own light

Result of Passionlessness
Love (agapē)

Mystical Knowledge (gnostikē)

Beginning: Contemplation of nature (physikē)

Purpose (purgative): Rid oneself of ignorance

Goal: Knowledge of the Trinity (theologia)

Purpose (positive): Acquire knowledge

Higher Level
Knowledge of God (theologikē)

Lower Level
Contemplation of Nature (physikē)

Contemplation of 2nd Nature (i.e., of bodies)

Contemplation of 1st Nature (i.e., of spiritual nature)

FIGURE 7.1. Evagrius's Map of Spiritual Progress.

progresses in the spiritual life, the psyche's faculties begin to come together, to reintegrate, to work the way God originally had made them to work.

Passionlessness and Its Offspring

The goal shaping this initial stage of ascetic practice is freedom. One seeks freedom from passions, from deep-rooted psychic obsessions and compulsions. Evagrius says that "the ascetic practitioner is one who has acquired passionlessness in the passionate part of his soul."[36] The key term here is *apatheia*, "passionlessness." This has nothing to do with apathy or lack of emotion; rather, "passionlessness is a quiet state of the rational soul; it results from gentleness and self-control."[37] The term *apatheia* had been originally used by the Stoics, but Christian theologians took it over and used for their own purposes. Church Fathers such as Athanasius used to speak of Christ as "passionless."[38] Evagrius's central concern was prayer, and in his view passions interfere with true prayer: "It is impossible to run while tied up, nor can a mind that is a slave to passions behold the place of spiritual prayer, for it is dragged and spun round by impassioned mental representations and it cannot achieve a stable state."[39]

Passionlessness, as Evagrius describes it, is not an all-or-nothing state. There are degrees of it. Think of health. One can be healthy in the sense of not being sick. Then there is the robust health and fitness of an elite athlete. For Evagrius, *apatheia* defines psychic health.[40] Just because one has arrived at passionlessness does not mean the ebbs and flows of thoughts cease. Rather, thoughts lose their ability to subvert self-control. The ascetic enjoys a measured calm during waking consciousness. This calm also extends to the unconscious, to dreams: "The test of passionlessness is that the mind...remains calm before haunting fantasies occurring during sleep."[41] Here Evagrius intuits an insight developed in twentieth-century psychology: that dreams offer telltale signs of our psychic health. Evagrius's passionlessness is a relative calm on the far side of the storm—and a realistic calm that still must face the daily upsets of life. To be passionless was a sign of advance, but it was no guarantee of holiness. Evagrius knew that even advanced monks could fall, and fall badly.[42] Still, he believed that after years of practice, the monk could—and should—arrive at a measure of genuine tranquility.

Evagrius says that "love (*agapē*) is the offspring of passionlessness"; "the ultimate goal of the ascetic life is love."[43] This is important and easy to overlook. The ascetic life is not about negativity, denying oneself this or that, but about learning to love. Ultimately, the ascetic life makes one free to love others, free of subtle compulsions and hidden agenda. It means loving others as they really are. Evagrius accents this in the concluding chapter of *The Monk*: "Love has the task of revealing itself to every image of God as being as nearly like its prototype as possible no matter how the demons ply their arts to defile them."[44] This takes a little decoding. When Evagrius says "every image of God," he means "every human being"; when he speaks of the "prototype" of that image, he means Christ. Evagrius is saying that love teaches us to see other human beings as sacred, as fragile glimpses of Christ, who is the true image of God and the prototype of what it means to be human. Seeing Christ in others is not easy because of "defilements." Some people hurt us, some annoy us, some have deep-seated evil propensities. Evagrius argues that the gaze of love must pierce through these defilements and see the God-given dignity that lies beneath. Evagrius was also realistic: "It is not possible to love all the brothers equally, but it is possible to conduct our relationships with all without passion and free from resentment and hatred."[45] Love becomes the doorway to the next stage, to mystical knowledge.[46]

Mystical Knowledge

Evagrius calls the second stage *gnostikē*, "the life of mystical knowledge," from the Greek word *gnōsis*, "knowledge." Here the monk embarks on a life of contemplation. This does not mean that he leaves behind the ascetic life. Ascetic disciplines continue and provide the foundation for progress. The starting point for this second stage is contemplating creation. The term Evagrius uses is *physikē*, literally "physics." He is not referring to the scientific study of nature. *Physikē* is the gift of seeing the divine presence in creation, of "revealing the truth hidden within all beings."[47] Evagrius calls this "natural knowledge" (*gnōsis physikē*) or "contemplation" (*theōria*). It has two sub-stages: "contemplation of the second nature," where the monk contemplates the visible beauty and order of created beings and of nature as a whole, whatever can be taken in by his senses; and "contemplation of the first nature," where the monk's contemplative vision pierces through the visible magnificence to grasp invisible created beings and the whole invisible order of creation. For Evagrius, the visible world was created by Christ, God's Word (*Logos*). Christ the Logos instilled in the visible world certain invisible "principles" (*logoi*) that form a hidden architecture and ecology beneath the world's visible surface and within history's unfolding.

In the first stage, passionlessness blossoms into love; in this second stage, contemplation blossoms into mystical knowledge of God. The term Evagrius uses is "theology" (*theologia*).[48] We tend to think of theology as an academic discipline—something studied in a classroom or read in a book. Evagrius thought of it not as academic enterprise, but as a contemplative exercise. Theology, in his view, is a knowledge of God that comes not from books, but from prayer. He did not doubt the value of reading, study, or reason; nor did he doubt the value of dogma, liturgy, and ecclesiastical authority. But for him, theology is the encounter of the praying mind with God. That is the point underlying his famous aphorism: "If you are a theologian, you will pray truly; and if you pray truly, you will be a theologian."[49] And what this praying mind encounters is the Trinity: Father, Son, and Holy Spirit. To know—experientially—the Holy Trinity is, according to Evagrius, the very definition of the kingdom of God.[50]

The "gnostic"—Evagrius's term for an advanced monk—was not only a contemplative, one who had achieved a measured calm of soul and a measured mastery over personal demons. The gnostic was also an *abba*. He had disciples around him and bore weighty responsibilities as a teacher and spiritual guide. Evagrius defines the gnostic as "one who plays the role of salt for the impure and that of light for the pure."[51] This division between "impure" and "pure," between beginners and advanced, mirrors his division between the life of ascetic practice and the life of mystical knowledge. The task for beginners, the "impure," is to purify the passions. Pedagogically, the gnostic needs to act as salt, preserving them, helping them endure the hard battles with demons. The task for the advanced, the "pure," is to move to a deeper knowledge. Pedagogically, the gnostic needs to act as light, enlightening disciples as they pass into an unfolding contemplation of creation, its principles, and ultimately the Trinity. Evagrius thus wanted the teacher to be salt and light, a preservative and an illumination.

THE SAPPHIRE LIGHT OF THE MIND

Evagrius's views on mystical experience and contemplation appear in his widely read *Chapters on Prayer* (*De oratione*) and his less well-known *Reflections* (*Skemmata*).

Pure Prayer

Evagrius speaks of the highest form of prayer as "pure prayer" (or sometimes "true prayer"). It has three qualities. First, it should be unceasing: "We have not been commanded to work, to keep vigil, and to fast at all times, but the law of unceasing prayer has been handed down to us."[52] The "law" Evagrius cites here is St. Paul's exhortation to "pray without ceasing" (1 Thess. 5:17). In the century after Evagrius, in fifth-century Palestine, a practical way of fulfilling this command would emerge: the Jesus Prayer, that unceasing repetition of a short phrase such as "Lord Jesus Christ, Son of God, have mercy on me."[53] This would become one of the most beloved devotions in Byzantine and Russian Orthodox spirituality. How did Evagrius expect this unceasing prayer to be carried out?[54] He does not say, but his disciple John Cassian advocated the unceasing repetition of Psalm 70:1: "God, come to my aid; Lord, make haste to help me."[55]

Second, Evagrius stressed that "pure prayer" be imageless: "When you pray do not form images of the divine within yourself, nor allow your mind to be impressed with any form, but approach the immaterial immaterially and you will come to understanding."[56] For Evagrius, God is utterly beyond material confines—beyond shape, beyond color, beyond time. Thus the one praying seeks complete transcendence. This is not simply for the advanced. In one striking passage, Evagrius remarks: "For my part I will say what I have said even to novices. Blessed is the mind which has acquired perfect freedom from the impressions of forms during the time of prayer. Blessed is the mind which prays without distraction and acquires an ever greater longing for God. Blessed is the mind which becomes immaterial and free from all things during the time of prayer."[57] This might give the impression that Evagrius was relentlessly apophatic. That distorts his context. Monks prayed over the scriptures, especially the Psalms, and these are packed with vivid images. For Evagrius, the praying monk springboards up, even if only briefly, from those scriptural images to the image-defying God that scripture itself teaches. These precious imageless intervals take place within the broader routine of chewing upon the scriptural word.[58]

Third, Evagrius suggests that "pure prayer" pass beyond words into wordlessness. Evagrius does famously define prayer as "the conversation of the mind with God."[59] His term "conversation" (*homilia*) implies that he thought of prayer as words. He certainly presumed that monks prayed the Psalms with heart and mind and tongue. And if one studies his *Scholia on the Psalms*, one sees how he saw the Psalms as medicinal, a sort of pharmacy for healing the soul's ills, and as a refining fire for honing one's contemplative vision of creation and world history. He also encouraged monks to use scriptural words as weapons against demonic attack—which was the whole reason he wrote his *Counter-Arguments*. But this "conversation," as Evagrius conceived it, is to move beyond words into wordless contemplation. Prayer in its higher forms meant not simply moving beyond words; it meant "laying aside mental representations."[60]

In another famous definition, Evagrius describes prayer as "the ascent of the mind to God."[61] Here and elsewhere Evagrius uses the word "mind" (*noũs*) to describe what in us prays. For most of us, "mind" implies logic, thinking, rational deduction. In the Greek theological tradition, the mind is our intuitive side. It enables us to know and recognize the truth of things instantly, whether a friend's face or a mathematical proof. For Evagrius, the way the mind knows God is through direct intuition, not logic: "for knowledge of God, one needs not a debater's soul, but a seer's soul."[62] In the Greek theological tradition, mind is the highest dimension of the human person. It is the image of God within us, that which is most like its creator. And since it is the most Godlike part of us, it is the faculty most capable of knowing God. Evagrius says that there is nothing more natural to us than praying: "Prayer is an activity befitting the dignity of the mind."[63] Furthermore, "undistracted prayer is the highest mindfulness of the mind."[64] Evagrius stresses that prayer is not just an activity of mind; it is a state of mind (*katastasis*). Prayer is not so much something one *does* as something one *is*. Nor does he think of this higher form of prayer as ecstatic—at least, not in the strict sense. Ecstasy (*ekstasis*) literally means to "stand outside" oneself. For Evagrius, prayer is not *ekstasis*, not leaving oneself; it is a *katastasis*, a coming to one's true state.

An Inner Mount Sinai

Entering into "pure prayer" was signaled by a vision of formless light. Such an experience was only accessible to the advanced, to one who had arrived at passionlessness.[65] Evagrius cites this experience of light as one of three signs that one has crossed the frontier from the life of ascetic practice to the life of mystical knowledge.[66] Where does this formless light come from? Is it a direct vision of God? Or is it the light of the mind itself? These were urgent questions for Evagrius, so urgent that he and a friend journeyed to consult John of Lycopolis, the famous "Seer of the Thebaid." (It must have been a demanding pilgrimage. When Palladius made the same journey some years later, it took him eighteen days, partly on foot through the desert, partly by boat down the Nile.) When Evagrius and his friend made it to Lycopolis, they asked John about this experience of prayer: Did the light come out of the purified mind itself (implying that the mind's nature is luminous)? Or did the light come directly from God, whose light then illuminated the mind (much as the sun illuminates the moon)? John's answer was somewhat evasive: "It is not in the power of human beings to explain it. Besides, the mind cannot be illuminated during prayer without the grace of God."[67]

Evagrius eventually came to his own decision on the matter: "When the mind—after having stripped off the old man—has been reclothed in the [new] one who comes from grace, then it will see its state, at the time of prayer, similar to sapphire or to the color of the sky. This is what Scripture describes as the 'place of God,' what the ancients saw on Mount Sinai."[68] This seeing "sapphire" or "sky-blue light" sounds like a visual experience, at least an interior one. But was it? Evagrius alludes here to the great theophany described in Exodus. The Bible says that Moses, Aaron, and the seventy elders climbed up Mount Sinai; there "they saw the God of Israel," and "under his feet there was something like a pavement of sapphire stone, like the very heaven for clearness" (Ex. 24:9–10). In other words, the experience of pure prayer marked a return to Mount Sinai. The monk could enjoy the same awe-inspiring experience of God's presence that Moses and the elders of ancient Israel enjoyed. The Hebrew text says bluntly that Moses and the elders "saw" God. But the Greek version of the Old Testament that Evagrius and other Greek-speaking Christians used—the Septuagint—says that the elders "saw" not God himself, but "the place of God."

What was this "place of God"? Evagrius defines it in his *Reflections*: "From holy David we have clearly learned what the 'place of God' is: 'His place is established in peace and his dwelling in Zion' (Ps. 75:3). The 'place of God' therefore is the rational soul, and his dwelling is the illuminated mind, which has renounced the pleasures of the world and has learned to contemplate the (underlying) principles of the earth."[69] Here Evagrius reads the biblical text allegorically. First, he transposes outer realities into inner ones. Mount Sinai, the "place of God," is not only a place on a map of the Holy Land; it is an inner landmark, a center in the geography of the soul. The encounter with God is not limited to some past theophany. The encounter is always possible because the place of encounter always lies at the core of who we are. Second, he uses the Bible to interpret the Bible. He notes that the phrase "place of God" appears both in Exodus 24 and Psalm 75. He thus reads Psalm 75 as a cipher for Exodus 24. This leads him to insist that the Mount Sinai of the mind is also a Mount Zion, that the inner mountain is an inner temple.[70] The human person is thus a sacred precinct, a holy of holies.

What then is Evagrius's view of mystical prayer? During pure prayer, the purified mind sees itself, its truest self, its true state. The self it sees is luminous. The luminosity that permits it to see itself is the divine light. In seeing itself as luminosity, as light like sapphire or sky blue, the mind discovers its Godlikeness. It also sees and knows by seeing—indirectly, as in a mirror—the uncreated, immaterial light that God is.[71] That is why for Evagrius prayer is both a moment of self-discovery and an encounter with ultimate mystery: "Prayer is the state of the mind that comes to be from the Holy Trinity's singular light."[72] This is the core of Evagrius's theology—and theology in his sense of it, the encounter of the praying mind with God. Antoine Guillaumont, the finest Evagrian scholar of the last century, has argued that "in this description of pure prayer, Evagrius is certainly referring to an experience, both real and personal."[73]

The Calligraphy of Christ

We should not detach Evagrius's accounts of "pure prayer" and of mystical glimpses of the "sapphire light of the mind" from his broader account of the journey to God. The monk-mystic is not the only one returning to God; all creation is. This is why "physics" (*physikē*) is so important. We saw Bonaventure's and Eckhart's metaphysics of flow, how they stressed that all things had come from God and were in the process of returning to God. A similar metaphysics is found here at the roots of the Christian mystical tradition. In his *Gnostic Chapters*, Evagrius speaks of creation charged with the signature of Christ: "Just as those who teach the alphabet to children trace the letters on tablets, so too Christ, in order to teach his wisdom to the rational beings, has inscribed it into corporeal nature."[74] Evagrius extends this metaphor in his *Letter to Melania*. He speaks of the world as a letter inscribed with Christ's beautiful handwriting. This letter-called-creation, however beautiful in itself, is meant to be read, for it offers instructions on our return to God. To decipher it, we need a certain spiritual literacy. Christ's calligraphy points to deeper realities, to God's awe-inspiring power and hidden wisdom. Still, Evagrius adds, we need to recognize that creation itself is a love letter. That is its deepest intention.[75]

Evagrius agreed with Origen's bold vision of a "restoration" (*apokatastasis*), the view that at the end of time God will restore all things to himself and all will become one in him. Like Origen, he speculated that fallen souls, in their return to God, might journey with different bodies and through different worlds. But in the end, all rational beings would recover their original spiritual nature and recover their long-lost primordial oneness with Christ. All that is tied up with the current creation—bodies, matter, time—would be shucked off, and God would become all in all. In his *Letter to Melania*, he plays upon the image of streams flowing into a vast sea: "When like torrents to the sea the minds return to him, he completely changes them to his own nature, colour, and taste: in his endless and inseparable unity, they will be one and no longer many, since they will be united and joined to him."[76] Evagrius moves from this cosmic vision to reflect on his own journey, its mystery and incompleteness:

> Now, my dear, I tell you that, just as astonishment seized the prophet when he saw these things and cried "Wonderful!," wonder likewise seizes me at all these things that happen to me along the way that I have taken. But I am kept from the goal that I began since I am bound by the mighty chains of loving those things that ceaselessly please me. I fall short of completing what I began . . . Just as the

journey of one seeking to arrive at the end of all torrents will arrive at the sea, likewise the one who seeks to arrive at the power of some created thing will arrive at the "Wisdom full of diversity" (Eph. 3:10) who established it. Anyone who stands on the seashore is seized by amazement at its limitlessness, taste, colour, and all it contains, and at how the rivers, torrents and streams that pour into it become limitless and undifferentiated in it, since they acquire its properties. It is likewise for anyone who considers the end of the intellects: he will be greatly amazed and marvel as he beholds all these various different knowledges uniting themselves in the one uniquely real knowledge and beholds them all become this one without end.[77]

Here we see Evagrius as he understood himself: a man driven by wonder and awe. And this wonder caused him to thirst for creation's origin, the unity at the heart of it all. Yet he found himself incomplete, "bound" by "mighty chains of loving" the awe-inspiring beauties of the universe. His sea image is intriguing, coming from a man who began his life near the grandeur of the Black Sea and who ended his days in an ocean of sand. He knew the incompleteness of being human, that for all his journeying, "I fall short of completing what I began."

A DESERT WELLSPRING

Evagrius may have spoken of himself as a desert's "waterless cloud," but the torrent of his ideas streamed down like rivers to the sea, quietly infusing the emerging Christian mystical tradition. Despite persecution, despite posthumous condemnation, that torrent of ideas flowed on. Evagrius's manuscripts were copied and recopied by desert calligraphers. In the Greek-speaking world, calligraphers quietly removed his name from the title page of manuscripts, but they continued both to copy and to imitate his proverblike "chapters." The great Orthodox mystical theologian Maximus Confessor (d. 662) would absorb Evagrius's key insights and fold them into his own profound theological synthesis.[78] Maximus's borrowings were deep but never uncritical. He took care to balance out Evagrius's imbalances. Maximus, for instance, meditated deeply on Christ's humanity, something Evagrius scarcely touched upon. Still Evagrius's insights gained currency via Maximus, diffusing out into the wider Orthodox mystical tradition.

Evagrius's manuscripts also spread further East, beyond the borders of the Roman Empire to Syriac-speaking Christians in Persia. There his name would be remembered and venerated. Isaac of Nineveh, a seventh-century native of

Qatar and bishop of what now is Mosul in Iraq, spoke fondly of *Mar* ("blessed") Evagrius, celebrating him as "the recipient of boundless spiritual revelations."[79] Isaac treasured and passed on Evagrius's theories about pure prayer and the sapphire light of the mind.[80] But Isaac too balanced Evagrius's imbalances, exploring the heart in greater depth and more positively than Evagrius. Playing on Evagrius's "physics," he spoke of the mystic's deep-felt compassion for all creation:

> And what is a merciful heart? . . . The heart's burning for all creation,
> for human beings, for birds and animals, and for demons, and ev-
> erything there is. At the recollection of them and at the sight of
> them his eyes gush forth with tears owing to the force of the com-
> passion which constrains his heart, so that, as a result of its abundant
> sense of mercy, the heart shrinks and cannot bear to hear or exam-
> ine any harm or small suffering of anything in creation. For this
> reason he offers up prayer with tears at all times, even for irrational
> animals, and for the enemies of truth, and for those who harm
> him, for their preservation and being forgiven . . . as a result of the
> immense compassion infused in his heart without measure—
> like God's.[81]

Evagrius's ideas also spread to the West. His old friend Rufinus translated some works into Latin, and Gennadius, the fifth-century historian, reports having access to much of Evagrius in Latin decades later. But Evagrius put his imprint on the Western mystical tradition much more profoundly, but more quietly, through John Cassian (d. 430s).[82] We know only bits and snatches about Cassian's life, but he was a great traveler and knew firsthand the wide range of early experiments in monastic living that were then springing up around the Roman Empire. A native of Scythia (now modern Romania), Cassian was bilingual, equally at ease in Greek and Latin. He became a monk in Bethlehem in the early 380s, but after hearing stories of Egyptian monks, he moved to Egypt and lived nearly fifteen years at Macarius's monastic settlement of Scetis. He both knew and passed on Evagrius's ideas, both great and small, but, interestingly, never once mentions Evagrius's name. Why? Scholars suspect it was because of the persecution of Evagrius's friends and disciples in 399. Cassian himself left Egypt that same year—why, he never says—and settled in Constantinople, where John Chrysostom welcomed him and ordained him deacon. After John's downfall a few years later, Cassian moved on to Rome and befriended key members of the papal curia, including the onetime archdeacon and later pope, Leo the Great. In the 410s Cassian settled in the port city of Marseilles in southern France. There, at the request of local bishops and abbots, he composed two works: *Institutes*, a book of core principles for monastic life; and *Conferences*, a collection of twenty-four dialogues with desert fathers he had met and admired.

Thanks to Cassian, Evagrius's ideas on the eight "thoughts" became part of the spiritual vocabulary of the Latin West. Cassian also repeated and furthered Evagrius's views about unceasing, imageless prayer. Like Evagrius, Cassian spoke of the mystical journey to God as mountain climbing. Where Evagrius had spoken of an inner Mt. Sinai, where the monk enjoyed the vision of God that Moses and the elders of Israel enjoyed, Cassian spoke of the monk climbing with Christ up the mountain of transfiguration, that "lofty mountain of the desert" where Christ "reveals the glory of his face and image of his brightness to those who deserve to look upon him with the clean gaze of the soul."[83] And whereas Evagrius spoke of theology as seeing the Trinity, Cassian spoke of our mystical union with God in Trinitarian terms:

> This [union] will be the case when every love, every desire, every
> effort, every undertaking, every thought of ours, everything that we
> live, that we speak, that we breath, will be God, and when that
> unity which the Father now has with the Son and which the Son has
> with the Father will be carried over into our understanding and our
> mind, so that, just as he loves us with a sincere and pure and in-
> dissoluble love, we too may be joined to him with a perpetual and
> inseparable love and so united with him that whatever we breath,
> whatever we understand, whatever we speak, may be God.[84]

Later Greek mystical theologians shared and extended Cassian's emphases. They would paint icons of the Transfiguration (such as the cover of this book) as a way of pointing not simply to Christ's transfiguration, but our own. They spoke, as Cassian does here, of this journey as *theōsis*, as our becoming "deified," "Godlike." Meanwhile, Western monks would read and commend Cassian's *Conferences*. Most famously, Benedict, in composing his massively influential *Rule*, insisted that Cassian become required reading for all his monks. In this way, Evagrius and the mystical traditions of the desert made their way into the medieval Christian West and beyond.

We saw earlier how Bonaventure drew together three different streams of the Christian mystical tradition and, by his synthesis, created something new. Here, in this study of Evagrius, we see the inverse: how, at the origins of the Christian mystical tradition, Evagrius served as fountainhead and wellspring for three new mystical streams in three languages. We thus get a glimpse of how dry deserts can become fertile torrents and how anonymous calligraphers can quietly rewrite memories of the journey to God.

8

Mysticism and Islam: Rumi

In the opening chapter, we saw William James's classic claim that mystics, whatever their religion of origin, share a common experience: "In mystic states we become one with the Absolute and we become aware of our oneness. This is the everlasting and triumphant mystical tradition, hardly altered by differences of clime or creed."[1] Evelyn Underhill, a contemporary of James and author of the widely read *Mysticism*, disagreed with him on many matters. But on this, she agreed:

> The jewels of mystical literature glow with this intimate and impassioned love of the Absolute; which transcends the dogmatic language in which it is clothed and becomes applicable to mystics of every race and creed. There is little difference in this between the extremes of Eastern and Western thought: between [Thomas] Á Kempis the Christian and Jalu'd Din [Rumi] the Moslem saint.[2]

Like James, she argued that mystics "speak the same language" because they "come from the same country."[3] This sunny universalism still flourishes. From the late nineteenth century until the 1970s, it reigned as a sort of scholarly orthodoxy.[4] One still sees it promoted, especially in popular accounts. But is it true?

We stand a century removed from James and Underhill and those pathbreaking turn-of-the-century scholars who made mysticism a serious academic concern. In the century between them and us scholarly understanding of the world's religions has advanced immeasurably. How? First, in the scholarly knowledge of religious literature—and this includes mastery of a vast array of foreign and ancient languages, the patient sifting and probing of vast libraries of surviving texts, and the publication of critical editions and careful translations. Second, in the intricate process of reconstructing religious histories, both at the micro and macro levels, and putting these religious histories into dialogue with contemporaneous political, social, and economic histories. Third, in the ongoing and necessarily relentless reflection on method, probing how we generalize—probing whether generalizations and concepts hide unspoken biases and thus distort the realities, ancient or modern, we try to talk about. The scale of scholarship on the world's religions over the last century has been staggering and has volumes to say about the study of mysticism in the West and beyond. Glib claims about the universality of the mystical and the casual setting of snippets from Christian mystics alongside quotations from Muslim Sufis or Hindu Vedantists or Zen Buddhists will no longer suffice.

In this chapter and the next, I want to take readers on two excursions to probe the issue of mysticism beyond the bounds of Christianity. I want to explore if claims like James's and Underhill's and those who repeat them still make any sense. I will continue, as before, with the same case-study approach, opening with a biographical sketch and then surveying key elements of the person's views on religious experience. In this chapter, we will explore the mystical traditions of Islam by focusing on the Sufi mystic that Underhill mentioned, Mowlānā Jalāl al-Din Rumi (1207–1273).[5] In the next chapter, we will look at Buddhism, focusing on Zen master Eihei Dōgen (1200–1253). Look at their dates. These two men were exact contemporaries, though they lived a half a world away from one another. They were also exact contemporaries of Thomas Aquinas and Bonaventure.

THE SUFI PATH

Jalāl al-Din Rumi was a Sufi and founded one of Islam's major Sufi orders, the Mevlevi, known in popular parlance as the "whirling dervishes." To appreciate his religious and mystical background, we need to sketch out a few basics on Sufism.

Sufism

The word *sufi* derives, it seems, from the word for wool (*sūf*) and refers to the woolen garment (*khirqah*), often blue, worn by early Sufi ascetics. Medieval Sufi theorists acknowledged this as one likely origin for the term. But some, such as Abū Bakr al-Kalābādhī (d. 995), opened their treatises on Sufism with long lists of definitions that used wordplay to tease out spiritual meanings of the term:

> Some say: "The Sufis were only named Sufis because of the purity (*safā*) of their hearts and the cleanliness of their acts"... Another said: 'The Sufi is he whose conduct towards God is sincere (*safā*), and towards whom God's blessing is sincere." Certain of them have said: "They were only called Sufis because they are in the first rank (*saff*) before God through the elevation of their desires toward Him."[6]

Al-Kalābādhī spoke of early Sufi ascetics in terms that may remind Western readers of early Christian monks:

> They were people who had left this world, departed from their homes, fled from their companions. They wandered about the land, mortifying the carnal desires, and... they took of this world's goods only so much as is indispensable for covering the nakedness and allaying hunger. For departing from their homes they were called "strangers"; for their many journeyings they were called "travelers"; for their travelling in deserts, and taking refuge in caves at times of necessity.[7]

Despite similarities to monks, Sufis noted a traditional saying (*hadīth*) attributed to the Prophet Muhammad: "There is no monasticism in Islam."[8] What defined Sufism was not simply outward asceticism, but inner detachment. When asked, "Who is a Sufi?" one early master replied: "He who neither possesses [material things] nor is possessed [by them]."[9] Rumi once offered his own spiritualized definition: "What is Sufism? To find joy in the heart at the coming of sorrow."[10]

Sufism emerged as a visible movement in Islam's second century, that is, in the early 700s. By Rumi's time, it had become a mystical tradition rich in literature, sophisticated in its theological formulations, and many-branched in organization. Nineteenth-century Western scholars tended to interpret Sufism as an ascetic movement at odds with Islam itself, a foreign derivative, something patched together out of the ascetic mélange that percolated around the Middle East among wandering gnostics, Christian monks, Manichaean elect,

Hindu sannyasi, and Buddhist bhikkhus. Treating Sufism like some foreign import simply does not stand up to critical scrutiny.[11] Sufis drew their deepest inspiration from and fashioned their distinctive self-understanding and practices out of Islam's own unique spiritual resources. We need to remember that ascetic practices and devotions lie at the very heart of Islam. One of Islam's "five pillars" is the five-times-per-day practice of prayer (salāt); another is the rigorous thirty-day fast of Ramadān. Sufis presumed, drew upon, and expanded upon both. They also drew inspiration from the life of Muhammad, especially his ascent (mi'raj) through the seven heavens to the throne of God. For the core of their mystical theology, they drew on that most central of Islamic affirmations, the shahāda ("there is no god but God"), and on the core doctrine that flows from it, the absolute oneness of God (tawhīd). This doctrine, as we will see, inspired the Sufi search for mystical union. And for that search, Sufis turned to the Qur'an, which—for Sufis as for all Muslims—is understood, quite literally, as God's word. As Michael Sells has noted, "Sufis view their thought and way of life as Qur'anic in every sense . . . Any passage in the Qur'an could be—and was—integrated into the Sufi view of life—or, conversely, the Sufi view of life was grounded in the Qur'an as a whole."[12]

Knowledge of God

We saw how Christian theorists such as Jean Gerson defined mystical theology as an "experiential knowledge of God" and how Evagrius spoke of this experiential knowledge as "gnosis" and of the advanced monk as a "gnostic." Sufis adopted similar terminology. They spoke of the advanced Sufi as a "knower" or "gnostic" ('arif) and stressed that the mystic's goal is "experiential knowledge" or "gnosis" (ma'rifa).[13] The earliest systematic treatise on Sufism, The Book of Flashes (Kitāb al-Luma') by Abū Nasr as-Sarrāj (d. 988), explores the nature of this mystical knowledge. He acknowledged two other traditional types of religious knowledge ('ilm) within Islam: the expertise of the traditionists, scholars who master the sayings traditions (hadīth) of the Prophet; and the expertise of the jurists, scholars who master the intricate legal traditions of Islamic morality (sharī'a). The Sufis, he claimed, possess a third, but no less essential, type of knowledge: knowledge of the heart.[14] This was the Sufis' unique expertise. Whereas other experts focused (legitimately) on religious externals, Sufis were specialists in the interior life. They possessed experiential knowledge of "manifestations, movements of spirit, gifts, and blessings, which its practitioners harvest from the ocean of divine largesse."[15] Just as one would not go to a layman for an expert legal opinion, so neither should one go to someone ignorant of this "science of the heart" for spiritual direction.[16] Sarrāj appealed to a favorite Qur'anic text: "If the ocean were ink to write the words of my Lord, the ocean would run out before the words of my Lord, even if We provided another like it" (18:109).[17] Since Sufism seeks knowledge of the infinite, it too is infinite: "The final objective of all the disciplines is knowledge of mystical realities. When someone ends up there, that person falls into a limitless ocean that is the science of hearts, the science of experiential knowledge (ma'rifa), the science of mysteries, the science of the inward, the science of Sufism."[18]

Sarrāj's treatise is the first of a long line within Sufism. Later authors charted, often with great subtlety, the unique experiential knowledge of the Sufis within the broader theological traditions of Islam. Modern accounts sometimes overplay the distinction between the scholars' 'ilm and the mystics' ma'rifa. While some Sufis leaders had little formal training in Islam's religious sciences, many others were highly trained and held eminent positions as religious scholars. Remember what we saw in the Christian mystical tradition, the way figures like Bonaventure and Eckhart combined philosophical dexterity and enormous erudition with their own profound mystical impulses. A number of leading Sufis combined the same dual vocation of religious scholar and mystic. Abū Hāmid al-Ghazālī (d. 1111) is one famous example; Rumi, as we will see, is another.

Stations and States

Sufis speak of this quest for an experiential knowledge of God as traveling "the path" (tariqa).[19] They developed intricate maps to chart this path of the spirit. Sufis traditionally distinguish between "stations" (maqāmāt) and "states" (ahwāl). Stations are the stages in the journey to God through which the mystic progresses stepwise. Sarrāj, in his Book of Flashes, outlined seven stations: (1) repentance, (2) watchfulness, (3) renunciation, (4) poverty, (5) patience, (6) trust, and (7) acceptance.[20] This list is but one of many, and the number and order differ, often widely, from theorist to theorist.[21] One may dwell within a station for years, for, as another of the great Sufi theorists, Abū l-Qāsim al-Qushayrī (d. 1074), once noted, "You cannot rise from one station to another until you have fulfilled [its] provisions."[22]

Sufi theorists contrast these longer-term, stepwise "stations" with brief, unexpected, passing "states." Qushayrī defined a state as "a mode of consciousness that comes upon the heart without a person's intending it, attracting it, or trying to gain it—a feeling of delight or sorrow, constriction, longing, anxiety, terror, or want"; thus, "states are bestowed, stations are attained."[23] "Stations" thus designate what the Sufi himself does; "states" are what God does to the Sufi. They are gifts of grace. Here again, lists of states vary from theorist to theorist. They are often listed in pairs. Qushayrī, for example, pairs "awe" (*hayba*), an intense holy fear of God, with its opposite, "intimacy" (*uns*), an intense holy yearning for God. Another classic pair is "union" (*jam'*) and "separation" (*farq*). According to Qushayrī, both are necessary: "Whoever has no separation has no worshipful-ness. Whoever has no union has no experience of knowing (*ma'rifa*)."[24] Another famous state is "drunkenness" (*sukr*). As Qushayrī notes, "Drunkenness is only for the ecstatics. If the attribute of beauty [of God] is unveiled to the servant, he attains drunkenness, his spirit is transported, and his heart is wander-lost."[25] Qushayrī took pains to emphasize that drunkenness has nothing to do with actually drinking alcohol, which is, of course, strictly forbidden in Islamic law. The image of the mystic reeling and staggering, drunk on God's heady wine, is, as we will see, one of Rumi's favorites.

Annihilation

The most controversial of the Sufi states is "annihilation" or "passing away" (*fanā'*). In annihilation, the Sufi mystic loses all sense of himself. He experiences his very being swallowed up within God's infinite being. God becomes, during this ephemeral state, his very existence. In such moments, Sufi mystics could shock hearers with ecstatic outbursts (*shathīyāt*). Bāyezīd Bistāmī (d. 875) once proclaimed, "Glory be to me," while al-Hallāj (d. 922) scandalously announced: "I am the Real." (The term "the Real" [*al-Haqq*] is a Qur'anic synonym for God.) Both men sounded as though they were claiming to be God. Al-Hallāj ended up being charged with incarnationalism (*shirk*), imprisoned, tortured, and brutally executed.[26] Later Sufi hagiography treated him as a Jesuslike figure, and Rumi revered him as a mystical saint.

Later Sufis theorists took pains to justify this "bewildered speech," as they called it. They routinely appealed to an extra-Qur'anic saying (*hadīth qudsī*) in which Allah says: "My servant continues to draw near to me through free acts of devotion until I love him. When I love him, I become the eye with which he sees, the hearing with which he hears, the tongue with which he speaks, the hand with which he grasps."[27] They also made distinctions between speech during ecstasy and speech during sober moments. The learned Sufi writer al-Ghazālī offered the classic defense:

> The gnostics, after having ascended to the heaven of reality, agree
> that they see nothing in existence save the One, the Real. Some
> of them possess this state as a cognitive gnosis. Others, however,
> attain this through a state of tasting. Plurality is totally banished from

them, and they become immersed in sheer singularity. Their rational faculties become so satiated that in this state they are, as it were stunned. No room remains in them for the remembrance of any other than God, nor the remembrance of themselves. Nothing is with them but God. They become intoxicated with such an intoxication that the ruling authority of their rational faculty is overthrown. Hence one of them [= al-Hallāj] says, "I am the Real!"; another [= Bistāmī], "Glory be to me, how great is my station!" . . . The speech of lovers in the state of intoxication should be concealed and not spread about. When this intoxication subsides, the ruling authority of the rational faculty—which is God's balance in His earth—is given back to them. They come to know that what they experienced was not the reality of unification but that it was similar to unification. It was like the words of the lover during a state of extreme passionate love: "I am He whom I love, / and He whom I love is I!"[28]

Al-Ghazālī admitted such outbursts were, in part, poetic exaggerations not unlike those of love-drunk lovers. Still, he felt that though ordinary Muslims may verbally confess God as absolute oneness, Sufis in the state of *fanā'* experience it, taste it.

Orders and Practices

The Christian mystics we studied belonged to a variety of religious orders, and within those orders they received their spiritual apprenticeship. A similar trend appears among Sufis. By Rumi's time, Sufism had spread about the Islamic world through dozens of orders. In its origins, Sufism centered on revered spiritual masters (*shaykhs* in Arabic, *pīr* in Persian) who guided circles of devoted disciples. Sufis insisted that to travel the spiritual path without a teacher was madness; according to an often-cited proverb, "When someone has no *shaykh*, Satan becomes his *shaykh*."[29] Rumi also warned of its hazards: "Though you be a lion, if you travel the Path without a guide, you will be a self-seer, astray and contemptible."[30] Sufi teachings were handed down, usually orally, generation to generation, and it became traditional for an order to trace its chain of mystical teaching from Muhammad down to the order's founder and from the founder down to the presiding *shaykh*. As we will see, such transmission chains (known as *silsila*) also figure prominently in Zen Buddhist spirituality.[31]

Discipleship within Sufism became formalized and carefully graded. An aspirant in Rumi's order, for example, spent three years working in the kitchen before gaining admittance. Rituals developed around formal initiation—for example, shaving one's head and receiving the Sufi cloak. Disciples also periodically undertook, under a *shaykh*'s guidance, forty-day retreats (*chilla*). These included rigorous fasting and intense prayer, often in a secluded and darkened room. Sufi orders eventually acquired lodges (*khāniqāh*), where they met for discussions, study, and prayer. These might have meeting areas for the study of the Qur'an, quarters for lodging visitors, and well-stocked libraries.

Sufis practiced what all observant Muslims practice: daily prayers, the yearly fast of Ramadān, the once-in-a-lifetime pilgrimage to Mecca, and so on. They also developed unique devotional practices. I mentioned their retreats. Sufis also more routinely gathered for late-night vigils, pointing to the Qur'an's admonition: "Keep vigil all night, save for a few hours . . . and with measured tone recite the Qur'an . . . Remember the name of the Lord and dedicate yourself to Him utterly" (73:2–8). Sufis, in their vigils, recited the sacred names of God. This form of prayer, the *dhikr* (literally, "remembrance"), is repeated like a mantra and, as the term suggests, is meant as a way to keep God quite literally always in mind. William Chittick has stressed that this "remembrance or invocation is *the* central spiritual technique of Sufism, but always under the guidance of a shaykh, who alone can grant the disciple the right and spiritual receptivity to invoke the Name of God in a systematic fashion."[32] Another fundamental—and controversial—practice was the *samā'* (literally, "audition"). This included instrumental music and ecstatic ritual dancing. The *samā'* not only served as the setting and inspiration for much of Rumi's poetry; it also became the setting and mode of his mystical prayer.

TO PRAISE THE SUN

For Rumi's biography, scholars have drawn on three major sources: a poem, *The Book of Beginnings* (*Ebtedā nāme*), by Rumi's son, Sultan Valad; a hagiographic work, *The Treatise* (*Resāle*), by Sepahsālār, one of Rumi's immediate disciples; and a later hagiographic history, *Acts of the Gnostics* (*Manāqeb al-'ārefin*), by Ahmad Aflāki (d. 1360). The first two were eyewitnesses, while the third had access to Mevlevi archives, but the three were hardly unbiased observers, and all make use of traditional hagiographic motifs. With the life of Rumi, as with that of so many mystics, sifting out the historically reliable from the hagiographic haze is a formidable task. Other tidbits can be gleaned from Rumi's own writings and from works by his father and his teachers.[33]

Family

Rumi's family spoke Persian and came originally from Balkh, in what is present-day Afghanistan. Rumi was born north of there, in Vakhsh, a small town in what is now Tajikistan.[34] His father, Bahā al-Din Valad (c. 1152–1231), was at the time a middle-aged cleric with a small but loyal circle of disciples. Rumi's father did not belong (apparently) to any known Sufi order, but he did have strong mystical inclinations. His surviving spiritual journal, preserved under the title *Gnostic Wisdom* (*Ma'āref*), records a hodgepodge of visions and contemplative experiences. In one striking entry, he reports: "I obliterated myself, stripping myself of all forms so that I could see God. I told myself I would obliterate God and strip God of all forms to see God and attain His blessings more immediately. I chanted 'God' and my consciousness joined to God and I saw God, in the guise of His Godhead and the attributes of perfection."[35]

The Islamic world was on the eve of a great crisis. This was the era of Genghis Khan and the Mongol invasion. Around 1216 Bahā al-Din moved his family out of northeast Persia, just before the Mongol armies poured into the area, leaving much of it devastated. He and his family, after a pilgrimage to Mecca and brief stays in Baghdad and Damascus, migrated to Anatolia (now central Turkey) and settled in Konya (the old Roman city of Iconium in Cappadocia). Konya was Anatolia's capital, and the court language under its Seljuk monarchy was Persian. In 1229 the sultan offered Rumi's father a teaching position at a local religious college (*madrasa*). Because Anatolia had, for centuries, been a province in the Roman Empire, it was known in the Muslim world as Rum. Rumi is therefore not Jalāl al-Din's name, but nickname. It simply means "the Roman."

Early Career

At age seventeen Rumi married Gowhar Khātun. They had two sons, Sultan Valad and Alā al-Din. Rumi's father died in 1231, two years after the family's arrival in Konya. Rumi was twenty-four at the time, and although his father had been grooming him to take over his teaching position, Rumi was neither old enough nor learned enough to do so. His father's senior disciple, Borhān al-Din Mohaqqeq, stepped in. He acted as Rumi's spiritual godfather, making sure that Rumi got the advanced education he needed. Rumi was sent off to Aleppo and Damascus, where he received top-notch training in the religious sciences. There he followed the traditional course of studies in the Qur'an, *hadīth*, theology, and jurisprudence. While in Damascus he may have attended lectures given by one of Sufism's most learned and controversial mystical theologians, Ibn 'Arabī (d. 1240).

Rumi returned to Konya around 1237 and assumed his father's post as a scholar and preacher. Borhān al-Din, who had taken up a comparable position in nearby Kayseri (ancient Caesarea in Cappadocia), had also overseen Rumi's formation as a Sufi. What we know of Borhān al-Din's teaching comes from an unpublished mystical journal, preserved under the same title Rumi's father had used for his own journal, *Gnostic Wisdom (Ma'āref)*. Borhān al-Din stressed an interior ascetic piety: "The kernel of worship is melting away the self and the rest of worship is merely the husk."[36] To spur on this "melting away" of self, he encouraged fasting: "The gnostic's body through self-abnegation becomes like a glass through which the light of faith shines."[37] In his poetry, Rumi would later celebrate elements of this ascetic spirituality: "Close your mouth to bread / for here comes the sugar of the fast / . . . Fly up from the dungeon world / to the heights / Acquire a God's-eye view with the eyes of the fast."[38] Under Borhān al-Din's guidance, Rumi undertook the rigors of the Sufi retreat, with its bread-and-water diet, its darkness, its isolation.[39] Borhān al-Din formally initiated Rumi as a Sufi, though Rumi had almost certainly picked up elements of mystical Sufism under his father's tutelage. During these years, Rumi began to study and deeply treasure his father's spiritual journal, absorbing its mystical accounts. Borhān al-Din died in 1241. A year or so later, Rumi's wife died. Rumi later married a widow named Kerrā Khātun, and from this marriage had two more children, a boy and a girl.

Shams al-Din Tabrizi

Rumi's life took an abrupt mystical turn. We even know the exact date: November 29, 1244. He was thirty-seven years old at the time, outwardly a well-respected professor of the religious sciences. As he strolled through Konya's marketplace, an old vagabond named Shams al-Din Tabrizi approached him and asked a provocative religious question: Who was greater, who enjoyed the greater mystical "station," the Prophet Muhammad or the Sufi mystic Bāyezīd Bistāmī? For Muhammad had proclaimed, "We do not know You (Allah) as we should," whereas Bistāmī had proclaimed in a shocking utterance of ecstatic union, "Glory be to me!"[40] The question left Rumi dizzy, ecstatic. So began a spiritual friendship that turned Rumi's life on its ear. For six months the two were inseparable, day and night. Rumi's old life fell away. He neglected his professorial duties, his students, his Friday sermons. He neglected family as well and spent long hours at the Sufi *samā'*, with its ecstatic music, its chanting, its dancing. Rumi was overwhelmed by Shams—not only his mystical teachings, but his very presence, which, for Rumi, seemed a prism of Allah's blinding light. Shams's name literally means "sun of faith," and so in poems that began to gush forth, Rumi celebrated that sunlight:

> A towering figure, lion-taming, drunk on love,
> a revolution in the beloved's presence,
> sober, on his own a madman,
> the shape of anger, the soul of peace,
> I've never seen in all the world such a sanguine stranger...
> Light would soak the world entire
> as once it did on Sinai's Mount
> if I reveal the ecstasy of my heart's fabliaux;
> Shall I call him candle, picture of love,
> heart-stealer, life-sustainer, pure spirit,
> tall statured, infidel, soul's beloved?...
> There I am, transfixed by this sage's light,
> the old man completely absorbed in the beloved...
> My knowledge and knowing, sagesse and wisdom and culture,
> see how all of it is drowned in the beauty
> of one rosy-cheeked and priceless pearl....
> That Tabrizi Sun of Truth and Faith, that Lord
> who turned this laggard by his love into a leader![41]

Under the glare of this "sun" called Shams, a revolutionary new Rumi emerged: Rumi the mystical poet. Poems, thousands of them, ecstatic love-drunk lyrics for God, poured forth, an eruption of poetic exuberance:

> Love for you took away my rosary and gave (me) verses and songs...
> At Love's hand, I became a singer of odes, hand-clapping;
> > love for you consumed reputation and shame and all that
> > > I possessed....
> If I am a mountain, yet I hold the echo of your voice;
> > and if I am chaff, in your fire I am reduced to smoke...
> To praise you in reality is to praise oneself,
> > for he who praises the sun thereby praises his own eyes.[42]

Older accounts treat Shams's arrival as though it marked the very beginnings of Rumi's mysticism. That interpretation, though not completely accurate, is understandable, given the extravagant praise that Rumi lavishes upon Shams. Recent scholarship has helped right the balance, noting that Rumi owed an earlier mystical formation both to his father and to Borhān al-Din. Even so, the revolutionary effect Shams had on Rumi cannot be downplayed.

Franklin Lewis, one of Rumi's finest recent commentators, has framed the shift this way:

> The encounter with Shams triggered the completion of a paradigm shift in Rumi's approach to piety and spirituality; he discovered that beyond the safe, dry and socially approved forms of obedience (prayer, sermonizing, discovering and applying the principles of law) and renunciation (fasting, controlling the passions and the ego), there is a meta-spirituality of love, which consists in joyously and creatively celebrating our relationship with God.[43]

Rumi's old religious world seemed like idolatry compared to the word-defying experiential knowledge of God: "I have carved idols enough to beguile every person; now I am drunk with Abraham . . . Seek another master for the shop of idol-making. I have cleared the shop of myself."[44] Sultan Valad looked back on his father's transformation and saw it as an eruption of spiritual drunkenness: "Through love, a fatwa-writing Shaykh turned poet / though ascetic, he grew intoxicate / but not from a wine which is made of grapes—/a spirit of light drinks only wine of light."[45]

Older accounts portray Shams as an uneducated Qalandar (wandering dervish). That, it turns out, is somewhat off the mark. Scholars have begun to revise this traditional estimate after the discovery of manuscripts of Shams's *Discourses* (*Maqālāt*). Despite the title, the work is not a set of speeches, but a rambling memoir, dictated in bits and snatches to Shams's or Rumi's disciples. The critical edition of the Persian original was published only in 1990, and the first English translation appeared only in 2004.[46] Contrary to the old view, Shams had a solid legal education and made his living humbly as a primary-school teacher who, it seems, had a gift for teaching children how to memorize the Qur'an.[47] While a Sufi, he was deeply critical of certain famous Sufis of the past, such as Bāyezīd Bistāmī, whose drunken ecstasies led to unlawful behavior. That is what lies behind Shams's initial test question to Rumi.[48] Shams had a deep devotion to the Prophet Muhammad, which he expressed in terms often shocking to traditional Muslim piety: "I do not revere the Qur'an because God spoke it. I revere it because it came out of Mohammad's mouth."[49] Shams's Muhammad is Muhammad the mystic: "Following Muhammad is that he went on the *mi'raj* [i.e., the mystical journey through the seven heavens]—you also should go in his tracks."[50] While learned, Shams was deeply critical of religious learning as a career tool:

> The reason these people study in the *madrasahs* is, they think, "We'll become tutors, we'll run *madrasahs*." They say, "Good deeds—one

must act beautifully!" They talk of such things in these assemblies so that they can get positions. Why do you study knowledge for the sake of worldly mouthfuls? This rope [of knowledge] is for people to come out of the well, not for them to go from this well into that well. You must bind yourself to knowing this: "Who am I? What substance am I? Why have I come? Where am I going? Whence is my root? At this time what am I doing? Toward what have I turned my face?"[51]

For Shams, religious knowledge must never be about empty words and mindless repetition of others' teachings. It had to be lived out, embodied. In one iconoclastic formulation, Shams insisted: "The meaning of the Book of God is not the text; it is the man who guides. He is the Book of God, he is its verses, he is scripture."[52]

Shams became a lightning rod, sparking fierce criticism from Rumi's disciples and congregation. He received threats, perhaps even death threats. Without warning he left town. Desperate, Rumi sent his son Sultan Valad to track down the old dervish. Sultan Valad found Shams in Damascus and cajoled him into returning to Konya. Shams was received back with celebration and effusive apologies from Rumi's inner circle. He even ended up marrying a woman from Rumi's extended household. But again he disappeared, never to return. What happened? No one knows for sure, but one thread within the hagiographic tradition claims that Shams was murdered by jealous disciples, the body thrown into a well, and that Rumi's son 'Alā al-Din was involved in the cover-up. The story seems to be groundless, a fanciful conspiracy theory. But one sees it repeated, even in modern scholarly accounts.[53] Whatever happened, Rumi was for a time deeply depressed, heartsick. He traveled to Damascus and elsewhere twice in search of Shams. Rumi finally resigned himself, sparking a breakthrough: "Since I'm him, for what do I search? I'm his mirror image and will speak myself."[54] Poems again began to pour forth. Rumi signed his poems not with his own name, but with Shams's.

Disciples and Friends

In the 1250s Rumi found a new source of mystical inspiration, a goldsmith named Salāh al-Din Faridun (d. 1258). Rumi's hagiographers tell the story of their meeting. One day Rumi was walking through the marketplace, past Salāh al-Din's workshop. Salāh, with his hammer, was busy tapping away, molding a gold piece. The hammer's rhythm caught Rumi's ear, and he broke into ecstatic dance, a whirling motion. Legend gives this as the origin of the ecstatic whirling dance for which the Mevlevi order would later earn its fame. The two may have known each other before this, because Salāh al-Din had been a leading disciple of Borhān al-Din. For the next few years Salāh al-Din served as Rumi's spiritual muse, much as Shams had. Rumi's spiritual friendship with Shams had set tongues to wagging. So did this one, but for different reasons. Shams, however gruff and iconoclastic, was at least learned, whereas Salāh al-Din was embarrassingly illiterate. Rumi fended off criticisms and defended Salāh al-Din's wisdom. Salāh al-Din's daughter ended up marrying Rumi's son Sultan Valad. One other key figure in Rumi's later years was his favorite student, Hosām al-Din Chelebi (d. 1284). Hosām served as Rumi's scribe, and it was to him and through him that Rumi dictated his mystical epic *Masnavi*.

Rumi had a knack for populist preaching and enjoyed strong support from the merchants and working classes. The religious elite chided him for his choice of disciples: "Wherever a tailor or a weaver or a greengrocer is, he will accept him!"[55] He was also courted by Konya's wealthy and ruling elite. Konya's second-in-command ("Parvāne"), Mo'in al-Din, counted himself as Rumi's disciple, and Rumi's surviving letters to him contain strong appeals on behalf of the poor. Politics then, as anytime, anywhere, could be fickle and ruthless, and Konya, which had Mongol armies on its doorstep, ended up as a Mongol satellite. Rumi was critical of the Parvāne's conduct. Once, when the Parvāne begged for advice, Rumi wrote back curtly: "If God's word and the sentences of the Prophet do not impress you, what shall I say?"[56]

Legacy

Rumi died on December 17, 1273. His funeral attracted huge crowds. Not only Muslims, but also Christians and Jews joined in the procession. Aflāki reports that the ceremony was ecumenical and included readings not only from the Qur'an but also from the Psalms, the Torah, and the Gospels. After Rumi's death, an elaborate mausoleum was constructed, the Green Dome, which still survives today. His more enduring legacy was the Mevlevi order. The term *Mevlevi* (the Turkish pronunciation of the Persian *Mowlavi*) simply means "my master" and refers to the title by which Rumi's disciples, both then and ever since, have called him. Rumi is venerated as the order's founder, but its flourishing and practical organization were due to his son's efforts. One last anecdote: Great *shaykhs* were expected to be great miracle workers. One of Rumi's disciples was asked what Rumi's greatest miracle was. His answer: that people of all faiths revered Rumi and treasured what he taught.[57]

LOVE'S ALCHEMY

In 1976 the American poet Robert Bly handed a friend of his, Coleman Barks, a copy of Rumi's lyrics. The translator, A. J. Arberry (1905–1969), had been a learned British Orientalist, a fine scholar of Persian, but no poet. Bly told Barks: "These poems need to be released from their cages."[58] And so over the next twenty years, Barks worked to unlock their power, starting with Arberry's and other scholars' technically precise but clunky translations, tinkering with them, refitting them into vibrant American free verse. In 1996 he compiled these "versions" (as he calls them), publishing them as *The Essential Rumi*.[59] The book, astonishingly, sold over 100,000 copies. Overnight, Rumi, a thirteenth-century Persian, became late-twentieth-century America's best-selling poet. Barks, who cannot read Persian, has faced criticism both from native speakers and from scholars. He has been chided for excising or downplaying the Qur'anic echoes and Islamic themes that pervade Rumi's poetry and for giving him a vague, "new age" feel.[60] Even so, Barks deserves credit for catapulting Rumi into the contemporary limelight. Translating any text is difficult. Translating poetry verges on the impossible since poets are so deeply, so inextricably, entrenched in the languages they speak. They are masters of compression and delight in exploiting the musicality of their native languages, the way words subtly echo with centuries of ancient voices, the way words subtly summon, especially when left half-spoken, vast palaces of feeling and labyrinths of meaning. As we come to Rumi the mystical poet, we must come aware of how much remains impossible to translate and how risky it is to interpret him if one's ear is not attuned both to his poetic and to his religious inheritances. So while sympathetic to Barks and other Rumi modernizers, I think it best to use Arberry's scholarly translations, even if they come off as "caged."

Divān-e Shams

Rumi was a staggeringly prolific poet. He composed over 60,000 lines of poetry, more than the collected output of Homer or Dante or Shakespeare. He authored two massive collections of mystical poetry. The first is *The Collected Poetry of Shams* (*Divān-e Shams*). It contains more than 3,000 poems. Most are *ghazals*, that is, brief love poems, roughly eight to ten lines, that extol, by turns, love's joy and love's anguish. Authors of *ghazals* traditionally wrote under pseudonyms. 'Attār, the Persian author of *Conference of the Birds*, was not the poet's real name, but a nickname that referred to his day job as a pharmacist.

This literary convention explains the title of Rumi's collection. Shams became Rumi's pen name. Rumi composed—or more precisely, dictated—these lyrics orally, spontaneously, often when swept up in mystical fervor. They were made to be recited aloud to the accompaniment of music and within the religious setting of the *samā'*. Rumi spoke of them as food to be eaten while hot:

> My poetry is like Egypt's bread—night passes over it,
>   and you can no longer eat it.
> Devour it the moment it is fresh, before the dust settles upon it.
> Its place is the warm climate of the heart;
>   in this world it dies of cold.[61]

We can do no more than touch on a scatter of themes from Rumi's oceanic output. Because his mystical theology comes to us (mostly) via poetry, his teaching defies system. While Rumi both knew and drew upon earlier Sufi theorists, his mystical theology is all the more evocative because it comes through the flash and clash of poetic image.

The Beloved

Love of God is Rumi's core theme, the gravitational center around which all his poetry revolves. As he once put it: "Love is the astrolabe of all we seek, / Whether you feel divine or earthly love, / Ultimately we're destined for above."[62] For Rumi, God—and God alone—deserves our whole heart. Since God alone is the Real, everything we love is a veil under which God at once hides and reveals himself. Rumi thus insists: "This is love: to fly to heaven, every moment to rend a hundred veils."[63] Rumi's poetry examines this love from every imaginable angle, in every imaginable mood. He is by turns ecstatic and depressed, panting with desire and anguished by absence, playful and tender, serious and stern, reserved and bawdy. Rumi has at his fingertips the stock images and motifs that love poets, no matter what culture, no matter what era, draw upon: roses and thorns, spring breezes and spring rains, wine and perfume, pining for nighttime and sighing for kisses, playful verbal sparring with the beloved and coquettish complaints over verbal slights. Rumi has the dizzying ability to move back and forth from human love to divine love, blending and blurring the two.

In many *ghazals*, Shams is the prism through which Rumi sees God's refracted presence and on whom Rumi lavishes love-drunk praises. Some commentators have, with some justice, compared Rumi's spiritualized love of Shams with Dante's spiritualized love of Beatrice. Some modern readers misread Rumi's works as paeans to gay love. Franklin Lewis, who has examined the issue at length, explains why such an interpretation is misguided:

Suggestions that the relationship between Shams and Rumi was a physical and homosexual one entirely misunderstand the context. Rumi, as a forty-year-old man engaged in ascetic practices and teaching Islamic law, to say nothing of his obsession with following the example of the Prophet, would not have submitted to the penetration of the sixty-year-old Shams, who was, in any case, like Rumi, committed to following the Prophet and opposed to the worship of God through human beauty. Rumi did employ the symbolism of homoerotic, or more properly, androgynous love, in his poems addressed to Shams as the divine beloved, but this merely adopts an already 300-year-old convention of the poetry of praise in Persian literature.[64]

What then was their relationship? Well, it was both like and very unlike that of a *shaykh* to a disciple. Rumi was already a mature spiritual master, with disciples of his own. But, as William Chittick has noted, Shams "did play the role of shaykh for Rumi in at least one important respect. He was the mirror in which Rumi contemplated God's Perfection."[65]

To see this theme of the Beloved, let us look at an extended example, *Divān* 1077. It opens with images and sentiments found in a thousand other love poems:

Each moment I catch from my bosom the scent of the Beloved;
    how should I not take my self every night into his bosom.
Last night I was in Love's garden; that desire ran into my head;
    his sun peeped out of my eye, so that the river began to flow.
Every laughing rose that springs from the bank of that river of love
    had escaped from the thorn of being....
Every tree and grass was a-dancing in the meadow.[66]

A garden, a rose, a lover's scent, trees dancing, grasses swaying—pretty conventional at first sight. But midway the poem takes an abrupt turn. Rumi announces that "our Cypress"—Shams—has appeared. Suddenly the whole garden goes mad, is "beside itself." Why? Because of Shams's burning presence: "Face like fire, wine like fire, love afire—all three delightful." At that point, the poem makes its mystical turn:

In the world of Divine Unity there is no room for number,
    but number exists of necessity in the world of five and four.
You may count a myriad of sweet apples in your hand;
    if you want to make one, squeeze them all together.
A myriad of grapes went forth from the veil of skin;

when skin no more remained, there remained the wine of
the Prince.
Without counting the letters, behold this speech of the heart:
unicolority.[67]

In our ordinary world—"the world of five and four"—there is manyness,
plurality; but not in the divine realm. Islam's solemn confession of faith—that
"there is no god but God"—means, according to traditional Islamic theology,
that "there is no real but Reality." That is why Rumi says that "in the world of
Divine Unity, there is no room for number." The oneness of God means—at
least, if one grasps reality rightly—the annihilation of manyness. Rumi invokes two examples here: sweet apples compressed and blended into the clear
sweetness of apple juice; grapes skinned and fermented into intoxicating wine.
This many-becoming-one-reality is refracted not only in nature—so too with
language. In the world of Divine Unity the many words the poet recites become
the unnumbered unspokenness of heart-speech. In that speech, the many-
colored universe becomes one color, "unicolority." It is important not to detach
the poem's mid-course mystical turn from its starting point—from "late night
in love's garden." Rumi is referring here, presumably, to the Sufi practice of
late-night prayer vigils or samā'. This mystical turn at the poem's center is
spurred not by abstract theological speculations on divine unity, but by the
heady experience of divine love. And—paradoxically—in the garden's darkness, Rumi sees "the sun," Shams, whose sunlight mirrors and focuses God's
light. This sunlight lies within Rumi's heart ("his sun peeped out of my eye").
The inward accent underlies and undercuts what seem stock images and
sentiments. Rumi opens another poem proclaiming, "Love is a rosegarden,"
but quickly adds that this is "an inward garden" whose fruit springs from the
"tree of poverty."[68] In still another poem, he calls out, "Come into the infinite
garden of the heart and behold its many sweet fruits!" but then abruptly ad-
monishes: "How long will you look at the form of the world's body? Return,
and behold its inward mysteries!"[69]

For Rumi, as for many Christian mystics, this intense experience of God's
love provided unique theological knowledge. We saw how Sufi treatises contrasted the mystic's inward experiential knowledge (ma'rifa) with the scholar's
knowledge of religious externals ('ilm). Rumi, despite his fine theological education, was often dismissive of scholarship: "Love resides not in science and
learning, scrolls and pages, whatever men chatter about, that way is not the
lover's way."[70] Love, Rumi insisted, offered it own course of study: "From Love
the soul learns a thousand manners of culture, such culture as cannot be found

from schools...The mind, though it be apprised of all the doctrines of the sects [of Islam], knows nothing and is bewildered by the doctrine of Love."[71] Love's knowledge requires self-emptying: "So long as you are desirous, know that this desire of yours is an idol; when you have become the beloved, after that there is no existence for the desirous."[72] Self-emptying thus ends in utter identification with the Beloved. Rumi sometimes drew upon Sufi technical vocabulary of stations and states. Rumi considered his own state that of the lover: "Someone asked: 'What is the state of a lover?' I answered: 'Don't ask what it means! The moment you become like me, you will see it. The moment He calls you, you will recite its tale.' "[73]

The Art of Turning

At the heart of Rumi's mystical practice was the Sufi ritual of *samā'*. *Samā'* was much more than music and dance. Rumi saw it as a carefully calibrated spiritual discipline, a method of contemplation and mystical prayer, a way of focusing mind and heart and body on God the Beloved. Listening to its music late at night inspired him, inspired those thousands of poems to gush forth. One of the finest scholars of Sufism, Annemarie Schimmel, has argued that *samā'* formed the spiritual axis of Rumi's poetry.[74] Those who read Rumi's poems in the original Persian can hear in their meter and rhyme echoes of the *samā'*—its rhythms, its drumbeats.[75] In some poems, Rumi speaks directly to the musicians; other times, he speaks of and even to their instruments.[76] But for Rumi, the true *samā'* is interior, the true music lies within:

> At the time of *samā'*, the Sufis hear another sound—
> from God's throne.
> You go ahead and listen to the (outer) form of the *samā'*,
> they have another ear.[77]

For Rumi, music awakens the heart: "*samā'* has become a window onto (God's) rosegarden"; through it "the ears and heart of lovers peer."[78] Rumi thus insists:

> What is the *samā'*? A message from those hidden within the heart.
> The heart—the stranger—finds peace in their missive.
> It is a wind which causes the branches of the intellect to blossom,
> a sound which opens the pores of existence.[79]

Rumi held theories about the origin and the mystical power of music akin to those of Hildegard. He speculated that all humanity had somehow been with Adam in Paradise and thus remembers, however faintly, the songs it had heard there; but in this present state, with humanity's mingling with the "earth of sorrow," music has become an up-and-down admixture of "treble and bass."[80] Still the music he and his fellow Sufis made and sang echo a larger cosmic music, the vast majestic turning of the celestial spheres.[81] He sees the whirling, circling dance performed during the Sufi *samā'* mirroring the vast turning of the cosmos around the gravitational force of God's love, for "love makes the millwheel of the heavens spin."[82] In the following *ghazal*, Rumi explores the symbolic resonances of this Sufi ritual of dance and spin:

> The wheel of heaven, with all its pomp and splendour,
>   circles around God like a mill,
> O my soul, circumambulate around such a Ka'aba;
>   beggar, circle about such a table.
> Travel like a ball around in His polo-field, . . . happy and helpless.
> Your knight and rook are circumambulating about the king,
>   even though you move from place to place on this
>   chessboard . . .
> Whoever circumambulates about the heart
>   becomes the soul of the world, heart-ravishing.
> The heart-forlorn becomes companion to the moth,
>   he circles about the tip of the candle,
> The mystic's soul circles about annihilation,
>   even as iron about a magnet,
> Because annihilation is true existence in his sight.[83]

Here, as so often, Rumi floods his verse with wildly diverse images: millstones and Kaaba, polo and chess, magnets and moths. Each has its own resonance. The turning of the millstone implies the hard grinding and harsh refining of the spiritual path.[84] The bouncing of the polo ball implies, as he says, both the joy of sport and the helplessness of our being knocked about by God. The chess moves of knight and rook imply that the heart of the game is to orient ourselves around God as king. The alignment of iron shards around a magnet imply the natural, irresistible force of God as our center. Rumi also invokes the deeply evocative Muslim ritual performed by pilgrims to Mecca, the solemn, majestic, *en masse* circumambulation of the Kaaba.[85] But this universe of circling has a mystical endpoint, a slow spiraling into the mystic state of "annihilation" (*fanā'*). Here Rumi appeals to a favorite image of a moth that spirals into a candle and burns itself up.[86] Mystic annihilation—that death of self—means, paradoxically, not eradication, but, as he says here, "true existence."

Ruby Mines, Ocean Pearls

Rumi saw life as a pilgrimage, a meandering, spiraling return to God:

> From God in the first place we sprang in the world;
>> to Him likewise we revert by revolving.
> Our cry is like the bell in the caravan,
>> or as thunder when the clouds travel the sky,
> Wayfarer, set not your heart upon a lodging-place,
>> coming weary at the time of attraction.[87]

But how does the spiritual wayfarer get past the fatigue? By "remembrance" (*dhikr*), that Sufi practice of ceaseless chanting of God's name. As Rumi remarks, "Remembrance makes people desire the journey"; "if you mention His Name in the depths of a well, He will make the well's depths the summit of paradise."[88] This invocation of God's name stirs the heart and fans its flames: "In the outside world, wind sets a tree in motion. In the inside, remembrance rustles the leaves of the heart's tree."[89]

Remembrance of God spurs the journey, but this requires not only movement toward God but also transfiguration of one's self. In one *ghazal*, Rumi introduces his favorite metaphors of transfiguration:

> When the drop departed from its homeland and returned,
>> it encountered a shell and became a pearl...
> And you—if you have no foot, choose to journey into yourself;
>> like a ruby-mine be receptive to an imprint from the sunbeams.
> Make a journey out of self into self, my master,
>> for by such a journey earth became a mine of gold.[90]

The journey to God is, as he says, a "journey out of self into self"; it moves inward. Rumi suggests here three metaphors for the transfigured self: the pearl, the ruby, and gold. To appreciate these and the network of associations they call to mind, let us take them one by one, in reverse order.

First, gold. Rumi stressed that the interior search led to interior riches: "The prophet of God said, 'Men are as mines'; the self is a mine of silver and gold and is truly full of gems...Discover yourself."[91] Yet this self-discovery requires painful self-transformation: "In quest of the philosopher's stone we are melting like copper."[92] Rumi speaks here and elsewhere of this spiritual transformation in terms of alchemy. Alchemy, of course, involved the arcane quest for a philosopher's stone by which one might transmute base metals into gold. Rumi insists, however, that it is God who transmutes our ordinary "copper" selves: "From myself I am copper, through you: gold."[93] Rumi also stresses that this purification burns. Gold comes out of the mine embedded in hard dark stone. It thus must suffer in a fiery furnace of love to become itself: the lover has "to live together with the fire in the midst of the furnace like gold."[94]

Second, the ruby. The ruby is famous for its dazzling reds. According to Middle Eastern folklore, sunlight is capable of transmuting ordinary stones into rubies.[95] That is why Rumi says in the *ghazal* above that "like a ruby-mine" one should "be receptive to an imprint from the sunbeams." Shams as the mirror of God's sunlight is like a magnifying glass "transmuting hearts of stone into precious rubies."[96] The ruby's red evokes others reds, blood and wine. It is thus lifeblood and intoxicant, and "were that ruby wine to bubble up at midnight, its lights would fill the heavens and the earth."[97]

Finally, the pearl. Pearls are gems from the sea. Rumi, to capture the immensity of the divine, routinely spoke of God as a vast ocean. Sometime he spoke, much as Evagrius had, of the mystic as a "torrent" of water flowing back to and disappearing into the ocean.[98] Other times he spoke of mystics as fish swimming in God's immensity.[99] But in the *ghazal* above, he plays on a different metaphor. He sees the mystic as a drop of water at the divine ocean's bottom, a drop that becomes encased in an oyster's shell, which, after long gestation, is transmuted into pearl. In another poem, Rumi has the Beloved speak: "You are a drop of my sea; why do you utter still? Become drowned, and fill the soul of the oyster shell with pearls."[100] In still another poem, the Beloved says: "I am wholly and completely within your heart, for the pearl of the heart was born of my ocean."[101] Rumi once used the pearl metaphor to denounce his own poems, their surface wordiness:

> Songs are spindrift on the face of the sea;
>   no pearl comes on the surface of the sea
> Yet know that the grace of the spindrift derives from the pearl,
>   the reflection of the reflection of whose gleam is upon us.[102]

FLUTE SONGS

Masnavi

The second great collection of Rumi's poetry is the *Masnavi* (or *Mathnawi*, as one often sees it transliterated). It is a sprawling six-volume epic poem, over 25,000 lines. The title means "couplets" and refers to the poem's rhyme scheme. Rhymed couplets are for Persian poetry what blank verse is for English, the vehicle of narrative. The *Masnavi* is a vast treasure trove of earthy fables, humorous parables, and exotic tales, a Sufi equivalent of the *Thousand and One Arabian Nights*. Few of its tales are original. Most are drawn not only from a backlog of Sufi lore, but also from the broader storehouse of Persian and Arabic literature, both secular and religious. Rumi's early English translator, Reynold Nicholson, once remarked that Rumi "borrows much but owes little; he makes his own everything that comes to hand."[103] A religious meaning lies beneath the "veil" of the winding, rambling tales he tells. As Rumi notes in the *Masnavi*'s early verses:

> "The loved one's secret's best kept veiled," I said,
>   "Listen to it in ecstasy instead,
> The lover's secret that's been kept concealed
>   Is best through tales of other loves revealed."[104]

Despite the poem's rambling narratives and intricate imagery, the message is always religious and often mystical. The *Masnavi* is numbered among Islam's greatest religious masterpieces. The fifteenth-century Persian poet Jāmī famously praised it, calling it "the Qur'an in the Persian language." Here again we can take no more than a couple of quick dips into its expansive ocean.

The Reed Flute

A routine subject of mystical literature is how we as human beings are capable of encountering God. Christian mystics typically explore this by meditating on Genesis 1:26, that human beings are made in God's image and likeness. A similar sort of meditation on the mystical roots of the human person appears in the famed opening verses of Rumi's *Masnavi*, the "Song of the Reed-Flute":

> Now listen to this reed flute's deep lament
>   About the heartache being apart has meant.
> "Since from the reed-bed they uprooted me
>   My song's expressed each human's agony
> A breast which separation's split in two
>   Is what I seek, to share this pain with you
> When kept from their true origin, all yearn
>   For union on the day they can return.
> Amongst the crowd, alone I mourn my fate,
>   With good and bad I've learnt to integrate,
> That we were friends each one was satisfied
>   But none sought out my secrets from inside;

My deepest secret's in this song I wail
>   But eyes and ears can't penetrate the veil:
Body and soul are joined to form one whole
>   But no one is allowed to see the soul.'
It's fire not just hot air the reed-flute's cry,
>   If you don't have this fire then you should die!
Love's fire is what makes every reed-flute pine,
>   Love's fervour thus lends potency to wine;
The reed consoles those forced to be apart,
>   Its notes will lift the veil upon your heart...
The few who hear the truths the reed has sung
>   Have lost their wits so they can speak this tongue...
While ordinary men on drops can thrive
>   A fish needs oceans daily to survive.[105]

The reed flute, or *ney*, that Rumi refers to here is the lead instrument used in the Sufi orchestra that performed the *sama'*. Here Rumi plays on obvious tidbits. First, a flute can only produce its melody if its bore is empty. Second, a flute sings not on its own, but because of something outside itself: the musician's breath. For Rumi, the reed flute symbolizes the human being. The connection is implied here, not stated. It appears explicitly in one of the *ghazals*:

A craftsman pulled a reed from the reedbed,
and cut holes in it, and called it a human being.
Since then, it's been wailing a tender agony
of parting, never mentioning the skill
that gave it life as a flute.[106]

For Rumi, human beings are like the reed flute. We are our true selves only if empty. Only then are we capable of beautiful music. Only then are we instruments in God's hands. His breath—or rather his fire, as Rumi says here—sounds the song. Playing the reed flute is an intimate act because the musician uses his lips, kisses it, so to speak. So too, by implication, the human being is played, is kissed, by God's lips. The melody is at once sweet and melancholy. The Anatolian flute was famous for its lonely haunting sound. For Rumi, its beautiful sadness is the beautiful sadness of the lover who longs for his absent beloved. The sad song of this flute-called-human-being springs from the experience of God's absence—though paradoxically, it is God's very breath that makes the song possible. Rumi says that the sweet tone of the reed flute comes from the fact it was harvested from sugar cane. In the same way, human beings have a sweetness that comes from their origins in God. Yet it is a melancholy sweetness—melancholy because of our separation from God. The reed's song evokes in its hearers—Rumi's fellow Sufis—the dizzying lifting of the veil of the heart, God's hiddenness within. It evokes drunkenness, bewilderment, ecstasy. Its song is life-giving water for those Sufi "fish" who need an ocean to survive in. The density of meanings in this passage, its echoes and evocations, is dazzling, and typical of Rumi.

The Shop of Unity

The "Song of the Reed Flute" is the doorway into the epic of the *Masnavi*. The poetry here is very different from the lyric intensity and deeply personal tone of the *Divān's ghazals*. The *Masnavi* is self-consciously didactic, a sort of madcap collection of homilies. On the surface, it is a disconnected scatter of folktales. Many are fables. Rumi delights in telling stories of parrots and peacocks, falcons and owls, ants and bees, gazelles who get trapped with idiotic donkeys, and mice who befriend frogs and lead camels by the nose ring.[107] He often starts a story, then in mid-stream breaks it off and starts another, only to return through roundabout ways back to the original. On occasion, he tells outrageously bawdy tales worthy of Chaucer and Boccaccio, for example, of a woman killed by having sex with a donkey.[108] As Rumi remarks, "My dirty jokes are not dirty jokes but instruction."[109] Of course, that is true of the whole work. There is always a moral—or rather, many morals—to his stories.

In this epic funhouse of mirrors, one finds tales of Sufis and meditations on Sufi spirituality. Sometimes he tells witty parables that satirize Sufi cuckolds and unmask Sufi pretenders.[110] He offers homilies on the need for a *shaykh* and reflections on mystical experience. Some of Rumi's Sufi contemporaries read the *Masnavi* as it was gradually being published and began giving it bad reviews:

> The *Masnavi* is lousy . . . There is no mention
> of theosophical investigations
> and the sublime mysteries towards which the saints make
> their steeds gallop,
> from the stations of asceticism to the passing away (*fanā'*),
> step by step to union with God,
> (It lacks) the explanation and definition of every station and stage
> so that by means of the wings a man of heart [= mystic] may
> soar.[111]

Rumi certainly knew his way around the standard treatises on Sufism, but he remarks that Noah (a prophet in the Islamic tradition) had lived some 900 years and preached God's mystical presence not by reading Sufi classics like Qusharyrī, but by reading the jeweled book of his heart.[112] What Rumi does discuss is venerable Sufis of the past. Two he returns to repeatedly are ones we saw earlier: Bistāmī, who in ecstasy scandalously proclaimed "Glory be to me!", and al-Hallāj, who just as scandalously proclaimed, "I am the Real." Meditating on these allowed him to meditate on *fanā'*. He defended al-Hallāj's ecstatic utterance.

> Asceticism is the labor of the sowing;
>   gnosis is the growth of the seed...
> The gnostic...is both the revealer of mysteries
>   and that which is revealed.
> When the Shaykh Hallāj said, "I am God"
>   and carried through to the end,
>   he throttled all the blind (skeptics).
> When a man's "I" is negated (and eliminated) from existence
>   then what remains? Consider, O denier.[113]

Yet, for Rumi, "annihilation" was more transmutation that disappearance. He compared al-Hallāj's proclaiming "I am the Real" to a piece of iron in a furnace proclaiming "I am fire." That fire-reddened iron challenges anyone who dares doubt the truth of its proclamation: "Test me! Touch me with your hand."[114]

Rumi also meditates on the prophets of the past, notably Jesus. Rumi's Jesus is the Jesus of the Muslim tradition: born of a virgin and renowned for healing the blind and deaf, walking on water, riding a donkey, and, as a child, turning clay pigeons into real ones.[115] Rumi plays on a tradition that Jesus apprenticed not as a carpenter, but as a dyer. Thus Rumi saw Jesus as an exemplar of Sufism, for he dyed hearts in his "dyer's vat" of "one-colouredness."[116] Rumi could even speak of Jesus in terms that his younger contemporary, Meister Eckhart, would have appreciated: "Every one of us has a Jesus within him, but until the pangs manifest in us our Jesus is not born."[117]

Rumi once joked that if he could say all that need be said, it would take forty camels to carry his *Masnavi*.[118] In a more serious moment, he spoke of his *Masnavi* in terms that echo the Qur'anic text that not even an ocean of ink could write God's self-revelation: "Even if all the forest should become pens and all the ocean ink, yet there is no hope of bringing the *Masnavi* to an end."[119] In the final volume, Rumi proclaimed: "Our *Masnavi* is the shop of Unity: anything that you see there except the One (God) is only an idol."[120] What does he mean? Rumi notes that in any Middle Eastern bazaar, one finds shops of all sorts, but each has its specialty items. Rumi's "shop" specializes in Divine Unity; that specialty unites all the rare and exotic stories that line its shelves. We have seen how Rumi and the broader Sufi tradition rooted the mystical experience in the doctrine of divine unity (*tawhīd*): that if God is the Real, then the mystic's existence must disappear. The *Masnavi* plays out the inverse side of this doctrine. If God is the Real, then the whole world must be the theater of his manifestations. The *Masnavi* is a "shop of Unity" in the sense that God's blazing singular light is allowed to refract in the beautiful and zany manyness of the everyday. What Rumi tries to show is how everyday things are the rainbow colors of God's unicolority. Rumi knew such things are hard to get across, but as he says in the *Masnavi*'s final line: "The speech in my heart comes from that auspicious quarter, for there is a window between heart and heart."[121]

MYSTIC AS PSEUDONYMOUS SILENCE

At the outset, I noted a commonplace claim, articulated by James, Underhill, and others: that mystics form a sort of worldwide confraternity, that the mystical experience is the same worldwide. And Underhill specifically cited Rumi as an exemplar of this claim. Well, is it true? Rumi himself seems, at first glimpse, a good candidate and spokesman for the thesis. In the *Masnavi*, he proclaims: "Every prophet, every saint has his path, but as they return to God, all are one";[122] or again, "the jugs are poured into one basin. / Inasmuch as the object of praise Himself is not more than One, from this point of view, (all) religions are but one religion."[123] Such passages, I should note, must not be pushed too far. Rumi, while deeply tolerant and warmheartedly ecumenical in many ways, had no doubts about the absolute truth of Islam nor about the deep theological errors and moral infidelities of other religions. But the issue here is more specific: Is the mystical experience the same worldwide? I do not want to preempt our look in the next chapter at the Buddhist experience, but let us try to bring a few things together, at least in some preliminary ways. I should caution, first, that we have looked only at Rumi and only at a few tidbits of his voluminous output. The Sufi mystical tradition is vast and varied, as wide-ranging and complex as the Christian mystical tradition. So we must be modest. Rumi's approach, while brilliant and striking, is only one. It highlights some features of Sufism and ignores others. Rumi's personality and mystical theology differ from those of other Sufis, whether the flamboyant martyr al-Hallāj, or the moderate and thoughtful al-Ghazālī, or the boldly speculative Ibn 'Arabī. I should also add that those who claim that mysticism is the same worldwide typically do so by laying texts from different mystics alongside one another in ways oblivious to context. That has not been the approach here.

I have tried, within this all-too-brief study, to situate Rumi in context, or rather in his many contexts, historical and biographical, literary and religious.

And so the question: What does the Sufi mystical tradition and Rumi's own mysticism illuminate about mysticism in a general sense? Or, more modestly, can one track convergences between Sufism and Christian mysticism? Well, there are convergences, often striking ones. Both traditions claim that God can be experienced, that that the experience of God provides gnosis, and that that gives the mystic—the gnostic—a measure of legitimate theological expertise. In Rumi's case—as in Bernard of Clairvaux's—that experiential knowledge comes from a heart-ravishing experience of God's love. Rumi, like Bernard, blended the mystical and the erotic in often flamboyant ways. Sufism shares with Christian mysticism a fondness for mystical map-making. Not all Christian mystics make much of such things; and, as we saw, Rumi knew of Sufi maps, but made little use of them. The Sufi tradition wedded the mystical with the ascetic. Sufis, much like Evagrius and the desert fathers, valued ascetic practices of fasting and vigils and unceasing prayer. Of course, Sufis knew Christian monks firsthand and disagreed with elements of Christian asceticism. Rumi and many other Sufis were not celibates, but married men with families and all the practical responsibilities that came with being husbands and fathers. Finally, the Sufi tradition in general and Rumi in particular deeply valued the ecstatic and embraced the often scandalous language of intoxication.

This case study also has highlighted features of mysticism too often ignored. Western theories about mysticism tend to go hand in hand with Western individualism—a linkage cemented by William James's individualist philosophy of religion. Sufism in general and Rumi in particular helps highlight that mysticism can be a communal enterprise. This communal character is obvious in the practices and structure of Sufi orders. Sufi mysticism is often a ritualized mysticism, or at least takes place within a ritual setting. This is obvious in Rumi's case, with his emphasis on samā'—with its recitations of the Qur'an, its prayers and poems, its music and dance. Modern theoreticians of mysticism have too often ignored or denied the role of scripture and of doctrine. We saw that ignoring or denying such fundamentals grossly distorts Christian mysticism. So too with Rumi and the whole Sufi tradition. If one cuts them off from the Qur'an and the broader Islamic theological tradition, one renders their religious experience unintelligible.

Christian mystical theologians tend to speak in terms of a mystic's "union" with God. Sufis, as we saw, sometimes adopted this same terminology in their systematic works. Rumi gives the impression—mainly, through his choice of metaphors—that he too worked from such a conception. But that impression is misleading. He, in the end, found such language not only imprecise, but deeply flawed. "Union" implies two existents, God and the mystic. This leads, in Rumi's view, to a miguided conception of the spiritual life: "In God's presence two I's cannot be contained. You say 'I' and He says 'I': either you die before Him, or He will die before you, so that duality may not remain."[124] Sufism's favored self-understanding was *fanā'*, annihilation, and that self-understanding was rooted in, oriented by, and flowed from Islam's confession of faith and its theological commitment to God's oneness. Rumi approached the issue not so much with theological abstractions as with poetic images. His poems display a kaleidoscope of metaphors to describe this annihilation in God. Some images imply eradication of the self (e.g., a moth consumed in a candle, a water-drop engulfed in an ocean); others imply transfiguration (e.g., the alchemical transmutation of copper into gold, of hard stone into sun-wrought rubies, of ocean droplets into gleaming pearl).

Western theoreticians, from William James onward, have tended to conceive of mysticism in experiential, psychological terms, and the gold standard for judging a mystic's authenticity has been autobiography. Sufism certainly stresses the experiential. So did Rumi. But how we well do know Rumi's experience? Remember that our access to his experience comes to us mainly through poems. His poems, especially the *ghazals* in the *Divān*, do use the first person. But we should not be naive. It is a freshman mistake to presume that the "I" of the poem is the "I" of the poet, that a poem is autobiography, pure and simple. A poem's speaker can never be presumed to be identical with the poet. That is obvious when one reads a poet-playwright such as Shakespeare. Poetry is full of artifice, not only the artifice of meter and rhyme, of metaphor and allusion, but also the artifice of voice and tone. Poets are masters of masks. Modern poets, from Ezra Pound and T. S. Eliot to Richard Howard and Norman Dubie, self-consciously write *persona* poems and speak from behind historical masks. Even self-consciously "confessional" poets such as Robert Lowell and Sylvia Plath have their masks. I am not denying that poems reflect a poet's experience in some ways. But there are no easy equations.

What about Rumi? He was unquestionably a profound mystic. But he was also a highly accomplished poet, utterly at ease with the intricate and subtle traditions of Persian and Arabic poetry, both secular and religious. He also, quite consciously, wrote under a mask. Shams was his pseudonym. We should not ignore the obvious: Rumi's mysticism was self-consciously pseudonymous, as paradoxical as that sounds. Shams may have been a favorite mask, but it was not his only one. Rumi consciously drew on the Sufi distinction between the states of separation and union. As Rumi complains, his poems are the expression of separation, not union; in union, one is speechless: "To utter words concerning Him is to shut the window through which He reveals himself: the very act of expression is the concealment of Him."[125] And so Rumi signs some poems not with his own name nor with Shams's, but with another pseudonym: *Khāmush*, "Silence!"[126] Rumi's poems, however one judges the mystical experiences that underlie them, were not words to be read. They were recited to Sufi disciples who had gathered around him and who lost themselves in the whirling dance of the *samā'*. Rumi as *shaykh* sought to lead them into the ineffable silence of God, into an experience of the speech-defying union of annihilation; and so again and again, at poem's end, he insisted to himself and his hearers that words must drop away:

> Be silent, be bewildered as silent ones,
>   so that He may say to you, "My silent and bewildered one!"[127]

9

Mysticism and Zen Buddhism: Dōgen

In 1967, a year before his death, Thomas Merton published a popular collection of essays entitled *Mystics and Zen Masters*. The essays ranged widely, from English mystics such as Julian of Norwich to Russians such as Seraphin of Sarov, from Orthodox hesychasts such as Gregory Palamas to Protestant ecstatics such as the Shakers. Half the book steps beyond Christian mysticism to include essays on classical Chinese figures such as Lao Tzu and Kung Tzu (or Confucius, as he is known in the West) and on other Eastern topics. This religious diversity was no hodgepodge in Merton's mind:

> The great contemplative traditions of East and West, while differing sometimes quite radically in their formulation of their aims and in their understanding of their methods, agree in thinking that by spiritual disciplines a man can radically change his life and attain to a deeper meaning, a more perfect integration, a more complete fulfillment, a more total liberty of the spirit . . . And they agree that a certain "purification" of the will and intelligence can open man's spirit to a higher and more illuminated understanding of the meaning and purpose of life, or indeed of the very nature of Being itself.[1]

The heart of Merton's book is three essays on Zen Buddhism, including the title essay. For Merton, mystics and Zen masters go together.

Zen as Merton knew it—and as much of the Western world knew it—came almost entirely from the pen of one man, Daisetz Teitaro Suzuki (1870–1966). As a young man, Suzuki was a disciple of Zen master Shaku Sōen (1859–1919). Sōen had been invited to come to the United States in 1893 for the World Parliament of Religions. In 1896 he summoned Suzuki to join him in the United States to serve as a translator. Suzuki stayed on, first working for Paul Carus of Open Court Publishing. In 1911 he married an American, Beatrice Lane. In the 1920s he began his teaching career at Otani University in Japan, where he and his wife founded the Eastern Buddhist Society. He continued coming to the United States off and on, including during the war years and again in the 1950s when he lectured at Columbia University. He was a masterful and prolific author, wonderfully at ease in English. His best-known works—*Introduction to Zen Buddhism*, the three-volume *Essays on Zen Buddhism*, and *Mysticism: Christian and Buddhist*—portray Zen in striking terms:

> There are in Zen no sacred books or dogmatic tenets, nor are there any symbolic formulae through which an access might be gained into the signification of Zen. If I am asked, then, what Zen teaches, I would answer Zen teaches nothing . . . We may say that Christianity is monotheistic and [Hindu] Vedanta pantheistic; but we cannot make a similar assertion about Zen. Zen is neither monotheistic nor pantheistic; Zen defies all such designations. Hence there is no object in Zen upon which to fix the thought. Zen is a wafting cloud in the sky . . . Zen wants to have one's mind free and unobstructed; even the idea of oneness and allness is a stumbling block and a strangling snare which threatens the original freedom of the spirit.[2]

Suzuki sometimes spoke of Zen as mysticism, even as a superior form because it was "more daringly concrete in its paradoxes than other mysticisms."[3] More often, he regaled his American readers with Zen's mind-teasing kōans ("What is the sound of one hand clapping?"), with its iconoclastic one-liners ("If you meet the Buddha on the road, kill him"), and with its flamboyant holy men. Such descriptions caught the imagination of a generation of American intellectuals, most famously the 1950s Beat poets and writers Jack Kerouac, Allen Ginsberg, and Gary Snyder, who admired the intuitive, iconoclastic, and nonconformist side of Zen. Suzuki's Zen seemed more an outlook on life than a religion. As Suzuki presented it, Zen's religious moorings—its monasteries, rituals, sects, hierarchies, hagiographies, and exacting meditation styles—were trappings, not its core.

Back to Merton: The title essay of *Mystics and Zen Masters* is devoted mostly to reviewing a new book Merton had been reading, Heinrich Dumoulin's *History of Zen Buddhism*.[4] Dumoulin (1905–1995) was a German Jesuit who spent his career in Japan, teaching philosophy and history of religions at Sophia University in Tokyo. Dumoulin's Zen looked very different from the Zen Merton had learned from Suzuki. It had a history. It also had figures Merton had never seen. One caught his eye: Zen master Eihei Dōgen (1200–1254).[5] Merton had never heard of Dōgen for a reason: Merton's Zen was Suzuki's, and Suzuki's Zen was decidedly sectarian, unbeknownst to Merton and other Western readers.[6] Dōgen was the founder of the Sōtō sect of Zen Buddhism, rival of Suzuki's Rinzai sect. Over the last generation, this once little-known figure has become, in the West, Zen's most written-about. Most of Dōgen's voluminous and brilliant writings have now been translated into English, accompanied by a rapidly growing body of learned commentaries and penetrating historical-critical studies. The English-speaking world is catching up on what Japanese philosophers and scholars have argued for nearly a century: that Dōgen is Japan's finest religious thinker, one who probed the nature of religious experience with philosophic profundity and startling poetic originality.

In this chapter, I would like to explore the issue of mystics and Zen masters by examining the life and writings of Dōgen. For many readers, Dōgen will be as new to them as it was to Merton. At the chapter's end, I will try and take up the question of how the language of mysticism is and is not appropriate to Zen. For the moment, I simply ask readers to take in (and hopefully enjoy) the story and to note here and there where things that bear uncanny resemblances to what we have seen earlier leap off the page. I do not think it an accident that Merton was haunted by Zen, convinced that it illumined his own contemplative quest.

ZEN CARICATURE

Over the centuries, Zen has inspired great works of art: calligraphy, landscape painting, poetry, architecture, even gardening. But one of its most brilliant art forms is caricature. Zen is respectfully irreverent, and it expresses veneration of its holy men by teasing and caricaturing them. Zen, I realize, is unfamiliar to many readers. So I need to spend a few pages creating a caricature of Zen itself. These are background items readers need to know if they hope to appreciate something of the Buddhist tradition that Dōgen loved and moved in, meditated on and quibbled with, joked about and argued over.

Zen and Zazen

The term *zen*, as Dōgen once noted, is short for *zazen*, which means "seated meditation."[7] Zen is thus the "meditation school" of Buddhism. Its origins lie in China. So one speaks of "Ch'an Buddhism" when speaking of its earlier Chinese forms and "Zen Buddhism" when speaking of its later Japanese forms. Most Westerners imagine that meditation is the heart of all forms of Buddhism, and it is, to some degree. But the specifics of practice vary considerably, and Buddhist life includes much else, including intricate (and sometimes esoteric) ritual practices, the chanting of sacred scriptures, doctrinal studies, and a rich complex of ethical precepts and ascetic disciplines. Early Japanese critics branded Zen as "single-practice Buddhism"—and it is, in a sense.[8] The fierce centrality that Zen pioneers such as Dōgen gave to zazen practice made them stand out from the wider Buddhist tradition of their time.

The Flower Sermon

Zen traces its origins back to the Buddha himself, back to his legendary "flower sermon." To use Dōgen's words: "Once Śakyamuni Buddha, on Vulture Peak in India, in the midst of a vast assembly of beings, held up an udumbara flower and winked." Buddha himself said nothing. The flower itself was the sermon. At this, a disciple named "Venerable Mahākāśyapa smiled. Then Śakyamuni Buddha said, 'I have the treasury of the true dharma eye, the inconceivable mind of nirvāna. This I entrust to Mahākāśyapa.' "[9] And so Buddha passed on his entire teaching (or dharma), in an instant, without words. Mahākāśyapa had his eye opened and signaled his understanding without words, with a simple smile. This story is an icon for the Zen tradition, that Buddha's dharma was and is passed master to disciple, wordlessly, mind to mind. For centuries Zen practitioners have presumed this founding legend was historical, but the story was coined, it seems, in medieval China, partly as a way for Ch'an to define itself and defend itself against rival Buddhist schools. The earliest known version appears only in 1036 in an encyclopedic Ch'an history.[10]

Bodhidharma

In Zen lore, the one who brought this teaching to China was Bodhidharma (late fifth to early sixth century), third son of an Indian prince. Zen tradition numbers him as the twenty-eighth Indian patriarch, that is, twenty-eight generations of passing on the Buddha-dharma from master to disciple. He is also numbered as the first Chinese patriarch.[11] He is remembered in the Ch'an and Zen traditions on several counts. First, he is remembered for meditating nine years, facing the wall of the cave where he lived. This wall-gazing meditation would become a hallmark of Ch'an and Zen practice. Second, his name is associated with a classic summary of Ch'an teaching: "A special transmission outside the scriptures; / Without depending on words and letters; / Pointing directly to the human mind / Seeing one's nature and becoming a Buddha." This slogan helped Ch'an define itself over against other Buddhist schools who, at the time, were engulfed in learned scholastic disputations over this or that Buddhist *sūtra*. Ch'an was antischolastic and did not depend on "words and letters." Its truth was discoverable by meditative introspection ("pointing directly to the human mind") and inherent in every person ("seeing one's nature"). The real shock is the first phrase: that Ch'an was, at least in principle, independent of the vast canon of Buddhist scriptures. Ch'an and Zen traditions have long presumed that this summary reflected Bodhidharma's own teaching, but twentieth-century scholars have shown that this summary, especially its controversial first phrase, appeared only in 1108— quite late in the developing Ch'an orthodoxy.[12]

Transmission of the Lamp

Christians use the term "apostolic tradition" as a catchphrase to describe how the message of Jesus and his apostles was and is faithfully and accurately passed from generation to generation. A similar concern pervades the Ch'an and Zen traditions. Ch'an Buddhists of medieval China were deeply—even obsessively—concerned about genealogy, about charting a lineal transmission of the Buddha dharma from generation to generation, from master to disciple. Ch'an Buddhists needed some way to certify authenticity and orthodoxy and did so by claims of spiritual genealogy. The writings that trace these genealogies are voluminous historical anthologies known as "transmission of the lamp" records, for example, the thirty-volume *Transmission of the Lamp in the Ching-te Era (Ching-te ch'uan-teng lu)*, compiled in 1004 by Ch'an monk Tao-yüan. The title plays on a classic Buddhist image: that the Buddha's teaching is passed on the way a single flame is passed from lamp to lamp.

That literature traces a lineal spiritual descent from Buddha to Mahākā-śyapa to the remaining Indian patriarchs, then to Bodhidharma and his Chinese heir, Hui-k'o, and so on, down to Hui-neng (638–713), the Sixth Patriarch. It then charts how lineages spread out and flowered over the centuries, coalescing into the so-called Five Houses. Two of these five are relevant here. One is the school of Ch'an master Lin-chi I-hsuan (d. 866). It made its way to Japan via Zen master Eisai (1141–1215) and became known as the Rinzai sect of Zen.

A second is the school of Ts'ao-tung, named after two Ch'an masters, Ts'ao-shan Pen-chin (840–901) and Tung-shan Liang-chieh (807–869).[13] This school made its way to Japan via Dōgen and became known as the Sōtō sect of Zen.

Modern understanding of Ch'an history has been revolutionized by the discovery of a huge library of Buddhist texts at Tun-huang in 1900, an archeological breakthrough that was for Buddhism what the 1945 discovery of the Dead Sea Scrolls was for Judaism and Christianity. In light of these new texts and of modern historical methodologies, scholars warn that one must read transmission-of-the-lamp histories and their genealogies with a critical eye, that the lineages and the stories they present are, in a number of cases, later inventions that gloss over ambiguities, conflicts, and gaps in the historical record. These accounts sometimes read later realities and later rivalries back into earlier eras and often romanticize, even fabricate, the past.[14] The actual teachings of individual schools shifted in dramatic ways over the centuries, and the exchange between lineages was complex. Because Ch'an monasteries enjoyed government patronage and oversight (much as medieval Christian monasteries did), one must always be alert to beneath-the-surface political dynamics. Those dynamics of patronage were equally at play (though with a different chemistry) when Ch'an lineages moved from Sung China to Kamakura Japan.

Kōans

Ch'an and Zen Buddhists are famed storytellers, and their best-known stories are the enigmatic kōans.[15] Typically kōans are short, often humorous, dialogues between a Ch'an master and his disciple or, on occasion, between two masters. Some sound like nonsense. For example, when a monk once asked Master Chao-chou (778–897), "What is the meaning of Bodhidharma's coming to China?" he answered, "The oak tree in the garden."[16] Another example: Once a monk asked Master Tung-shan (d. 900), "What is Buddha?" Tung-shan's reply: "Three pounds of flax."[17] Some kōans are shockingly irreverent. For example, when a monk once asked Yün-mei (864–949) the same question, "What is Buddha?" Yün-mei said: "A dried piece of shit."[18] Kōans recount not just shocking words. Once Master Nan-chüan (748–834) saw two factions in the monastery arguing over a cat. So he grabbed the cat and said, "If you can give an answer, you will save the cat. If not, I will kill it." Neither could answer, and so he cut it in two.[19] We find a story like this shocking, but Buddhists, who vow to save all sentient beings, find such behavior from a reputed holy man deeply disturbing. However bizarre such stories appear to outsiders, those within the tradition claim the stories are perfectly reasonable and intelligible, that they manifest enlightened behavior and states of mind.

The Japanese word *kōan* comes from the Chinese word *kung-an*, a judicial term meaning "public case" and, by extension, a "public record" or judgment on a case. Kōans were originally stories that appeared in the larger transmission-of-the-lamp literature or in collections of sayings of famous masters. They were singled out and became "public cases" discussed between masters and monks. Ch'an masters were asked to render formal judgment on them, much as a judge does on a case. In time, classic cases, together with later masters' commentaries and judgments, were compiled into anthologies. Two famous ones were *The Blue Cliff Record* (*Pi-yen lu*; Japanese: *Hekiganroku*), compiled by Yüan-wu K'o-ch'in (1063–1135), and *The Gateless Gate* (*Wu-men kuan*; Japanese: *Mumonkan*), compiled by Dōgen's contemporary, Wu-men Hui-k'ai (1183–1260).

Kōans came to be seen not simply as *reflections* of how enlightened masters spoke and acted; they came to be used as *tools* for provoking enlightenment. The one credited with this innovation is Ta-hui Tsung-kao (1089–1163), a Ch'an master of the Lin-chi school. He made kōans the focus of monks' meditation, what was called "the Ch'an of contemplating words" (*k'an-hua ch'an*; Japanese: *kanna-zen*). Over the centuries, this kōan-introspection meditation underwent elaborate codification in the Rinzai tradition. In this tradition—and this is the one best-known in the West, thanks to D. T. Suzuki—kōans came to be seen as psychological devices designed to frustrate rational analysis. As Cheng-feng, a thirteenth-century master, once put it, cases "such as 'the oak tree in the courtyard,' 'three pounds of flax,' and 'a dried piece of shit' which are impenetrable to the intellect, were devised and given to people to bore into. This is like having to penetrate a silver mountain or a steel wall."[20] Kōans were (and are) used to provoke a spiritual crisis (or "great doubt") in the meditator in hopes of sparking a breakthrough, a sudden enlightenment experience (*satori*). The editor of *The Gateless Gate* claims that if you concentrate on a kōan with all your might, then:

> You will go hand in hand with the successive patriarchs, entangling your eyebrows with theirs, seeing with the same eyes, hearing with the same ears... Carry [the kōan] continuously day and night... It will be just as if you swallowed a red-hot iron ball, which you cannot spit out even if you try. All the illusory ideas and delusive thoughts accumulated up to the present will be exterminated, and when the time comes, internal and external will be spontaneously united...
> Then all of a sudden an explosive conversion will occur, and you will astonish the heavens and shake the earth.[21]

One sometimes reads that Dōgen's Ts'ao-tung/Sōtō lineage did not use kōans. That is simply not true. Dōgen personally compiled a 300-case kōan anthology, and his writings teem with kōan commentaries. Dōgen did disagree with Ta-hui, sometimes sharply, and the kōan-introspection method that Ta-hui recommended was not Dōgen's approach. But kōans form a central thread in Dōgen's literary genius and spirituality.

This caricature of Zen—dashed off with a few quick, crude brushstrokes—must suffice for background. For life-size portraits of Zen and its history, follow up with the scholarly works recommended in the bibliography. Let us now turn to Dōgen himself.

DROPPING AWAY BODY-MIND

The main lines of Dōgen's career can be charted from autobiographical remarks scattered through his own writings, from reminiscences of early disciples, and from the precise ways he and his disciples dated his writings. Over the centuries, scholars within the Sōtō Zen school drew on these to create learned but often uncritical hagiographies that masked ambiguities and shifts of mind, that glossed over tense political undercurrents (both secular and religious), and that read later doctrines and later debates back into earlier events. With Dōgen, as with so many other religious figures, both East and West, sorting out biography from the hagiographic haze is a formidable (and ongoing) task.[22]

Dōgen was born in Kyoto, then Japan's capital and imperial seat. He was an aristocrat by birth: his father was a high government official, and his mother was a Fujiwara, a member of one of Japan's ruling families. Dōgen received a traditional elite education, mastering Chinese and its canon of literary classics. He faced tragedy early. His father died when he was two, and his mother, when he was seven. When he was twelve, a relative offered to train him for a political career at the imperial court. He declined and became a monk, setting off for Mt. Hiei, then the spiritual center of Japanese Buddhism. In the early thirteenth century, the Buddhist establishment was dominated by the Tendai sect, which offered an eclectic blend of Buddhist doctrine and esoteric rites. It also positioned itself as a guardian of Buddhist orthodoxy around the country, overseeing appointments at temples and monasteries and suppressing new sects, either through secular authorities or, on occasion, with its own armed monastic militias. Dōgen settled at Mt. Hiei and received tonsure as a monk at age thirteen. There he studied the canon of Buddhist scriptures (the *Tripitaka*) as well as the *Lotus Sūtra*, a favorite in Tendai circles.

The Great Doubt

As a young man, Dōgen confronted what seemed an inscrutable intellectual contradiction, one at the very heart of Buddhism. Traditional Tendai doctrine taught that every human being possesses an innate Buddha nature. This "original enlightenment" (*hongaku*), as it was called, was distinguished from the "acquired enlightenment" (*shikaku*), which the Buddha experienced and preached.[23] To Dōgen, this seemed a contradiction: if we are already enlightened, if we already possess enlightened Buddha-nature, then "why have the buddhas of all ages had to awaken the longing for and seek enlightenment by engaging in ascetic practice?"[24] The question haunted Dōgen. It fueled his quest both intellectually and spiritually—not unlike the way that the question "*Unde malum?*" (Where does evil come from?) haunted the young Augustine. Hagiographic sources claim that this question led Dōgen to abandon Mt. Hiei and seek guidance elsewhere. Dating his "great doubt" this early seems hard to prove, but it certainly appears as a burning issue from his earliest writings.

Zen Teachers

One brand of Zen had recently arrived on Japan's shores, brought back from China by the Tendai priest-turned-Zen master Eisai (1141–1215). Eisai, while on pilgrimage in China, received dharma transmission from the Lin-chi school and so is counted as founder of its Japanese counterpart, the Rinzai sect. Like other religious innovators of his time, such as Shinran and Nichiren, Eisai faced opposition from the Tendai establishment. His temple was shut down for a few years, from 1194 to 1200, but he wrote a tract defending the venerable antiquity of his teachings and methods and argued how they would help the nation's well-being. His propaganda campaign succeeded, and he was allowed to set up the first Zen temple in Kyoto, the Kenninji. Eisai's successor was Myōzen (1185–1225), and under Myōzen, the young Dōgen first studied Zen at Kenninji for some six years, from 1217 to 1223. Dōgen deeply admired his old teacher: "Priest Myōzen alone, as a senior disciple of ancestor Eisai, correctly transmitted the unsurpassable Buddha-dharma; no one can be compared to him."[25]

Pilgrimage to China

In 1223 Dōgen accompanied Myōzen on a pilgrimage to China. Sea-travel in those days could be hazardous. This journey "to the flourishing kingdom of Sung China" required, as Dōgen remarked, "a voyage of many miles, during which I entrusted my phantom body to the billowing waves."[26] Dōgen spent four decisive years in China, from the spring of 1223 to the fall of 1227. For two years he wandered and "visited masters on both sides of the Zhe River, and heard the teaching of the Five Schools."[27] This itinerancy stemmed from his being denied full access to training because local Ch'an monasteries did not initially accept his Japanese monastic credentials.[28] Only in 1225 did Dōgen gain full admittance at one of the major centers, the monastery on Mount T'ien-t'ung. Its new abbot, Ju-ching (1163–1228), a Ch'an master of the Ts'ao-tung line, welcomed him and, according to Dōgen, granted him ready access to the abbot's quarters, an unusual privilege for a newcomer. Dōgen claims in an autobiographical memoir (the *Hōkyōki*) that, though still a novice, he impressed the Ch'an master, who told him: "Although you're still young, there is a look of deep accomplishment in your face. It will be good for you to live in a deep mountain or quiet valley so that you can slowly gestate in the womb of buddha ancestors. Then you will certainly arrive at the place of enlightenment of the ancient sages."[29] Ju-ching linked his teachings with venerable antiquity, with the "buddha ancestors in India and China." His instruction touched something profound in Dōgen as he listened: "I was so moved that I cried until the lapel of my robe became soaked with tears."[30] During this apprenticeship under Ju-ching, Dōgen's old friend and teacher Myōzen died.

Enlightenment

At Mount T'ien-t'ung, Dōgen experienced enlightenment. A narrative account appears only in later hagiographic sources and as such must be viewed guardedly. Here is the classic story: Ju-ching reportedly held monks to a rigorous regimen, practicing meditation for long hours, day and night. In 1225, during the annual summer retreat, Dōgen was up late meditating in the monk's hall. Ju-ching entered and scolded a nearby monk whom he found sleeping: "To study Zen is to drop off body-mind. Why are you engaged in single-minded seated slumber rather than single-minded seated meditation?"[31] The words, though addressed to another, shook Dōgen to the core, and he experienced a sudden breakthrough, an enlightenment that shattered everything. Brimming with joy, he rose, left the meditation hall, lit incense, and gave thanks to the Buddha. He then sought out Ju-ching, who interviewed him, probing the depth of the awakening and later ratifying its authenticity.

Dōgen himself, in his surviving writings, does not tell this story, but the catchphrase that sparked his awakening—"dropping off body-mind" (*shinjin datsuraku*)—appears repeatedly in his writings.[32] He does allude to his experience of awakening in one of his earliest essays, remarking: "Finally, I practiced under Zen master Ju-ching at Mount T'ai-pai [= Mount T'ien-t'ung], and there I resolved the one great matter of Zen practice for my entire life."[33] Years later, Dōgen spoke of the interview with Ju-ching after his breakthrough: "Upon this occasion he transmitted dharma, finger to finger, face to face, and said to me, 'The dharma gate of face-to-face transmission from buddha to buddha, ancestor to ancestor, is realized now.'"[34] Dōgen received formal cer-tification of dharma-transmission (shisho) from Ju-ching. He stayed on two more years at Mount T'ien-t'ung, leaving soon after Ju-ching's death.

Return to Japan

In October 1227 Dōgen sailed back to Japan. He returned, as he famously said, "empty-handed"—without the usual tourist paraphernalia of relics and icons. He himself had been transformed to his very core: "Recently I returned to my homeland with empty hands. And so this mountain monk [as Dōgen often referred to himself] has no Buddha Dharma. Trusting fate, I just spend my time. Morning after morning, the sun rises in the east. Evening after evening, the moon sets in the west. The clouds disperse and mountain valleys are still."[35] Traditional accounts have claimed that within weeks of his arrival, in 1227, he wrote a brilliant essay, Recommending Zazen to All People (Fukanza-zengi), that proclaimed his new and revolutionary view of Buddhism. That clear-cut inauguration to his ministry does not seem to have been the case. The earliest surviving version dates from some six years later.[36] We simply do not know much about this key transition in Dōgen's career other than that he returned, quietly it seems, to his former monastery at Kenninji.

In 1230 he moved—why, we are not sure—and set up residence in Fu-kakusa (just outside Kyoto) at An'yōin temple. During this early period, he authored the first of his great essays, Negotiating the Way (Bendōwa). In an au-tobiographical preface, he set out his deep-felt sense of mission:

> I came back to Japan with the hope of spreading the teaching and
> saving sentient beings—a heavy burden on my shoulders. However,
> I will put aside the intention of having the teaching prevail every-
> where until the occasion of a rising tide. I think of wandering about
> like a cloud or a water-weed, studying the wind of the ancient sages.
> Yet there may be true students who are not concerned with fame and
> gain and who allow their thought of enlightenment to guide them,
> and they may be confused by incapable teachers and obstructed
> from the correct understanding. Indulging in smug self-satisfaction,
> they may sink into the land of delusion for a long time. How can they

nourish the correct seed of wisdom (*prajña*) and have the opportunity to gain the way? If I am wandering about, which mountain or river can they call on? Because I feel concerned for them, I would like to record the standards of Zen monasteries which I personally saw and heard in Great Song [China] as well as the profound principle which has been transmitted by my master. I wish to leave for the students of the way the teaching of the buddha's house. This is indeed the essence.[37]

Note his accents: (1) shouldering a bodhisattva's "heavy burden" of "teaching and saving sentient beings"; (2) renouncing the carefree joys of enlightenment so to be available as a teacher (for "if I am wandering about, which mountain or river can [students] call on?"); and (3) writing. The writings Dōgen envisioned were to focus on two core matters: Ch'an monastic practices and the "profound principle . . . transmitted by my master."

This intense sense of mission soon took practical shape. In 1233 Dōgen opened the monastery of Kōshōji, just outside the modern city limits of Kyoto. It was Japan's second Zen temple (Eisai's Kenninji being the first). What struck contemporaries was its large Chinese-style Monks' Hall, where monks practiced zazen. This gave architectural prominence to Dōgen's central message of the virtues of zazen. At Kōshōji, Dōgen began his extraordinary preaching and lectures. He soon attracted a following. Most important among early disciples was Koun Ejō (1198–1280). Ejō was a refugee of sorts, a former member of a banned Zen sect, the Daruma-shū ("Bodhidharma sect"), whose monastic center had been destroyed in 1228 by armed Tendai monks. Ejō became Dōgen's close personal assistant, editor, and eventual successor.

Shōbōgenzō

In 1233 Dōgen began composing what is now regarded as his masterpiece, *Treasury of the True Dharma Eye* (*Shōbōgenzō*). Masao Abe, one of Japan's leading philosophers, has acclaimed Dōgen's *Treasury* "a monumental document in Japanese intellectual history"; in it, Dōgen displays "a rare combination of religious insight and philosophical ability," comparable in scope and depth to that of his contemporary Thomas Aquinas.[38] Dōgen drew the title from what Buddha had said at the Flower Sermon: that he possessed a liberating seeing (the "dharma eye") and had transmitted this "treasury" wordlessly to his disciple, the smiling Mahākāśyapa. Dōgen's magnum opus is not a single composition, but a sprawling anthology of essays and sermons, over 700 pages in modern English translations. Topics of individual essays (or "fascicles") range widely. Some, such as *Being-Time* (*Uji*) and *Birth and Death* (*Shōji*), plumb profound philosophic depths; others, such as *Plum Blossoms* (*Baika*) and *Mountains and Waters Sūtra* (*Sansui-kyō*), are rich poetic excursions; some focus on traditional Buddhist doctrines, such as *Buddha-Nature* (*Busshō*) and *Karmic Retribution* (*Sanji gō*); others are practical, even earthy—for example, *Washing the Face* (*Semmen*) and *Rules for the Lavatory* (*Senjō*). Most fascicles are precisely dated in a closing colophon and list the recorder-editor, who in most cases was Ejō. The majority were delivered at the Kōshōji, and most date from a limited but intensely creative period, from 1240 to 1244.[39]

Dōgen delivered these pathbreaking lectures in Japanese, not Chinese. This was a major innovation. For thirteenth-century Japanese Buddhists, classical Chinese, not vernacular Japanese, was the respectable language of spiritual discourse, much as Latin was in the medieval West. In these lectures, Dōgen pioneered a new vernacular spirituality of great depth—not unlike what Meister Eckhart would do a few years later when he transformed Latin mystical theology into a vivid German vernacular. Dōgen's Japanese lectures (or *jishu*) were delivered to select—and often advanced—disciples, usually in the evening or late at night in the abbot's quarters.

The standard modern edition of Dōgen's *Treasury* has 95 fascicles. This version was edited centuries after his death, in 1690, by the Sōtō scholar Kōzen, who arranged the fascicles in chronological order. In recent years text critics have been probing earlier manuscript traditions that collect different numbers of fascicles (75, 12, 60, 84, 28), placed in different orders and with textual variants. All this poses complex issues for scholars as they try to sort out Dōgen's original design and, beneath it, his deeper intentions. Of the competing recensions, both the 75- and the 12-fascicle *Treasury* have good claim to go back to Dōgen himself.[40]

Dōgen has two other works that use the same title, *Shōbōgenzō*. The two are very different in content and style and length. One is *Shōbōgenzō Zuimonki* (*Treasury . . . Record of Things Heard*), a six-chapter collection of informal talks he gave between 1235 and 1238, recorded by Ejō. The other is *Mana Shōbōgenzō* (*Chinese Treasury . . .*), a collection of 300 kōans that Dōgen himself selected from a wide range of Chinese sources and put together around 1235. Scholars view this work (only recently accepted as genuine thanks to recent manuscript discoveries) as Dōgen's personal workbook or sourcebook.[41] Other kōan collections, like *The Blue Cliff Record* or *The Gateless Barrier*, offer mind-teasing commentaries on each kōan case. Dōgen's sourcebook simply narrates the bare-bones stories. His extensive and mind-teasing commentaries appear elsewhere, within the essays in his voluminous vernacular *Treasury*.

Eiheiji

In 1243, after the annual summer retreat, Dōgen and his disciples quite suddenly packed up and abandoned Kōshōji. They left Kyoto altogether and began setting up a new monastery in the remote mountainous countryside of Echizen province. Dōgen himself never says why he and his followers so abruptly and so decisively abandoned the imperial capital for the hinterland. Scholars have speculated at length, and competing theories have attempted to account for this sudden and career-altering move. Was it political fall-out? Had Dōgen run afoul of the Tendai authorities? That is possible. In 1241 Dōgen had accepted a flock of new disciples from the proscribed Daruma sect. Was it Dōgen's own reaction to competition from a rival Zen group? Again, that is possible. A rival Zen master, Enni Ben'en, who had just returned from his own pilgrimage to China, was appointed abbot of a new Zen monastery, the Tōfukuji, just down the road from Dōgen's. This monastery was massive and would have dwarfed Dōgen's own community. Was it the influence of a new patron? A leading samurai, Hatano Yoshishige, had become a supporter and political patron of Dōgen and offered to establish a full-scale monastery within his fiefdom. Political winds in Japan were certainly shifting away from the old imperial seat of Kyoto and toward the emerging military center of Kamakura, where the shogunate were based. Whatever the decisive reason—and all three likely played some role—Dōgen's future and the future of his movement lay in the mountainous countryside.

For the harsh winter of 1243–1244, Dōgen and his disciples set up small hermitages. Despite the hardships, it remained an intensely creative period for Dōgen, who composed twenty-eight new fascicles for his *Treasury*. In the spring of 1244 construction began on a major new monastery, initially named Daibutsuji (Great Buddha Monastery). In 1246 he renamed it Eiheiji (Eternal Peace Monastery), alluding to the "eternal peace" era (58–75 CE) when the first Buddhist scriptures had been imported into China. I should add here that in medieval Japan, as in medieval Europe, an abbot's home monastery became part of his name. Thus Dōgen is called Eihei Dōgen (as Bernard is called Bernard of Clairvaux).

A shift in literary output paralleled the shift in locale. One focus became monastic legislation. Such matters had been a concern from an early date, evident, for example, in his innovative *Instructions for the Head Cook* (*Tenzo kyōkun*). But with the move to Echizen, he saw the need to craft a more thorough body of rules and instructions, eventually known as *Eihei shingi*, that dealt with everything from monastic officers to decorum in monastic clothing to conduct in the library. Dōgen's concern was to create a "pure community," drawing on the best legislation and practices he had witnessed among the great Ch'an monasteries of Sung China.

Eihei kōroku

A second literary focus was his *Extensive Record* (*Eihei kōroku*), edited by Ejō and other disciples. This work gathers speeches and writings, mostly from his last ten years, into ten large volumes. The first seven volumes are collections of his brief, dense, and allusive sermons (known as *jōdō*) delivered in Chinese from the high seat in the main Dharma hall. Some could be exceptionally brief. Dōgen once ascended his seat and gave a one-line sermon: "If this greatest cold does not penetrate into our bones, how will the fragrance of the plum blossoms pervade the entire universe?"[42] At that, he stepped down. Few, I should add, are that terse.

The eighth volume of the *Extensive Record* has informal talks and some letters; the ninth, a collection of kōans, each case footed with a verse commentary; and the tenth, a collection of his poetry. All told, the work is nearly 700 pages in the remarkable English translation published only in 2004. This often difficult work has received little attention from Western scholars, but its recent translation has begun to spark new assessments of Dōgen's later years and of the overall cast of his thought.[43]

Last Years

Despite his remote mountain monastery, Dōgen continued to attract attention from the highest political officials in Japan. In the spring of 1247 he was summoned to Kamakura to meet with the shogun, Hōjō Tokiyori (1227–1263). Dōgen was apparently offered the abbacy of Kenchōji temple, what would become the new Zen center of Kamakura Japan. This would have meant tremendous prestige and powerful political patronage. But Dōgen disapproved of the way Tokiyori sought to combine Zen spirituality with the way of the samurai and turned down the offer. He returned to the Eiheiji in the late fall. After rubbing shoulders with the nation's elite, Dōgen's preaching took a decided shift. He now stressed karma and its stark retribution for evil deeds.

Dōgen's health began going downhill in the fall of 1252. Early in 1253 he composed one last fascicle for his *Treasury*. By mid-1253 his condition had worsened, and at Hatano's urging he returned to Kyoto for medical attention. He died a few weeks later. Just before his death, he expressed his profound inner joy, even exuberance, in a final *waka* poem: "For fifty-four years following the way of heaven; now leaping beyond, shattering every barrier, Amazing! To cast off all attachments; while still alive, plunging into the Yellow Springs."[44]

JUST SITTING

A good entry into Dōgen's thought is his pathbreaking essay *Recommending Zazen to All People*.[45] An extraordinary early manuscript of it, dating from 1233, written in Dōgen's own hand, was discovered in the archives of the Eiheiji and first shown to the public in 1922. The better-known version is the so-called Vulgate manual, a revised edition from ten years later, later appended to volume 8 of his *Extensive Record*. It sets out Dōgen's stripped-down, back-to-basics Buddhism briefly and pungently. The heart of the text is a practical how-to-meditate manual, and for this Dōgen both drew on and brilliantly rewrote an earlier Ch'an text.[46] He set out precise directions for seated meditation: pick a quiet room; sit on a round cushion atop a mat; cross legs in either full-lotus or half-lotus; bring hands together, palms up, thumbs together; sit straight, leaning neither right nor left, forward nor back; close lips; keep eyes open, alert.[47] He adds psychological directives: "Let go of all involvements and let myriad things rest. Do not think good or bad. Do not judge right or wrong. Stop conscious endeavor and analytic introspection."[48]

Nonthinking

For Dōgen, seated meditation is not about chanting mantras or deciphering kōans or counting breaths. It is "just sitting" (*shikantaza*). It is hard, very hard, just to sit and do nothing but sit. Within seconds, the mind leaps off in a thousand directions. Dōgen addressed the problem and advised: "Think of not-thinking. How do you think of not-thinking? Nonthinking. This in itself is the essential art of zazen."[49] His terms, "thinking (*shiryō*) of not-thinking (*fu-shiryō*)" and "nonthinking" (*hi-shiryō*), sound like wordplay or simple non-sense. They are neither. Thinking means distinguishing, discriminating, sorting out this thing from that thing. Zazen is not about thinking, whether rationally or intuitively, whether about one's life or the world or something religious. Nor is it not-thinking, the cessation of thought, the shutting down of consciousness, the cultivating of some out-of-body trance state. What then does he mean by "nonthinking"? Like many Zen masters, Dōgen can be artfully opaque at the most pivotal of moments—and this is a pivotal moment because, as he claims, "nonthinking ... *is* the essential art of zazen." Nonthinking, it seems, lies beyond both thinking and not-thinking; it "neither affirms nor denies, accepts nor rejects, believes nor disbelieves"; it is presencing, a real-izing of the "pure presence of things as they are."[50]

Buddha and Zazen

Dōgen insisted that zazen is not one pious Buddhist practice among many. It is the heart of the matter, it is Buddhism itself, "the supreme of the supreme," as he says in *Negotiating the Way*: "From the first time you go before your master and receive his teaching [on zazen], you no longer have need for incense-offerings, homage-paying, chanting Buddha's name, penance disciplines, or sūtra-reading. Just cast off your body and mind in the practice of zazen."[51] Dōgen did not deny the value of some scripture study—it was useful for understanding the Buddha's teachings—but reading without practicing is like reading prescriptions without bothering to take the medicine. As for chanting, "If you merely raise your voice in endless recitation, you are in no way different from a frog in a spring field—although you croak from morning to nightfall, it will bring you no benefit at all."[52]

Dōgen saw his "zazen-alone" approach as a return to and restoration of the Buddha's own way. Dōgen's was a Buddha-centered spirituality. He sensed that amid competing schools and competing lineages, competing doctrines and competing practices, the stark simplicity and centrality of the Buddha's own way had gotten lost to sight. Dōgen claimed that his old teacher, Ju-ching, had denounced all talk of a Zen sect: "To call the wide road of the buddhas and ancestors 'the Zen School' is thoughtless talk. 'The Zen School' is a false name used by bald-headed idiots, and all sages from ancient times are aware of this."[53] Dōgen himself did not mince words about this: "If you call the Buddha Dharma the Zen school, your tongue will fall out."[54] In *Recommending Zazen*, Dōgen insisted his focus was the Buddha's focus: "Look at the Buddha himself, who was possessed of a great inborn knowledge—the influence of his six years of upright sitting is noticeable still."[55] It was equally the focus of patriarchs such as Bodhidharma who transmitted this teaching to China: "Still celebrated is Master Bodhidharma of the Shaolin Temple, who sat facing the wall nine years although he had already received the [Buddha's] mind seal."[56] Dōgen's point, in part, is that if one follows Buddha and the patriarchs, then one does what they did. As he remarked in a later essay, *Admonitions on Zazen (Zazenshin)*: "What has been inherited by successor after successor is just this message of seated meditation; one who does not participate in the unique transmission of this message is not a Buddha or a Patriarch."[57] While zazen was not Buddha's sole teaching or sole practice, it was the centerpiece, and "when one is not clear about this one dharma, he is not clear about the ten thousand dharmas or about the ten thousand practices."[58] Christian mystics have insisted that one cannot really live the Christian life without contemplation at its center. In a similar way, Dōgen insisted that one cannot be Buddhist without zazen.

Practice-Realization

Dōgen's point went much deeper. Note his stress on time: the Buddha's "six years of upright sitting"; Bodhidharma's "nine years" of wall-facing. Dōgen focused on the fact that Buddha and Bodhidharma practiced zazen even *after* they experienced enlightenment. This meant that Buddhas and patriarchs did not practice zazen in order to be enlightened; they were already enlightened and *therefore* practiced zazen. Zazen itself is the practice of enlightenment. This is the heart of Dōgen's message. Zazen is not a means to an end. Dōgen rejected all means-ends thinking. Practice is itself enlightenment: "The zazen I speak of is not *learning* meditation . . . It is the practice-realization of totally culminated enlightenment. It is things as they are in suchness."[59] Note Dō-gen's compound term "practice-realization" (*shushō-ittō*). It encapsulates a core insight teased out in his early essay *Negotiating the Way*:

> In the Buddha Dharma, practice and realization are one and the same. As your present practice is practice within realization, your initial negotiation of the Way is in itself the whole of original realization. That is why from the time you are instructed in the way of practice, you are told not to anticipate realization apart from practice. It is because practice points to original realization.[60]

Zazen is thus not a practice for the unenlightened to become enlightened; it is itself "practice within realization." That is why in *Recommending Zazen* Dōgen encouraged students to "have no designs on becoming a Buddha."[61] For Dōgen, there was a sort of sacred purposelessness to zazen. We take to it naturally, "like the dragon when he reaches the water, like the tiger when he enters the mountain."[62] Zazen is not about becoming a buddha; it is being Buddha:

> When just one person does zazen even one time, he becomes, im-perceptibly, one with each and all of the myriad things and permeates completely all time, so that within the limitless universe, through-out past, future, and present, he is performing the eternal and cease-less work of guiding beings to enlightenment. It is, for each and every thing, one and the same undifferentiated practice, one and the same undifferentiated realization.[63]

These are remarkable claims: that zazen, performed but once and by but one person, unites the practitioner with the universe, with each and every thing; that the practitioner does what Buddha does, that is, guide myriad beings to enlightenment. In those precious moments of zazen, dualities vanish: "The seer and the seen, the reflecter and the reflected, are one; practice and enlightenment are one."[64] Zazen is itself mystical practice.

Dōgen's core insight—that zazen is at once practice-in-realization and realization-in-practice—answered the great doubt that had once haunted him. As a young man, he had pondered why one works to acquire enlightenment if, as Tendai doctrine taught, one already innately possesses Buddha-nature ("original enlightenment"). The Tendai doctrine seemed to dissolve, even deny, any difference between delusion and enlightenment. It seemed to make the long, hard road of seeking enlightenment a useless quest. On the far shore of his own awakening, Dōgen saw things with new eyes. At the heart of the quest, there lay a subtle dialectic: "The *dharma* is amply present in every person, but without practice, it is not manifested; without realization, it is not attained."[65] According to Masao Abe, the mature Dōgen recognized that both realization and practice are "equally real and equally indispensable to human existence"; realization is "the ground or basis," whereas practice is the "the condition or occasion."[66] Practice reveals that original awakening had been there from the very beginning; without practice there is no revealing. But practice also reveals something quite unexpected. We might imagine that enlightenment means entering into some unchanging perfection, some eternal fixity. Dōgen insisted that it was no such thing: "As it is, from the very first, realization in practice, realization is endless; as it is the practice of realization, practice is beginningless."[67] Enlightenment is neither a goal reached nor a prize attained. Rather, enlightenment unfolds—to use Kazuaki Tanahashi's apt phrase.[68] It unfolds endlessly, an endless beginning, an ever-fresh start into long-familiar territory.

Polishing the Tile

Dōgen faced criticism. His teaching sounded as though he was reducing Buddhism to mere quietism, that he was advocating "silent illumination," an approach sharply criticized by the old Ch'an master Ta-hui.[69] Critics then and since have cited against Dōgen and his followers one of Zen's most famous anecdotes. According to the story, Ch'an master Ma-tsu Tao-i (709–788) used to spend all day practicing seated meditation. He was confronted by his teacher, Ch'an master Nan-yüeh (677–744): "What are you figuring to do, sitting there in meditation?" Ma-tsu replied: "I'm figuring to make a Buddha."

And so Nan-yüeh took up a piece of tile and began rubbing it. Ma-tsu asked Nan-yüeh what he was doing: "I'm polishing this to make a mirror." Ma-tsu scoffed, "How can you make a mirror by polishing a tile?" Nan-yüeh rebutted, "How can you make a Buddha by sitting in meditation?"[70] On first hearing, the story seems an obvious rebuke to Dōgen's approach, implying that his practice of seated meditation is as ridiculous as trying to turn a terracotta tile into a polished mirror. The story is especially poignant since the mirror is a traditional symbol of Buddha's enlightened mind.

This story, it turns out, was one of Dōgen's favorites. He considered it a kōan and included it among the 300 kōans in his personal anthology.[71] He also commented on it in several essays in the *Treasury*. Far from seeing it as a critique, he appealed to it as a profound commentary on and confirmation of his deepest convictions. In his essay *The Ancient Mirror* (*Kokyō*), he argued that people have misunderstood the story, that they misread Nan-yüeh's action as provoking and criticizing Ma-tsu. Dōgen says that, in fact, polishing a tile to make a mirror is exactly "the bones and marrow of the Buddha and the Patriarchs." To explain, he launches into a rapid-fire chain of Zen logic: "When the polishing of the tile becomes a mirror, Ma-tsu makes a Buddha; and when Ma-tsu makes a Buddha, Ma-tsu quickly becomes Ma-tsu. When Ma-tsu becomes Ma-tsu, zazen quickly becomes zazen."[72]

Dōgen's kōan commentary here is classic Zen: turning a topsy-turvy parable topsy-turvy. He treats the ridiculous—turning a tile into a mirror—as a fact obvious to anyone who looks, as down-to-earth common sense. He then yanks up a pungent truth: that the absurd practice of seated meditation does indeed make Ma-tsu a Buddha, that Ma-tsu's terracotta-tile-mind is the Buddha's mirror-mind. And so Dōgen adds, in his leapfrogging chain of logic, that in seated meditation, the Ma-tsu who becomes Buddha is the Ma-tsu who becomes himself ("Ma-tsu quickly becomes Ma-tsu"). Zazen, in other words, reveals the true self. Dōgen adds:

Accordingly, the tile becomes the ancient mirror [= original Buddha mind] and when we polish the mirror we will find untainted and pure practice. This is done, not because there is dust on the tile, but simply to polish the tile for its own sake. In this, the virtue of becoming the mirror will be realized. This is the basis of the practice and observation of the Buddhas and Patriarchs. If we cannot make the mirror by polishing a tile, we cannot make the mirror even by polishing the mirror. Who understands this? In the action itself [of polishing] is the realization of Buddha and the actualization of the mirror.[73]

Zazen is not about purification (removing "dust on the tile"); it is practice-realization ("polish the tile for its own sake"). Dōgen's accent is not on the static image ("mirror"), but the activity ("polishing"). Activity reveals reality: "Zazen quickly becomes zazen."

Tea and Rice

Dōgen was firmly rooted in the "sudden enlightenment" tradition of Zen. He often cited classic stories of sudden awakenings such as that of Hsiang-yen Chih-hsien (d. 898), who experienced enlightenment after hearing a pebble strike bamboo, or of Ling-yün Chih-ch'in (ninth century), who awakened after seeing peach blossoms.[74] In *Record of Things Heard*, Dōgen alluded to both stories and teased out links between practice, enlightenment, and the everyday:

> Look. There was one who was enlightened with the sound of a bamboo being struck and another who clarified his mind upon seeing peach blossoms. Is the bamboo bright or dull, deluded or enlightened? Are peach blossoms shallow or deep, wise or foolish? Although flowers blossom year after year, not everyone who sees them is enlightened. When a bamboo cracks, not everyone who hears it realizes the way. Enlightenment and clarity of the mind occur only in response to the sustained effort of study and practice. Endeavoring in the way ripens the conditions of your practice. It is not that the sound of the bamboo is sharp or the color of the blossoms is vivid. Although the sound of the bamboo is wondrous, it is heard at the moment when it's hit by a pebble. Although the color of blossoms is beautiful, they do not open by themselves but unfold in the light of springtime. Studying the way is like this. You attain the way when conditions come together ... A stone is turned to a jewel by polishing. A person becomes a sage by cultivation. What stone is originally shiny? Who is mature from the beginning? You ought to polish and cultivate yourself.[75]

Dōgen's fondness for such everyday awakening stories point to a centerpiece of his teaching: contemplative practice does not send one off one into some otherworldly realm. It moves one into the mundane. It gives one eyes to see the everyday world as it is—as sacred. As he puts it in his essay *Continuous Practice* (*Gyōji*): "Do not wait for great enlightenment, as great enlightenment is the tea and rice of daily activity."[76]

BUDDHA-NATURE

Christians hold that every human being has a sacred dignity, that every human being is made in God's image. This conviction led Christian mystics such as Bernard and Bonaventure and Eckhart to explore how human nature bears within itself a sacred meeting-ground of the divine and human. Just as Christian thinkers have meditated on human nature as a way to probe the sacred vocation of every human being, so Buddhist thinkers have meditated on Buddha-nature as a way to probe the sacred vocation of all life. Dōgen explored this theme of Buddha-nature in unique and sometimes startling ways in various essays. Let me touch on a couple of examples.

Study Self, Forget Self

One exploration appears in Dōgen's famous essay *Actualizing the Fundamental Point (Genjōkōan)*. The thrust of his inquiry is about seeing life as it is and living out of that core insight. Note that the Japanese title contains the word *kōan*. The other term, *genjō*, means "becoming manifest" or "presencing." Thus one Dōgen scholar has translated the title as "The Kōan Realized in Life."[77] This highlights that the essay is not a kōan commentary (though he does cite one), but rather a commentary on life itself as a sort of kōan. Early in the essay, Dōgen launches into a classic logic chain:

> To learn the Buddha Way is to learn one's self. To learn one's self is to forget one's self. To forget one's self is to be confirmed by all dharmas. To be confirmed by all dharmas is to cast off one's body and mind and the bodies and minds of others as well. All trace of enlightenment disappears, and this traceless enlightenment continues on without end.[78]

Let me try and break this down phrase by phrase. Dōgen speaks of learning the Buddha Way. He could expect his listeners to understand how this occurs. It begins for most, as it did for Buddha himself, with facing sickness, facing poverty, facing death. Dōgen's early biographers claimed that it began for him at his mother's funeral, that in the anguish of his loss, he noticed the clouds of incense rising up, how they swirled and vanished. The Buddhist quest begins when we seek to understand suffering and death. We thirst and quest for liberation and recognize that what binds us and what provokes suffering are illusions we hold about ourselves and about the world. And so, as Dōgen says here, one learns the Buddha Way by learning one's self. One learns the self by zazen, and its inward-turning vision reveals our self-centeredness for what it is. We discover the falsity of our worldview: that we act and see the world as if we ourselves were the fixed center of the universe. Dōgen invokes an intriguing analogy to highlight this:

> When a man is in a boat at sea and looks back at the shoreline, it may seem to him as though the shore is moving. But when he fixes his gaze closely on the boat, he realizes it is the boat that is moving. In like manner, when a person tries to discern and affirm things with a confused notion of his body and mind, he makes the mistake of thinking his own mind, his own nature, is permanent and un-changing. If he turns back within himself, making all his daily deeds immediately and directly his own, the reason all things have no selfhood becomes clear to him.[79]

Dōgen here emphasizes, with an analogy Albert Einstein could appreciate, that we think and behave as though we were a fixity; in reality we are a relativity, a constantly shifting self in a constantly shifting world. This helps explain Dō-gen's second phrase, "To learn one's self is to forget one's self." The spiritual life means unmasking the emptiness of the self we thought we were. It is self-abnegation, self-lessness, no-self-ness.

This brings us to Dōgen's next phrase: "To forget one's self is to be con-firmed by all dharmas." When he says "all dharmas," he means "all things," the myriad of ever-fluid phenomena that swirl about us and within us. What he is saying here is that the moment we forget self, the whole world and every-thing in it bursts forth and shimmers with teaching.[80] As Dōgen remarks in his earlier *Negotiating the Way*:

> The trees, grasses, and land involved in all this emit a bright and shining light, preaching the profound and incomprehensible Dhar-ma; and it is endless. Trees and grasses, wall and fence expound and exalt the Dharma for the sake of ordinary people, sages, and all liv-ing things.... Each and every thing is, in its original aspect, endowed with original practice—it cannot be measured or comprehended.[81]

Each and every thing teaches truth by being itself, by manifesting itself as it is. This, by the way, explains why some Dōgen specialists have translated the Japanese title *Genjōkōan* as "manifesting suchness."[82]

In that self-forgetting that is simultaneously all things manifesting themselves, dualities drop away, or, in Dōgen's terminology, one "casts off one's body and mind." This, of course, is the catchphrase that had sparked Dōgen's own decisive awakening. The Christian mystical tradition, like the wider Western philosophical tradition, has tended to work from a body-mind dualism. It has tended to claim that there is something within us—"mind" or "soul"—that is a timeless reality, a "substance" somehow preserved beneath and despite the ceaseless changes (both physical and psychic) that we ourselves are. Dōgen denies such dualisms. Awakening is awakening to the nondual person ("body-mind"). Other splits also drop away, including that between oneself and others. Thus Dōgen says here that one not only "casts off one's body and mind" but also "the bodies and minds of others as well." The nondual person awakens nondually into a nondual seeing of others and of the world itself. One thus moves into a new world that was always there: the original interconnectedness of self-and-others-and-world.

Finally, Dōgen insists that true enlightenment means that "all trace of enlightenment disappears." "Trace" here may refer to mystical phenomena that the Buddhist tradition presumed accompanied the breakthrough experience of awakening. "Traces" might include world-shattering insights about the origin and nature of the cosmos; they might include heightened states of consciousness, powers of mind-reading, remembering past lives, psychic travel; they might be affective states of bliss, of joyous freedom, of a peace that passes all understanding.[83] For Dōgen, enlightenment is beyond all clinging, beyond clinging even to the enlightenment experience itself: "When Buddhas are truly Buddhas, there is no need for them to perceive they are Buddhas. Yet they are realized, fully confirmed Buddhas—and they go on realizing Buddhahood continuously."[84]

Enlightened Impermanence

Let us turn briefly to another of Dōgen's essays, *Buddha-Nature* (*Busshō*). It is the longest and among the most subtle in his *Treasury*. I will do no more than touch on a few highlights. Dōgen opens with a key quotation from the *Nirvāna Sūtra*: "Shakyamuni Buddha said, 'All sentient beings without exception have the Buddha-nature.'"[85] This is for Buddhism what Genesis 1:26 (which says that every person is made in God's "image and likeness") is for Christianity. It is a touchstone for the Buddhist tradition to think about the sacredness of life, the way Genesis is for Christians. One key difference: Christians limit this sacred dignity to human beings; Buddhists locate it more broadly and treasure the sacred dignity of all sentient beings.[86]

Dōgen takes this key scripture text and deliberately misreads it to uncover a deeper (and arguably more deeply Buddhist) meaning. He reads "all sentient beings . . . have the Buddha-nature" as "every being is the Buddha-nature." Two subtle shifts in the wording shift everything. First, Dōgen changes "all sentient beings" to "every being." Philosophically, this breaks down any dichotomy between sentient beings and insentient beings, between living and nonliving, and reveals reality's nondual nature. Religiously, this word shift moves the borderline of what counts as sacred. It means that not only sentient beings are revered as sacred; every being is, all being is. A brief aside to illustrate this: Once in a sermon, Dōgen recalled the story of a monk-scholar named Tao-sheng who, when he heard that all things can become Buddha, went out and preached Buddhism to a mountain. "The lifeless rocks," Dōgen insisted, "nod their heads again and again."[87]

Second, Dōgen changes "*have* the Buddha-nature" to "*is* the Buddha-nature." This subtle shift transforms one's worldview. Philosophically, it goes after under-the-surface assumptions. "Having Buddha-nature" could imply two wrong ways of thinking, at least in Dōgen's view. One could read "having Buddha-nature" to imply that we have some eternal self, some hidden unchanging inner nature. This claim matches, more or less, the commonplace Western mystical (and philosophical) view of the soul. Dōgen reminds readers that within the Buddhist tradition, this view is heresy.[88] For Dōgen and the wider Buddhist tradition, there are no eternal substances, neither within us nor within the world. One might read "having Buddha-nature" to imply that we have within us this Buddha-nature as some hidden potential, like a seed that, when nourished by truth, sprouts and blossoms into enlightened Buddhahood. Dōgen dismisses this as "a supposition . . . bred from illusion in the unenlightened mind."[89] This would imply one has to wait until some future date for Buddha-nature to show itself. Dōgen insisted instead: "There can be no Buddha-nature that is not Buddha-nature manifested here and now."[90]

Dōgen goes on to claim (in a phrase that sounds clumsy in English) that "entire being is Buddha-nature." This meant that in seeing everything and everyone, we are seeing Buddha-nature: "Seeing mountains and rivers is seeing the Buddha-nature. Seeing the Buddha-nature is seeing a donkey's jowls or a horse's mouth." This is a dash of Dōgen's humor. Buddha-nature is seen not just in the beautiful ("mountains and rivers"), but in the ordinary, even the ridiculous ("donkey's jowls"). For Dōgen, contemplation transforms how one sees everything. At one point in the essay, he quotes Ch'an master Po-chang Huai-hai: "If you wish to know the Buddha-nature's meaning, you must contemplate temporal conditions."[91] This contemplating shatters all dichotomies:

> The way to contemplate temporal conditions is through temporal conditions . . . [Po-chang's phrase] "*must contemplate*" has nothing to do with someone contemplating or with something contemplated. It has no correspondence to "right" contemplation or to "false"

contemplation. It is just contemplating. It is "Look !!! temporal conditions!!!" It is the Buddha-nature's emancipated suchness. It is "Look !!! Buddha! Buddha!!!" It is "Look nature!! nature!!!"[92]

Just as Dōgen advocated zazen as "just sitting," so he advocated "just contemplating." Dōgen took Po-chang's terminology seriously: one contemplates "temporal conditions" by seeing the world as Buddha-nature, by seeing it not from some eternal vantage point, but from the right-here, right-now, right-before-your-eyes.

This leads to one of Dōgen's most startling teachings: "impermanence-Buddha-nature" (mūjo-busshō). In the essay Buddha-Nature, he quotes Hui-neng the Sixth Patriarch: "Impermanence is the Buddha-nature." This remark turns Buddhist common sense topsy-turvy, as Dōgen himself notes: "Those holding the narrow views of the Lesser Vehicle [= Theravada Buddhists], Buddhist scholars of the sutras and shastras, and the like will be suspicious, surprised and frightened by these words of the Sixth Patriarch."[93] Traditional Buddhism stresses that all things—both self and world—are impermanent, that one seeks liberation from impermanence by attaining the permanence of Buddhahood. Dōgen disagrees. The world in all its buzzing, blooming impermanence is Buddha-nature itself:

> The very impermanence of grass and tree, thicket and forest is
> the Buddha-nature. The very impermanence of people and things,
> body and mind is the Buddha-nature. Lands and nations, mountains
> and rivers are impermanent because they are Buddha-nature. Su-
> preme, complete enlightenment, because it is the Buddha-nature, is
> impermanent. Great nirvana, because it is impermanent, is the
> Buddha-nature.[94]

This seeing sees the sacred in the everyday and the everyday in the sacred. As Masao Abe has noted, Dōgen's radical view forces Buddhism to rethink what emancipation really is. If nirvāna is liberation from impermanence, then one is attached to permanence and not really liberated; "true compassion can be realized only by transcending nirvāna to return to and work in the midst of the sufferings of the ever-changing world."[95]

Moonlit Water

We have seen Dōgen in his more philosophical mood. Let me return to his essay Actualizing the Fundamental Point and explore his more poetic side. He talks at one point about enlightenment, what it is and how it unfolds us:

The attainment of enlightenment is like the moon reflected on the water. The moon does not get wet, and the surface of the water is not broken. For all the breadth and vastness of its light, the moon comes to rest in a small patch of water. The whole moon and the sky in its entirety come to rest in a single dewdrop on a grass tip—a mere pinpoint of water. Enlightenment does not destroy man any more than the moon makes a hole on the surface of the water. Man does not obstruct enlightenment any more than the drop of dew obstructs the moon or the heavens.[96]

For Dōgen, Buddha-nature is a light that lights up the world. It does so whether we notice or not. All things reflect it entirely, even the infinitesimally small— like a dewdrop on a blade of grass. It does not swallow up the individuality of any single thing; it lights it up. If we are to be ourselves, we need to be a stillness like a small patch of moonlit water that serenely soaks in and mirrors back the magnificence around us. "There are," he says, "inexhaustibly great virtues in mountains and seas. We must realize that this inexhaustible store is present not only all around us, it is present right beneath our feet and within a single drop of water."[97]

ENTANGLING VINES

Before closing, I need to say something about Dōgen's approach to words. Words were central to Dōgen's spirituality, and his approach dismantles two widespread Western stereotypes about Zen.

Oneness of Zen and Scriptures

The first stereotype comes from a simplistic interpretation of the slogan that Zen is a "special transmission outside the scriptures / without reliance on words and letters" (kyōge betsuden / furyū monji). This could imply (and did imply in some circles) that Zen needed no scriptures, that it was independent of them, that Zen was ultimately about wordlessness. Dōgen both agreed and disagreed with this traditional slogan. He agreed that there had been a "special transmission," that the Buddha dharma had for centuries been passed wordlessly from master to disciple. He once devoted a whole essay to it: Mind-to-Mind Transmission (Menju).[98] Another brief essay of his, Buddha Ancestors (Busso), carefully listed his own spiritual ancestry, a spiritual genealogy he reckoned from the Buddhas down to his own Chinese mentor, "old Buddha"

Ju-ching, as Dōgen fondly called him.[99] Still, Dōgen insisted that though this special transmission may have been "outside the scriptures," that did not mean that it was contrary to the scriptures, nor was it ignorant of them. Quite the opposite. He insisted that the transmission signified a "oneness of Zen and scriptures" (kyōzen itchi).[100] Scriptural formulations pervaded his writings even if his exegesis, as we saw, could be bold. Recent studies have highlighted the powerful and multifaceted shapings of the Lotus Sūtra on both the content and style of his thinking.[101]

Kōans and the Art of Entanglement

The second stereotype Dōgen dismantles has to do with Zen's most famous words: kōans. I mentioned earlier the widespread view—prevalent in the West thanks to Suzuki—that kōans are a sort of holy nonsense meant to draw in the conscious mind and entrap it in a conceptual labyrinth; that through their double binds, kōans provoke a psychological crisis that breaks through the barrier into enlightenment. This view gained momentum in the pedagogical innovations of Ch'an master Ta-hui. One also sees scholars who say Dōgen's tradition did not use kōans. That, as we have seen, is simply not true. Dōgen himself produced two massive kōan anthologies, the 300-case Mana Shōbōgenzō ("Chinese Treasury...") and the 90-case collection with poetic commentaries preserved in volume 9 of the Extensive Record. And the essays and sermons in Dōgen's own Shōbōgenzō are mostly kōan commentaries.

Dōgen certainly knew of Ta-hui's views on kōans, and opposed him and his followers in the strongest terms. In his essay The Mountains and Rivers Sūtra (Sansui-kyō), he says that "in great Sung China today there are a group of scatterbrained people" who claim that kōans "are incomprehensible utterances"; these "scatterbrains" claim "the past masters often employed these as skillful means which cut off entangling vines... because such things were beyond comprehension." Dōgen fiercely disagreed: "People who utter such nonsense have not yet met a true master; hence they lack the eye of proper study... What these pseudo-Buddhists regard as 'incomprehensible utterances' are incomprehensible only to them, not to the buddhas and patriarchs."[102]

The Ch'an tradition knew that Buddhists—like religious people the world over—can get caught up in fighting over words, that words often become entanglements that snare and divert seekers from the spiritual quest. Ta-hui and the tradition that followed him saw kōans as a way to "cut off entanglements." He used what became known as the "short-cut" approach and had disciples focus on the kōan's "critical phrase" or "punch line" (watō). Take, for example, Ta-hui's favorite kōan: Chao-chou's dog. One day, a monk approach Master Chao-chou and asked "Does a dog have buddha-nature?" Chao-chou answered, "No!" (wu; Japanese mu). To appreciate this kōan, we need to re-member that in medieval China, dogs were not household pets; dogs were thought of as fleabags, scavengers who scoured trash heaps for food scraps. Thus, the force of the question: can one find the Buddha in fleabags and trash heaps?[103] Chao-chou's answer was the real shock. His "no" seemed, on the face of it, to deny that most fundamental of Buddhist doctrines, namely, that all sentient beings, even mongrel dogs, have Buddha-nature. Thus begins the quandary, thus the double bind. How could Chao-chou possibly, in good Buddhist conscience, say "no"? And, even worse, how could a master like Ta-hui give this apparent heresy to a disciple to meditate on as though it were sacred truth? This is only one of many, many double binds that soon ensnare the unwary meditator.[104] Ta-hui taught disciples to ignore the story and focus solely on the punch line, on Chao-chou's "no!" According to Ta-hui: "This character [Chao-chou's 'no!'] is the rod by which many false images and ideas are destroyed in their very foundations. To it you should add no judgement about being or non-being, no arguments, no bodily gestures ... Words have no place here. Neither should you throw this character away into the nothingness of emptiness."[105] Ta-hui thus advocated abbreviation in the service of spiritual iconoclasm. His punch-line approach stripped away the kōan's dialogue, its disciples and masters, its questions and questioners, and forced the meditator to the very brink of wordlessness. Ta-hui's punch-line pedagogy has been aptly compared to the "one-word" prayer method advocated by the desert fathers and others in the Christian mystical tradition.[106]

Dōgen opposed Ta-hui's spirituality and his spiritual pedagogy. Dōgen valued kōans every bit as much as Ta-hui did, but Dōgen took them in a sharply different direction. He knew, of course, that words could entangle believers. But he also believed that words could liberate. In his essay *Entangling Vines* (*Kattō*), he played on this theme of "word-tangles" and argued:

> Generally, although all Buddhist sages in their training study how
> to cut off entanglements at their root, they do not study how to cut off
> entanglements by using entanglements. They do not realize that
> entanglements entangle entanglements. How little do they know
> what it is to transmit entanglements in terms of entanglements. How
> rarely do they realize that the transmission of the Dharma is itself
> an entanglement.[107]

This gives some hint of why Dōgen opposed Ta-hui. He was convinced the whole kōan—and *not just* the punch line—transmitted the dharma. Yes, words could entangle, but the Buddha himself had used the entanglements of words to liberate. And so Dōgen's whole pedagogy used words as liberating entanglements. Dōgen treated the wide-ranging kōan tradition as a well-honed spiritual lexicon, a sort of enlightenment vocabulary for talking about enlightenment. This often makes Dōgen difficult reading, partly because few of us have kōan cases at our fingertips the way his disciples (at least the advanced ones) did. Most essays in Dōgen's *Treasury* are kōan commentaries, and most tap on multiple kōans pitting one against another. The effect is entangling and disconcerting. One has to wrestle with Dōgen's words—and he meant hearers and readers to wrestle with his words. Over and over again, sometimes every few paragraphs, he says to his hearers: "You should examine thoroughly the meaning . . ."; "you should study [this] further . . ."; "you should investigate this thoroughly. . . ."[108]

One Bright Pearl

Let me illustrate Dōgen's word-tangle spirituality with a fairly straightforward example, the poetic essay *One Bright Pearl* (*Ikka Myōju*). Dōgen opens with a kōan about Ch'an master Tsung-i Ta-shi of Mount Hsüan-sha. Hsüan-sha (as Dōgen calls him) was a simple man, an ex-fisherman, and after his enlightenment he used to instruct people by saying: "All the universe is one bright pearl." A monk once asked Hsüan-sha, "I've heard you have said that all the universe is one bright pearl. How can I gain an understanding of that?" Hsüan-sha answered, "All the universe is one bright pearl. What is there to understand?" The next day, Hsüan-sha asked the monk how he understood the phrase. The monk answered, "All the universe is one bright pearl. What need is there to understand?" Hsüan-sha then answered, "Now I know that you are living in the Cave of Demons on Black Mountain."[109] The punch line is shocking: Hsüan-sha was declaring that his disciple had condemned himself to the deepest depths of Buddhist hell (a realm a bit like Mordor in Tolkien's *Lord of the Rings*).[110]

Dōgen's commentary, which makes up the rest of the essay, does not reduce the kōan to its punch line. Rather, he expounds it phrase by phrase. All phrases count equally, and his commentary modulates between varied vantage points— some philosophical, some poetic, some religious. For instance, he takes the phrase "all the universe" and offers a playfully Buddhist perspective on cosmology: "The entire universe is not vast and large, not minute and small, or square or round . . . 'All the universe' is an unceasing process, pursuing things and making the self, pursuing the self and making it things."[111] He then takes up the phrase "one bright pearl" and argues: " 'One bright pearl' is able to express

Reality without naming it, and we can recognize this pearl as its name. One bright pearl communicates directly through all time... That stalk of grass, this tree, is not a stalk of grass, is not a tree; the mountains and rivers of this world are not the mountains and rivers of this world. They are the bright pearl."[112]

Mention of a pearl reminds him of a parable from the *Lotus Sūtra* about a man who met a wealthy friend and went out drinking. The wealthy man had to leave, and his drunk friend had fallen into a deep sleep. So the man sewed a pearl into his friend's clothing. When the drunk woke up, he did not realize he held a priceless pearl and spent years wandering in terrible deprivation until finally he ran into his rich friend again, who told him of the hidden pearl.[113] Dōgen interprets the kōan in terms of this parable:

> The pearl is attached within the lining of clothes... Make no utterance that tries to attach it to on the surface. Do not attempt to sport it on the surface. When you are drunk, there is a close friend who will give the pearl to you, and you as well must without fail impart the pearl to a close friend. When the pearl is attached to someone, he is invariably drunk. It being thus, it is the one bright pearl—all the universe. So although its face seems to keep on changing, turning and stopping, it is the same bright pearl... Should we not cherish the bright pearl? Such infinite colorations and brilliance? Each of the many facets of its radiant variegations containing the merit of the entire universe—who could possibly usurp it?[114]

Drunkenness is a traditional metaphor for delusion. The point is that even in our delusion we possess the measureless riches of enlightenment. Dōgen here spins out, with subtle inferences, elements of his own spirituality. The pearl imparted to the "close friend" is the dharma passed "without fail" from generation to generation. The pearl not attached to the surface seems to allude to his view that one not be attached even to enlightenment. The pearl, with its "infinite colorations and brilliance" that keep on "changing, turning, and stopping," seems to allude to Dōgen's teaching on "impermanence-Buddha-nature." At the essay's end, Dōgen addressed seekers who felt depressed, who felt as though they dwelt in hell. To them he offered hope that even in the darkest places, all is sacred: "Even when you are perplexed or troubled, those perplexed or troubled thoughts are not apart from the bright pearl. As there are no deeds or thoughts produced by something that is not the bright pearl, both coming and going in the Black Mountain Cave of Demons are themselves nothing but the one bright pearl."[115]

Steven Heine, one of Dōgen's finest modern interpreters, closes his analysis of Dōgen's use of kōans by playing on the story of Chao-chou's dog.[116]

Heine playfully yet poignantly asks: Does a kōan have Buddha-nature? Just as Chao-chou had answered "no!" to the question about the dog and Buddha-nature, so Dōgen's nemesis, Ta-hui, had effectively answered "no!" about kōans. Ta-hui had chopped kōans down to their punch line, then chopped that punch line down to a world-stopping wordless "no!" meant to burst the meditator into seeing apophatic Buddha-nature. Dōgen, in his essay *Buddha-Nature*, stressed that in the original dog-kōan, Chao-chou answered not only "no" (*mu*) but "yes" (*u*).[117] Dōgen approached kōans with a similar yes-and-no. Heine notes that Dōgen disentangled by entangling, pitting text against text, image against image, not to chop down mystical meanings, but to let them flower, bloom, and overgrow. Dōgen treated kōans as "polysemous," as words that "over-mean," that pile up until they overspill their banks and flood the world with meaning. Given the brevity and the introductory nature of this study, I cannot begin to take readers through Heine's intricate postmodern literary analysis. Here, as on other scores, I must give Dōgen short shrift. But let this one case remind us that for Dōgen kōans are beautiful entanglements, vines that not only twist but flower. They are like peach blossoms meant to awaken hearers to the sound of bamboo. They are terracotta tiles that, after Dōgen's wordy polishing, glisten back as mirrors. They are themselves nothing but one bright pearl.

MOUNTAINS, RIVERS, AND ECHOES

Heine has remarked that

> Dōgen's writing is like a mighty river flowing from the mountains in which we—Zen scholars, students, practitioners, and other more casual and merely curious readers and observers—are fishing for big and small catches by using our impressions and opinions as edible bait. Yet we must also realize that while we are valiantly trying to reel in the best of the prey as the stream rushes by, there are so many more fish going uncaught or undetected.[118]

Our fishing expedition here has been a modest one. It has, no doubt, missed some big fish. I hope that with this modest catch, we might at least sort out some ways that Dōgen and the wider Zen tradition can both illuminate and disabuse certain claims about mystics and mysticism. As I noted in the last chapter, there are great risks in singling out any individual, however remarkable, as emblematic of any vast and varied religious tradition. That is no less a problem here. Still, many of the most famous Ch'an/Zen figures—

Bodhidharma, Hui-neng, Ma-tsu—are so deeply shrouded in myth that it becomes all but impossible to sort out history from hearsay and legend. Because of the volume, depth, and variety of Dōgen's writings (not to mention, the volume, depth, and variety of scholarship on him), we can reel in at least a few snatches of him as a historical figure and as a religious thinker.

So let us confront the question: Is Zen Buddhism mystical? Or at least, is Dōgen's Zen mystical? If one defines mysticism as it is often defined, as the experience of the soul's union with God, then clearly Dōgen is no mystic. He is utterly silent about God's existence, let alone about any claim of union with God. That silence, I should add, is not untypical of the Buddhist tradition. With Rumi and the Sufis, we at least moved in deeply monotheist waters, and so the language of mysticism transferred rather easily, even if mystical currents differed in marked ways. Any use of mystical language must undergo serious redefining if it is to be applied to Zen or to any of a variety of Eastern traditions. But it is not just the question of theism. Dōgen, like the wider Buddhist tradition, denied anything like a substantial, eternal self, whether one calls it "soul" or "mind" or whatever. If there is no-self, the language of "union" simply makes no sense: What is "it" that can possibly unite to "whatever"?

Yet in other ways Zen seems deeply mystical—in fact, more self-consciously mystical than either Christianity or Islam. Buddhism (and Dōgen's especially) places at its very center a carefully calibrated and exacting contemplative discipline: zazen. And Buddhism (and Zen especially) focuses its practitioners' best energies on seeking a sudden awakening experience. This enlightenment is a life-altering, world-shattering breakthrough. It offers an utterly new way of seeing, thinking, feeling, acting, being. That experience is said to open a radical, nondual way of seeing that shatters both illusory distinctions between and false conflations of self and others and world. The language applied to that new worldview has fascinating parallels to Western mystical languages. It is sometimes poetic, sometimes philosophical, often paradoxical, even cryptic. And Zen, in its literature at least, celebrates a flamboyant and at times outrageously irreverent account of this enlightened life. Christian apophaticism seems tame by comparison. Zen, one might even argue, has created a thoroughgoing institutional framework for mystical cultivation. Its hierarchy centers around mystically awakened masters. It has created a sizable mystical literature that charts and records enlightenment encounters between masters and disciples. And some of that literature, namely its kōans, is set out as the intense focus of mystical sermons and commentaries (as we saw in Dōgen's case) and even as the intense focus of meditative practice (as in the case of Ta-hui and the Rinzai tradition). Zen has gone on to ceremonialize, even bureaucratize, the mystical. There is, for example, careful tracing and recording of one's spiritual genealogy, linking one's own awakening to the mystical awakening of one's spiritual forebears. Zen has also honed elaborate procedures for testing the authenticity and depth of one's mystical awakening. It even practices the handing on of formal certificates that officially testify to a practitioner's dharma transmission.

That said, the case of Dōgen offers nuances to, even refutations of, this picture. Dōgen's insistence that zazen is realization-in-practice and his insistence that enlightenment endlessly unfolds shatters outsiders' presumptions that one practices meditation to reach enlightenment. Zen, as portrayed by Suzuki and others, has often been described as "pure experience" unfettered by traditions or dogmas. That claim simply does not hold up. It is clear that, for Dōgen, tradition mattered deeply and was in many ways a centerpiece of his spirituality. He deeply revered the idea that the dharma had been transmitted from master to disciple, wordlessly, mind to mind, that one dharma lamp had lit another down through the centuries. And Dōgen insisted that that spiritual tradition took, and often required, institutional form in the Ch'an monastic framework he learned in China, especially from Ju-ching, and its handing on via a monastic framework was something he came to see as the heart of his life's work. Finally, Dōgen stressed the unsurpassable value of traditional Buddhist doctrine as expressed in and through the vast canon of Buddhist scriptures and also in and through the no less vast Ch'an transmission-of-the-lamp and kōan literatures. Dōgen appreciated, indeed celebrated, the inherently wordless ineffability of Buddhist teaching. At the same time he deeply valued the wonderfully liberating "entanglements" of words, both the words of Buddhist scriptures and the words of Ch'an/Zen kōans.

Earlier generations of Western scholars have sometimes described Zen as "nature mysticism." That, I believe, is wildly off the mark. Dōgen had a deep love of nature, a sense of mystical intimacy with mountains and rivers and peach blossoms and moonlight flickering in the tiniest dewdrops. But Dōgen's sense of nature looks nothing like the vague "nature mysticism" of nineteenth-century romantic poets or American transcendentalists. Dōgen's mysticism is *not* a nature mysticism. It is, if anything, a *Buddha-nature* mysticism: all being and every being is impermanence-Buddha-nature.

How Dōgen's Buddha-nature mysticism compares to, intersects with, or illuminates Western varieties is an open question. Unraveling that is not the goal here. The goal has been much more modest: to take up and to take on the widespread claim that "all religions are all the same at the top," that "mystics are all experiencing the same thing," that one can simply peel away a religion's doctrine from a mystic's writings, as though it were so much hardened crust, to reveal beneath it some pristine universal mystical experience. I hope I've shown here and in the last chapter that such claims are simply nonsense, that those who make them have simply not done their homework. It is incredibly hard work even to begin to enter into the world of Buddhist discourse and self-understanding, to address with some measure of fairness and precision what a thinker as sophisticated and nuanced as Dōgen is saying about religious experience. It is also urgent to take seriously his and others' claims that the language he and they use does, in fact, tell us something about their religious experience. If one were to strip away Dōgen's views on the Buddha dharma or on the Buddha-nature as though they were just so much dogmatic crust, then one would strip away the very heart of his message. One cannot simply rummage through a writer's works and then cherry-pick appealing quotes out of context, whether historical or literary or religious, and claim that they offer proof of some unmediated universal mystical experience. Nor can one claim that autobiographical passages about so-called mystical experiences are really about experiencing some transcendental eternal Absolute even when a writer of Dōgen's philosophical self-awareness adamantly denies that there is any such transcendental eternal Absolute. I am not saying that there are no cross-cultural, cross-religious points of convergence. There certainly are. But mapping them takes time and care and sensitivity. One must carefully tune one's ear to individual thinkers and to individual traditions. Comparative religion is a tricky enterprise, and even the most well-meaning and most eminently skilled have often bungled the effort. One must approach such matters with great humility, listening first, last, and always. We can, and indeed we must, learn to speak and listen across the chasms that separate one religion from another, but we must also be wary of hearing only our own echo coming back to us.

10

Reading Mystics: Text, Community, Experience

To this point we have focused on individual mystics. Now we need to confront broader issues, especially one tough question: What is mysticism? This core question will guide us here. I will certainly give my own take on it. But my real concern is to bring readers to the doorway of a many-sided, long-standing, and ongoing scholarly conversation on the nature of mysticism. I will not try to summarize this century-long conversation, but rather will give readers tools to follow its terms and assess its claims.[1] First, a few words on the design that has guided this study: The approach used here says something, I believe, about how best to take on broader questions of mystics and mysticism. Let me expand on points first raised in the preface, points that may have greater poignancy now that we stand on the far side of these eight case studies.

The case-study method used here has focused more on mystics than on mysticism, thus the title of the book. I singled out individuals routinely given the moniker of "mystic" but tried, in analyzing their lives and their writings, not to impose some predefined, extrinsic framework for assessing their mysticism. I sought, instead, to let their own language and their own categories come to the fore. To aid that search, I have given preference to scholars who are specialists in the individual being studied rather than those who are generalists in the study of mysticism. Specialists, I believe, are more likely to have their ear tuned to a mystic's texts, categories, and contexts. I have especially presumed that history matters. That required that we probe, however briefly, not simply a mystic's teaching but also his or her life story. This was meant to avoid or redress two common methodological shortcomings. The first is to detach a mystic's account(s) of peak experiences from his or her wider biography. William James and those who followed his lead tended toward a sort of mystical anecdotalism, plucking out reports of odd or dramatic psychological experiences. Long ago Evelyn Underhill argued against James's method, noting that "mysticism is no isolated vision, no fugitive glimpse of reality, but a complete system of life carrying its own guarantees and obligations."[2] The second is cherry-picking of another sort: that is, fixating on quotable mystical teachings in isolation from their historical, religious, and literary contexts. Many studies, especially older ones, treat mysticism as though it were a gnostic enterprise, bloodless and ahistorical—as though mystics uttered verities from eternity rather than in the thick of texts wrought at specific historical moments for specific historical communities in languages inherited from specific religious traditions. History is messy, and studying history is a convoluted business, fraught with all sorts of methodological pitfalls. If we hope to understand mysticism, we are required to throw ourselves into the unavoidable messiness of history and the pitfall-laden path of historiography.

My case-study approach has built-in risks. Much depends, of course, on which cases one chooses to study and which cases one chooses to ignore. Selection always creates bias. Balancing a mystic's life story with a mystic's mystical theology has meant that we did not grapple with pivotal mystical writers about whom we know almost nothing—for example, the sixth-century Pseudo-Dionysius or the fourteenth-century *Cloud of Unknowing* writer. I can be chided for incompleteness on many scores. I included no Protestant mystic. Beyond Christianity, I included neither a Jewish mystic nor a Hindu. We must not lose sight of the modest, introductory scope of this study.

Let me touch on three other biases. First, because mystics have so often been portrayed as otherworldly cranks or as psychological misfits, I singled out individuals whose careers demonstrated down-to-earth leadership skills. Hildegard of Bingen, as we saw, was not only an abbess who guided a sizable monastic community, but also a mover and shaker of her day, respected by popes, reformers, and emperors. Bernard of Clairvaux was even more prominent, not only as a leader of the Cistercians, but as an internationally renowned preacher, a sort of medieval celebrity. Eckhart too had leadership gifts. He spent his career in high-profile posts, both administratively and academically. As provincial of Saxonia, he was a leading figure in the Dominican order. Even more striking is Bonaventure who spent half his career as the head of the Franciscan order. The mystical sensibilities of these four posed no roadblock to their practical ones. In fact, mystical views fueled practical drives and reform efforts. My choices have meant that I ignored one thread within the history of mysticism, namely, those mystical neurotics, eccentrics, and holy fools, whether the fourteenth-century Richard Rolle or the nineteenth-century Thérèse of Lisieux. Such figures, while intriguing and often entertaining, are not the norm, and undue focus on them distorts the historical record. A second bias: I chose some mystics committed to the intellectual life. Too often mystics have been written off as advocates of irrationality or purveyors of empty-headed emotionalism. Such judgments are off the mark. Bonaventure and Eckhart were leading academics of their day. Evagrius, too, valued a rigorous philosophic and theological rationality and used the best intellectual tools he knew to chart forces that distort the psyche and to map the mind's upward journey to God. Respect of intellect is not limited to the Christian mystical tradition. We saw in Dōgen one whose philosophical turn of mind has been aptly called "rational Zen."[3] A third bias: I opted for diversity. I thought it best to show as broad an array as possible, to illustrate how mystics range widely in historical context, cultural background, artistic expression, and ideological position. Some readers might, by this point, be wondering whether the range has been so broad that the very category of mystic does not make much sense. That question must be considered a live option.[4]

In this chapter, I will draw on our earlier case studies as a database to think through more general questions on mysticism, on its nature and varieties. I will pull things together under three broad headings: (1) mystical texts, (2) mystical communities, and (3) mystical experiences. These headings provide a framework within which to address questions and tease out perspectives that have been simmering beneath the surface and that have been quietly guiding earlier analyses. These three headings may provide aids for readers to take on other mystics whose lives and theologies we did not take up. This three-sided optic provides, I believe, a way of mapping and defining the mystical. Its multiple lenses offer a grid for ongoing interpretation and may help correct otherwise one-sided approaches.

RAIDS ON THE INEFFABLE: MYSTICAL TEXTS

T. S. Eliot, in his famous *Four Quartets*, explored the poet's struggle with ineffability:

> Words strain,
> Crack and sometimes break, under the burden

> Under the tension, slip, slide, perish,
> Decay with imprecision, will not stay in place . . .
>
> And so each venture
> Is a new beginning, a raid on the inarticulate
> With shabby equipment always deteriorating. . . .[5]

Mystics, like poets, are professional raiders on the ineffable, and they, like Eliot and other poets, sometimes complain about "shabby equipment," those words that "slip, slide, perish, decay with imprecision." We need to take mystics' complaints with a grain of salt. For all the hand-wringing about the ineffability of the mystical, mystics rarely abandon words or lapse into silence. They are a singularly talkative lot and a singularly gifted group of talkers. Some, like Teresa of Ávila, may adopt an artless and chatty persona, but the figures we studied possessed considerable literary gifts, and their writings are, in the main, well-crafted works of literature, constructed with circumspection and artistic self-consciousness.

This should remind us of matters both obvious and too often ignored. First, virtually all that we know of mysticism comes to us via words on a page. Reading mystics is, first of all, *reading*, and mystical texts are, first of all, *texts*. We need to keep our literary wits about us whenever we grapple with mystics and their texts. This study has, I hope, demonstrated ways that one brings to mystical texts those fundamentals of interpretation that one would bring to any decent work of literature. Those fundamentals include paying attention to genre and to audience, to design, outline, and authorial intent. They include being alert to sources authors quote or allude to and to the many-sided metaphors they tap on. They include charting how and why a text was preserved through the centuries, including ways it might have been altered, disguised, suppressed, or simply mislaid. They also include reflecting on the often heavy and sometimes misguided agenda that we moderns bring to older texts.

What defines a mystical text? Let me suggest a working definition: A mystical text is a religious text that describes a profound experiential knowledge of God or of ultimate reality.[6] Such texts often, *but not always*, discuss pathways to seeking out and arriving at such knowledge. Such texts also often, *but not always*, offer the author's own experience of seeking out and arriving at that knowledge. A few remarks: First, I place the accent not on experience, but on experiential knowledge. The modern interest in psychology and the modern focus on a self that experiences things only imperfectly match the literature we have studied. That literature focuses more on God and other life-defining realities than on autobiographical testimony. Second, we need to see mystical literature not in either/or terms, but on a sliding scale. Some texts are wholly mystical, some only in spots. Bonaventure's *Journey of the Mind into God*, Merton's *New Seeds of Contemplation*, and Eckhart's *German Sermons* are largely mystical in focus, whereas Hildegard's *Letters* and Merton's *Conjectures* are so only episodically. Third, definitions can only roughly define a canon. Think of the difficulty involved in precisely defining what constitutes a philosophical text. Such a definition would be expected to include an uncomfortable range: Plato's *Dialogues*, Aristotle's *Metaphysics*, Augustine's *Confessions*, Thomas Aquinas's *Summa Theologica*, Nietzsche's *Thus Spake Zarathustra*, Wittgenstein's *Philosophical Investigations*, and Foucault's *Madness and Civilization*. Definitions help, but scholarly consensus also plays a role in defining what does and does not fit in a canon of literature.

Mystical Genres

Let us explore some literary issues. Take the case of genre. The span of mystical genres we came across was wide. It included:

- autobiography (Merton's *Seven Storey Mountain*)
- letters (Merton, Hildegard, Evagrius)
- journals (Merton's *Conjectures of a Guilty Bystander* and *Asian Journal*, the *Gnostic Wisdom* of Rumi's father and mentor, Dōgen's *Hōkyōki*)
- sermons (Bernard's *Sermons on the Song of Songs*, Eckhart's *German Sermons*, Dōgen's *Extensive Record*)
- essays and treatises (Merton's *Mystics and Zen Masters*, Bernard's *On Loving God*, Bonaventure's *Journey of the Mind into God*, Eckhart's *Book of Divine Consolation*, Dōgen's *Fukanzazengi* and *Bendōwa*)
- scripture commentaries (Bonaventure's *Collations on the Six Days of Creation*, Eckhart's *Commentary on Exodus* and *Commentary on the Gospel of John*, Evagrius's *Scholia* on Psalms and Proverbs, fascicles in Dōgen's *Treasury*)
- theological summae (Hildegard's *Scivias*)
- poetry of various types (Hildegard's antiphons, Rumi's *ghazals* in the *Divān* and his epic *Masnavi*, Dōgen's brief *waka* poems)
- proverbs (Evagrius's *The Monk* and *Chapters on Prayer*)
- dialogues (*Sayings of the [Desert] Fathers*, Cassian's *Conferences*, Ch'an and Zen kōan collections such as *The Gateless Gate* and Dōgen's *Mana Shōbōgenzō*)
- hagiographies (William of St. Thierry's *Life of Saint Bernard*, Godfrey's *Life of Saint Hildegard*, Palladius's *Lausiac History*, Sultan Valad's *Book of Beginnings*, Ch'an and Zen "transmission of the lamp records," the *Kenzeiki* [on Dōgen's life])

We looked only at a handful of mystics and only at their best-known works. The list gets much longer, the wider the range of mystics one studies. We also saw that some mystical texts were, in fact, multimedia works. Hildegard may have designed the main body of her *Scivias* as a theological summa, but she appended both a morality play and a cluster of poems she had set to music. Eventually her text included carefully crafted and quite original manuscript illuminations of her visions. Merton too not only produced texts, but late in life used photography as a medium to explore and express his own contemplative vision of the world.

Because we moderns tend to relegate mysticism to psychological experience (an instinct we owe, in part, to William James), we look to autobiography as the privileged form of mystical literature. This long list of genres should disabuse us of this bias. Autobiography is only one of many genres. We did touch upon one classic autobiography, Merton's *Seven Storey Mountain*. There are other even more famous ones, such as Augustine's *Confessions* or Teresa of Ávila's *Book of Her Life* (*Libro de la Vida*). Some writers we studied sprinkled autobiographical reminiscences within other works. Merton's journals record key breakthroughs, Bernard of Clairvaux touched on his mystical experiences here and there in the course of sermons, and Hildegard handed on autobiographical testimonies to her later biographers and to recipients of her letters. Autobiographical snippets popped up also in the works of Rumi and Dōgen.

We cannot be naive about autobiography as a genre or as a mode of discourse. Neither autobiographies nor journals nor other first-person accounts offer unmediated access to personal experience. Rarely does one come across firsthand reports immediately after a mystical encounter. Hildegard's reports appear in a text she spent ten years crafting. Or take the case of Merton. Only with the recent publication of his private journals did scholars realize that his famous account of the Fourth-and-Walnut episode was rewritten eight years after the event. Does immediacy guarantee authenticity? Not necessarily. A mystical experience, like any pivotal experience, acquires meaning and depth only after long years of reflection. Hindsight is the overlooked crucible of the mystical. Also, autobiographies, even the most artless and unselfconscious, are never straightforward narrations of events. They are unashamedly biased. Writers of autobiographies have many motives, only some of which they are willing to admit. Common motives include self-defense and self-justification, and such motives often flicker beneath the surface of mystical self-accounts.

Scriptures and the Mystical

Steven Katz, in his recent collection of essays, *Mysticism and Sacred Scriptures*, has noted that if one reviews a century of scholarly literature on mysticism from William James onward, one discovers shockingly little acknowledgment and even less analysis of the way scriptures shape mystical texts. The neglect comes, in Katz's view, from a widespread but largely misconceived theory of mysticism, namely, that mystics and their experiences transcend their history, their culture, even their home religion.[7] Katz is right to complain. Many mystical texts, as we have seen, are scriptural exegeses, whether sermons on specific biblical verses or commentaries on specific biblical books. Think back on Bernard. On the one hand, he did much to introduce the term "experience" into Christian mystical discourse. On the other hand, his own mystical language is saturated with biblical quotations, biblical turns-of-phrase, biblical images. His overarching metaphor for the mystical encounter was marriage, but he lifted this metaphor not from personal experience of marriage, but from the biblical Song of Songs. But this one biblical book was only one of many he appealed to. Like other mystical writers, Bernard loved to mine scripture's nooks and crannies. To voice his sense of God's omnipresence, he cited Acts 17:38 ("In him we live and move and have our being"); to define the nature of mystical union, he cited 1 Corinthians 6:17 ("He who is united to the Lord becomes one spirit with him"); to explore the deep affinity of God and the soul, he cited Genesis 1:26 ("Let us make man in our image and likeness").

Other mystics appealed to other scriptural episodes, motifs, and verses. Evagrius appealed to Moses and the theophany on Mt. Sinai as the bedrock for his teaching on the sapphire light of the mind. Eckhart appealed to St. Paul's knockdown encounter with the risen Christ for his stress on seeing all things in and through God. Bonaventure spoke of the crucified Christ as the climax of the mystical journey. He also drew upon fairly arcane biblical imagery, such as the Mercy Seat above the Ark of the Covenant.

Scriptural imagery and exegesis are in no way limited to the Christian tradition. As we saw, Rumi's *Masnavi* has been called the "Qur'an in the Persian language" precisely because it is so deeply saturated with the Qur'an's language and imagery. Dōgen too focused on scripture. We noted his careful and ingenious uses of the *Nirvāna Sūtra* and the *Lotus Sūtra*. Contrary to Western descriptions of Zen as "pure experience" and contrary even to Zen's self-description as "a transmission outside the scriptures," Dōgen insisted on "the unity of Zen and scriptures" (*kyōzen itchi*).

This may seem like needless harping on the obvious, but as Katz rightly argues, too many grand surveys of mysticism have ignored the obvious. One other obvious point: mystics understand themselves not as mystics but as Christians, as Muslims, as Buddhists, and so on. For mystical writers, the mystical is not so much about experience, even if experience may be at play as one crucial element. Mysticism is about the revelation of hidden truths, truths about who we are as human beings, about what the nature of the universe is, and—at least in Western traditions—about who God is. It should come as no surprise that mystics turn their gaze to their own traditions' scriptures for definitive insights. In this, mystics do not differ from their coreligionists. Mystics often exegete scriptures in ways quite like their coreligionists. What distinguishes them then? Sometimes mystics appeal to scriptural verses, scriptural terminology, or scriptural images as a way to articulate, even map, the contours of their own (or others') most profound interior experiences. Other times mystics appeal to scripture as a public standard to judge their own (or others') experiences—to judge whether they be true or false, orthodox or heterodox, divinely inspired or demonic. The modern accent on experience distorts the usual mystical balance: scriptures measure experience, not vice versa. A third permutation—one we did not study—is that the very act of exegesis is itself mystical experience. The clearest exemplar of this in the Christian tradition is Origen of Alexandria, who saw biblical exposition as a Spirit-inspired enterprise and who passionately probed and sorted and expounded what he saw as the polysemous layers densely compressed within biblical texts.[8] Mystical exegesis is at the heart of much Jewish mysticism, especially in traditions surrounding the *Zohar*.[9] It is equally at work in Islam, notably in Rumi's contemporary, Ibn 'Arabī.[10]

Theology and the Mystical

Just as classic surveys of mysticism have ignored the role of scripture, so they have ignored, or even dismissed, the theological. William James's disregard is emblematic of this much wider trend. Even when scholars do acknowledge theological themes in mystical texts, a common move has been to downplay their significance. Mystics, they claim, are simply imposing on their mystical experiences interpretations drawn from their home religions. Theological interpretations are thus regarded as an extrinsic crust that can be conveniently and neatly peeled away.

How true is such a claim? Consider the case of Hildegard. Her most famous text, *Scivias*, offers verbal accounts and visual presentations of her personal visionary experiences, but her text's overarching focus is using those visions to expound Christian doctrine. Or take the case of Meister Eckhart. At the heart of his mysticism is his teaching on the unceasing birth of God in the soul. This teaching is founded upon and inextricably bound to the classic fourth-century Christian doctrine of the eternal, unceasing generation of the Son from the Father. To dismiss this doctrinal core of Eckhart's teaching is to render his mysticism unintelligible. Or take the case of Bonaventure. Bonaventure's is a single-mindedly Christ-centered mysticism. Christ is the "middle" (*medium*), the center of the Trinity who originates from the Father and co-originates the Spirit, the Father's self-expression and artistry, creation's prototype and exemplar, the mediator between God and humanity and thus the vehicle of salvation and of mystical ascent. The entire intelligibility of Bonaventure's mystical map would be blotted out beyond recognition if one discounts or dismisses its Christ-centered compass.

The language of doctrine forms a central thread not only in the Christian mystical tradition, but beyond. At the heart of Rumi's mysticism is the fundamental Islamic doctrine on the oneness of God. It undergirds and renders intelligible his dazzling paradoxes and poetic imagery. So too with Dōgen. At the heart of his teaching are fundamental Buddhist doctrines on the Buddha-nature and the transmission of the Buddha dharma. To strip out such doctrines from his teaching is to strip away the core of his mysticism.

The widespread intertwining of the doctrinal and the mystical is no accident. It cannot be reduced to mystics' concerns to justify their own orthodoxy. Theological bravado, in fact, got some mystics into hot water with their coreligionists. Theology lies at the very heart of the mystical enterprise. Mystics often set forth their (or others') experiences as the *experience of doctrine*. This sets mystical theologies apart from other ways of doing theology. Mystical theologies work from the conviction that doctrine is not extrinsic, not some outer standard or mere verbal measure of the truth. Rather, doctrine itself lies within the realm of the experiential. Mystics are convinced that key doctrines— whether of the Trinity or of the oneness of Allah or of the reality of Buddha-nature—can be and, in some cases, must be experienced. Jean Gerson was right, therefore, to speak of the mystical precisely as a form of doing *theology*. The issue, as Bonaventure noted, is the theologian's vocation itself: "The theologian considers how the world, which was made by God, will be brought back to God."[11] Mystics may allude to their own experiences, but the mystic's vision goes far beyond documenting personal experiences. Their concern spans the breadth of humanity, indeed, of the cosmos itself. Religious doctrines and theological languages provide mystics with time-tested, well-honed grammars for articulating such breadth of vision and for rendering its intelligibility to others.

Inheriting Tradition, Creating Tradition

Scripture and doctrine are two elements in the grammar that defines mystical texts. A third is the way mystical authors tap on earlier mystical texts, quoting them openly or alluding to them obliquely, reworking them consciously or soaking them in unwittingly. Take the case of Bernard. His *Sermons on the Song of Songs* drew on a long-standing tradition of mystical exegesis that dated back to Origen in the third century and had made its way to the Latin West via Ambrose and Gregory the Great. Bernard not only made that earlier tradition his own, but so reinvigorated it that he set off a fashion in Christian mystical discourse that lasted centuries. Or take the case of Bonaventure. He claimed that the outline shaping his *Mind's Journey into God* came from Francis's extraordinary mystical experience on Mount La Verna, which included a vision of a seraph and receiving the marks of Christ. The seraph's six wings marked out six stages of mystical ascent. Bonaventure went on to match pairs of stages to three distinct Christian mystical traditions, those of Francis, of Augustine, and of Pseudo-Dionysius. This is partly what made Bonaventure such a striking case study. He demonstrated what one might call "mystical multilinguism," that ability to negotiate earlier mystical languages so seamlessly that one creates a new mystical language out of older ones. The case of Merton, while less obvious, is no less striking. Merton drew heavily from earlier mystical languages, from Pseudo-Dionysius's apophaticism to the desert fathers' monologistic prayer methods to Eckhart's language of a "spark" at the soul's very core. But Merton's borrowings, embedded in passing turns of phrase or in passing images, come so thoroughly digested as to be nearly invisible except to those with ready and wide familiarity with Christian mystical literature. Merton even tapped on a broader linguistic palette. He both knew and drew on mystical vocabulary beyond Christianity, including that of Sufism and of Zen.

This sometimes subtle cross-referencing of earlier mystical discourses is not limited to the Christian mystical tradition. Rumi self-consciously knew and drew on earlier Sufi traditions, whether the flamboyant expostulations of the controversial al-Hallāj or the language of "states" and "stations." The case of Dōgen is even more obvious. His literary masterpiece, *Treasury of the True Dharma Eye*, is itself a mystical commentary on the earlier mystical literature of kōans, which enshrine the enlightenment dialogues of Ch'an masters and their disciples.

Mystical texts, like texts of any sort, have ancestors, and tracing their ancestry is at one level part and parcel of good disciplined reading. It has its risks. Source criticism always risks dissolving mystical texts into a patchwork of borrowed voices. The challenge is to step beyond tracing a text's complex genealogy and take in the finished fabric's broad pattern, whether its threads be borrowed or not. Tracing a mystical text's ancestry reminds us that mystics speak languages that they may well have improved on but did not invent. It also reminds us that just as ordinary languages always belong to quite specific human communities, so mystical languages always belong to specific mystical communities. (More on this in a moment.)

One other point: In writing—unlike in nature—one creates one's own ancestors. Great writers, by the way they self-consciously draw upon earlier genres or styles, earlier poetics or thematics, define their own literary ancestry. Writers, by the very act of writing, define a canon of classic literature. So too mystical authors. They create a mystical canon by the very way they draw on, imitate, even disagree with earlier mystical texts. Some modern critics have argued that the Christian mystical tradition is an artificial construct.[12] If so, it is a construct that mystical writers themselves have constructed, whether consciously or unconsciously, by their quoting of, alluding to, and backward glancings at earlier mystical texts.[13] This means that mystical discourse is no fixity. It shifts constantly. Writers, in the unique way they draw on, bring together, and transfigure earlier voices, are always creating a new literary nexus. Each new work, in turn, opens for later generations new linguistic possibilities by which one may create new modes of mystical discourse. Mystical literature remains a moving target, however unsettling that may be to those who want clear and distinct definitions.

Linguistics of the Mystical

Scholarship on mysticism has, in recent years, tended to move away from older psychological categories ("mystical experience," "mystical consciousness") and toward linguistic ones. Partly this stems from frustration with the literary naiveté and methodological conundrums of William James and other psychoanalysts of the mystical. Partly this comes from excitement over the potential of postmodern literary theories, such as those of Georges Bataille, Jacques Lacan, Jacques Derrida, and Michel de Certeau.[14] Some postmodern critics have gone so far as to claim that mysticism is nothing but language.[15] That takes things far too far.

Even so, mysticism dwells, in part, within worlds constructed out of language, and so language studies remain a necessary laboratory for analyzing a mystic's chemistry. If mystics, like poets, are raiders on the ineffable, they, like poets, deploy varied strategies for bringing to speech realities that defy speech. At one level, of course, all experience is beyond words. To explain even the simplest everyday experience can be staggeringly difficult. It is hard to put things clearly, to bring alive not only facts, but feelings, to chart out the wider dimensions and deeper implications of an event, to anticipate what one's audience knows and does not know, to pick and choose words that can flare up and bring to sight an event in our hearers' minds and hearts. All of us learn to express ourselves, for better or for worse, with a language we did not invent. We all begin speaking a borrowed tongue. Over time, we take the language we inherit as children and gradually make it our own. We draw upon its vast repertoire of words and phrases, its syntax and sounds, and somehow make of this stuff a vehicle for our own self-expression. However much we may complain to one another about how hard it is to talk about this or that everyday experience, we do somehow find a way. We do somehow, by some miracle, communicate with one another and bring the ineffable stuff of ordinary life to speech.

Mystics do something similar. They are born into and inherit a "language" called Christianity, or Islam, or Buddhism, or whatever. They draw upon their religion's inherent grammar and inherited vocabulary, its semantics and its syntax, its vast library of written texts and its equally vast repertoire of oral utterances. Mystics also draw upon prior mystical dialects—which, in themselves, possess prepackaged clusters of scriptural prooftexts, doctrinal phraseology, and poetic imagery. And from these intricate linguistic inheritances, they gradually bring to speech their personal experiences of mystery and their distinctive vision of a God-drenched world. They may and do complain of the difficulty, of the way that words betray them and mislead their hearers. I grant that the ineffability of what mystics try to bring to speech is vastly greater and more mysterious than what most of us try to bring to speech from our ordinary but ineffable experience. Still, we must not miss the obvious fact that mystics are unusually good wordsmiths. Earlier generations of scholars presumed, often naively, that one can pierce through a mystic's language to get at his or her psychological experience. Current scholars stress that mystical languages cannot be treated offhandedly, cannot be treated as wrapping paper to be ripped away and discarded. Mystical languages need to be acknowledged in their manyness and mapped for their unique geographies. To presume otherwise presumes that mystics do not know what they are talking about.

Mystical Languages of Unsaying

Some elements of mystical language—for example, quoting scriptures, citing doctrines—overlap with other types of religious speech. One element, however, is native to and distinctive of mystical speech: apophasis, or negative theology. Mystics often assert that certain realities—God, the soul, the universe, mystical union—are ineffable. Mystics assert these speech-defying realities by negating—often in shocking fashion—traditional religious ways of speaking. Eckhart, for example, spoke about a God beyond God and asserted that calling God "good" or "just" was telling lies and sinning. This linguistic habit figured prominently not only in Eckhart, but also in Evagrius, Bonaventure, and Merton. Apophatic speaking not only crosses the centuries. It also crosses religious traditions and shows up, as we saw, in Sufis such as Rumi and in Zen Buddhists such as Dōgen.

Michael Sells, a specialist in Islamic mysticism, has probed this in his recent study, *Mystical Languages of Unsaying*. His analysis has charted its presence and varieties across religious traditions: in pagans (Plotinus), in Christians (John the Scot Eriguena, Marguerite Porete, Meister Eckhart), and in Muslims (Ibn 'Arabi). He has also sought to uncover the linguistic dynamic that fuels the production of mystical speech. He notes that whenever mystics assert, for example, that "God is beyond names," they instantly recognize that that very claim contains an inescapable dilemma (what Sells calls *aporia*): it names what is beyond-name; it therefore contradicts the reality of the real God-beyond-names. Therefore, the mystic must negate his or her own claim, must negate the negation. Sells argues that apophasis, while described as "negative theology," is more precisely an "un-saying" (as the etymology of the Greek *apo phasis* implies). Mystical unsaying, Sells insists, has a built-in dynamic that produces speech:

> Every act of unsaying demands or presupposes a previous saying. Apophasis can reach a point of intensity such that no single proposition concerning the transcendent can stand on its own. Any saying (even a negative saying) demands a correcting saying, an unsaying. But that correcting proposition which unsays the previous proposition is in itself a "saying" that must be "unsaid" in turn. It is in the tension between the two propositions that the discourse becomes meaningful. That tension is momentary. It must be continually re-earned by ever new linguistic acts of unsaying.[16]

Mystical speech necessarily feeds off other, previous religious language. It presupposes positives ("God is one," "God is truth") for its negatives ("God is not one the way this-or-that is one," "God is not truth the way this-or-that is true"). Its unsayings can feed off prior claims in scripture or in doctrine, assertions from older mystical texts or from a mystic's own prior sayings. To speak the truth as experienced, the mystic must keep speaking to undo the earlier undoings.

Mystical speech has a double trajectory. One trajectory veers towards silence. Here words are used to purge us of words. Here words are stripped down and stripped away to let us see the reality that words block us from seeing. Words become fingers pointing at the moon. It is no accident that Rumi ended so many of his poems with his signature "*Khāmush*," "Silence!" The other trajectory veers toward a wordy overflowing fullness. Think back on Dōgen. For Dōgen, words are "entangling vines," things that trap us, but these same "entangling vines" can also disentangle us. Dōgen pointed out that mystical speech is liberating speech, that the way past the entanglement of religious words is, paradoxically, through entangling religious words.

"ABBA, GIVE ME A WORD": MYSTICAL COMMUNITIES

Robert Gimello, an expert in Buddhist mysticism, has pinpointed a deep flaw in older studies of mysticism. These works, he points out, portray mystics as figures who "stand aloof from and independent of the religious traditions 'of the masses'"; they type-cast mystics as "a transcultural aristocracy of *illuminati*."[17] Behind such portraiture lie old-fashioned romantic notions about the genius of the individual. Gimello warns of such hyperindividualist readings and argues against yanking mystics up out of their deep social roots.

Our case studies may have zeroed in on individuals, but we read them within, not apart from, their social worlds. The mystics we studied all belonged to larger mystical communities. Merton and Bernard were Cistercians; Hildegard was a Benedictine; Bonaventure, a Franciscan; Eckhart, a Dominican. Their ordinary lives and their extraordinary mystical teachings were nurtured by and cultivated within the religious orders to which they belonged. In the Western Christian tradition, mystical communities often take institutional shape as religious orders. But such mystical communities are hardly limited to Christianity. Rumi was heir to long-standing Sufi traditions and, in the end, created his own Sufi order, the Mevlevi, which exists to this day. So too Dōgen, who founded a still vibrant mystical community, the Sōtō sect of Japanese Zen. He repeatedly stressed his great debts to his monastic training in the Ch'an monasteries of Sung China, to his Ts'ao-tung Ch'an lineage, and to his Ch'an master Ju-ching.

I coin the term "mystical community" here. What do I mean? A mystical community is a religious community that self-consciously commits its members and its communal resources to religious perfection, however it may define that perfection. Mystical communities are religious elites. By this, I do not mean what Gimello criticizes, namely, some illumined spiritual aristocracy, let alone one that transcends its culture or its religion. Nor by speaking of "elites" do I mean that individual mystics are elitists or arrogant in any sense. Mystics, as a rule, tend to be humble and self-effacing. Mystical communities are elites in a quite narrow and quite specific sociological sense: they are professionals. They profess to commit themselves to living out their religious commitments at a radical level. That does not mean they always, or even often, succeed at it. It does mean that they invest the best resources of their individual and corporate lives—intellectual, emotional, physical, economic, ritual—to living out their commitments. For mystical communities, being religious means being single-mindedly committed to perfection. That perfection is some religious ideal, perhaps poverty or preaching or contemplative prayer or charitable service. And the community pursues it with intense focus and great personal and corporate energy. Pursuing perfection requires training in and the practice of contemplation. Pursuing it presumes renunciations, often radical ones (e.g. leaving family, abandoning property, renouncing marriage), as well as ascetic disciplines (e.g., fasting, vigils, intellectual study, psychological exercises). That does not mean that every member or even many members of a mystical community are mystics of some exalted type. But many enjoy periodic but little-publicized mystical experiences, and many cultivate contemplative outlooks. All this makes up the routine stuff of religious life. Because competing mystical communities embrace competing spiritual perfectionisms, their pursuits can spark and spawn intense rivalries. The Middle Ages witnessed notorious clashes between Dominicans and Franciscans. Bernard of Clairvaux used to spin out hilarious, if unfair, satires of his Benedictine rivals from Cluny. Similarly, Dōgen did not mince words about what he saw as failures of rival Ch'an and Zen lineages. My point is that we need to step back behind the individual mystics we have studied and chart how the mystical communities to which they belonged shaped the contours of their mysticism.

Transmission of the Lamp

Let us start not with the Christian experience, but the Buddhist, because it illuminates something overlooked within the Christian tradition itself. We saw how medieval Ch'an and Zen Buddhists created a vast hagiographic literature known as "transmission of the lamp records." These anthologies not only recorded stories of mystical awakenings of individual Ch'an and Zen masters; they also rooted these masters within a centuries-long spiritual genealogy, charting how the Buddha dharma passed from master to disciple, just as a single flame may pass from one lamp to another. Historical-critical studies have challenged the historical foundation of these accounts and various links (especially early ones) in their genealogies. That is not the point. The Ch'an and Zen traditions understand that mystical awakenings pass from generation to generation *in community*.[18] It is the Ch'an or Zen master who oversees the community's contemplative training. It is also the Ch'an or Zen master who serves as arbiter and judge of what constitutes authentic awakening and what does not. And while the Ch'an and Zen communities were and are deeply literate and have produced loads of texts, their mystical transmission remains oral, and beyond that, wordless. Nothing highlights this more than the kōan literature. Kōans, as we saw, are (mostly) excerpts from that bulkier "transmission of the lamp" literature. Most are dialogues between masters and disciples, and dialogues often end by announcing a disciple's mystical awakening. This literature highlights that mystical experiences are not private affairs. They are dialogical, even communal. Disciples learn from masters. And their experiences remain subject to masters' discernment, judgments, and certification.

Kōan literature has intriguing parallels in the Christian tradition, notably the stories of the fourth- and fifth-century desert fathers, stories that came to be collected first in Evagrius's *The Monk* and later in the *Sayings of the Fathers* (*Apophthegmata Patrum*). That literature illustrates that the Christian mystical tradition at an early date relied upon an oral master-disciple dynamic. Again and again the desert fathers' stories open with that classic question: "Abba, give me a word." We saw how that oral word was a prophetic word, a word announcing that the *abba* had read a disciple's heart and expected the disciple to enact that word in his life. What the disciple sought and what the *abba* offered was insight into a way of salvation and a way of encountering God here and now, in this life.

The literature of the desert fathers highlights patterns of oral instruction that remain alive and well within later, more institutionalized mystical communities. Let me offer a personal anecdote—something I normally avoid doing, but I think relevant here. I myself belong to one of these mystical communities, the Society of Jesus, founded in 1540 by a flamboyant Basque mystic, Ignatius of Loyola (1492–1556). Every Jesuit at least twice in his life must go through Ignatius's *Spiritual Exercises*. The *Exercises* (to vastly oversimplify it) requires that one undergo a thirty-day silent retreat in which one converses only with a spiritual director. During that month, one prays a minimum of five hours a day using a wide repertoire of prayer forms. The most famous is what Ignatius called *contemplatio*, that is, praying with one's imagination through the major episodes of the life of Jesus. I remember, in the middle of my thirty-day retreat as a novice, noting in my spiritual journal a key realization: Jesuit mystical spirituality cannot be written down; it is, at its very core, oral. Some books, whether on athletic training or car repair or computers, require performance. Ignatius's *Spiritual Exercises* certainly does. It is not a text to be read; it is a text to be worked through, enacted, and made one's own.[19] Ignatius's text provides a rough outline for this thirty-day retreat, but by Ignatius's own insistence, the director must adapt things, shifting constantly in light of the retreatant's prayer reports, shifting things in light of what the director judges to be God's discernible presence. I realized that Jesuit spirituality, like Zen spirituality, is a lamplight transmitted generation to generation, orally, from teacher to disciple. It is impossible to write it down. While texts play key roles within mystical communities, oral teaching, however difficult to catch a glimpse of, is the ever-fluid bedrock in which the mystical gets adapted and ever so precisely fitted to each individual within the community. Mystical texts are inevitably one-size-fits-all. Spiritual masters are their custom tailors.

Mysticism as Liturgical Performance

Mystical communities, like all religious communities, have their rituals. Obvious, but too often ignored. Yet to miss this fact is to miss much of what constitutes mysticism. Mystics' words may come down to us as written texts, as words fixed and frozen on the pages of books, but often those words preexisted as oral speech. In their genesis, those words poured forth from live speakers before live audiences. In their genesis, those words were enacted, delivered, performed. And this live oral performance took place within a wider ritual enacted by a specific mystical community. Think back on Bernard and Eckhart. Their best-known mystical texts are sermons. Those sermon texts have been reworked and, in Bernard's case, given considerable literary polish. But in their origin, they were performed within public worship, either as part of a eucharistic celebration or a Liturgy of the Hours. As oral performance, they not only presume a live audience; they also presume quite specific qualities in that live audience: an easy familiarity with scripture, a high degree of religious commitment, a deep moral seriousness. (More on this in a moment.)

Ritual venues are hardly limited to the Christian mystical tradition. Take the case of Rumi's lyrics in the *Divān*. These were not crafted in some private bookish study. They burst forth orally and were hurriedly transcribed by devoted disciples in the noisy late-night *samāʿ* where Rumi and fellow Sufis orally, publicly recited ecstatic poems in praise of God. These artful poetic outbursts formed but one thread in a much larger mystical performance that included ecstatic music, dance, and fervent chanting of God's names. So too with Dōgen. The bulk of his *Extensive Record* includes transcriptions of oral sermons (*jōdō*) delivered in Chinese from the high altar in the Dharma Hall to monks ready to embark on long hours of zazen. Dōgen's oral sermons might have been written down and treasured by disciples as the outpourings of an enlightened master. But Dōgen intended both his own words and the kōans he cited as explosive devices meant to shatter illusions and provoke mystical awakenings among his hearers.

The ritual backdrop of mystical texts should be obvious. Yet if one scans older classic studies of mysticism, one gets no hint of this. Their fixation on mysticism as psychological experience glosses over the far more common landscape of mysticism as liturgical performance. Here again, William James and his idiosyncratic philosophy of religion has skewed the scholarship and led commentators to ignore what is right before their eyes. They too often treat mysticism solely as private, not public; as individual, not communal. Classic studies are not only the culprits here. Even many excellent contemporary studies focus so narrowly on texts and textuality that they neglect oral performance and liturgical setting. We need to remember that many mystical texts, like musical scores or scripts of plays, presuppose live performance. To miss the performative is to miss much of the dynamic.

Consider sermons. Sermons, according to Augustine's classic formulation, are meant to instruct, to delight, and to move.[20] They instruct hearers in religious content; they delight hearers if only to keep them attentive as hearers; and they move hearers—or, at least, try to move them—to moral action and religious practice. Not all sermons do this successfully, of course, nor do even the best ones achieve all three ends simultaneously. But all sermons are performative. What then sets mystical sermons apart? Sometimes it is content. Mystical sermons may, content-wise, instruct hearers how they may encounter God here and now, within the depths of their hearts or within the fabric of their lives. But most mystical sermons are not just mystical in content. They are mystical in their ultimate end, in the way they strive to move hearers to a mystical encounter with God (or in the case of Buddhism, to an encounter with ultimate reality). This means that mystical sermons focus not on the speaker's mystical experience(s), but on the hearers'. Bernard did use sermons as a vehicle to discuss his own mystical experiences, but that fact probably tells us more about his personality and his personal rhetorical style than it does about mystical speech in general. Eckhart's example better highlights the performative. Eckhart, as we saw, discussed mystical content, namely, that "God's ground and the soul's ground are one ground." But he did more. He sought to enact that identity, marshaling a complex of verbal strategies—metaphors, startling logic, that odd first-person-eternal voice—to awaken his hearers to a union present here and now.

Apprenticeship into the Mystical

Mystics are almost never prodigies and almost never autodidacts. Most spend long years of apprenticeship within the confines of their religious communities. There they receive training at many levels—intellectual, moral, ritual, contemplative. And mystics, in their maturity, spend much time and, on occasion, considerable literary energy training disciples. If one focuses solely on mystical texts, as has become fashionable, one risks losing sight of this. Merton may be well known for his writings on contemplation, but he spent much time and much energy training Cistercian novices and scholastics in the basics of Cistercian life. His talks to beginners focus more on the rudiments of the spiritual life than on its mystical peaks. Or consider Eckhart. He certainly delivered subtle and erudite mystical sermons, but he also wrote an important but unmystical treatise, *Talks of Instruction*, for his Dominican novices. So too with Evagrius, who, for all his mystical interests, composed a decidedly unmystical work for beginners, *The Foundations of Monastic Life*. Or consider Dōgen. While the fascicles of his *Treasury* presume advanced disciples and learned readers, he devoted much care in his later years to crafting monastic legislation as a framework for cultivating a "pure" community.

The modern fascination with peak experiences may miss these less glamorous but no less vital disciplinary programs. We saw the issue vividly in Evagrius, in what he called "ascetic practice" (*praktikē*). Evagrius's writings on the "eight thoughts" offer a demanding program for naming and rooting out deep and often subtle psychic vices. His innovative analyses not only named an array of personal demons; they also offered a thoroughgoing program for reforming habits and cultivating a life of virtue. Evagrius presumed that the mystical life (*gnostikē*) came only after a long apprenticeship in prayer and disciplined self-knowledge. Evagrius's reflections on ascetic practice presumed a community with high standards and profound commitments. His reading public was monks who had already renounced marriage and family, wealth and career, even the humblest comforts and simplest possessions. Some were foreigners, like John Cassian, who had traveled far from their homeland and settled into the obscurity of the Egyptian desert. Just being a member of Evagrius's community at Kellia presumed one knew lots of basics on how to fast, how to pray, how to contemplatively do manual labor.

The mystical journey is often compared to mountain climbing. The analogy is apt. Mountain climbers' first mountain is never Everest. Climbers spend long years winding their way up lesser peaks, slowly mastering their sport. Mystical ascents, like mountain climbing, can be a dangerous business. Most mystical texts presume a long and disciplined apprenticeship within a community of climbers. As the desert fathers used to say, "If you see a young man climbing up to heaven by his own will, catch him by the foot and pull him down to earth for it is not good for him."[21]

Calligraphers of the Ineffable

Easy to overlook are those disciples who circle round mystics and zealously record their words and deeds. Here again, Zen practices put in high relief patterns found worldwide. Much of Dōgen's work, both the oral sermons in his *Extensive Record* and the late-night kōan commentaries in his *Treasury*, come to us from transcriptions scribbled down by Ejō and other devoted disciples. Similar circles surrounded many of the figures we studied. We saw, in Rumi's case, how Hosām al-Din faithfully spent years transcribing Rumi's meandering mystical epic *Masnavi*. Disciples play key roles as stenographers and manufacturers of mystical texts. They work hard to transcribe and preserve fleeting spoken words. They also quietly select which words deserve transcription. They may preserve, but they also filter out things in ways quite difficult to measure.

No less important but even less visible are the generations of copyists who after that first generation of disciples quietly and anonymously reproduce mystical texts they consider worth preserving. We stand profoundly in their debt. Text critics, those scholars who create modern critical editions from surviving manuscripts, are acutely aware of the virtues and vices of such copyists. Copyists of mystical texts, like copyists the world over, are inveterate tinkerers, quietly "correcting" all sorts of things in the manuscripts under their gaze. They may correct what they judge to be bad grammar or odd vocabulary; they may clean up what they perceive as inaccurate scriptural citations; they may alter turns of phrase they judge heterodox. So while copyists do preserve, they also, here and there, subtly disfigure things. They are a complex lot. I noted the way monastic copyists quietly translated Evagrius's writings into Syriac, Armenian, Coptic, Ethiopic, and Arabic. Some also quietly removed Evagrius's name and inserted another's because they associated Evagrius with Origenist heterodoxy.

These two groups—the transcribers of the oral and the copyists of the written—are often active members of larger mystical communities. Both are what I would call *calligraphers of the ineffable*. Evagrius, as we saw, was a calligrapher in the literal sense. He made his living copying books. But he was also a calligrapher of the ineffable. He had apprenticed in the monastic life under leading desert fathers such as Macarius the Egyptian. Evagrius consciously preserved such oral wisdom. His treatise *The Monk* contains the earliest written collection of sayings of the desert fathers. Evagrius was equally self-conscious about why he preserved this oral wisdom. He wanted to record "the upright ways of the monks who have gone before us and to correct ourselves with respect to these," for "it is they who anoint us for the struggles and who heal the wounds inflicted by the wild beasts."[22] This oral wisdom thus marked a pathway for the follower and a corrective for the wayward, an anointing for the inevitable struggle and a medicine for the inevitable wounds.

These disciples and these scribes work from a *spirituality of memory*—to coin yet another term. They take great pains to remember accurately. But theirs is not accuracy for accuracy's sake. Theirs is not the accuracy of modern scholars. Theirs is accuracy for the sake of mystical spirituality. Mystical communities work to remember because they are convinced that remembering provides access to the holy. They preserve mystics' memories and mystics' writings because they desire holiness and seek pathways to holiness. Memories of mystics—their words, their deeds, their very memories—provide precious landmarks. Those landmarks offer pathways across the demon-ridden landscape of the human heart. They also offer passageways inward and upward to a God who is a trackless infinitude, who waits at 10,000 doorways to embrace those called, willing, and graced to make the passage.

THROUGH A GLASS DARKLY: MYSTICAL EXPERIENCES

William James set the terms and trajectory for the modern study of mysticism. That is no accident. James was a pioneer of psychology, an academic field emblematic of modernity in many ways. Few things define our world more than the fascination with psychology, with the intricate twists and turns of our half-known, half-hidden motives, with the subtle interplay and beneath-the-surface contradictions between what we know of ourselves and what we end up doing with our lives. This taste for the psychological plays itself out in the novels we read and in the movies we watch, in our taste for talk shows and reality television and in the everyday ways we talk about relationships that define our loves and our lives. Given this culture, it seems all too natural to isolate the psychological as the centerpiece of the mystical. But is it adequate? Clearly not, given what we have seen of mystical texts and mystical communities. Nonetheless, psychology remains one vital thread in any analysis. The problem with James and so many other philosophers and psychoanalysts of the mystical is methodological naiveté, their propensity for leaping to what they diagnose as a subjective core and, in that leap, sidestepping the often difficult and messy literary, historical, sociological, and theological analyses that must come with any disciplined reading. Let us reflect here on the personal, experiential dimension of the mystical—but with a critical eye.

The Overlooked Ordinary

An anecdote: In graduate school, I took a course on sixteenth-century spirituality from John O'Malley, S.J., a renowned Renaissance and Reformation scholar. As we made our way through texts by Erasmus and Luther and Teresa of Ávila, O'Malley repeatedly asked us a down-to-earth question: how did the writers we read—given what their texts say about the spiritual life—go about "filling up" their day? This is a vital and overlooked starting point. How did the mystics we studied fill up their day? Well, they did many things, but one important thing they did was pray. Prayer was part and parcel of their daily experience. They became recognized experts in prayer and contemplation because they had prayed and contemplated daily, often for long hours and often for long years at a stretch. I point out this not to be pedantic, but because in scholarly studies of mysticism, both classic and contemporary, this obvious fact is given short shrift or overlooked altogether.

Think back on the mystics we studied. The Christians would have experienced Christian rituals, notably, the weekly (and for some, daily) Eucharist and the many-times-per-day Liturgy of the Hours. They also had personal devotional practices. One was sacred reading (*lectio divina*), that slow, meditative chewing on biblical texts. One reason mystics such as Bernard or Evagrius could speak in scripture-saturated prose or leap from biblical text to biblical text to explain their points is the simple fact that they had prayed over the Bible for years. Many also practiced wordless contemplation. Merton stresses this, but we also saw how Evagrius, at the genesis of the Christian mystical tradition, advocated such practice. John Cassian brought that Evagrian insistence to the Latin West, and Benedict, when he set about writing his influential *Rule*, insisted that his monks read Cassian. The very Psalm phrase Cassian advocated repeating unceasingly as a mantra ("God, come to my assistance; Lord, make haste to help me") was adopted as the opening phrase of every monastic Liturgy of the Hours. Both word-centered praying and wordless contemplation form the wider experiential grounding for mystical experience within the Christian tradition. As Evagrius emphasized, "If you are a theologian, you will pray truly; and if you pray truly, you will be a theologian."[23]

This applies equally to Muslims like Rumi and to Buddhists like Dōgen. Rumi may not have spoken much about it, but as a devout Muslim, he prayed five times a day. As a Sufi, he also practiced the *dhikr* ("remembrance"), that unceasing recitation of the names of God. Even in a nontheist tradition such as

Zen, contemplation formed the very heart of Dōgen's practice and the locus for his decisive views on enlightenment. His single most famous teaching is "practice-realization" (shushō-ittō), the inseparable oneness of zazen and enlightenment.

To savor what the disciplined experience of prayer involves, let me suggest comparisons with two other types of disciplined practitioners. First, think about musicians. In public concerts, they can dazzle us with their virtuosity and move our hearts in profound and hard-to-articulate ways. But long before musicians ever step onto the stage and into the limelight, they master their instruments and their craft slowly, often tediously, through long hours and over lonely years. No matter how gifted, these artists acquire their technical virtuosity, their improvisational spontaneity, and their brilliant expressiveness slowly, fitfully. Their artistry is the quiet fruit of practice, practice, and more practice. Second, think about Olympic athletes. They come to our attention but once every four years. We see them only at their peak and are amazed at their record speeds, their extraordinary endurance, and their dazzling grace of movement. What we do not see is their grueling ordinary workouts begun at five in the morning and carried on for hours every day for years. Nor do we see what their commitments have cost them, the sacrifices, both great and small. We are blissfully ignorant of their daily aches and pains and the anguish of their slow-to-heal injuries. Olympic highlight reels may make for exciting viewing, but they hardly let one know how the games are played, let alone how individual athletes train to play.

Too often scholarly studies of mystical experiences remind me of sports highlight reels or greatest-hits compilations. Too often they zoom in on dazzling moments of spiritual virtuosity, abstracting them from the disciplinary routine. Unless we read mystical texts from start to finish—and not simply anthologies—and unless we see how mystical communities actually live, we are liable to miss the ordinary, the slow, and the often fitful and painful progress done outside the limelight. Too often, as we read mystical texts and, even more, as we read scholarly analyses of mystical experiences, we may miss the subtle editing out of the ordinary. Ironically, scholars—who should know better—can get so taken up with the abstracting of brief peak experiences from the unremarkable everyday routine of being religious that they lose their bearings. For all the scholarly interest in "experience," the experiences they describe are treated in ways utterly abstracted from experience. We need to see that the everyday center for the mystic is the everyday routine of prayer and contemplation. That, of course, is not all they do to fill up their day. But it remains a highly disciplined, time-intensive, and usually off-camera center of their lives. Mystical experiences may appear like sudden eruptions, but they erupt from this quiet and too often overlooked center. Mystical experiences are the extraordinary moments of prayer within a lifetime of ordinary moments of prayer. To abstract them from this more pedestrian routine renders them not only abstract, but rootless and unintelligible.

Varieties

James entitled his classic work *The Varieties of Religious Experience*. The key word is "varieties." James was hardly alone in charting this variety. Centuries earlier, Jean Gerson had done the same, listing "contemplation, ecstasy, rapture, liquefaction, transformation, union, exultation, . . . jubilation beyond the spirit, of being taken into a divine darkness, of tasting God, of embracing the bridegroom."[24] We studied only a handful of cases, but we too came across extraordinary variety. Hildegard reported frequent visions. She seems, at first glance, to play out the stereotype of the mystic: an experiencer of strange visions or voices or other psychological oddities. Yet Hildegard understood visions in ways that move against the grain of our expectations: as revelations that helped interpret Christian doctrines or served as prophetic judgments on the politics of her day. This, as I noted, has led some to question her mystical credentials. But as I argued, at least as important as her visionary gifts was an underlying mystical vision of a God-drenched world, encapsulated in her articulations of God's presence within the world's "greenness" and within the cosmos's musicality.

If Hildegard was at once conventional and unconventional, so too were others we studied. Bonaventure reported not his own mystical experience, but Francis of Assisi's. That experience included a vision of a seraph and its physical aftermath, the stigmata. This was no mere psychological event. It was profoundly physical, and its physicality lay at the center of its mystical meaning: Francis had imitated Jesus even unto enduring the wounds of the cross. Francis thus became an enfleshed icon of the crucified Christ. Some today may choose to question Bonaventure's report or the event's authenticity. However one judges things, Francis's experience serves as a cautionary tale to modern theorists who reduce the mystical solely to psychology.

Still, the reports we saw were, in the main, interior ones. Bernard, who pioneered the very language of "experience," reported profound interior experiences and found in the biblical Song of Songs both a vocabulary and a measure for his experiences. For much of the Middle Ages, Bernard was the mystic's mystic. Dante famously chose Bernard as his guide to the highest spheres of paradise, so much was his contemplative expertise respected.[25] Even so, Bernard reported neither visions nor voices nor other psychic phenomena.

His language turned apophatic the moment he spoke of the mystical encounter itself. Nor did his negations articulate it in psychological terms, as an event of "mystical consciousness." They highlighted how his mystical experiences unveiled both the soul's vast depths and God's elusive omnipresence. What came through in Bernard was not psychological specificity, but an almost dizzying affective intensity. Bernard seems to have self-consciously avoided sensory language ("seeing God," "hearing God"), and invoked the terminology of the "inner senses" only to negate it. Bernard's restraint proved no restraint to later mystics, such as the thirteenth-century Beguines or the sixteenth-century Carmelites, who mined his marriage motifs and wove them into the fabric of their own florid visionary encounters and ecstatic states.

Evagrius described experiences of "sapphire light" at the "peak of the mind." It is hard to know how literally to take his sapphire language, given that Evagrius self-consciously alludes to the biblical account of the theophany of Moses and the elders of Israel on Mount Sinai. Evagrius saw this experience as seeing God's uncreated light refracted in the mind's pure mirror. Just as Bernard's language of mystical marriage inspired a centuries-long tradition within the mysticism of the Latin West, so too Evagrius's language of sapphire light inspired a centuries-long tradition in the Greek East and Syriac Middle East. His light-mysticism was expanded upon by authors as diverse as Diodochus of Photice, Isaac the Syrian, Pseudo-Dionysius, Maximus Confessor, and Gregory Palamas.

Such interior peak experiences—visions, ecstatic union, inner light—attract the bulk of attention and analysis from psychologists and philosophers of religion. At least as common and at least as important are peak experiences of another sort: contemplative awakenings or breakthroughs. Remember Merton's Fourth-and-Walnut episode. Merton did not see visions or hear voices. His was no out-of-body experience. He retained full, sober consciousness. There was nothing "ecstatic" about it. He saw ordinary people on the streets of Louisville charged with God's presence. It marked a breakthrough that enabled Merton to see the right-here, right-now world with transfigured eyes. This was not Merton's first mystical experience, nor would it be his last. Remember his striking experience at Polunnawara. The Fourth-and-Walnut episode, while intense, was emblematic of what he had already written about frequently and would go on writing about frequently: contemplation. It was an experience notable for its intensity, not for its difference from his routine contemplative experience as a hermit.

Breakthroughs into new ways of seeing have intriguing parallels in Zen Buddhist literature—which explains, in part, why Merton was so intrigued with Buddhism in general and Zen in particular. Cultivation of a breakthrough into enlightenment is at the heart of Ch'an and Zen religious experience. We saw one dramatic instance of it in the hagiographic account of Dōgen's awakening, what he (and the later Sōtō tradition) came to speak of as "dropping off mind-body." For Dōgen, this new seeing opened up a new world that had been right before his eyes all along. As he counseled, "We must realize that inexhaustible store is present not only all around us, it is present right beneath our feet and within a single drop of water"; one should "not wait for great enlightenment, as great enlightenment is the tea and rice of daily activity."[26] For Dōgen, as for Merton, breakthroughs are just the beginning of what was always there.

"Breakthrough" was important for Eckhart, but it was not an experiential category. I note this because some modern authors (e.g., D. T. Suzuki and Rudolph Otto) have claimed a kinship between Eckhart and Buddhists.[27] But is this claim accurate? For Eckhart, breakthrough meant a return to or a rediscovery of one's eternal identity within the divine ground of being. I find it intriguing that many contemporary commentators see Eckhart as the mystic's mystic when he shows astonishingly little interest in "mystical experiences."[28] I say this not to impugn Eckhart's mystical credentials, but to note what it says about contemporary sensibilities. We saw a second mystical theme in Eckhart, the birth of God in the soul. He normally spoke of this birth not in experiential terms, but in ontological ones—as God's dynamic creativity within us. Eckhart did speak of this, though rarely, in psychological terms, as taking place in the soul's "noblest part," and he did say that "this birth . . . always comes with fresh light," using the analogy of a lightning flash.[29] Still, Eckhart, the contemporary mystic's mystic, is largely unexperiential in focus. Eckhart often uses the word "I" in mystical-sounding ways, but more as a rhetorical device, what I called his "first-person-eternal voice," as a way of speaking of our preexistence in the mind of God. Eckhart's experiential thrust is more implied than stated. His words are performative; they point not to Eckhart's experiences, but to his hearers'.

Mapmaking

What does one do with such variety? One long-standing strategy within mystical traditions, both West and East, is mapmaking. We looked at two influential mapmakers, Bonaventure and Evagrius. Bonaventure charted a seven-stage journey: finding God outside us (1) through and (2) in creation; finding God within us (3) through and (4) in God's image in the soul; and finding God beyond us (5) through and (6) in his name as oneness and Trinity; arriving finally (7) in ecstatic union with the Crucified Christ. Evagrius, centuries earlier, charted a broad two-stage map: (1) ascetic practice (*praktikē*), that "spiritual method for purifying the passionate part of the soul" and for acquiring a ecology of virtues that allow the soul's three parts to reintegrate and work as God had originally made them to work; and (2) mystical knowledge (*gnostikē*), with its two substages, (2a) contemplating God's presence in the created world (*physikē*) and (2b) contemplating God as Trinity (*theologikē*). We did not study other famous mapmakers, such as John Climacus, whose *Ladder of Divine Ascent* charts a thirty-step process, or Teresa of Ávila, whose *Interior Castle* charts seven "dwelling places." Arguably the most influential map comes from Pseudo-Dionysius, who spoke of three dynamics: purgation, illumination, and union.[30] Mapmaking and stage charting are common not only in the Christian tradition, but beyond. In Sufism, there is the "path" (*tarīqa*) with its stations and states. In Buddhism, there are incredibly elaborate and detailed schemes and maps.[31]

We need to read mystical mapmakers and their maps with care. Some maps may well reflect a mystic's own spiritual journey. But the autobiographical is not the only narrative that may lie behind such spiritual maps. Some maps may be drawn from scriptures, because mystics see scripture as the decisive measure of experience. Some maps may also reflect the mystic's experience as a spiritual director. Many figures we studied spent long hours directing others in the spiritual path. Merton certainly did. So did Eckhart and Evagrius. So, certainly, did Dōgen. These served not only as spiritual directors of individual seekers, but as leaders of and spiritual pedagogues for larger communities of seekers. Numbering stages has great pedagogical value. It is easier for hearers to remember a numbered hierarchy. We should also be alert to the absence of maps and to rejections of a hierarchy of mystical experiences. The Zen tradition, with its stress on sudden awakenings, tends to reject gradualist schemes of the spiritual life, and thus stage theories. One has to ask why Meister Eckhart, who certainly knew of Pseudo-Dionysius's and Bonaventure's writings and who, as a theologian, had a scholastic's fondness for numbering arguments, never plots stages or numbers progress in the spiritual life. Mystics themselves seem to take experiential maps with a grain of salt. Bonaventure may be famous for his seven-stage *Itinerarium*, but he is also the author of another text, *The Mystical Vine*, which expounds the three-stage Dionysian scheme of purgation, illumination, and union. Mystical maps, in other words, may be as much heuristic as experiential.

Unio mystica

Odysseys, including spiritual ones, seek a homecoming. Modern theorists often speak of "mystical union" (*unio mystica*) as that endpoint.[32] Evelyn

Underhill, for example, saw it as the defining issue: "Mysticism, in its pure form, is . . . the science of union with the Absolute, and nothing else, and . . . the mystic is the person who attains to this union, not the person who talks about it."[33] This assertion is not without its difficulties. The term "mystical union" appears rather late in the Christian tradition, only becoming prominent in seventeenth-century treatises.[34] While this joining of the adjective "mystical" with the noun "union," is late, the noun "union" or adjective "unitive" or metaphors of oneness appear much, much earlier. We saw it in Jean Gerson's classic definition: that "mystical theology is an experiential knowledge of God that comes through the embrace of unitive love."[35] Gerson admired Bernard, and Gerson's accent on love as the uniting force comes from Bernard. Bernard was quite explicit and theologically precise about this: God and the soul become "one in spirit" and *not* "one in being." Bernard took pains to distinguish the soul's love-wrought union with God from the Son's ontological union with the Father. For Bernard, the overarching metaphor of union was marriage, and he boldly explored its erotics: of kissing, of breasts, of bridal chambers. For all his boldness, Bernard's mystical erotics seem tame by comparison with the flamboyant imagery and accounts of mystical union in the thirteenth-century Beguines and sixteenth-century Carmelites.

But Bernard's marriage metaphors were only one account of union. Bonaventure also saw union as the climax of the journey. But his sense of union was different because he worked from a different christology. Whereas Bernard's Christ was the bridegroom of the soul, Bonaventure's, like Francis's, was the crucified. For Bonaventure, union meant sharing in the radical self-emptying, self-abnegating union with Christ crucified. Union involved entering into a divine darkness. Eckhart too spoke of oneness; his notion was not of mystical union, but of mystical identity—that "God's ground and the soul's ground are one ground." He underlined such claims with a cluster of images, such as "the ground" as a vast trackless desert. Eckhart focused on this mystical identity not as an experience, but as a realizable metaphysical truth. What interested Eckhart was its reality and its implications rather than its experience. Eckhart's theology of mystical identity had harsh critics. Even if his inquisitors did not target his speaking of a "breakthrough into the ground," they did single out and condemn the way he spoke of us and Christ as "one and the same Son."

At the origins of the Christian mystical tradition, Evagrius insisted that theology in its deepest and truest sense meant seeing the Trinity that God is. Evagrius also spoke of unity with God and expressed his deep regrets about the incompleteness for his own journey. For Evagrius, while seeking unity might be something experienced by individuals, this search itself was emblematic of a vast cosmic movement, a return of all things into God. He drew on the metaphor of rivers streaming and gushing down to a vast sea: "Like torrents to the sea, minds return to [God, and] he completely changes them to his own nature, colour, and taste; in his endless and inseparable unity, they will be one and no longer many."[36]

The Sufi tradition also emphasized union. The Islamic doctrine of *tawhīd*, of the oneness of God, both fueled that language of union and put a brake on it. Rumi spoke of mystical unity in an erotic language more flamboyant than, but not unlike that of, Bernard. He also, like other Sufis, embraced the language of *fanā'*, "annihilation," and invoked the metaphors of the ocean, of the faint drops of individuality vanishing into an oceanic vastness, and of moths plunging into and burning up in the firelight.

What about Buddhism? It is difficult to say, and the difficulty should not be underplayed. Dōgen, like most Buddhists, emphasizes the nondual and took pains to unmask false, illusory splits within oneself ("body-mind"), between oneself and others, or between oneself and the wider world. On the other hand, he spoke of "impermanence-Buddha-nature," a thoroughgoing accent on the buzzing, blooming manyness of things, a deep appreciation of the utter uniqueness of each and every thing in its particularity—thus rejecting a mystical vision that blends all things into some cosmic unity. There are other moments when, as in his essay *One Bright Pearl*, Dōgen points to a magnificent unity of beauty. While this language—that this thing or that thing is "one bright pearl"—is one way he pointed to the radically nondual, it cannot be presumed he is speaking of a oneness within ultimate reality that is anything like what Christians or Muslims speak of, much less what Hindus mean when they speak of a deeper monism.

The claim by Underhill and others that "mystical union" defines mysticism risks distorting the history of mystical literature. McGinn, who oversaw a book-length interreligious study of the issue, concluded that "the study of mystical tradition indicates that the language of union is *only one* of the linguistic strategies used by mystics to try to describe, or at least to point to, what they contend is the ultimately ineffable nature of their contact with God."[37] The modern focus on experiences of mystical union misses countercurrents and critiques within the Christian mystical tradition. One key voice we touched upon but did not explore was Augustine's. Augustine was deeply interested in mystical ascents and recorded several famous (and much disputed) accounts in his *Confessions*.[38] He remained adamant about their limits. He saw them as pointers to or hints of a future life with God, and cited St. Paul's phrase that we see God "now through a glass darkly, but then face to face" (1 Cor. 13:12). Seeing God in all things and seeing all things in God may be glimpsed here and now, but for Augustine this world remains opaque, and its opacity will lift only in an unimaginable future life with God.[39]

Augustine's challenge is one countervoice. A second comes from Evagrius's disciple, John Cassian. Cassian thought that the union of the Father and the Son bespoke a possible union of God and us. He also insisted that monastic life offered here-and-now foretastes of eternal life and that the monastic life might be seen as an ascent with Christ up the mountain of transfiguration. It could include ecstatic moments, fiery prayer, or fugitive glimpses, but Cassian thought the mystical life involved more than this or that experience, however dazzling. The deeper process was what the Greek mystical tradition came to call "deification" (theōsis), that graced transfiguration of the ordinary. For Cassian, the goal is that "every love, every desire, every effort, every undertaking, every thought of ours, everything that we live, that we speak, that we breath, will be God."[40] For Cassian, the journey is about the ordinary stuff of life: loving, striving, thinking, speaking, breathing. While that journey may include fugitive glimpses of Christ transfigured, it foreshadows and, in the end, requires our own transfigured life.

DEFINING MYSTICISM

A Common Core? Or Contextualist?

How are we to interpret this variety of mystical experiences? What about the varied conceptions of mystical union? William James may have called his book *The Varieties of Religious Experience*, but he embraced not mystical variety, but mystical unanimity. He held the thesis that mystics, however diverse their reports, are experiencing the same thing. And Evelyn Underhill, whose *Mysticism* remains one of the most widely read classic studies, agreed. They are but two of a long line of theorists to embrace this "common core" hypothesis. Others theorists include Aldous Huxley, Rudolph Otto, Joseph Maréchal, William Johnston, Mircea Eliade, and Ninian Smart.[41]

The most often cited defender of the common-core view is Walter T. Stace (1886–1967), whose influential *Mysticism and Philosophy* (1961) claims to offer a systematic study of the issue. Stace argues, as his central hypothesis, "that the experience of all [mystics] are basically the same . . . but that each puts upon his experiences the intellectual interpretations which he has derived from the peculiarities of his own culture."[42] To argue that different reports do not indicate different experiences requires "a distinction between a mystical experience itself and the conceptual interpretations which may be put upon it."[43] According to

Stace, "experience" and "conceptual interpretations" can be neatly separated; one can "penetrate through the mantle of words to the body of the experiences which it clothes."[44] In practice, Stace handles texts in ways oblivious to their original context, whether historical or literary or religious, and interprets them in almost willfully arbitrary fashion.[45] When a text mentions anything religiously specific ("God," "Allah,""nirvāna"), Stace judges it "interpretation"; when the same text mentions a term he thinks descriptive ("light," "darkness," "union," "essential unity," "imageless," "nothingness," "silence," "nakedness"), he judges it "experiential."[46] Stace says that "it seems to be clear that if we strip the mystical experience of all intellectual interpretations such as that which identifies it with God, or with the Absolute, or with the soul of the world, what is left is simply the undifferentiated Unity."[47]

What happens when mystics speak not of "undifferentiated unity" but of "union with God"? Stace admits that some, such as Teresa of Ávila, preferred speaking of mystical "union with God." Teresa's problem, according to Stace, was that "she was a woman of extremely simple Christian piety with no interest in theory, or in abstract thinking, or in philosophical distinctions and analyses, and no capacity for them."[48] Because of this, she was not capable of correctly interpreting her own experiences:

> "Union with God" is not an uninterpreted description of any human being's experience. It is a theistic interpretation of the undifferentiated unity. St. Teresa's uninterpreted experience is the same as Eckhart's, but she is incapable of distinguishing between experience and interpretation so that when she experiences divisionless oneness of the mystical consciousness she jumps at once to its conventional interpretation in terms of Christian beliefs.[49]

Stace goes on to claim that while Eckhart was certainly capable of such philosophic distinctions, he too wrongly interpreted his "experience" of "undifferentiated unity" because he read things in terms of the Christian doctrine of the Trinity.[50] What permits Stace's interpretative bravado (or arrogance, depending on one's view) is the presumption that mystical experience is radically ineffable. If mystical experience is so truly and thoroughly ineffable, then we do not really have to pay attention to what mystics actually say about their own experiences. Stace is convinced that he, as meta-interpreter, can actually render a more accurate interpretation of what mystics are experiencing than they themselves are capable of.

The once-reigning common-core hypothesis has come under repeated and detailed fire, and its most articulate critic has been Steven Katz. Over the last few decades, Katz has edited several influential collections of essays: *Mysticism* and *Philosophical Analysis* (1979), *Mysticism and Religious Traditions* (1983), *Mysticism and Language* (1992), and *Mysticism and Sacred Scriptures* (2000). Katz starts in a different spot. He argues that "there are *no* pure (i.e. unmediated) experiences," that "all experience is processed through, organized by, and makes itself available to us in extremely complex epistemological ways."[51] Mystical experience enjoys no exemption from this complexity. Katz denies Stace's account of the way mystics bring experience into words. He denies that a mystic has some ineffable "whatever" experience and then imposes on this ineffable "whatever" a religious interpretation. Katz argues that "a right understanding of mysticism" requires not only paying attention to mystical reports, but also "acknowledging that the experience itself, as well as the form in which it is reported, is shaped by concepts which the mystic brings to, and which shape, his experience."[52] This means that "pre-mystical consciousness informs the mystical consciousness."[53] Thus a Christian mystic's experience is genuinely *different* from a Buddhist's experience. The two are not simply verbally different; they are experientially different. Katz also points out that mystical experiences do not come out of the blue. They are the culmination of broader experiential pathways. Since each religion's pathway begins from a different understanding of the problem of being human, each ends with a different culminating mystical experience:

> Thus the Sufi *tariq*, the Taoist *Tao*, the Buddhist *dharma* and the Christian *via mystica* are all "intentional," i.e. intend some final state of being or non-being, some goal of union or communion, some sense of release, exaltation, blessedness, or joy. And the *tariq*, the *Tao*, and the *via mystica* seek different goals because their initial, generative, problems are different. The Sufi and the Christian mystic begin with the "problem" of finitude, sin, and distance from God, while the Buddhist begins with the problem of suffering and *anitya* or impermanence ... The respective "generating" problems at the heart of each tradition suggest their respective alternative answers ... The Buddhist experience of *nirvāna*, the Jewish of *devekuth*, and the Christian of *unio mystica*, the Sufi of *fana*, the Taoist of *Tao* are the *result*, at least in part, of specific conceptual influences, i.e., the "starting problem" of each doctrinal, theological system ... Indeed, it appears that the different states of experience which go by the names *nirvāna, devekuth, fana*, etc. are not the ground but the *outcome* of the complex epistemological activity which is set in motion by the integrating character of self-consciousness employed in the specifically mystical modality.[54]

This more holistic vantage point means recognizing religious differences for what they are. This also means we have to take mystic's language seriously:

> Mystical reports do not merely indicate the postexperiential description of an unreportable experience in the language closest at hand. Rather, the experiences themselves are inescapably shaped by prior linguistic influences such that the lived experience conforms to a preexistent pattern that has been learned, then intended, and then actualized in the experiential reality of the mystic.[55]

We must therefore take mysticism seriously as a linguistic reality. We need to be attuned to genre and metaphor, to scriptures and theology. Katz refers to his own position as "contextualist," insisting that we interpret mysticism *in context*, or rather in many overlapping contexts—historical, literary, religious, theological.[56] Not only has Katz argued for this; he and his contributors have demonstrated it in practice in essays that target specific mystics, specific mystical themes, and specific mystical traditions.

Katz has won over a broad range of contemporary scholars because he articulates an epistemology that matches the actual methods and practices of working historical theologians and religious scholars. The case-study method I have used here shares many of Katz's concerns and demonstrates how those concerns play out when applied to individual mystics. I share with Katz and his colleagues a commitment to historical-critical and literary-critical methods, which requires listening quite precisely to mystics, to paying attention to what *they say* their experiences are and to what literary vehicles *they use* to say what they say. It requires rooting them in complex local religious traditions and charting their historical distinctiveness. All this is simply good historical methodology and scholarly objectivity. It respects the uniqueness of individual mystics and the uniqueness of individual mystical traditions. But if Katz's position is taken to its logical extreme—and I'm not sure he goes this far—it risks dissolving mysticism into *mysticisms*. It risks making individual mysticisms so disconnected from one another that we lapse into nominalism. In other words, we bestow a common name, "mysticism," on them even though they bear no real relationship to one another and thus have no real basis for sharing the name. This makes for incommensurable mysticisms. This absurdly implies that religious traditions cannot really talk to one another, that mystics cannot really talk to one another, that they are each locked into some self-contained hermetically sealed hermeneutics.

Terminology: Experience? Consciousness? Presence?

This particular debate on mystical experience points to complex philosophical questions and competing philosophical understandings. Front and center is epistemology, that is, the philosophical study of how we know what we know. All of us claim to know things on the basis of personal experience. It is one thing to claim such knowledge; it is another to formulate a coherent and convincing philosophical theory that accounts for our everyday, ordinary knowledge. One way to read the long history of Western philosophy is to read it as a history of competing epistemologies. If formulating a coherent and convincing theory of ordinary experience is difficult, formulating a coherent and convincing theory of mystical experience is singularly daunting. But the issue—no matter how daunting—is real. Mystics do make knowledge claims. They claim to know something experientially about who God is or what ultimate reality is. William James was right to point to a "noetic" element in mystical experience.

The problem is that "experience" is a very slippery and wonderfully vague term. What constitutes "experience"? For example, I can read about New York City; I can talk to someone who has been there; I can even see a movie about New York. Reading a book, hearing a report, seeing images—these are all experiences, and they do give some real knowledge of New York. But they are all secondhand. If I actually go to New York and walk around, then I experience it firsthand, directly. But then a tourist's experience is not a native New Yorker's. This rough distinction between secondhand and firsthand experience seems to be the way most of us imagine the difference between ordinary religious experience and mystical experience. We may have read about God, heard others talk about God, or seen images of God through icons or rituals. Mystics claim to experience God "directly"—or at least, that is how their claims are often read. The problem is that God as an *experienced* reality is not experienced as we experience places or objects or persons. In fact, if mystical reports are taken seriously, Christian mystics *experience* God as *transcendent*, as here but beyond here, as real but like no other reality, as a personal presence but like no other personal presence. Mystical experience, in other words, is experience of a radically different order than the ordinary. In ordinary experiences, our senses play a key role. Not so in mystical experience—at least, according to certain mystical theologians. Eckhart used to mock those who "want to see God with their own eyes, just as they see a cow."[57] Eckhart and Evagrius both strongly insisted on a radical withdrawal from the senses and from the memory, from images, both external and internal, even from words and from concepts. But that is only one thread within the Christian mystical tradition itself. Visionaries, such as Hildegard, are quite aware of hallucinations and the dangers of delusion, and they take pains to distinguish and defend their mode of perception as being something other, a gift, a mode of seeing and understanding utterly unlike normal experiential and cognitive modes. I do not want to try and analyze, let alone resolve, this complex issue here. My concern is simply to highlight ambiguities, to alert readers to the often subtle philosophical issues at play both within mystical texts and among their scholarly interpreters.

Because of such ambiguities, some scholars and philosophers shift the terminology from "mystical experience" to "mystical consciousness." This gives any analysis, willy-nilly, a psychological slant. "Consciousness," I should add, is not a common term in Christian mystical texts. It finds favor mostly in modern scholarly accounts, especially among scholars of Hinduism and of comparative religions. The one who has argued most strongly for its usage is Robert K. C. Forman. He opposes Katz strongly, and following Katz's own strategy, he has gathered sympathetic colleagues and edited two volumes of essays aimed at dismantling Katz's new scholarly status quo.[58] Forman acknowledges, at least in principle, the interpretative deficiencies of older common-core theorists and comes at issues with somewhat greater sensitivity to distinctive religious terminology and religious contexts. But he remains convinced of cross-cultural, interreligious commonalities and, especially, of a core universal mystical experience, what he calls a "pure consciousness event." He defines this experience as a "wakeful though contentless (non-intentional) consciousness."[59] He claims to find evidence of it in a range of contemporary experiences—including his own experience of transcendental meditation under the guidance of the Maharishi Mahesh Yogi and Ram Dass—and claims to find such reports confirmed in mystical literature ranging from Meister Eckhart to Dōgen to the Hindu *Upanishads*.[60] He recognizes his theory of "pure consciousness" does not fit a broad range of experiences and texts traditionally referred to as "mystical," namely, reports of visions, voices, and others that retain sensory language (however understood). Forman therefore sharply distinguishes "mystics" from "visionaries."[61] This exclusion, however defended, means excluding many of the great women mystics, not only figures like Hildegard, but also Mechthild of Magdeburg and Teresa of Ávila. As Amy Hollywood has argued, the visionary tradition became important for women who, because of their gender, had been excluded from the wider theological marketplace and who, therefore, drew on the biblical visionary tradition to lay claim to the religious authority to interpret scripture and religious experience.[62] Forman seems unaware of this gender bias.

A third often-used term is "presence." Bernard McGinn has argued for this as a preferred term and has entitled his massive multivolume history of Christian mysticism *The Presence of God*. Both "experience" and "consciousness" move the accent in a psychological direction, that is, toward a mystic's subjectivity. However, mystics, especially Christians, do not speak of their search as a search for subjective experiences. They are seeking God. They see practices of prayer and contemplation not as *experiences* (on the subjective side), but as *encounters* (on the objective side) with the presence of the living God. Remember the way Evagrius defined prayer. It is a "communion (*homilia*) of the mind with God." And he appended to this definition a question that defines the quest in a decidedly mystical slant: "What sort of state does the mind need so that it can reach out to its Lord without turning back and commune with him without intermediary?"[63] This states the issue: God is the end (*telos*) of the search, and the God who is sought is an objective reality, albeit a transcendent one. The subjective side concerns the seeker's state of mind that makes the objective encounter possible. Thus "presence" shifts the focus from subjective experience to the objective (though transcendent) reality the mystic seeks.

McGinn argues that "presence" is "a more central and more useful category for grasping the unifying note in the varieties of Christian mysticism."[64] He draws on an early-twentieth-century theorist, Friedrich von Hügel, who spoke of three intertwined elements within any religion: the institutional, the intellectual, and the mystical.[65] McGinn includes von Hügel's distinction in his definition of Christian mysticism: "The mystical element in Christianity is that part of its beliefs and practices that concerns the preparation for, the consciousness of, and the reaction to what can be described as the immediate or direct presence of God."[66] McGinn's definition has strengths. He focuses not simply on "experiences," but on a wider lifelong process ("preparation for," "the reaction to"). He also refuses to exclude the religious ("practices") and the theological ("beliefs"). This is evident not only in his definition but in his actual efforts at interpreting individual figures. Does "presence" as a category work beyond Christianity? Perhaps not. But it is a helpful category to articulate that the Christian mystical experience is not simply a psychological event—though it includes that—but an encounter with the Other.

A History of Hyperinflation

Mysticism as a concept and as a disciplinary focus has suffered the ill effects of conceptual hyperinflation. Its currency value has spiraled out of control, the victim of a century of scholars, philosophers, and psychologists who have overloaded it by overinterpreting it and overapplying it. I believe that its value can be reclaimed if it is restricted to properly religious venues.

Let me give an all-too-brief excursus on the term. "Mystic" comes from the Greek μυστικός and is derived from the verb μύω, meaning "to close," as in "to close one's eyes." Greeks, before the Christian era, applied it not to secret revelations or secret knowledge of the divine, but to the secret rites of mystery cults. The earliest Christian writers to use the word did *not* draw on this mystery-religions meaning. Early Christian usage, as Louis Bouyer has argued, "applies it to the least Greek thing about Christianity: the Bible."[67] Christian biblical commentators such as Clement of Alexandria and Origen spoke of the Bible's "mystical," that is, "hidden," meaning. That hidden meaning was Christ:[68] Christ was the mystical key that unlocked the hidden meaning of biblical texts. Fourth-century Church Fathers continued this use, but also began extending it to a second domain. Bishops, especially in mystagogical sermons delivered to the newly baptized during Easter week, unveiled the hidden "mystical" meanings of the Christian rites of baptism, chrismation, and eucharist.[69] The mystical key that unlocked the hidden meanings of the liturgy's symbols was the same mystical key that unlocked the hidden meaning of the scriptures: Christ.[70] If one wanted to speak of "mystical experience" as the early Church Fathers would have understood the term, one would speak of it as the ordinary faith experience of *all* baptized Christians. That is not to say that mystical experience in the modern sense was not found in ancient Christianity. It clearly was, as we saw in our study of Evagrius and the desert fathers. But the desert fathers and later monastic thinkers spoke of their experience not as "mystical experience," but as "contemplation"; they spoke of themselves not as "mystics," but as "contemplatives."

The great popularizer of the adjective "mystical," the one who cemented its place within Christian parlance, was Pseudo-Dionysius, that sixth-century author of *The Mystical Theology*. His use of the word "mystical" largely overlaps with earlier patristic uses. "Mystical" refers to the hidden meaning of the scriptures and of the Church's liturgies. But Dionysius extends it to a third, though related, domain. For him, "mystical" refers not to subjective psychological experience, but to the experiential encounter with the utterly transcendent reality that God is.[71]

Lorenzo Valla, the Renaissance philologist who demonstrated that Dionysius was really Pseudo-Dionysius, once remarked: "A new reality requires a new word."[72] In Valla's time, "mystical" was still an adjective; a century and a half later, it had become a noun, a substantive: "mysticism" (*la mystique*). This new word, according to Michel de Certeau, signaled a new historical reality. The sixteenth century spoke of "contemplatives" and "spirituals"; the seventeenth century began calling them "mystics."[73] By the seventeenth century, mysticism in the modern sense had begun to appear. As de Certeau notes, *la mystique* began referring to "an experiential understanding which was slowly detached from traditional theology or from ecclesial institutions and which was characterized by a consciousness—whether acquired or received—of a passivity in which the 'I' loses itself in God."[74] Mysticism, in the hands of seventeenth-century theorists, came to be characterized by "special experiences." It emerged as an inward-gazing "science," with both experimentalists (the mystics) and theoreticians (mystical theologians) who classified and catalogued their observations. In the end, this new experimental science of religious experience languished on the margins, eclipsed in the very era that created the outward-gazing physical sciences.[75]

When nineteenth-century Western scholars began doing serious and sympathetic (though sometimes deeply flawed) studies of non-Christian religions, the terms "mystic" and "mysticism" were ready-to-hand concepts. Scholars applied them to disciplines and doctrines, to practices and experiences, found among Hindus and Buddhists and beyond. They cited convergences between Western mystical texts and what they found in the East. But generalizations ran ahead—sometimes wildly ahead—of the evidence. Some comparative religionists used "mysticism" to argue for the superiority of Christianity over the "natural" religions of the East.[76] Others drew on those initial and limited researches into Eastern religious texts and traditions to forge a new meta-theory of religion, claiming to found a universal theory of religion upon a theory of universal mystical experience. They cast mystical experience as the bedrock of all religion and argued that those who founded religions or those who reformed religions were all mystics. Mysticism became romanticized, globalized, bloated. It got applied to any and all manner of vague cosmic feelings.[77] Terminological inflation was, in other words, well under way when James and others detached it from actual religious practices and practitioners. He and they not only psychologized the mystical, atomizing it into disconnected mystical experiences; they also detached it from scriptures, from theology, from public worship, from religious communities. They applied it quite carelessly to drug experiences, to the "nature mysticism" of romantic poets, to a bizarre host of altered states of consciousness. All this paved the way for terminological hyperinflation.

Mysticism as Macro-concept

I think the terms "mystic," "mystical," and "mysticism" still have a rightful and useful place in the study of religion, but only if we are willing to use them more modestly and with greater circumspection. The terms are useful as macro-concepts to highlight worldwide religious trends. Think of other macro-concepts in comparative religions: "scripture" or "ritual" or "priesthood" or "prophecy" or "doctrine" or, for that matter, "God." Take the macro-concept of "scripture." It highlights that all the world's major religions have sacred texts. Scripture as an idea is originally a Jewish one. But that does not reduce its usefulness as a macro-concept. Any knowledgeable student recognizes that the world's religions have created, used, venerated, and understood sacred texts in varied ways, that the way Christians use and understand the Bible is not the way that Jews use and understand the Tanakh, nor is it the way that Muslims use and understand the Qur'an, nor is it the way the Buddhists use and understand the Tripitaka. There is great pluralism among the world's religions. There is also great pluralism among major traditions within every single religion, say, between Orthodox and Catholics and Protestants. There is even great pluralism among influential figures within the same Christian tradition, say, between Origen and Maximus Confessor, or between Augustine and Aquinas, or between Luther and Calvin. That pluralism does not empty the concept of "scripture" of its meaning. Quite the contrary. Both broad comparisons and microscopic analyses of scriptural usage and interpretation shed much light on all concerned. Similar pluralism comes to light as one probes other macro-concepts, such as "ritual" or "priesthood." So too with "mysticism." Mysticism highlights a worldwide trend in experiential religious perfectionism. The study of mysticism, like the study of scripture or the study of ritual, marks out a domain of research. And that study includes not only recognizing, but also mapping out the enormous pluralism among religions, among traditions, and among individuals.

With that in mind, what then is mysticism? It is a domain of religion that deals with the search for and the attainment of a profound experiential knowledge of God or of ultimate reality. It takes its literary form in mystical texts, its organizational form in mystical communities, and its practical form in the remarkable experiences and the broader lives of individual mystics. The mystical encounter is usually, but not always, experienced by individuals as a profound revelation of who we are, what the world is, and especially (for the religions of the West) who God is. It is usually, but not always, notable for its psychological intensity and for its life-altering aftereffects. It includes the reported varieties what we have seen: visions, experiences of ecstasy and peace, claims of union with the divine, illuminations that shatter illusions and open new vistas, psychic reorientations, and much else. I speak of mysticism as a domain of religion. I do not think it properly includes *non-religious* testimonies, such as those gathered by James and others—that vast and varied sprawl of autobiographical accounts of aesthetic trances, ecstatic transports, and drug-induced highs. Such testimonies can be thought-provoking, but to call them "mystical" bloats the term and the domain beyond all conceptual value. The terminology of mysticism fits best within the religion that first formulated it: Christianity. It can be meaningfully and insightfully applied beyond that, to the theistic religions of Judaism and Islam. It can be applied, though only with care and with appropriate nuance, to the religious traditions of the East, notably Hinduism and Buddhism. This extension beyond theistic traditions has real hazards and risks distorting how Hindus and Buddhists understand themselves. It also has rewards in what it highlights about worldwide religious trends. I have tried, both at the end of chapter 9 and throughout this chapter, to suggest ways that "mysticism" might be circumspectly applied to Buddhism, which advocates contemplative disciplines and experiential breakthroughs and a liberating knowledge of the deeper truths about the self and others and world, but which does so in nontheistic terms and which denies anything like a substantial self (and thus any "experiencer"). The points of convergence are real; so too are the points of divergence; both are illuminating, but should not be overdrawn.

WHY MYSTICS MATTER

Before closing, let me return to the anecdote with which I opened this book, to that classroom of students who, after a few weeks of reading mystics, began wondering openly about their own mystical propensities. Why did they feel that they had understood what the mystics were talking about? Were they mistaken? Naive? Some might dismiss their enthusiasm as one or the other or both. I disagree. I think that they sensed, however intuitively, however partially, some continuity between the mystics' account of the spiritual life and their own. Despite the real historical gulfs and despite the profound cultural chasms, the mystics they read spoke to their experience. The mystics' brilliant raids on the ineffable gave voice to what my students had some taste of, to what they knew but had not known how to talk about.

I fear that three accents in this chapter could be read as undermining their intuition. First, I have stressed reading mystical texts within their historical, literary, and religious contexts. This always risks turning mystical texts into remote, foreign objects, intelligible only to professional historians of religion. Second, I have stressed interpreting mystics as members of broader mystical communities. This risks distancing mystics from readers who may not belong to communities marked off by such a self-conscious religious profession.

Third, I have stressed mystics' experiences as rooted in disciplined practices of prayer and contemplation. This risks distancing mystics' experiences from those who lack such training or do not practice such contemplative routines. While I stand by my emphases as necessary lenses for a disciplined reading of mystics and their texts, I do think my students' (and others') intuition names something essential. It names why mystics matter.

Think back on my comparison of mystics with musicians and athletes. The vast majority of us are neither professional athletes nor professional musicians. Still, most of us can be swept up into the excitement of sports and the expressiveness of music. Why? Because we do actually understand what is going on. Not perfectly, of course. We may not have a coach's seasoned eye nor a musicologist's well-tuned ear. But we do have eyes and ears, and most of us have some real, if limited, experience of sports and music. We may have played high school football or played piano as kids. Our talents and our expertise may be limited, but we are not without some experience. So too, many of us, perhaps all of us, have had genuine religious experiences. Most of us have prayed and meditated and contemplated and encountered in those experiences some real but hard-to-name mystery within us and around us. Many of us who come across mystics' texts find that their words highlight for us experiences we may well have had but have never named or even knew how to name. And many of us come to mystics' texts having been raised in churches or religious cultures that focus all too often on religious externals, whether scriptures or rituals or behaviors or authoritative pronouncements. What draws in first-time readers is not simply mystics' verbal virtuosity. It is their breathtaking insistence that God and that ultimate truth can be encountered here and now, however dimly, with whatever difficulty, in both the ordinary and the extraordinary, in certain peak moments of prayer and in certain peak, though unexpected, encounters with a mystery that runs in and through and beyond the world that swirls about us.

Few theologians have explored why mystics matter more systematically than Karl Rahner (1904–1984), a German Jesuit and one of the finest and most influential theologians of the twentieth century.[78] His writings are a vast library, written in a difficult and often technical prose style. Most famous are his twenty-three volumes of essays collected under the title *Theological Investigations* (*Schriften zur Theologie*). Rahner was raised in a religious culture and a theological world that regarded mystics with deep suspicion or that turned them into inimitable exceptions, rare birds graced with supernatural experiences of infused contemplation. Rahner disagreed. He insisted that mystics' experiences, while certainly extraordinary, point to something essential about being human. A good entry into his thinking on mystical experience and mystical theology is found in a late essay written on the occasion of Pope Paul VI's official naming of Teresa of Ávila as a Doctor of the Church. This event led Rahner to reflect on what Teresa as "Doctor" could teach the wider Christian faithful.

> Even today it is still possible, indeed it is more urgent than ever, to have a theology and, even beyond this, an initiation into the human being's personal experience of God . . . If these older mystics are able to help us in this task, we must of course assume for our part that in every human being (as a result of the nature of spirit and of the grace of the divine self-communication always offered to everyone) there is something like an anonymous, unthematic, perhaps repressed, basic experience of being orientated to God, which is constitutive of man in his concrete makeup (of nature and grace), which can be repressed but not destroyed, which is "mystical" or (if you prefer a more cautious terminology) has its climax in what the older teachers called infused contemplation.[79]

Rahner's prose here, as throughout his works, is convoluted and may seem a bit daunting to first-time readers. This style comes from his constant concern for theological precision and balance, for giving theological claims the nuances they require. Let me put starkly what Rahner says with nuance. He thinks that mystics are, in fact, the normal ones, that they are the real norms of what it means to be truly human. It's the rest of us who are abnormal. The rest of us have, in principle, the mystical within our experiential repertoire, but we have repressed it. Still, it remains constitutive of who we are as human beings. So often it remains under the surface and unarticulated, or as Rahner puts it here, "anonymous" and "unthematic." That we happen to be anonymous mystics or repressed mystics is, for Rahner, precisely what makes it possible of us to grasp something of what the mystics are talking about. As he sees it, all of us already have some experience of God, however anonymously, however "unthematically," in our very constitution as human beings.

Rahner's theological starting point is to focus on what it means to be human. He is convinced that mystics illustrate something important about human nature. He often speaks of human beings as "hearers of the word" (the title of one of his early works).[80] What does he mean? If I speak to you, I presume that you have an ear to hear me. Your ear is what Rahner calls "the condition of the possibility" of your hearing anything I say. Having an ear, you are structured as a human being to be a hearer. You may choose not to. You may block up your ears. You may distract yourself with a thousand other sounds. But you are constituted, by your structure as a human being, to be a

hearer of words. Rahner argues that if God speaks to us—which is what
Christianity and other religions of the West claim—then we must be structured by our very constitutions as human beings to be hearers of God. Our
very human constitution as hearers lies prior to our hearing any particular
revelation of God. For Rahner, what mystics point to in their often unusual
and profound experiences is our deeper but often ignored human constitution as hearers of God. Mystics represent thematically what remains for most
of us unthematic: that we have the condition of the possibility of encountering God.

For Rahner, as for the Christian mystical tradition as a whole, mystical
experiences are graced experiences. They are God's freely bestowed gifts. We
have no right to experience God. Still, as Rahner emphasizes, God in God's
own radical freedom does choose to communicate to us. We may experience
God's self-communication in any number of ways—as a voice or in a vision, as
a blinding insight or as a felt presence. But beneath any experience is an
encounter that is at once God's self-revelation and self-communication. For
Rahner, mystical experiences, however dramatic, are not discontinuous from
ordinary graced experiences. Mystics' experiences serve as pointers and paradigms. They point to the human condition, to its ever-present possibility of a
radical encounter with the mystery that God is:

> Christian theology, at least in Catholicism, will not cease to regard
> such mystical experience of transcendence at least as a possible
> *stage* on the way to perfection . . . This however does *not* mean simply
> that mystical experience as such could be or ought to be regarded
> merely as a single and rare exceptional case in individual human
> beings and Christians which is granted to the latter either by psycho-
> technical effort or by a special grace of God as rare privilege or by
> both together, without really having any constitutive importance of
> the actual way to perfect salvation . . . It seems to me . . . to be the
> task of Christian theology as a whole and the Christian theology of
> mysticism in particular to show and to render intelligible the fact
> that the real basic phenomenon of mystical transcendence is present as
> innermost sustaining ground (even though unnoticed) in the simple
> act itself of Christian living in faith, hope, and love, that such (as we
> may say) implicit transcendence into the nameless mystery known
> as God is present by grace in this very believing, hoping, and loving; it
> seems to us that mysticism in an explicit experience has therefore
> (conversely) a paradigmatic character, an exemplary function, to make
> clear to the Christian what really happens and is meant when his faith

tells him that God's self-communication is given to him in grace and accepted in freedom whenever he believes, hopes, and loves.[81]

For Rahner, mystics matter because they are paradigms of the human condition. They make clear a God who reveals God's self. Their explicit and profound experiences of transcendence point to our much more common, much more routine experiences of transcendence. For most of us most of the time, that transcendence takes place less dramatically in the ordinary course of religious living, in those everyday, underestimated, and overlooked acts of living in faith and hope and love. For Rahner, both dramatic mystical experiences and ordinary unspectacular experiences point to the same "nameless mystery known as God."

Rahner's is but one theoretical framework that tries to account for the widespread human thirst for the mystical and for the diverse particularity of individual mystics and mystical traditions. While thought-provoking, it provides no grounds for adjudicating mystics' experiences or their conflicting theological claims; nor does it offer criteria to distinguish true from false, authentic from inauthentic. On one crucial point, I think Rahner is correct: mystics' experiences are not discontinuous from our own. Think about color, about the spectrum of light. It is one thing to say "that thing is purple"; it is quite another to see purple within the broader color spectrum. Against that spectrum, it seems arbitrary, even impossible, to define the light frequency of purple as it fades back to red or up to ultraviolet. Ordinary religious experience may be a "lower" frequency in some sense, a "yellow" or "orange" or "red"— less intense somehow, but still light, still in continuity with that more intense, higher light frequency that moves ever so gradually from purple to violet to ultraviolet invisibility.

Mystics matter for other reasons. They are pioneers who explore the frontiers and limits of being human. Not all of us can climb Everest or circumnavigate the globe, but explorers show what is possible for human beings. Mystics are interior explorers, and they too show us the possible. Because mystics probe interiorly and know all too well our all-too-human knack for self-deception, they map the tangles and perils that lie within the human heart. Think back on Merton's image of the contemplative as "fire watcher," as one who stands vigil at night in a lonely belfry, overlooking a dark landscape, an eye ever alert to the arsonist's fire. Merton reminded readers that as he gazed out from his monastic perch, he saw a world burning with racism and madly dabbling with nuclear weapons, and he insisted that if one peered into the human heart's darkness, one could see where such mad fire making is first devised and rationalized beneath the masks of the false self. Mystics, in their watchfulness, remind us of that all-too-human darkness. But they insist that that darkness is not the last word. Far from it. That is because they see another darkness, the divine darkness. That darkness, blinding in its superluminosity, lies at once within and beyond our field of vision. The mystics, with their sensitized night vision, remind us that we too have such visual acuity. They see—and help us see—much more than visions. They have learned to peer into the divine darkness long and hard enough to see a God-drenched world, dizzying in its beauty. They remind us that we too have eyes to see those fragile ephemeral beauties where drops of dew glisten like sapphires for a few fleeting moments in an inbreaking dawnlight through which most of us routinely sleep.

Abbreviations

ACW   Ancient Christian Writers (New York: Newman Press and Paulist Press)

Arberry 1   A. J. Arberry, trans., *Mystical Poems of Rūmī: First Selection, Poems 1–200* (Chicago: University of Chicago Press, 1968)

Arberry 2   A. J. Arberry, trans., *Mystical Poems of Rūmī 2: Second Selection, Poems 201–400*, ed. Ehsan Yarshater (Chicago: University of Chicago Press, 1991)

Baird   Joseph L. Baird and Radd K. Ehrman, trans., *The Letters of Hildegard of Bingen*, 3 vols. (New York: Oxford University Press, 1994)

Casiday   A. M. Casiday, ed. and trans., *Evagrius Ponticus*, Early Church Fathers (London: Routledge, 2006)

CCCM   Corpus Christianorum, Continuatio Medievalis (Turnholt)

CCSL   Corpus Christianorum, Series Latina (Turnholt)

CF   Cistercian Fathers Series (Kalamazoo, MI: Cistercian Publications; Collegeville, MN: Liturgical Press)

Combes   André Combes, *Ioannis Carlerii de Gerson: De Mystica Theologia* (Lugano, Switzerland: Thesarus Mundi, 1958)

Cousins	Ewert Cousins, trans., *Bonaventure: The Soul's Journey into God, The Tree of Life, The Life of St. Francis*, Classics of Western Spirituality (New York: Paulist Press, 1978)
CS	Cistercian Studies Series (Kalamazoo, MI: Cistercian Publications; Collegeville, MN: Liturgical Press)
CSCO	Corpus Scriptorum Christianorum Orientalium (Louvain)
CWS	Classics of Western Spirituality (New York: Paulist Press)
D	Heinrich Denzinger, ed., *Enchiridion symbolorum definitionem et declarationum de rebus fidei et morum*, 40th ed. by Peter Hünermann (Freiburg: Herder, 2005)
Davies	Oliver Davies, *Meister Eckhart: Selected Writings* (New York: Penguin Book, 1994)
DW	Josef Quint and Georg Steer, eds., *Meister Eckhart: Die deutschen und lateinischen Werke heraugegeben im Auftrag der deutschen Forschungsgemeinschaft; Die deutschen Werke*, 5 vols. (Stuttgart: W. Kohlhammer, 1958–)
Ep.	*Epistula [Letter]* of Bernard of Clairvaux, Hildegard of Bingen, Evagrius Ponticus, et al.
Essential	Edmund Colledge and Bernard McGinn, trans., *Meister Eckhart: The Essential Sermons, Commentaries, Treatises, and Defense*, Classics of Western Spirituality (New York: Paulist Press, 1981)
Evans	G. R. Evans, trans., *Bernard of Clairvaux: Selected Works*, Classics of Western Spirituality (New York: Paulist Press, 1987)
Frankenberg	Wilhelm Frankenberg, ed., *Euagrios Ponticus*, Abhandlungen der königlichen Gesellschaft der Wissenschaften zu Göttingen; Philol. His. Klasse, Neue Folge, 13.2 (Berlin, 1912)
Glorieux	Palemon Glorieux, ed., *Jean Gerson: Oeuvres complètes* (Paris: Desclée & Cie, 1960–1973)

Hart Mother Columba Hart and Jane Bishop, trans.,
Hildegard of Bingen: Scivias, Classics of Western
Spirituality (New York: Paulist Press, 1990)

Heart Norman Waddell and Masao Abe, trans., *The
Heart of Dōgen's Shōbōgenzō* (Albany, NY:
SUNY Press, 2002)

Hexaem. Bonaventure, *Collationes in Hexaemeron* [*Collations on the Six Days of Creation*]

Itin. Bonaventure, *Itinerarium mentis ad Deum* [*Journey
of the Mind into God*]

Leighton Taigen Dan Leighton and Shohaku Okumura,
trans., *Dōgen's Extensive Record: A Translation of
the Eihei Kōroku* (Boston: Wisdom Publications,
2004).

Lewis Franklin D. Lewis, *Rumi: Past and Present, East
and West; The Life, Teachings and Poetry of Jalāl
al-Din Rumi* (Oxford: One World, 2000)

LW Josef Koch et al., eds., *Meister Eckhart: Die deutschen
und lateinischen Werke: Die lateinischen Werke*, 5
vols. (Stuttgart: W. Kohlhammer, 1956–)

McGuire Brian Patrick McGuire, trans., *Jean Gerson: Early
Works*, Classics of Western Spirituality (New
York: Paulist Press, 1998)

Mojaddedi Jawid Mojaddedi, trans., *Rumi: The Masnavi; Book
1*, Oxford World's Classics (New York: Oxford
University Press, 2004)

Muyldermans J. Muyldermans, "Evagriana," *Muséon* 44 (1931):
37–68; "Note additionnelle: Evagriana," *Muséon*
44 (1931): 369–383

Nicholson Reynold A. Nicholson, trans., *The Mathnawī of
Jalālu'ddin Rūmī*, 3 vols. (1926; reprint:
Warminster: Aris & Phillips, 1990)

PG Patrologia Graeca, ed. J. Migne (Paris)

PL Patrologia Latina, ed. J. Migne (Paris)

PO Patrologia Orientalis (Paris)

Qrc *Doctor Seraphici S. Bonaventurae Opera Omnia*, 10
vols. (Quaracchi: Collegium S. Bonaventurae,
1882–1902)

Renard   John Renard, trans., *Knowledge of God in Classical Sufism*, Classics of Western Spirituality (New York: Paulist Press, 2004)

SBO   *Sancti Bernardi Opera*, 8 vols., ed. J. Leclercq, H.-M. Rochais, and C. H. Talbot (Rome: Editiones Cistercienses, 1957–1977)

SC   Sources chrétiennes (Paris: Éditions du Cerf)

SCC   Bernard of Clairvaux, *Sermones super Cantica Canticorum* [*Sermons on the Song of Songs*]

Sells, *EIM*   Michael Sells, trans., *Early Islamic Mysticism: Sufi, Qur'an, Mi'raj, Poetic and Theological Writings*, Classics of Western Spirituality (New York: Paulist Press, 1993)

Sinkewicz   Robert E. Sinkewicz, ed. and trans., *Evagrius of Pontus: The Greek Ascetic Corpus*, Oxford Early Christian Studies (New York: Oxford University Press, 2003)

Tanahashi, *EU*   Kazuaki Tanahashi, trans., *Enlightenment Unfolds: The Essential Teachings of Zen Master Dōgen* (Boston: Shambhala, 1999)

Tanahashi, *MD*   Kazauki Tanahashi, trans., *Moon in a Dewdrop: Writings of Zen Master Dōgen* (New York: North Point Press, 1985)

Tanahashi, *TDE*   Kazuaki Tanahashi and John Daido Loori, trans., *The True Dharma Eye: Zen Master Dōgen's Three Hundred Kōans* (Boston: Shambhala, 2005)

Teacher   Bernard McGinn, trans., *Meister Eckhart: Teacher and Preacher*, Classics of Western Spirituality (New York: Paulist Press, 1986)

Walshe   Maurice O'C. Walshe, *Meister Eckhart: Sermons & Treatises*, 3 vols. (Rockport, MA: Element Books, 1979–1987)

WB   *Works of Bonaventure, Cardinal Seraphic Doctor and Saint*, trans. José de Vinck, 5 vols. (Patterson, NJ: St. Antony Guild Press, 1960–1970)

WSB   *Works of Saint Bonaventure*, ed. George March and F. Edward Coughlin (St. Bonaventure, NY: Franciscan Institute)

Notes

PREFACE

1. Bernard McGinn, "General Introduction," in *The Foundations of Mysticism: Origins to the Fifth Century*, vol. 1 of *The Presence of God: A History of Western Christian Mysticism* (New York: Crossroad, 1991), xiv.

CHAPTER 1

1. For the Latin text of Gerson's *De mystica theologia*, see Combes. For a partial translation, see McGuire, 262–333.

2. Gerson, *De mystica theologia*, I.28.4–7 (Combes, 72); trans. my own.

3. On the rise of this terminology, see the brilliant but difficult work of Michel de Certeau, *The Mystic Fable*, vol. 1, *The Sixteenth and Seventeenth Centuries*, trans. Michael B. Smith, Religion and Postmodernism Series (Chicago: University of Chicago Press, 1992). We will examine this in chapter 10.

4. Gerson, *De mystica theologia* I.2.5 (Combes, 10); trans. McGuire, 267.

5. Gregory the Great, *Hom. in Ev.* 27.4 (PL 76:1207A): *amor ipse notitia est.*

6. Gerson, *De mystica theologia*, prol. (Combes, 1); trans. McGuire, 262.

7. See Mark A. McIntosh, *Mystical Theology: The Integrity of Spirituality and Theology*, Challenges in Contemporary Theology (Malden, MA: Blackwell, 1998).

8. John XXII, *In agro dominico* (D §979). On Eckhart, see chapter 6.

9. Gerson, *De mystica theologia* I.3.1–4 (Combes, 11–12); McGuire, 267–268.

10. Gerson, *De mystica theologia*, annotatio (Combes, 219–220); McGuire, 332–333.

11. Joseph Adelson, "Still Vital After All These Years," *Psychology Today* 16, no. 4 (April 1982): 52, quoted in Gerald E. Myers, *William James: His Life and Thought* (New Haven: Yale University Press, 1986), 485 n. 6.

12. Rebecca West, *Henry James* (New York: Holt, 1916), 11, quoted in Myers, 21.

13. Walter Lippmann, quoted in Linda Simon, *Genuine Reality: A Life of William James* (New York: Harcourt Brace, 1998), xv.

14. William James, *The Varieties of Religious Experience: A Study in Human Nature, Being the Gifford Lectures on Natural Religion delivered at Edinburgh in 1901–1902*, The Works of William James, ed. Frederick H. Burkhardt, Fredson Bowers and Ignas K. Skrupskelis (Cambridge, MA: Harvard University Press, 1985), 12.

15. James, *Varieties*, 20.

16. James, *Varieties*, 19.

17. James, *Varieties*, 23.

18. James, *Varieties*, 26.

19. James, *Varieties*, 12.

20. James, *Varieties*, 15.

21. James, *Varieties*, 33.

22. James, letter to Henry W. Rankin (June 16, 1901), in *The Letters of William James*, ed. Henry James (Boston: Atlantic Monthly Press, 1920), 2:149–150.

23. James, *Varieties*, 301.

24. James, *Varieties*, 302.

25. James, *Varieties*, 302.

26. James, *Varieties*, 302.

27. James, *Varieties*, 302.

28. James, *Varieties*, 303.

29. James, *Varieties*, 303.

30. Bruce Whilshire, "The Breathtaking Intimacy of the Material World," in *The Cambridge Companion to William James*, ed. Ruth Anna Putnam (Cambridge: Cambridge University Press, 1997), 111.

31. James, *Varieties*, 304.

32. James, *Varieties*, 307–308.

33. James, *Varieties*, 332.

34. James, *Varieties*, 34.

35. James, *Varieties*, 341. Earlier, he puts forward this basic view in different terms: "Our impulsive belief is here always what sets up the original body of truth, and our philosophy is but its showy verbalized translation. The immediate assurance is the deep thing in us, the argument is but a surface exhibition. Instinct leads, intelligence does but follow" (*Varieties*, 67).

36. James, *Varieties*, 341.

37. James, *Varieties*, 352.

38. McGinn, *Foundations of Mysticism*, xvi.

39. James, *Varieties*, 334.

CHAPTER 2

1. Thomas Merton, "Contemplation in a World of Action," in *Contemplation in a World of Action*, ed. Robert Coles (1971; reprint: Notre Dame: University of Notre Dame Press, 1998), 154. This essay is reprinted in Lawrence Cunningham, *Thomas Merton, Spiritual Master: The Essential Writings* (New York: Paulist Press, 1992), 368–387.

2. Merton, "Contemplation in a World of Action," 160.

3. Merton, "Contemplation in a World of Action," 160–161.

4. Merton, *The Seven Storey Mountain*, 50th anniversary ed. (New York: Harcourt Brace, 1998), 3.

5. Lawrence S. Cunningham, *Thomas Merton and the Monastic Vision*, Library of Religious Biography (Grand Rapids, MI: William B. Eerdmans, 1999), 6–7.

6. Merton, *Seven Storey Mountain*, 235–236.

7. Merton, *The Sign of Jonas* (New York: Harcourt, Brace, 1953), 3.

8. Merton, journal entry from April 7, 1941, in *The Intimate Merton: His Life from His Journals*, ed. Patrick Hart and Jonathan Montaldo (San Francisco: HarperSanFrancisco, 1999), 28.

9. James O. Supple, *Chicago Sun* (December 28, 1948); cited in William H. Shannon, "*The Seven Storey Mountain*," in *Thomas Merton Encyclopedia*, ed. William H. Shannon, Christine M. Bochen, and Patrick F. O'Connell (Maryknoll, NY: Orbis Books, 2002), 423.

10. Merton, "Is the World a Problem?," in *Contemplation in a World of Action*, 141.

11. Merton, *A Thomas Merton Reader*, ed. Thomas P. McDonnell (New York: Harcourt, Brace & World, 1962), 17.

12. Merton, *Sign of Jonas*, 89.

13. Michael Mott, *The Seven Mountains of Thomas Merton* (Boston: Houghton Mifflin, 1986), 189.

14. Merton, *Conjectures of a Guilty Bystander* (Garden City, NY: Doubleday, 1966), 21. This reworks the original entry in his private journals of April 28, 1957: see *Intimate Merton*, 110.

15. Merton, "Day of the Stranger," in Cunningham, *Thomas Merton: Spiritual Master*, 216.

16. Merton, "Day of the Stranger," 215.

17. Mott, *Seven Mountains*, 435–454. Merton's own account is found in his 1966–1967 private journals published as *Learning to Love: Exploring Solitude and Freedom; The Journals of Thomas Merton*, vol. 6 (San Francisco: HarperSanFrancisco, 1997). See James A. Wiseman, "Learning to Love and Learning the Price: Thomas Merton and the Challenge of Celibacy," *Merton Annual* 12 (1999): 85–102.

18. Merton, *The Inner Experience: Notes on Contemplation*, ed. William H. Shannon (San Francisco: HarperSanFrancisco, 2003), 67. On this, see Philip Richter, "Late Developer: Thomas Merton's Discovery of Photography as a Medium for His Contemplative Vision," *Spiritus* 6 (2006): 195–212.

19. Merton, "Monastic Experience and East–West Dialogue," in *The Asian Journal of Thomas Merton*, ed. Naomi Burton, Patrick Hart, and James Laughlin (New York: New Directions, 1973), 212–213.

20. Merton, *Asian Journal*, 231–236.

21. Merton, *Seven Storey Mountain*, 461–462.

22. Merton, *Conjectures*, 156.

23. Merton, journal entry from March 10, 1958, in *Intimate Merton*, 124.

24. For a translation and analysis of the two versions of Julian's work, see Edmund Colledge and James Walsh, eds., *Julian of Norwich: Showings*, CWS (New York: Paulist Press, 1978).

25. See Sidney H. Griffith, "Thomas Merton, Louis Massignon, and the Challenge of Islam," *Merton Annual* 3 (1990): 151–172.

26. Louis Massignon, "Mystique musulmane et mystique chrétienne au moyen age," quoted in Griffith, 167.

27. William H. Shannon, *Thomas Merton's Dark Path*, rev. ed. (New York: Farrar, Straus, Giroux, 1987), 4.

28. Merton, *New Seeds of Contemplation* (New York: New Directions, 1962), 9–11.

29. Merton, *New Seeds*, 1.

30. Merton, *New Seeds*, 1.

31. Merton, *New Seeds*, 2–3.

32. Merton, "The Contemplative and the Atheist," in *Contemplation in a World of Action*, 167.

33. Merton, *New Seeds*, 3.

34. Merton, *New Seeds*, 226–227.

35. Merton, *New Seeds*, 291–292.

36. Merton, *New Seeds*, 254–255.

37. Merton, *New Seeds*, 31.

38. Merton, *New Seeds*, 31–32.

39. Merton, *New Seeds*, 33.

40. Cunningham, *Thomas Merton and the Monastic Vision*, 96.

41. Merton, letter to Ch. Abdul Aziz (Jan 2, 1966), in William H. Shannon, *Hidden Ground of Love: The Letters of Thomas Merton on Religious Experience and Social Concerns* (New York: Farrar, Straus, Giroux, 1985), 62–63.

42. Merton, "Epilogue: The Fire Watch, July 4, 1952," *Sign of Jonas*, 350.

43. Merton, *Sign of Jonas*, 352.

44. Merton, *Sign of Jonas*, 359–360.

45. Merton, *Sign of Jonas*, 362.

CHAPTER 3

1. Bernard of Clairvaux, *De diligendo Deo*, prol. (SBO 3:119). For a critical edition of the Latin text of Bernard's writings, see SBO. For a selection of Bernard's mystical texts, see Evans. The dating of Bernard's *On Loving God* is notoriously difficult to pin down, though most date it early in Bernard's literary career, around 1128;

see Emero Stiegman, trans., *Bernard of Clairvaux: On Loving God; An Analytical Commentary*, CF 13B (Kalamazoo, MI: Cistercian Publications, 1995), 59–66.

2. Bernard of Clairvaux, *De diligendo Deo* 1 (SBO 3:119); trans. my own.

3. Bernard of Clairvaux, *De diligendo Deo* 1.1–2.2 (SBO 3:120–121); Evans, 175–176.

4. Bernard of Clairvaux, *De diligendo Deo* 7.18–21 (SBO 3:134–137); Evans, 188–190.

5. Bernard of Clairvaux, *De diligendo Deo* 6.21–22 (SBO 3:137); trans. Evans, 191.

6. Bernard of Clairvaux, *De diligendo Deo* 10.27 (SBO 3:142); trans. my own.

7. On the hagiographic distortions of Bernard's biography, see Adriaan H. Bredero, *Bernard of Clairvaux: Between Cult and History* (Grand Rapids, MI: Wm. B. Eerdmans, 1996); Jean Leclerq, *A Second Look at Bernard of Clairvaux*, trans. Marie-Bernard Saïd, CS 105 (Kalamazoo, MI: 1990).

8. The standard critical history is that of Louis J. Lekai, *The Cistercians: Ideals and Reality* (Kent, OH: Kent State University Press, 1977). Constance Hoffman Berman, *The Cistercian Evolution: The Invention of a Religious Order in Twelfth-Century Europe* (Philadelphia: University of Pennsylvania Press, 2000), offers a controversial revisionist reading of Cistercian expansion. She challenges, for example, the tendency to overestimate Bernard's role in the order's growth, as well as the dating of and "myths" in the foundational Cistercian documents.

9. Bernard of Clairvaux, *Apologia* V.10–XII.28 (SBO 3:90–105). For a translation, see Michael Casey, ed., *St. Bernard's Apologia to Abbot William: Cistercians and Cluniacs* (Kalamazoo: Cistercian Publications, 1970).

10. Bernard of Clairvaux, *De conversione* 1.2–3.4 (SBO 4:72–74); trans. Evans, 67.

11. Bernard of Clairvaux, *De conversione* 12.24 (SBO 4:97); trans. Evans, 84.

12. Bernard of Clairvaux, *De conversione* 13.25 (SBO 4:99); trans. Evans, 85.

13. Bernard of Clairvaux, *De consideratione* IV.3.6 (SBO 3:453); trans. John D. Anderson and Elizabeth T. Kennan, *Bernard of Clairvaux: Five Books on Consideration*, CF 37 (Kalamazoo: Cistercian Publications, 1976), 24.

14. Bernard of Clairvaux, *Ep.* 239 to Pope Eugenius III (SBO 8:120); trans. Bruno Scott James, *The Letters of St. Bernard of Clairvaux* (1953; reprint: Kalamazoo, MI: Cistercian Publications, 1998), 280.

15. Bernard of Clairvaux, *Ep.* 250.4 to the Carthusian Prior Bernard of Porto (SBO 8:147); trans. James, *Letters of St. Bernard*, 402.

16. Étienne Gilson, *La théologie mystique de saint Bernard* (Paris: Librarie Philosophique J. Vrin, 1947), 19; published in English as *The Mystical Theology of St. Bernard*, trans. A. H. C. Downs, CS 120 (1940; reprint: Kalamazoo, MI: Cistercian Publications, 1990), 7.

17. Jean Leclerq, *Bernard of Clairvaux and the Cistercian Spirit*, trans. Claire Lavoie, CS 16 (Kalamazoo, MI: Cistercian Publications, 1976), 32.

18. For the Latin text of Bernard's *Sermones Cantica Canticorum* (*SCC*), see vols. 1 and 2 of SBO. Besides the partial translation of Evans, I have drawn here on the complete translation in Kilian Walsh and Irene Edmonds, *Bernard of Clairvaux: On the Song of Songs*, CF 4, 7, 31, and 40 (Kalamazoo, MI: Cistercian Publications, 1971–1980), cited hereafter as "CF" with the volume number. At times, I give my own translations to try and capture the flavor of Bernard's poetic prose.

19. Jean Leclerq, "Introduction: Were the Sermons on the Song of Songs Delivered in Chapter?" in CF 7, vii–xxx; and Leclerq, "Introduction: The Making of a Masterpiece," in CF 40, ix–xxiv.

20. Bernard McGinn, "The Language of Love in Christian and Jewish Mysticism," in *Mysticism and Language*, ed. Steven T. Katz (New York: Oxford University Press, 1992), 202–235. On Origen's and Ambrose's use of the Song, see McGinn, *Foundations of Mysticism*, 117–126, 205–215.

21. Bernard of Clairvaux, *SCC* 1.7–8 (SBO 1:6); trans. CF 4:5.

22. Bernard sometimes interprets "bride" as the whole Church; see *SCC* 69.1 (SBO 2:201–202), where he debates whether to interpret a certain passage in a collective or in an individual sense.

23. Bernard of Clairvaux, *SCC* 83.3 (SBO 2:299); trans. CF 40:182.

24. Bernard of Clairvaux, *SCC* 8.9, 31.6 (SBO 1:41, 223).

25. Bernard of Clairvaux, *SCC* 71.7 (SBO 2:220); trans. CF 40:54.

26. Bernard of Clairvaux, *SCC* 67.8 (SBO 2:193); trans. CF 40:12.

27. Bernard of Clairvaux, *SCC* 67.10, 45.8 (SBO 2:195, 2:54); trans. CF 40:14, 7:238.

28. Bernard of Clairvaux, *SCC* 2.3, 8.8 (SBO 1:9–10, 1:41).

29. Bernard of Clairvaux, *SCC* 8.9 (SBO 1:41); trans. CF 4:52.

30. Bernard of Clairvaux, *SCC* 3.1 (SBO 1:14); trans. CF 4:16.

31. Paul Verdeyen, "Un théologien de l'expérience," 557–578, in *Bernard de Clairvaux: Histoire, mentalités, spiritualité*, Colloque de Lyon-Cîteaux-Dijon, SC 380 (Paris: Éditions du Cerf, 1992).

32. Bernard of Clairvaux, *SCC* 41.3 (SBO 2:30); trans. CF 7:206.

33. Bernard of Clairvaux, *SCC* 85.14 (SBO 2:316); trans. CF 40:210.

34. Bernard of Clairvaux, *SCC* 23.15 (SBO 1:148).

35. Harvey D. Egan, *An Anthology of Christian Mysticism*, 2nd ed. (Collegeville, MN: Liturgical Press/Pueblo, 1991), 170.

36. Bernard of Clairvaux, *SCC* 74.5 (SBO 2:242–243); trans. Evans, 255.

37. Bernard of Clairvaux, *SCC* 74.5 (SBO 2:242–243); trans. Evans, 255.

38. Bernard of Clairvaux, *SCC* 74.6 (SBO 2:243); trans. Evans, 255–256.

39. Bernard of Clairvaux, *SCC* 74.6 (SBO 2:243); trans. Evans, 255–256.

40. Bernard of Clairvaux, *SCC* 74.5 (SBO 2:243); trans. Evans, 255.

41. Bernard of Clairvaux, *SCC* 74.7 (SBO 2:243–244); trans. Evans, 256.

42. Bernard of Clairvaux, *Liber de praecepto et dispensatione* 19.60 (SBO 3:293): "*Praesens igitur Deo est Deum amat in quantum amat.*"

43. Michael Casey, "Bernard's Biblical Mysticism," *Studies in Spirituality* 4 (1994): 14.

44. Bernard of Clairvaux, *SCC* 36.5 (SBO 2:7); cf. *SCC* 27.6 (SBO 1:184), *Sermones de diversis* 40.4 (SBO 6:237), 42.2–3 (SBO 6:256–258), *De gratia et libero arbitrio* 32 (SBO 3:188). Bernard likely drew the phrase from Augustine's *Confessions* 7.10.16, in which at the peak of a mystical encounter, Augustine discovers his own moral and ontological distance from God. Augustine uses a similar phrase to describe his sinfulness: "I have made myself a region of destitution" (*Confessions* 2.10.18: *factus sum*

mihi regio egestatis). For its use in Bernard's works, see Gilson, *Mystical Theology*, 33–39; see also Michael Casey, *Athirst for God: Spiritual Desire in Bernard of Clairvaux's Sermons on the Song of Songs*, CS 77 (Kalamazoo, MI: Cistercian Publications, 1988), 171–182.

45. Bernard of Clairvaux, *SCC* 81.1, 82.1, 83.1 (SBO 2:284, 292, 298).

46. E.g., *SCC* 18.6, 21.6, 24.5–6, 25.7, 77.5 (SBO 1:107, 1:125, 1:156–157, 1:167, 2:264). On Bernard's anthropology of desire, see Casey, *Athirst*, 133–170.

47. Bernard is not always consistent in his theology of image and likeness, that is, in qualities he attributes to the image and those he attributes to the likeness. Variants come up especially in the final *Sermons on the Song of Songs*. Bernard himself was alert to this and makes a brief apology: *SCC* 81.11 (SBO 2:291).

48. Bernard of Clairvaux, *SCC* 80.2 (SBO 2:277). Bernard uses other terms such as *propinquitas* ("nearness"), *convenientia* ("compatibility"), and *vicinitas naturae* ("closeness of nature"). See, e.g., *SCC* 69.7 (SBO 2:206); see Casey, *Athirst*, 164.

49. Bernard of Clairvaux, *SCC* 24.5–6 (SBO 1:156–157); trans. CF 7:46: "God indeed gave man an upright stance of body, perhaps in order that this corporeal uprightness, exterior and of little account, might prompt the inward man, made to the image of God, to cherish his spiritual uprightness; that the beauty of this body of clay might rebuke the deformity of the mind. What is more unbecoming than to bear a warped mind in an upright body?" See *Sermones de diversis* 12.1 (SBO 6:127–128); *SCC* 80.3–4 (SBO 2:278–280); also Gilson, *Mystical Theology*, 51–54.

50. Bernard of Clairvaux, *SCC* 82.5 (SBO 2:295); trans. my own.

51. Bernard of Clairvaux, *SCC* 83.1 (SBO 2:298); trans. my own.

52. Bernard of Clairvaux, *SCC* 83.1 (SBO 2:298–299); trans. CF 40:180.

53. Bernard of Clairvaux, *SCC* 83.2 (SBO 2:299); trans. Evans, 271.

54. Bernard of Clairvaux, *SCC* 83.4 (SBO 2:300); cf. *SCC* 18.6 (SBO 1:107).

55. Bernard of Clairvaux, *SCC* 83.4 (SBO 2:300); trans. Evans, 272.

56. Gerson, *In festo S. Bernardi* (Glorieux, 5:325); trans. McGuire, 129.

57. Bernard of Clairvaux, *SCC* 1.11 (SBO 1:7–8); trans. CF 4:6–7.

CHAPTER 4

1. Hildegard of Bingen, *Ep.* 1 to Bernard, Abbot of Clairvaux (CCCM 91:3–5); trans. Baird, 1:27–28. I have altered the translation of *viriditas*, substituting "greenness" for Baird's "fruitfulness." On this key term, see below. On this episode, see Amy Hollywood, "Ca. 1147: Hildegard of Bingen Writes to Bernard of Clairvaux," in *A New History of German Literature*, ed. David E. Wellbery (Cambridge, MA: Harvard University Press, 2004), 39–44.

2. Barbara Newman, "Sibyl of the Rhine: Hildegard's Life and Times," in *Voice of the Living Light: Hildegard of Bingen and Her World*, ed. Newman (Berkeley, CA: University of California Press, 1998), 1.

3. Bernard McGinn, *The Growth of Mysticism: Gregory the Great through the 12th Century*, vol. 2 of *The Presence of God: A History of Western Christian Mysticism* (New York: Crossroad, 1996), 333.

4. Godfrey of Disibodenberg, *Vita s. Hildegardis* I.1 (CCCM 126:6); trans. Anna Silvas, *Jutta and Hildegard: The Biographical Sources*, Brepols Medieval Women Series (University Park, PA: Pennsylvania State University Press, 1998), 138.

5. Hildegard of Bingen, *Ep.* 95 (CCCM 91A:250–251); Baird, 2:10–11.

6. Hildegard of Bingen, *Ep.* 85r/b (CCCM 91:207); trans. Baird, 1:195.

7. Hildegard of Bingen, *Ep.* 52r (CCCM 91:129–130); trans. Baird, 1:129.

8. Tengswich, *Ep.* 52 to Hildegard (CCCM 91:126); trans. Baird, 1:127.

9. Hildegard of Bingen, *Ep.* 52r (CCCM 91:128–130); trans. Baird, 1:128–130.

10. Hildegard of Bingen, *Scivias*, Protestificatio (CCCM 43:3–4); trans. Hart, 59.

11. Hildegard of Bingen, *Ep.* 2 to Pope Eugenius (CCCM 91:7-8); Baird, 1:32–33.

12. Hildegard of Bingen, quoted in Theodore of Echternach, *Vita S. Hildegardis* II.v [*Secunda visio*] (CCCM 126:27); trans. Silvas, 164.

13. E.g., the denunciation of the Cologne clergy in *Ep.* 15r (CCCM 91:34–44); Baird, 1:55–63.

14. Guibert of Gembloux, *Ep.* XVI [= *Ep.* 102 in Hildegard's letters] (CCCM 66:219–220); trans. Baird, 2:18.

15. Guibert of Gembloux, *Ep.* XVII [= *Ep.* 103 in Hildegard's letters] (CCCM 66:223); trans. Baird, 2:20.

16. Hildegard of Bingen, *Ep.* 103r to Guibert of Gembloux (CCCM 91A:258–262); trans. Baird, 2:21–23. Godfrey considered this letter a definitive statement and quotes it at length in his biography of Hildegard: *Vita S. Hildegard* I.8 (CCCM 126:14–15); Silvas, 149–150.

17. Oliver Sacks, *Migraine: Understanding a Common Disorder* (Berkeley: University of California Press, 1985), 106–108. For an assessment, see Sabina Flanagan, *Hildegard of Bingen, 1098–1179: A Visionary Life*, 2nd ed. (New York: Routledge, 1998), 185–204.

18. Newman, *Voice of the Living Light*, 10.

19. Hildegard of Bingen, *Scivias*, Protestificatio (CCCM 43:3); trans. Hart, 59.

20. Hildegard of Bingen, *Scivias* II.1 (CCCM 43:111–112); trans. my own.

21. Hildegard of Bingen, *Scivias* I.3 (CCCM 43:41); trans. Hart, 94. Cf. *Scivias* I.2, I.5, II.1, II.2.

22. Madeleine Caviness, "Artist: 'To See, Hear, and Know All at Once,' " in Newman, *Voice of the Living Light*, 110.

23. Caviness, "Artist," 115.

24. Hildegard of Bingen, *Scivias* II.2 (CCCM 43:124); trans. Hart, 161.

25. Hildegard of Bingen, *Scivias* II.2.2 (CCCM 43:125–126); trans. Hart, 161–162.

26. Hildegard of Bingen, *Scivias* II.2 (CCCM 43:127–130); trans. Hart, 163–164.

27. Peter Dronke, "Hildegard's Inventions," in *Hildegard von Bingen in ihrem wissenschaftlicher Kongreß zum 900 jährigen Jubiläum, 13.–19. September 1998, Bingen am Rhein*, ed. Alfred Haverkamp (Mainz: Verlag Philipp von Zabern, 2000), 314.

28. Hildegard of Bingen, *Scivias* III.13 (CCCM 43A:615); trans. Hart, 525.

29. Hildegard of Bingen, *Scivias* III.13 (CCCM 43A:621); trans. Hart, 529.

30. Odo of Soissons, *Ep.* 40 to Hildegard (CCCM 91:102); trans. Baird, 1:119.

31. Richard Crocker, "Medieval Chant," in *The New Oxford History of Music*, 2nd ed., vol. 2, *The Early Middle Ages to 1300* (New York: Oxford University Press, 1990), 301.

32. Hildegard of Bingen, "O viridissima virga," song 19 in *Symphonia armonie celestium revelationum*. The Latin text is from Barbara Newman, ed., *Saint Hildegard of Bingen: Symphonia; A Critical Edition of the Symphonia armonie celestium revelationum*, 2nd ed. (Ithaca, NY: Cornell University Press, 1998), 126; the translation is my own. For a recording, see Sequentia, *Canticles of Ecstasy: Hildegard von Bingen*, track 11.

33. Hart and Bishop, whose translation in CWS is the widely used standard, do not consistently reflect the original Latin term in their English translation. They use various terms to translate *viriditas*: "freshness" (Hart, 86, 103, 212, 252, 402, 405), "vitality" (161), "fertility" (113, 177, 251), "fecundity" (129, 220, 440), "fruitfulness" (154, 226, 404, 439), "growth" (258). Constant Mews, "Religious Thinker: 'A Frail Human Being' on Fiery Life," in Newman, *Voice of Living Light*, 211 n. 24, has argued: "The archaic *viridity* perhaps deserves to be restored in translations of Hildegard."

34. Gregory the Great, *Moralia in Job* VI.16 (CCSL 143:298), defines *viriditas* as the life of trees and plants; he uses the word forty-three times. See Mews, "Religious Thinker," 212 n. 28.

35. Hildegard of Bingen, *De divinorum operum* I.1.2; *Scivias* I.4.17 (CCCM 43:78–79); *Scivias* I.4.5 (CCCM 43:70): "cum virtutes in me uiriditatem suam ostendere incipient."

36. Hildegard of Bingen, *Scivias* II.1.3 (CCCM 43:114); trans. Hart, 151. Note that I have substituted "greenness" for Hart's "freshness."

37. Barbara Newman, *Sister of Wisdom: St. Hildegard's Theology of the Feminine* (Berkeley: University of California Press, 1987), 192, notes that Hildegard has a "special predilection for natural images—branch, foliage, and flower—suggested by the standard play on *virgo* and *virga*."

38. G. M. Dreves and Clemens Blume, *Analecta hymnica mediiaevi* (Leipzig, 1886–1922), 484; cited in Newman, *Saint Hildegard of Bingen: Symphonia*, 32 n. 74.

39. Hildegard of Bingen, *Ep.* 1 to Bernard, Abbot of Clairvaux (CCCM 91:5); trans. Baird, 1:28.

40. Hildegard of Bingen, *Ep.* 23 (CCCM 91:63–64); trans. Baird, 1:78.

41. Hildegard of Bingen, *Ep.* 23 (CCCM 91:64); trans. Baird, 1:78.

42. Hildegard of Bingen, *Ep.* 23 (CCCM 91:64); Baird 1:77–78.

43. Hildegard of Bingen, *Ep.* 23 (CCCM:91:64); trans. Baird, 1:79.

44. Hildegard of Bingen, *Ep.* 23 (CCCM:91:64); trans. Baird, 1:79.

45. Barbara Newman, "Hildegard and Her Hagiographers: The Remaking of Female Sainthood," in *Gendered Voices: Medieval Saints and Their Interpreters*, ed. Catherine M. Mooney (Philadelphia: University of Pennsylvania Press, 1999), 16–34.

46. Caroline Walker Bynum, preface, in Hart, 3.

47. McGinn, *Growth of Mysticism*, 335.

CHAPTER 5

1. Étienne Gilson, *The Philosophy of St. Bonaventure*, trans. Illtyd Trethowan and Frank J. Sheed (Paterson, NJ: St. Anthony Guild Press, 1965), 1.

2. Bonaventure, *Letter in Response to an Unknown Master* 13 (Qrc 8:336); trans. Dominic Monti, *St. Bonaventure's Writings Concerning the Franciscan Order*, WSB 5 (St. Bonaventure, NY: Franciscan Institute, 1994), 54.

3. On this clash, see C. H. Lawrence, *The Friars: The Impact of the Early Mendicant Movement on Western Society* (London and New York: Longman, 1994), 153–159; John Moorman, *History of the Franciscan Order: From Its Origins to the Year 1517* (1965; reprint: Chicago: Franciscan Herald Press, 1988), 124–131.

4. Joachim of Fiore, *Liber concordiae novi et veteris testimenti*. The classic study of Joachim is by Marjorie Reeves, *The Influence of Prophecy in the Later Middle Ages: A Study in Joachimism* (1969; reprint: Notre Dame: University of Notre Dame Press, 1993). See also Bernard McGinn, ed., *Apocalyptic Spirituality*, CWS (New York: Paulist Press, 1979); the passage from *Liber concordiae* quoted here is on p. 123.

5. R. Colt Anderson, *A Call to Piety: Saint Bonaventure's Collations on the Six Days*, Studies in Franciscanism (Quincy, IL: Franciscan Press, 2002), 19.

6. David Burr, *Olivi and Franciscan Poverty: The Origins of the Usus Pauper Controversy* (Philadelphia: University of Pennsylvania Press, 1989), 4.

7. David Burr, *The Spiritual Franciscans: From Protest to Persecution in the Century after Saint Francis* (University Park: Pennsylvania State University Press, 2003), 32–41.

8. Bernard McGinn, *The Flowering of Mysticism: Men and Women in the New Mysticism, 1200–1350*, vol. 3 of *The Presence of God: A History of Western Christian Mysticism* (New York: Crossroad, 1998), 105.

9. Bonaventure, *Itin.* prol. 5 (Qrc 5:296); trans. Cousins, 57.

10. Cousins, introduction, 21.

11. Bonaventure, *Itin.* 1.2 (Qrc 5:297); trans. Philotheus Boehner and Zachary Hayes, *Works of St. Bonaventure II: Itinerarium Mentis in Deum*, rev. ed., WSB 2 (St. Bonaventure, NY: Franciscan Institute, 2002), 47.

12. Bonaventure, *Legenda maior* 13.3 (Qrc 8:543); trans. Cousins, 305–306.

13. Bonaventure, *Itin.* prol. 2 (Qrc 5:295); Cousins, 54.

14. Bonaventure, *Itin.* prol. 3 (Qrc 5:295); trans. Cousins, 54.

15. Bonaventure, *Itin.* 1.5 (Qrc 5:297); trans. Cousins, 61.

16. Bonaventure, *Itin.* 1.5 (Qrc 5:297), notes other biblical sixes: the theophany that Moses experienced atop Mt. Sinai took place "after six days" (Ex. 24:16); so too did the theophany that the apostles experienced during Jesus's transfiguration (Mt. 17:1–2).

17. Bonaventure, *Itin.* 1.2 (Qrc 5:297); trans. Cousins, 60.

18. Bonaventure, *Itin.*, capitula (Qrc 5:296); trans. Boehner and Hayes, WSB 2:43.

19. Bonaventure, *Itin.* 1.2 (Qrc 5:297); trans. Cousins, 60.

20. Bonaventure, *Itin.* 1.2 (Qrc 5:297); trans. Cousins, 60.

21. Bonaventure, *Itin.* 1.2 (Qrc 5:297); trans. Cousins, 60.

22. Bonaventure, *Itin.* 1.5 (Qrc 5:297); trans. Cousins, 61: "Any one of these [three] ways can be doubled, according to whether we consider God as the Alpha and the Omega. Or in each of these ways we can see him through a mirror or in a

mirror . . . Therefore it is necessary that these three principal stages be multiplied to a total of six."

23. Bonaventure, *Commentarius in I librum Sententarium* distinctio 3, pars 1, articulus 1, quaestio 3 (Qrc 1:74); trans. from Denys Turner, "Hierarchy Interiorised: Bonaventure's *Itinerarium Mentis in Deum,*" in *The Darkness of God: Negativity in Christian Mysticism* (Cambridge: Cambridge University Press, 1995), 111.

24. For the three types of theology, see *Itin.* 1.7; for the three laws, see *Itin.* 1.12; for the six powers of the soul, see *Itin.* 1.6; for the seven properties of creature: *Itin.* 1.14. Cf. *Hexaem.* 5.24 (Qrc 5:358).

25. Bonaventure, *Itin.* 2.10 (Qrc 5:302); trans. Cousins, 75: "Number is the foremost exemplar in the mind of the Creator" (quoting Boethius, *De institutione arithmetica* I.2).

26. Bonaventure, *Itin.* prol. 4 (Qrc 5:296); trans. Cousins, 56.

27. Bonaventure, *Itin.* prol. 1 (Qrc 5:295); trans. Cousins, 53.

28. Bonaventure, *Itin.* prol. 1 (Qrc 5:295); trans. Cousins, 53.

29. Francis of Assisi, *Canticle of the Creatures* (1225); see Regis J. Armstrong, J. Wayne Hellmann and William J. Short, eds., *Francis of Assisi: Early Documents,* vol. 1, *The Saint* (Hyde Park, NY: New City Press, 1999), 113–114.

30. Bonaventure, *Legenda maior* 9.1 (Qrc 8:530); trans. Cousins, 262–263.

31. Zachary Hayes, "Bonaventure: Mystery of the Triune God," in *The History of Franciscan Theology,* ed. Kenan Osborne (St. Bonaventure, NY: Franciscan Institute, 1994), 56–57.

32. Bonaventure, *Itin.* 2.11 (Qrc 5:302); trans. Cousins, 75–76.

33. Bonaventure, *Itin.* 1.14 (Qrc 5:299); trans. Cousins, 67.

34. Grover A. Zinn, "Book and Word: The Victorine Background of Bonaventure's Use of Symbols," in *San Bonaventura, 1274–1974,* ed. Jacques Guy Bougerol (Rome/Grottaferrata: Collegio S. Bonaventura, 1974), 2:151–164.

35. Bonaventure, *Hexaem.* 13.12 (Qrc 5:390); trans. my own.

36. Bonaventure, *Itin.* 3.1 (Qrc 5:303); trans. Cousins, 79.

37. Augustine, *Confessions* 10.27.38. For the Latin text, see J. J. O'Donnell, *Augustine: Confessions,* vol. 1, *Introduction and Text* (Oxford: Clarendon Press, 1992); my own translation here.

38. Bonaventure, *Itin.* 3.1 (Qrc 5:303); trans. Cousins, 80.

39. Augustine, *Confessions* 13.11.12 (O'Donnell, 188); trans. Henry Chadwick, *Saint Augustine: Confessions* (New York: Oxford University Press, 1991), 279.

40. Augustine, *De trinitate* X.9.18 (CCSL 50A:330–331). Augustine ultimately discarded this and his other intra-mental analogies in Book XV. In this case, each who possesses this triad is one person, whereas God is three; and the three powers do not belong to one God, but *are* the one God. See Augustine, *De trinitate* XV.7.12 (CCSL 50A: 476–477).

41. Bonaventure, *Itin.* 3.5 (Qrc 5:305); trans. Cousins, 84.

42. Bonaventure, *Itin.* 4.1 (Qrc 5:306); trans. Cousins, 87.

43. Bonaventure, *Itin.* 4.3 (Qrc 5:306); trans. Cousins, 89.

44. Bonaventure, *Itin.* 4.4 (Qrc 5:307); trans. Cousins, 90.

45. Bonaventure, *Itin.* 4.7 (Qrc 5:307); trans. Cousins, 92.

46. Bonaventure, *Itin.* 5.1 (Qrc 5:308); trans. Cousins, 94.

47. Bonaventure, *Itin.* 3.1 (Qrc 5:303); Cousins, 79.

48. Bonaventure, *Itin.* 5.1 (Qrc 5:308); trans. Cousins, 94.

49. Bonaventure, *Itin.* 5.1 (Qrc 5:308); trans. Cousins, 94.

50. Bonaventure, *Itin.* 5.8 (Qrc 5:310); trans. my own.

51. Bonaventure, *Itin.* 5.7 (Qrc 5:309); trans. Cousins, 119.

52. Pseudo-Dionysius, *De caelesti hierarchia* 1.1–2 (PG 3:120–121); trans. Colm Luibheid, *Pseudo-Dionysius: The Complete Works*, CWS (New York: Paulist Press, 1987), 145–146. On Pseudo-Dionysius's influence, see Georges Duby, *The Age of the Cathedrals: Art and Society, 980–1420*, trans. Barbara Thompson (Chicago: University of Chicago Press, 1983); Otto von Simson, *The Gothic Cathedral*, rev. ed. (Princeton: Princeton University Press, 1988).

53. Pseudo-Dionysius, *De caelesti hierarchia* 1.3 (PG 3:121); trans. Luibheid, 146.

54. Suger of St.-Denis, *De administratione* 33; trans. Duby, 102. For Suger's Latin text, together with a complete translation, see Erwin Panofsky, *Abbot Suger on the Abbey Church of St.-Denis and Its Art Treasures* (Princeton: Princeton University Press, 1946). For an analysis, see Paula Lieber Gerson, ed., *Abbot Suger and Saint-Denis: A Symposium* (New York: Metropolitan Museum of Art, 1986).

55. Suger of St.-Denis, *De administratione* 27 (Panofsky, 48); trans. Panofsky, 49.

56. Bonaventure, *Hexaem.* 12.14 (Qrc 5:386); trans. WB 5:179.

57. Bonaventure, *De reductione artium ad theologiam* 5 (Qrc 5:321); trans. Zachary Hayes, *St. Bonaventure's On the Reduction of the Arts to Theology*, WSB 1 (St. Bonaventure, NY: Franciscan Institute, 1996), 45.

58. Bonaventure, *Itin.* Prol. 1 (Qrc 5:295); trans. Cousins, 53.

59. Bonaventure, *Hexaem.* 1.17 (Qrc 5:332); trans. my own.

60. Bonaventure, *Hexaem.* 12.14 (Qrc 5:386); trans. WB 5:179.

61. Bonaventure, *Breviloquium* 2.12 (Qrc 5:230); trans. WB 2:105.

62. Hayes, "Bonaventure: Mystery of the Triune God," 118.

63. Bonaventure, *Hexaem.* 1.17 (Qrc 5:332); trans. my own.

64. Bonaventure, *Itin.* 5.1 (Qrc 5:308); trans. Cousins, 94.

65. Bonaventure, *Itin.* 5.4 (Qrc 5:309); trans. Cousins, 96.

66. Bonaventure, *Itin.* 5.4 (Qrc 5:309); trans. Cousins, 96.

67. Bonaventure, *Itin.* 3.3 (Qrc 5:304); Cousins, 82.

68. Bonaventure, *Itin.* 5.4 (Qrc 5:309); trans. Cousins, 97.

69. Bonaventure, *Itin.* 5.4 (Qrc 5:309); trans. Cousins, 97.

70. Bonaventure, *Quaestiones disputatae de scientia Christi*, concl. 21 (Qrc 5:43); trans. Zachary Hayes, *Saint Bonaventure's Disputed Questions on the Knowledge of Christ*, WSB 4 (St. Bonaventure, NY: Franciscan Institute, 1992), 195–196.

71. Pseudo-Dionysius, *De mystica theologia* 3 (PG 3:1032–1033); Luibheid, 138–140. On this famous distinction, see Paul Rorem, *Pseudo-Dionysius: A Commentary on the Texts and An Introduction to Their Influence* (New York: Oxford University Press, 1993), 194–205.

72. Bonaventure, *de scientia Christi*, concl. 21 (Qrc 5:43); trans. Hayes, WSB 4:195–196.

73. Bonaventure, *Itin.* 7, *cap.* (Qrc 5:312); trans. Cousins, 110.

74. Bonaventure, *Itin.* 7.5 (Qrc 5:313); trans. Cousins, 114; quoting Pseudo-Dionysius, *De mystica theologia* 1.1 (PG 3:997).

75. Bonaventure, *Hexaem.* 1.10 (Qrc 5:330–331); trans. my own.

76. Ewert Cousins, "Francis of Assisi: Christian Mysticism at the Crossroads," in *Mysticism and Religious Traditions*, ed. Steven T. Katz (New York: Oxford University Press, 1983), 166–175.

77. Bonaventure, *Itin.* 7.3 (Qrc 5:312); trans. Cousins, 112.

78. Bonaventure, *Itin.* 7.3 (Qrc 5:312); trans. Cousins, 112–113.

79. Bonaventure, *Itin.*, prol. 3 (Qrc 5:295); trans. Cousins, 54.

80. Bonaventure, *Itin.* 4.2 (Qrc 5:306); trans. Cousins, 88.

81. Bonaventure, *Itin.* 4.1 (Qrc 5:306); trans. Cousins, 88.

82. Bonaventure, *Commentarius in I librum Sententarium* d. 27, p. 2, art. 1, q. 2, concl. (Qrc 1:485). Cf. *De reductione* 23.

83. Bonaventure, *Itin.* 6.5 (Qrc 5:311); Cousins, 107.

84. Bonaventure, *De reductione* 23 (Qrc 5:325); trans. Hayes, WSB 1:59, modified.

85. Bonaventure, *Itin.* 7.1 (Qrc 5:312); trans. Cousins, 111.

86. Bonaventure, *Itin.* 7.6 (Qrc 5:313); trans. Cousins, 116.

87. Turner, "Hierarchy," 102–103.

88. Cousins, "Francis of Assisi: Christian Mysticism," 182.

89. Bonaventure, *Itin.* 1 (Qrc 5:296); trans. my own.

90. Bonaventure, *Itin.* 7.2 (Qrc 5:312); trans. my own.

91. Bonaventure, *Hexaem.* 1.37 (Qrc 5:335); trans. from Hayes, "Bonaventure," 52.

CHAPTER 6

1. Meister Eckhart, *Predigt* 52 (DW 2:492–504). For Eckhart's Middle High German writings, see DW. The translation here is from *Essential*, 200–203.

2. This chapter owes much to the magisterial work of Bernard McGinn, especially his recent study, *The Mystical Thought of Meister Eckhart: The Man from Whom God Hid Nothing* (New York: Herder & Herder/Crossroad, 2001); this reappears in briefer (and slightly updated) form in the recent volume of his history of Christian mysticism: *The Harvest of Mysticism in Medieval Germany*, vol. 4 of *The Presence of God* (New York: Herder & Herder/Crossroad, 2005), 94–194. On Eckhart's biography (and much else), see also Kurt Ruh, *Meister Eckhart: Theologe, Prediger, Mystiker* (Munich: Verlag C. H. Beck, 1985). For a compendium of source documents, see Loris Sturlese, ed., *Acta Echardiana*, LW 5 (1988): 153–193. Some older surveys claim Eckhart was of noble birth, but the evidence is not clear. Some also give Eckhart's first name as "John"; there is no evidence for this. An early document speaks of him as being from Hochheim; the problem is that there are two Hochheims, one near Erfurt and one near Gotha.

3. Eckhart, *Responsio ad articulos sibi impositos de scriptis et dictis suis* (LW 5:156); trans. *Essential*, 72. This is from what is usually called Eckhart's *Defense* (*Rechtfertigungsschrift* or *Verteidigung*); for the critical edition, published in 2000, see LW 5:247–354.

4. Eckhart, *Sermo Paschalis* n. 15 (LW 5:145), where he mentions Albert's (oral) teaching.

5. The *Opus tripartitum* was, until recently, presumed to be from Eckhart's second tenure in Paris (1311–1313). Loris Sturlese has demonstrated, on the basis of manuscript evidence, that it was earlier, in the first decade of the fourteenth century. See McGinn, *Mystical Thought*, 7, 186–187.

6. See Ellen Babinsky, ed., *Marguerite Porete: The Mirror of Simple Souls*, CWS (New York: Paulist Press, 1993). On links between her and Eckhart, see Bernard McGinn, ed., *Meister Eckhart and the Beguine Mystics: Hadewijch of Brabant, Mechthild of Magdeburg, and Marguerite Porete* (New York: Continuum, 1994).

7. Matthew Paris, *Chronica Majora*. For the Latin, see Henry Richards Luard, vol. 4, Rolls Series (London, 1877), 278; the translation here is from R. W. Southern, *Western Society and the Church in the Middle Ages* (New York: Penguin Books, 1970), 319.

8. Robert Lerner, *The Heresy of the Free Spirit in the Later Middle Ages*, 2nd ed. (Notre Dame: University of Notre Dame Press, 1997). Lerner does much to unmask the patent distortions that made their way into some of these pronouncements.

9. Council of Vienne, *Decreta* 16. For the Latin text and translation, see Norman P. Tanner, ed., *Decrees of the Ecumenical Councils*, 2 vols. (Washington, DC: Georgetown University Press, 1990), 1:374.

10. Council of Vienne, *Decreta* 16 (Tanner, 1:374).

11. Maria Lichtmann, "Marguerite Porete and Meister Eckhart: *The Mirror of Simple Souls* Mirrored," in McGinn, *Meister Eckhart and the Beguine Mystics*, 65–86.

12. See the helpful comments of Michael Sells, "The Pseudo-Woman and the Meister: 'Unsaying' and Essentialism," in McGinn, *Meister Eckhart and the Beguine Mystics*, 143.

13. Thomas Aquinas, *Summa Theologiae* II a II ae, q. 188, a.6c. For a discussion, see McGinn, *Harvest*, 11 ff.

14. Eckhart, *Daz buoch der götlîchen trœstunge* (DW 5:60); trans. *Essential*, 239.

15. Eckhart, *Daz buoch der götlîchen trœstunge* (DW 5:61); trans. *Essential*, 239.

16. The original edition of Eckhart's sermons in Middle High German was done by Franz Pfeiffer, *Meister Eckhart*, vol. 2 of *Deutsche Mystiker des vierzehnten Jahrhunderts* (1857; reprint: Scientia Verlag Aalen, 1962). Pfeiffer attributed 110 sermons to Eckhart. Not all have been accepted as authentic. Josef Quint, who oversaw the original volumes of the critical edition (DW 1–3), pared this number down to 86. However, Georg Steer, the editor of the nearly completed final volume (DW 4), now lists the final total as 114 authentic sermons. Unfortunately, scholars and translators of Eckhart have not agreed upon a standardized system for numbering the German sermons. Some scholars and some translators (such as M. O'C. Walshe) have

used the older Pfeiffer numbering; other scholars and other translators (such as Bernard McGinn and Frank Tobin) follow the numbering of the Quint-Steer edition (DW 1–4); and still others (such as Oliver Davies) make up their own numbering. This can make tracing down references confusing for nonspecialists and for students. Throughout these pages, I will use the numbering of DW (the Quint-Steer edition) even when I rely on translators such as Davies and Walshe who (unfortunately) use other numbering.

17. McGinn, *Mystical Thought*, 10.

18. Bruce Milem, *The Unspoken Word: Negative Theology in Meister Eckhart's German Sermons* (Washington, DC: Catholic University of America Press, 2002), 3. For details, see Georg Steer, "Zur Authentizität der deutschen Predigten Meister Eckharts," in *Eckhardus Theutonicus, homo doctus et sanctus: Nachweise un Berichte zum Prozeß gegen Meister Eckhart*, ed. Heinrich Stirnimann and Ruedi Imbach, Freiburger Zeitschrift für Philosophie und Theologie 11 (Freiburg, Schweiz: Üniversitätsverlag Freiburg, 1992), 127–168.

19. Matthew Paris, *Chronica Majora* (Luard, 4:278); trans. Southern, 319.

20. The general chapter's decrees are in *Monumenta Ordinis Praedicatorum Historia*, tome 4, *Acta Capitulorum Generalium*, vol. 2 (Rome, 1899), 160–161; quoted in McGinn, *Mystical Thought*, 14.

21. On Eckhart's trial and the complex politics behind it, see Oliver Davies, "Why Were Eckhart's Propositions Condemned?" *New Blackfriars* 71 (1990): 433–445; also McGinn, "Eckhart's Condemnation Reconsidered," *Thomist* 44 (1980): 390–414; Ruh, *Meister Eckhart*, 168–187.

22. Eckhart, *Responsio* I, n. 80 (LW 5:277); trans. *Essential*, 72.

23. Eckhart, *Responsio* II, n. 147 (LW 5:353); trans. *Essential*, 75.

24. Eckhart, *Responsio* I, n. 126 (LW 5:293); trans. *Essential*, 74.

25. Eckhart, *Responsio* I, n. 126 (LW 5:293); trans. *Essential*, 74.

26. John XXII, *Cum inter nonnullas* (D §930 [p. 397]); in Edward Peters, trans., *Heresy and Authority in Medieval Europe: Documents in Translation* (Philadelphia: University of Pennsylvania Press, 1980), 247.

27. Geoffrey Barraclough, *The Medieval Papacy* (New York: W. W. Norton, 1979), 147, perceptively notes that John's attacks on the Franciscans were "one of the factors most effective in undermining respect for the papacy; for the genuine spirituality of the friars was beyond all dispute, and it seemed wicked for a pope living in luxury in his palace in Avignon to condemn them for maintaining the doctrine of apostolic poverty. Wicked, self-interested, and worldly."

28. Walter Senner, "Meister Eckhart in Köln," in Klaus Jacobi, *Meister Eckhart: Lebensstation-Redistuationen* (Berlin: Akademie Verlag, 1997), 233, has argued, drawing on a seventeenth-century Dominican source, that Eckhart was prayed for on January 28 in German convents, implying that in Dominican circles Eckhart was remembered to have died on January 28, 1328.

29. John XXII, *In agro dominico* (D §979 [p. 404]); trans. *Essential*, 80.

30. John XXII, *In agro dominico* (D §980 [p. 404]); trans. *Essential*, 81.

31. Johannes Tauler, *Predigt* 15. The German text is in Ferdinand Vetter, *Die Predigten Taulers*, Deutsche Text des Mittelalters 11 (Berlin, 1910), 69; trans. McGinn, *Harvest*, 247.

32. Eckhart, *Responsio* I n. 79 (LW 5:276); *Essential*, 72.

33. McGinn, *Mystical Thought*, 71. The coinage comes originally from Alain de Libera, who had applied it to Albert the Great: see *Albert le Grand et la philosophie* (Paris: Vrin, 1990).

34. Eckhart, *Predigt* 53 (DW 2:536–537); trans. *Essential*, 205. Cf. *Sermo* XXV.1.259 (LW 4:273).

35. On Arius and Nicaea, see R. P. C. Hanson, *The Search for the Christian Doctrine of God: The Arian Controversy, 318–381* AD (Edinburgh: T & T Clark, 1988); Lewis Ayres, *Nicaea and Its Legacy: An Approach to Fourth-Century Trinitarian Theology* (New York: Oxford University Press, 2004). On Athanasius, see Khaled Anatolios, *Athanasius: The Coherence of His Thought* (New York: Routledge, 1998).

36. Eckhart, *Predigt* 6 (DW 1:109); trans. *Essential*, 188. Also: *Predigt* 43 (DW 2:319–320); *Daz buoch der götlîchen trœstunge* (DW 5:43–44).

37. Eckhart, *Predigt* 4 (DW 1:72); trans. *Teacher*, 251.

38. Eckhart, *Predigt* 75 (DW 3:299); trans. Walshe, 2:281–282.

39. Eckhart, *Predigt* 6 (DW 1:109); trans. *Essential*, 187.

40. Eckhart, *Predigt* 49 (DW 2:434–435); Walshe, 2:288.

41. Eckhart, *Expositio Libri Exodi* n. 16 (LW 2:21–22); trans. *Teacher*, 46. Cf. *Predigt* 35 (DW 2:180).

42. Eckhart, *Expositio Libri Exodi* n. 16 (LW 2:22); trans. *Teacher*, 46. *Predigt* 38 (DW 2:243–244; trans. Walshe, 1:221) uses the image of two springs.

43. Eckhart, *Predigt* 109 (DW 4:766); trans. Davies, 233. Quint originally questioned the authenticity of this sermon but later included it in his own *Meister Eckhart: Deutsche Predigten und Traktate* (Munich: Carl Hanser, 1963), 271–73. See Georg Steer, DW 4:750–757, for a discussion of its authenticity.

44. Eckhart, *Predigt* 12 (DW 1:199–200); trans. *Teacher*, 269.

45. Eckhart, *Predigt* 109 (DW 4:772–773); trans. Davies, 234.

46. Eckhart, *Predigt* 83 (DW 3:437–438); trans. *Essential*, 206.

47. Eckhart, *Predigt* 48 (DW 2:420); trans. *Essential*, 198.

48. Eckhart, *Predigt* 2 (DW 1:43–44); trans. *Essential*, 181.

49. *Processus contra mag. Echardum*, n. 69 (LW 5:223). See the discussion in Alain de Libera, "L'Un ou la Trinité," *Revue des sciences religieuses* 70 (1996): 39.

50. Bernard McGinn, "Meister Eckhart on God as Absolute Unity," in *Neoplatonism and Christian Thought*, ed. Dominic O'Meara (Albany, NY: SUNY, 1982), 128–139; also *Harvest*, 129–131.

51. Eckhart, *Sermo* XI n. 118 (LW 4:112); trans. McGinn, *Harvest*, 130.

52. Eckhart, *Predigt* 10 (DW 1:173); trans. Davies, 174.

53. Eckhart, *Predigt* 38 (DW 2:234); trans. Davies, 114.

54. Eckhart, *Sermo* XI n. 118 (LW 4:112); trans. McGinn, *Harvest*, 130.

55. Eckhart, *Expositio libri Sapientiae* n. 154 (LW 2:490); trans. *Teacher*, 169.

56. Eckhart, *Predigt* 10 (DW 1:173); trans. Davies, 174.

57. John XXII, *In agro dominico*, art. 24 (D §974 [p. 403]); trans. *Essential*, 79. This is citing a passage from Eckhart's sermon *Of the Nobleman* (*Von dem edeln Menschen*), appended to his *Book of Divine Consolation* (DW 5:115; *Essential*, 244). Art. 23 (D §973 [p. 402]; *Essential*, 79), attacks Eckhart's views on *unum* and indistinction, quoted from *Expositio libri Exodi* nn. 58–60 (LW 2:55–56).

58. On this, see John D. Caputo, "Fundamental Themes in Meister Eckhart's Mysticism," *Thomist* 42 (1978): 211.

59. Eckhart, *Predigt* 109 (DW 4:772); trans. Davies, 234.

60. Eckhart, *Predigt* 52 (DW 2:492–493); trans. *Essential*, 200.

61. Eckhart, *Predigt* 83 (DW 3:448); trans. *Essential*, 208.

62. Eckhart, *Predigt* 53 (DW 2:529); trans. *Essential*, 203.

63. Eckhart, *Predigt* 83 (DW 3:441–442); trans. *Essential*, 206–207.

64. John XII, *In agro dominico*, art. 28 (D §978 [p. 403]); *Essential*, 80.

65. McGinn, "Theological Introduction," *Essential*, 31.

66. Johannes Tauler, *Predigt* 1. For a translation, see Johannes Tauler, *Sermons*, CWS, trans. Maria Shrady (New York: Paulist Press, 1985), 35–39.

67. On the theme of birth of God in the soul in Eckhart, see Frank Tobin, *Meister Eckhart: Thought and Language* (Philadelphia: University of Pennsylvania Press, 1986), 94–115. Also useful is a classic article: Karl G. Kertz, "Meister Eckhart's Teaching on the Birth of the Divine Word in the Soul," *Traditio* 15 (1959): 327–363. For readings of *Predigt* 6, see Milem, *Unspoken Word*, 112–142; Kurt Flasch, "Predigt 6: 'Iusti vivent in aeternum," in *Lectura Eckhardi: Predigten Meister Eckharts von Fachgelehrten gelesen und gedeutet*, ed. Georg Steer and Loris Sturlese, 2 vols. (Stuttgart: Verlag W. Kohlhammer, 1998, 2003), 2:40–51.

68. Eckhart, *Predigt* 6 (DW 1:109–110); trans. *Essential*, 187–188.

69. Eckhart focuses on this traditional theme in various sermons, most famously in *Predigt* 16b (DW 263–276; *Teacher*, 275–279). As usual, Eckhart gives it an unusual interpretation. See Milem, *Unspoken Word*, 86–111; Susanne Köbele, "Predigt 16b: 'Quasi vas auri solidum,'" in Steer and Sturlese, *Lectura Eckhardi*, 1:52–74.

70. Milem, *Unspoken Word*, 48–49, 131–132; also Michael A. Sells, *Mystical Languages of Unsaying* (Chicago: University of Chicago Press, 1994), 172–173.

71. Kertz, "Meister Eckhart's Teaching," 329, refers to this as "the eternal eidetic pre-existence of the soul in God."

72. John XXII, *In agro dominico* art. 21 (D §971 [p.402]); trans. *Essential*, 79.

73. Eckhart, *Responsio* II, n. 134–136 (DW 5:350–351); trans. my own. He is addressing a similar text from *Predigt* 10 (DW 1:166–167).

74. Eckhart, *Expositio sancti Evangelii secundum Iohannem* n. 106 (LW 3:90; *Essential*, 162); *Expositio s. Evang. secundum Iohannem* n. 123 (LW 3:107; *Essential*, 170).

75. Eckhart, *Predigt* 22 (DW 1:382–383); trans. *Essential*, 194.

76. The classic study of the history of this theme is Hugo Rahner, "Die Gottesgeburt: Die Lehre der Kirchenväter von der Geburt Christi aud dem Herzen der Kirche und der Gläubigen," *Zeitschrift für katholische Theologie* 59 (1933): 333–418. Eckhart cites Origen in *Predigt* 41 (DW 2:293).

77. McGinn, *Harvest*, 559, n. 502, gives the most complete listing: *Predigten* 2, 3, 4, *5a*, 5b, *6*, 10, 11, 12, 13, 14, *16b*, 18, 19, 22, 24, 25, 26, 28, 29, 30, 31, 37, *38, 39*, 40, 41, 42, *43*, 44, 46, 49, 50, *54b*, 59, *75*, 76, 84, 86, 87, 91, 98, 99, and *101–104*. The numbers in italics are cases where Eckhart treats the subject in more detail.

78. Among Eckhart's Latin works, the theme of the birth appears in: *Sermones* VI nn. 57–59, XL n. 405, XLII nn. 422–423, XLIV n. 441, LI n. 518, LV n. 544; *In Gen.* II nn. 180, 191; *In Sap.* nn. 55, 67, 279–288; *In Ioh.* nn. 118–119, 341, 573.

79. Eckhart, *Predigt* 38 (DW 2:227–228); trans. Walshe, 1:215.

80. These were first published as sermons I–IV by Pfeiffer, but Quint, the editor of Eckhart's German works, did not include them in his original critical edition (DW 1–3). Because of this, scholars have tended not to use them extensively. But Quint himself later included three of them in his own *Meister Eckhart: Deutsche Predigten und Traktate* (Munich: Hanser, 1959), numbering them QT 57–59. Their authenticity has since been verified by Georg Steer. For Steer's commentary as well as the critical edition of the texts, see DW 4:279–505. See also the extensive commentary in McGinn, *Mystical Thought*, 53–70.

81. Eckhart, *Predigt* 101 (DW 4:335–336); trans. Walshe, 1:1.

82. Eckhart, *Predigt* 101 (DW 4:354); trans. Walshe, 1:6.

83. Eckhart, *Predigt* 101 (DW 4:343–344); trans. Walshe, 1:3.

84. Eckhart, *Predigt* 37 (DW 2:211); trans. Walshe, 1:229.

85. Eckhart, *Predigt* 48 (DW 2:419–420); trans. *Essential*, 198.

86. John XXII, *In agro dominico*, art. 27 (D §977 [p. 403]); trans. *Essential*, 80.

87. Eckhart, *Predigt* 2 (DW 2:42–44); trans. *Essential*, 181.

88. Eckhart, *Predigt* 101 (DW 4:341); trans. Walshe, 1:2.

89. Eckhart, *Predigt* 101 (DW 4:340–341); trans. Walshe, 1:2.

90. Eckhart, *Predigt* 102 (DW 4:417); trans. Walshe, 1:19.

91. Eckhart, *Predigt* 102 (DW 4:419); trans. Walshe, 1:20–21.

92. Eckhart, *Predigt* 102 (DW 4:421); trans. Walshe, 1:21–22. This point sounds reminiscent of how, in medieval art, the Virgin Mary is portrayed at becoming pregnant at the Annunciation by hearing God's word; Eckhart does not, to the best of my knowledge, touch on this theme in his exegesis.

93. Eckhart, *Predigt* 103 (DW 4:487–488); Walshe, 1:44–45.

94. Eckhart, *Predigt* 102 (DW 4:412–413); trans. Walshe, 1:16–17.

95. Eckhart, *Predigt* 103 (DW 4:488); trans. Walshe, 1:45.

96. Eckhart, *Predigt* 103 (DW 4:487); trans. Walshe, 1:44.

97. Eckhart, *Predigt* 10 (DW 1:166–167); trans. Davies, 171, 173.

98. Eckhart, *Predigt* 37 (DW 2:218–219); trans. Walshe, 1:231.

99. Tobin, *Meister Eckhart*, 114–115.

100. Eckhart, *Predigt* 2 (DW 1:40); trans. *Essential*, 180.

101. Eckhart, *Predigt* 28 (DW 2:66); trans. Davies, 121. Cf. *Predigt* 24 (DW 1:418; *Teacher*, 285).

102. Eckhart, *Predigt* 28 (DW 2:66); trans. Davies, 121.

103. Eckhart, *Predigt* 6 (DW 1:106); trans. *Essential*, 187—modified. Colledge and McGinn originally translated *istikeit* as "is-ness." McGinn, in a note to me, recommended changing "is-ness" to "self-identity" because of recent philological studies which show that *istikeit* is derived not from *ist* ("is"), but from *istic* ("self-ness").

104. Eckhart, *Predigt* 15 (DW 1:253); trans. *Essential*, 192.

105. Eckhart, *Predigt* 24 (DW 1:419); trans. *Teacher*, 285.

106. McGinn, *Harvest*, 83–93, 118.

107. Bernard of Clairvaux, *SCC* 71.7 (SBO 2:220); trans. CF 40:54.

108. Josef Quint, "Mystik und Sprache, Ihr Verhältnis zueinander, insbesondere in der spekulativen Mystik Meister Eckeharts," in *Altdeutsche und altneiderländische Mystik*, ed. Karl Ruh (Darmstadt: Wissenschaftliche Buchgesellschaft, 1964), 141. See also McGinn, *Harvest*, 85.

109. Eckhart, *Predigt* 10 (DW 1:171–172); trans. *Teacher*, 265.

110. Eckhart, *Predigt* 42 (DW 2:309); trans. McGinn, *Mystical*, 44.

111. Eckhart, *Predigt* 51 (DW 2:478.5–9); trans. McGinn, *Mystical*, 29.

112. Eckhart, *Predigt* 52 (DW 2:504–505); trans. *Essential*, 203.

113. *Schwester Katrei*. For the German text, see Franz-Josef Schweitzer, ed., *Der Freiheitsbegriff der deutschen Mystik* (Frankfurt am Main: Peter Lang, 1981), 322–370; for a translation, see the appendix to *Teacher*, trans. Elvira Borgstädt, 349–387; this passage is on 358.

114. Heinrich Suso, *The Little Book of Truth*. For the text, see Karl Bihlmeyer, *Heinrich Seuse: Deutsche Schriften* (Stuttgart: Kohlhammer, 1907), 552–557; for a translation, Frank Tobin, *Henry Suso: The Exemplar, with Two German Sermons*, CWS (New York: Paulist Press, 1989), 326–329.

115. Eckhart, *Predigt* 16b (DW 1:274); trans. *Teacher*, 278.

116. Eckhart, *Predigt* 86 (DW 3:481–482); trans. *Teacher*, 338.

117. Eckhart, *Predigt* 71 (DW 3:211–212); trans. *Teacher*, 320.

118. Eckhart, *Predigt* 103 (DW 4:488–489); trans. Walshe, 1:45.

119. Eckhart, *Predigt* 6 (DW 1:106); trans. *Essential*, 187, modified. See n. 103.

120. Eckhart, *Responsio* II, n. 92 (LW 4:340); trans. McGinn, *Mystical Thought*, 15.

121. Eckhart, *Responsio* I, n. 81 (LW 5:277); trans. *Essential*, 72.

122. McGinn, *Harvest*, 105.

123. Eckhart, *Predigt* 22 (DW 1:384); trans. *Essential*, 195.

124. This position has been argued by Kurt Flasch, "Die Intention Meister Eckharts," in *Sprache und Begriff: Festschrift für Bruno Liebrucks*, ed. Heinz Röttges (Meisenheim am Glan: Hain, 1974), 292–318; also Burkhard Mojsisch, *Meister Eckhart: Analogy, Univocity, and Unity*, trans. Orrin F. Summerell (Amsterdam and Philadelphia: B. R. Grüner, 2001).

125. On Eckhart's sermons as mystical performances, see Milem, *Unspoken Word*, 20–21.

126. Ruh, *Meister Eckhart*, esp. 187–188.

127. Eckhart, *Predigt* 66 (DW 3:113–114); trans. Walshe, 2:91.

CHAPTER 7

1. Athanasius, *Vita Antonii* 14 (SC 400:174); trans. Robert C. Gregg, *Athanasius: The Life of Antony and The Letter to Marcellinus*, CWS (New York: Paulist Press, 1980), 42–43. On the desert fathers, see William Harmless, *Desert Christians: An Introduction to the Literature of Early Monasticism* (New York: Oxford University Press, 2004).

2. *Apophthegmata Patrum* Macarius 23 (PG 65:272); trans. Benedicta Ward, *The Sayings of the Desert Fathers*, CS 59 (Kalamazoo, MI: Cistercian Publications, 1984), 132.

3. On Evagrius's life and theology, see Harmless, *Desert Christians*, 311–371. See also Luke Dysinger, *Psalmody and Prayer in the Writings of Evagrius Ponticus*, Oxford Theological Monographs (New York: Oxford University Press, 2005).

4. For a translation, see Robert T. Meyer, ed., *Palladius: The Lausiac History*, ACW 34 (New York: Newman Press, 1965).

5. On the authenticity and importance the Coptic *Life of Evagrius*, see Adalbert de Vogüé and Gabriel Bunge, *Quatre érmites égyptiens: D'après les fragments coptes de l'Histoire Lausiaque*, Spiritualité orientale 60 (Begrolles-en-Mauges: Abbaye de Belle-fontaine, 1994); for a translation, see Tim Vivian, trans., *Four Desert Fathers: Pambo, Evagrius, Macarius of Egypt, and Macarius of Alexandria;: Coptic Texts Relating to the Lausiac History of Palladius* (Crestwood, NY: St. Vladimir's Seminary Press, 2004), 69–92.

6. Rufinus, *Historia monachorum in Aegypto* XXI.1.3–1.6. For the Latin text, see Eva Schulz-Flügel, ed., *Tyrannius Rufinus Historia Monachorum sive De Vita Sanctorum Patrum*, Patristische Texte und Studien 34 (Berlin, 1990), 356–357; for a translation, see Norman Russell, *The Lives of the Desert Fathers: The "Historia monachorum in aegypto*," CS 34 (Kalamazoo, MI: Cistercian Publications, 1981), 148. The original *Historia monachorum in Aegypto* was written in Greek around 400 and published anonymously; Rufinus translated it into Latin, adding comments (such as these) from his own experience. See Harmless, *Desert Christians*, 277–279.

7. In 1964, Antoine Guillaumont discovered the buried ruins of Kellia. On this discovery, see Guillaumont, "Kellia," in *Coptic Encyclopedia*, ed. Aziz S. Atiya (New York: Macmillan, 1991), 5:1396–1410.

8. Rufinus, *Historia monachorum in Aegypto* XXII.2.1–4 (Schulz-Flügel, 358); trans. my own.

9. *Historia monachorum in Aegypto* 23.1. For the Greek text, see André–Jean Festugière, *Historia Monachorum in Aegypto: Édition critique du text grec et traduction annoté*, Subsidia hagiographica 53 (Bruxelles: Société des Bollandistes, 1971), 130–131; the translation here is from Russell, 113.

10. Evagrius Ponticus, *Praktikos* 29. For the Greek text, see Antoine Guillaumont and Claire Guillaumont, eds., *Évagre le Pontique, Traité pratique ou le Moine*, SC 171 (Paris: Éditions du Cerf, 1971), 566–568; the translation here is from Sinkewicz, 102–103.

11. Socrates, *Historia ecclesiastica* 4.23 (PG 67:516); trans. my own.

12. Palladius, (Coptic) *Life of Evagrius* 17. For the Coptic text, see E. Amélineau, ed., *De Historia Lausiaca* (Paris, 1887), 114–115; the translation here is by Vivian, 83–84.

13. *Historia monachorum* XX.15 (Festugière, 123); trans. Russell, 107.

14. Evagrius Ponticus, *Ep.* 58.5, quoted in Jeremy Driscoll, ed., *Evagrius Ponticus: Ad Monachos*, ACW 59 (Mahwah, NJ: Paulist Press, 2003), 290.

15. I outline the history of this scholarship in "Monasticism," in *The Oxford Handbook of Early Christian Studies*, ed. David Hunter and Susan Ashbrook Harvey (New York: Oxford University Press, forthcoming).

16. Louis Bouyer, *History of Spirituality*, vol. 1, *The Spirituality of the New Testament and the Fathers* (1963; reprint: New York: Seabury Press, 1982), 381.

17. Hans Urs von Balthasar, "The Metaphysics and Mystical Theology of Evagrius," *Monastic Studies* 3 (1965): 183.

18. Merton, *Inner Experience*, 67–68.

19. John Eudes Bamberger, ed., *Evagrius Ponticus: The Praktikos; Chapters on Prayer*, CS 4 (Kalamazoo, MI: Cistercian Publications, 1981). Jean Leclerq, in the preface, notes that it was Merton "who first encouraged this translation" (xxi).

20. Sinkewicz has translated the surviving Greek materials except Evagrius's *scholia*. Other previously untranslated works, including some *scholia* and works only preserved in Syriac, are now available in Casiday. This also includes a fresh translation of the *Letter on Faith* and *Letter to Melania* (*Ep. ad Melaniam*).

21. Evagrius Ponticus, *De oratione* 60 (PG 79:1180); trans. Sinkewicz, 199.

22. Evagrius Ponticus, *De oratione* 35 (PG 79:1173); trans. Sinkewicz, 196.

23. Evagrius Ponticus, *Praktikos*, prol. (SC 171:492); Sinkewicz, 96.

24. Evagrius Ponticus, *Praktikos* 91 (SC 171:692); trans. Sinkewicz, 112.

25. Evagrius Ponticus, *Praktikos* 100 (SC 171:710); trans. Sinkewicz, 113.

26. Evagrius Ponticus, *Praktikos* 6 (SC 171:506–508); Sinkewicz, 97–98.

27. John Cassian, *De institutis* V.1, X.1 (SC 109:90, 384).

28. Evagrius Ponticus, *Praktikos* 12 (SC 171:520–526); trans. Sinkewicz, 99.

29. Evagrius Ponticus, *De octo spiritibus malitiae* 6.6 (PG 79:1157); trans. Sinkewicz, 84. I have followed Sinkewicz's renumbering of the paragraphs of this treatise.

30. Evagrius Ponticus, *De octo spiritibus malitiae* 6.14 (PG 79:1160); trans. Sinkewicz, 84.

31. Evagrius Ponticus, *De octo spiritibus malitiae* 6.14 (PG 79:1160); trans. Sinkewicz, 84.

32. David Brakke, *Demons and the Making of the Monk: Spiritual Combat in Early Christianity* (Cambridge, MA: Harvard University Press, 2006), 48–77.

33. Evagrius Ponticus, *Praktikos* 78 (SC 171:666); trans. Sinkewicz, 110, modified. Sinkewicz translates *praktikē* as "practical life," an overly literal choice, easy for English-speakers to misinterpret.

34. This three-part psychology goes back to Plato, but Evagrius, in *Praktikos* 89 (SC 171:680; Sinkewicz, 111), says that he learned it from his old mentor, Gregory of Nazianzus, whom refers to as "our wise teacher." On this, see Guillaumont, SC 171:683–684.

35. Evagrius Ponticus, *Praktikos* 89 (SC 171:688); trans. Sinkewicz, 111–112.

36. Evagrius Ponticus, *Gnostikos* 2. For (remnants of) the Greek text, see Antoine Guillaumont, ed., *Évagre le Pontique: Le gnostique ou a celui qui est devenu digne de la science*, SC 356 (Paris: Éditions du Cerf, 1989), 90. The translation here is my own.

37. Evagrius Ponticus, *Skemmata* 3. For the Greek text, see Muyldermans. The text here is on p. 374. The translation is from William Harmless and Raymond Fitzgerald, "The Sapphire Light of the Mind: The *Skemmata* of Evagrius Ponticus," *Theological Studies* 63 (2001): 498–529.

38. Athanasius, *Orationes contra Arianos* 3.34 (PG 396–397).

39. Evagrius Ponticus, *De oratione* 71 (PG 79:1181); trans. Sinkewicz, 200.

40. Evagrius Ponticus, *Praktikos* 56 (SC 171:630); Sinkewicz, 107.

41. Evagrius Ponticus, *Praktikos* 64 (SC 171:648); trans. my own.

42. Jeremy Driscoll, *Steps to Spiritual Perfection: Studies on Spiritual Progress in Evagrius Ponticus* (Mahwah, NJ: Newman Press/Paulist Press, 2005), 94–123.

43. Evagrius Ponticus, *Praktikos* 81, 84 (SC 171:670, 674); trans. my own.

44. Evagrius Ponticus, *Praktikos* 89 (SC 171:680–688); trans. my own.

45. Evagrius Ponticus, *Praktikos* 100 (SC 171:710); trans. Sinkewicz, 113.

46. Evagrius Ponticus, *Praktikos*, prol. (SC 171:492); trans. my own.

47. Evagrius Ponticus, *Gnostikos* 49 (SC 356:190–191); trans. my own.

48. Evagrius Ponticus, *Praktikos* 84 (SC 171:674); *Gnostikos* 49 (SC 356:190–191).

49. Evagrius Ponticus, *De oratione* 60 (PG 79:1180); trans. Sinkewicz, 199.

50. Evagrius Ponticus, *Praktikos* 3 (SC 171:500); Sinkewicz, 97.

51. Evagrius Ponticus, *Gnostikos* 3 (SC 356:90); trans. my own.

52. Evagrius Ponticus, *Praktikos* 49 (SC 171:610–612); trans. Sinkewicz, 106.

53. Kallistos Ware, "The Origins of the Jesus Prayer: Diadochus, Gaza, Sinai," in *The Study of Spirituality*, ed. Cheslyn Jones, Geoffrey Wainwright, and Edward Yarnold (New York: Oxford University Press, 1986), 175–184; Gabriel Bunge, " 'Priez sans cesse': Aux origines de la prière hésychaste," *Studia Monastica* 30 (1988): 7–16.

54. In excavations at Kellia, archeologists have discovered inscriptions on the wall of a cell from the sixth century that show that the Jesus prayer was part of the devotional pattern. See Antoine Guillaumont, "The Jesus Prayer among the Monks of Egypt," *Eastern Churches Review* 6 (1974): 66–71.

55. Cassian, *Collationes* 10.10 (SC 54:85–90); for a translation, see Boniface Ramsey, *John Cassian: The Conferences*, ACW 57 (New York: Paulist, 1997), 379–383.

56. Evagrius Ponticus, *De oratione* 66 (PG 79:1181); trans. Sinkewicz, 199.

57. Evagrius Ponticus, *De oratione* 117–120 (PG 79:1193); trans. Sinkewicz, 206.

58. Dysinger, *Psalmody and Prayer*, 5–6, 196–198.

59. Evagrius Ponticus, *De oratione* 3 (PG 79:1168); trans. my own.

60. Evagrius Ponticus, *De oratione* 70 (PG 79:1181); trans. my own.

61. Evagrius Ponticus, *De oratione* 35 (PG 79:1173); trans. my own. There is a discrepancy in the numbering of the Greek text at this point; the recension reproduced in the *Philokalia* lists this as no. 36.

62. Evagrius Ponticus, *Kephalaia gnostica* 4.90. For the Syriac text, see Antoine Guillaumont, *Les six centuries des "Kephalaia gnostica" d'Évagre le Pontique: Édition*

critique de la version syriaque commune et édition d'une nouvelle version syriaque, PO 28, fasc. 2 (Paris: Firmin Didot, 1958), 175. The translation here is my own.

63. Evagrius Ponticus, *De oratione* 84 (PG 79:1185); trans. my own. Cf. *Praktikos* 49 (SC 171:612).

64. Evagrius Ponticus, *De oratione* 34a; trans. my own. The Greek text of this chapter is not found in manuscript tradition found in PG, but in the *Philokalia*; see Hausherr, *Les leçons d'un contemplative: Le* Traité de l'oraison d'Évagre le Pontique (Paris: Beauchesne, 1960), 52–53.

65. Evagrius Ponticus, *Gnostikos* 45 (SC 356:178); *Skemmata* 2 (Muyldermans, 38).

66. Evagrius Ponticus, *Praktikos* 64 (SC 171:648); Sinkewicz, 109.

67. Evagrius Ponticus, *Antirrhetikos* VI.16. For the Syriac text, see Frankenberg, 524. The translation here is my own.

68. Evagrius Ponticus, *Peri logismon* 39 (SC 438:286–288); trans. my own. Cf. *Skemmata* 2 and 4 (Muyldermans, 38); *Ep.* 39 (Frankenberg, 592).

69. Evagrius Ponticus, *Skemmata* 25 (Muyldermans, 41); trans. Harmless and Fitzgerald, 526.

70. Evagrius Ponticus, *Skemmata* 23 (Muyldermans, 41); trans. Harmless and Fitzgerald, 525.

71. Evagrius Ponticus, *Kephalaia gnostica* 1.35 (PO 28:33): "God, in his essence, is light."

72. Evagrius Ponticus, *Skemmata* 27 (Muyldermans, 41); trans. my own.

73. Antoine Guillaumont, "La vision de l'intellect par lui-même dans la mystique évagrienne," in *Études sur la spiritualité de l'Orient chrétien*, Spiritualité orientale 66 (Bégrolles-en-Mauges: Abbaye de Bellefontaine, 1996), 148–149.

74. Evagrius Ponticus, *Kephalaia gnostica* 3.57 (PO 28:121); trans. my own.

75. Evagrius Ponticus, *Ep. ad Melaniam* 5–6. Frankenberg knew only the first half of the Syriac text and published it in *Euagrios Pontikos*, 610–619; the remainder is found in Gösta Vitestam, *Seconde partie du traité, qui passe sous le nom de "La grande lettre d'Évagre le Pontique à Mélanie l'Ancienne," publiée et traduite d'après le manuscrit du British Museum Add. 17192*, Scripta minora 31 (Lund: Regiae Societatis Humaniorum Litterarum Lundensis, 1964). The translation here is from Casiday, 65–66.

76. Evagrius Ponticus, *Ep. ad Melaniam* 27; trans. Casiday, 69.

77. Evagrius Ponticus, *Ep. ad Melaniam* 64–66; trans. Casiday, 76–77.

78. On Maximus's use of Evagrius, see Andrew Louth, *Maximus the Confessor*, Early Christian Fathers (London: Routledge, 1996), esp. 35–38.

79. Isaac of Nineveh, *Discourse* II.35.12. For the Syriac text, with an English translation, see Sebastian Brock, ed., *Isaac of Nineveh: "The Second Part," Chapters IV–XVI*, CSCO 554 (Louvain, 1995), 142–143. On the life and teachings of Isaac, see Hilarion Alfeyev, *The Spiritual World of Isaac the Syrian*, CS 175 (Kalamazoo: Cistercian Publications, 2000).

80. Isaac of Nineveh, *Discourse* II.22. For this, see Sebastian Brock, ed., *The Syriac Fathers on Prayer and the Spiritual Life*, CS 101 (Kalamazoo, MI: Cistercian Publications, 1987), 262–263.

81. Isaac of Nineveh, *Discourse* I.71; trans. Brock, *Syriac Fathers*, 251.

82. On Cassian, see Harmless, *Desert Christians*, 373–413; Columba Stewart, *Cassian the Monk*, Oxford Studies in Historical Theology (New York: Oxford University Press, 1998).

83. Cassian, *Collationes* 10.6 (SC 54:80); trans. Ramsey, ACW 57: 375.

84. Cassian, *Collationes* 10.7.2 (SC 54:81); trans. Ramsey, ACW 57: 375–376.

CHAPTER 8

1. James, *Varieties*, 332.

2. Evelyn Underhill, *Mysticism: A Study in the Nature and Development of Man's Spiritual Consciousness* (1901; reprint: Oxford: OneWorld, 1999), 86–87.

3. Underhill, *Mysticism*, 80.

4. Other leading scholars who hold one or another variant of this view include Aldous Huxley, Rudolph Otto, Joseph Maréchal, William Johnston, Mircea Eliade, W. T. Stace, and Ninian Smart. I discuss this issue in greater detail in chapter 10.

5. Sufi names and terms get transliterated into English in various ways, partly because of the varied linguistic expertise—whether Arabic, Persian, or Turkish—of the various scholars and translators who study Rumi and his Sufi background. For example, Rumi's name, Jalāl al-Din, is spelled variously as Jalāloddin (e.g., in Annemarie Schimmel), Jelaluddin (e.g., in Coleman Barks), or Jalālu'ddin (e.g., in Reynold Nicholson). To preserve some consistency, for the names and terms in the history of Sufism I follow Sells, *EIM*; for names and terms relating specifically to Rumi I use the transliterations from Lewis. On this issue, see Sells, *EIM*, 5–8, and Lewis, xvi–xvii.

6. Abū Bakr al-Kalābādhī, *Kitāb at-ta'arruf li-madhhab ahl at-tasawwuf* (*Book of the Exploration of the Teachings of Those Who Subscribe to Sufism*); trans. A. J. Arberry, *Doctrine of the Sufis* (Cambridge: Cambridge University Press, 1935), 5.

7. al-Kalābādhī, *Kitāb at-ta'arruf*; trans. Arberry, *Doctrine of the Sufis*, 5.

8. Cited in Carl W. Ernst, *The Shambhala Guide to Sufism* (Boston: Shambhala, 1997), 99. Rumi alludes to this *hadith* in *Masnavi* V.575.

9. al-Kalābādhī, *Kitāb at-ta'arruf*; trans. Arberry, *Doctrine of the Sufis*, 6.

10. Rumi, *Masnavi* III.3261; trans. Nicholson, 2:183.

11. For an overview of the history of Western scholarly understanding (and misunderstanding) of Sufism, see Ernst, *Shambhala Guide*, 1–18. On the Islamic sources of Sufism, see Ernst, *Shambhala Guide*, 32–57; for key texts, see Sells, *EIM*, 29–74. On the "innate originality" of Sufism, see the classic 1922 monograph by Louis Massignon, *Essay on the Origins of the Technical Language of Islamic Mysticism*, trans. James Clark (Notre Dame: University of Notre Dame Press, 1997).

12. Sells, *EIM*, 29.

13. The one credited with introducing this terminology is the Egyptian Sufi Dhū 'n-Nūn (d. 859). For texts on Sufi mystical epistemology, see Renard.

14. Abū Nasr as-Sarrāj, *Kitāb al-Luma'* (*Book of Flashes*) 12; trans. Renard, 83.

15. Sarrāj, *Kitāb al-Luma'* 8; trans. Renard, 79.

16. Sarrāj, *Kitāb al-Luma'* 9; trans. Renard, 80–81.

17. Sarrāj, *Kitāb al-Luma'* 8, 122; trans. Renard, 79, 99.

18. Sarrāj, *Kitāb al-Luma'* 122; trans. Renard, 99.

19. For an overview, see Annemarie Schimmel, *Mystical Dimensions of Islam* (Chapel Hill: University of North Carolina Press, 1975), 98–148.

20. Abū Nasr as-Sarrāj, *Kitāb al-Luma' (Book of Flashes)*; trans. Sells, *EIM*, 199–211.

21. See Ernst, *Shambhala Guide*, 98–106.

22. 'Abd al-Karīm ibn Hawāzin al-Qushayrī, *Ar-Risāla al-qushayrīya (The Treatise on Sufism)*; trans. Sells, *EIM*, 102–103.

23. Qushayrī, *Risāla*; trans. Sells, *EIM*, 103.

24. Qushayrī, *Risāla*; trans. Sells, *EIM*, 117.

25. Qushayrī, *Risāla*; trans. Sells, *EIM*, 125.

26. The classic study is by Louis Massignon, *La passion de Husayn Ibn Mansūr Hallāj: Martyr mystique de l'Islam exécuté à Baghdad le mars 29 922; Étude d'histoire religieuse*, 2nd ed., 4 vols. (Paris: Gallimard, 1973). For an abridged version in English, see *Hallaj: Mystic and Martyr*, trans., ed., and abridged Herbert Mason (Princeton: Princeton University Press, 1994). For a translation of one of his surviving texts, *Tawāsīn*, see Sells, *EIM*, 266–280.

27. This famous "hadith of superogatory devotions" (*hadīth al-nawāfil*) is cited by Sarrāj, *Kitāb al-Luma'* 124.6, in defense of Bistāmī's claims (Sells, *EIM*, 218). See also Michael Sells, "Bewildered Tongue: The Semantics of Mystical Union in Islam," in *Mystical Union in Judaism, Christianity, and Islam: An Ecumenical Dialogue*, ed. Moshe Idel and Bernard McGinn (1989; reprint: New York: Continuum, 1999), 87–124.

28. Abū Hamid al-Ghazālī, *Mishkat al-anwar (The Niche of Lights)*, 45–46; for the Arabic text with an English translation, see David Buchman, ed., *Al-Ghazālī: The Niche of Lights*, Islamic Translation Series (Provo, UT: Brigham Young University Press, 1998), 17–18.

29. Cited in Schimmel, *Mystical Dimensions*, 103.

30. Rumi, *Masnavi* IV.543; trans. William C. Chittick, *The Sufi Path of Love: The Spiritual Teachings of Rumi* (Albany, NY: SUNY, 1983), 139. Cf. *Masnavi* I.2955.

31. Schimmel, *Mystical Dimensions*, 234.

32. Chittick, *Sufi Path of Love*, 150–151. See also Schimmel, *Mystical Dimensions*, 167–178.

33. For a magisterial study of Rumi's life, see Lewis, 41–275. Lewis carefully weighs subtle threads and contradictions between the hagiographic materials and is the first author in English to extensively use original texts from Rumi's father and from his mentors, Borhān al-Din and Shams al-Din Tabrizi.

34. Most accounts list Balkh as Rumi's birthplace; on Vakhsh, see Lewis, 47–49.

35. Bahā al-Din Valad, *Ma'āref* 1.169; trans. Lewis, 41. For partial translations, see A. J. Arberry, *Aspects of Islamic Civilization, as Depicted in the Original Texts* (London: Allen and Unwin, 1964), 228-255; Coleman Barks and John Moyne, *The Drowned Book: Ecstatic and Earthy Reflections of Bahauddin, the Father of Rumi* (New York: Harper Collins, 2004).

36. Borhān al-Din, *Ma'āref* 19; trans. Lewis, 99.

37. Borhān al-Din, *Ma'āref* 14–15; trans. Lewis, 99.

38. Rumi, *Divān-e Shams* 2307; trans. Lewis, 379.

39. Aflāki, *Manāqeb al-'ārefin* (*Acts of the Gnostics*), 82–83, claims that Rumi underwent a 120-day retreat, because at the end of both 40 days and 80 days, Borhān al-Din found his disciple entranced in meditation. On this episode, see Lewis, 116.

40. This encounter assumes mythical proportions in the hagiography that surrounds Rumi. For a thorough analysis of Shams and of his teaching and influence on Rumi, see Lewis, 134–202.

41. Rumi, *Divān* 2789; trans. Lewis, 169–170.

42. Rumi, *Divān* 940; trans. Arberry 1:105–106 (#122). Arberry's numbering of the poems does not match the numbering in the Persian edition. Therefore, I give the poem number from the critical edition of the Persian and follow it with the volume and page number from Arberry's translation, followed by Arberry's numbering of the poem in parentheses and marked with "#".

43. Lewis, 171.

44. Rumi, *Divān* 2449; trans. Arberry 2:85–86 (#313).

45. Sultan Valad, *Ebtedā nāme* 53; trans. Lewis, 173.

46. For a translation, see William C. Chittick, ed., *Me and Rumi: The Autobiography of Shams-i Tabrizi* [*Maqālāt*] (Louisville, KY: Fons Vitae, 2004). In translating the disheveled text Chittick chose not to follow the order of the Persian edition, but to regroup sayings around themes. Therefore, one has to follow his chart on pages 406–407 to match his numbering of paragraphs with that of the Persian original.

47. Whereas Rumi was a Hanafi, Shams was a Shafi'i; see Shams al-Din, *Maqālāt* 182; Chittick, *Me and Rumi*, 133. On Shams as a school teacher, see *Maqālāt* 343, 340, 291–294; Chittick, *Me and Rumi*, 8–12.

48. Shams al-Din, *Maqālāt* 685; Chittick, *Me and Rumi*, 210.

49. Shams al-Din, *Maqālāt* 691; trans. Chittick, *Me and Rumi*, 71.

50. Shams al-Din, *Maqālāt* 645; trans. Chittick, *Me and Rumi*, 79.

51. Shams al-Din, *Maqālāt* 178; trans. Chittick, *Me and Rumi*, 50–51.

52. Shams al-Din, *Maqālāt* 18; trans. Lewis, 136.

53. The original story appears in Aflāki, 766. Leading Iranian scholars such Abdülbāki Gölpinarli gave it credence, and it has been repeated widely by some of the best Rumi scholars writing in English, notably Annemarie Schimmel, *The Triumphal Sun: A Study of the Works of Jalāloddin Rumi*, Persian Studies 8 (Albany, NY: SUNY, 1993), 20–22. Lewis, in an extended analysis ("Murder Most Foul?," 185–193), has debunked much of the evidence, concluding: "This murder rumor arises late, circulates in an oral context, and is almost certainly groundless" (193). Lewis's arguments have gained acceptance; for instance, Chittick, introduction, *Me and Rumi*, xiv.

54. Sultan Valad, *Ebtedā nāme* 61; trans. Lewis, 185.

55. Cited in Schimmel, *Triumphal Sun*, 30.

56. The story is preserved by Aflāki, 165. On Rumi's relation with the Parvāne, see Schimmel, *Triumphal Sun*, 28–30; Lewis, 279–281.

57. The story is preserved by Aflāki, 519; see Lewis, 284.

58. Coleman Barks, *The Soul of Rumi: A New Collection of Ecstatic Poems* (San Francisco: HarperSanFrancisco, 2001), xv.

59. Coleman Barks, *The Essential Rumi*, 2nd ed. (San Francisco: HarperSan-Francisco, 2004).

60. On Barks's strengths and weaknesses as a translator and popularizer, see Ernst, *Shambhala Guide*, 169–173, and Lewis, 589–594.

61. Rumi, *Divān* 981; trans. Arberry 1:107 (#125), modified.

62. Rumi, *Masnavi* I.110–111; trans. Mojaddedi, 11.

63. Rumi, *Divān* 1919; trans. Arberry 2:31 (#237).

64. Lewis, 324. See his discussion on 320–324.

65. Chittick, *Sufi Path of Love*, 139. Shams, in *Maqālāt* 777–778 (Chittick, *Me and Rumi*, 212), denies that he was Rumi's *shaykh* in the traditional sense and insists that no human being could have been, that Rumi was already a saint.

66. Rumi, *Divān* 1077; trans. Arberry 1:114 (#136).

67. Rumi, *Divān* 1077; trans. Arberry 1:114 (#136).

68. Rumi, *Divān* 1125; trans. Chittick, *Sufi Path of Love*, 285.

69. Rumi, *Divān* 1101; trans. Chittick, *Sufi Path of Love*, 285.

70. Rumi, *Divān* 395; trans. Arberry 1:42 (#47).

71. Rumi, *Divān* 232; trans. Arberry 1:27 (#28).

72. Rumi, *Divān* 395; trans. Arberry, 1:42 (#47).

73. Rumi, *Divān* 2733; trans. Schimmel, *Triumphal Sun*, 336; Chittick, *Sufi Path of Love*, 195.

74. Annemarie Schimmel, *Rumi's World: The Life and Works of the Greatest Sufi Poet* (Boston: Shambhala, 2001), 200.

75. Schimmel, *Rumi's World*, 38–39. On Rumi's metrics and poetics, see Lewis, 330–335.

76. Rumi, *Divān* 304 (Arberry 1:32 [#34]); this notes the rebec's music; in *Divān* 441 (Arberry 1:46 [#51]), Rumi speaks of himself as the rebec and Love as the rebec player. The reed flute also figures prominently: *Divān* 1628 (Arberry 2:2 [#202]), 2135 (Arberry 2:55 [#269]). See below on the *Masnavi* prologue, "Song of the Reed Flute." For more on this, see Schimmel, *Triumphal Sun*, 210–222.

77. Rumi, *Divān* 105; trans. Chittick, *Sufi Path of Love*, 328.

78. Rumi, *Divān* 2404; trans. Chittick, *Sufi Path of Love*, 327.

79. Rumi, *Divān* 1734; trans. Chittick, *Sufi Path of Love*, 326.

80. Rumi, *Masnavi* IV.735–738; Nicholson, 2:313.

81. Rumi, *Masnavi* IV.733; Nicholson, 2:312.

82. Rumi, *Divān* 127; trans. Chittick, *Sufi Path of Love*, 160.

83. Rumi, *Divān* 260; trans. Arberry 1:30–31 (#32).

84. On the millwheel, see Rumi, *Divān* 181; trans. Arberry 1:22 (#21).

85. Cf. Rumi, *Divān* 2997. On Kaaba as a symbol, see Schimmel, *Triumphal Sun*, 291–293.

86. The image is a common one; see Rumi, *Divān* 2789.

87. Rumi, *Divān* 304; trans. Arberry 1:32–33 (#34).

88. Rumi, *Divān* 3136 and 820; trans. Chittick, *Sufi Path of Love*, 159.

89. Rumi, *Divān* 820; trans. Chittick, *Sufi Path of Love*, 159.

90. Rumi, *Divān* 304; trans. Arberry 1:32–33 (#34).

91. Rumi, *Divān* 409; trans. Arberry 1:42 (#48).

92. Rumi, *Divān* 314; trans. Arberry 1:34 (#36).

93. Rumi, *Divān* 179; trans. Schimmel, *Triumphal Sun*, 73.

94. Rumi, *Divān* 1848; trans. Schimmel, *Triumphal Sun*, 73.

95. Rumi alludes to this in *Masnavi* V.2025 (Nicholson, 3:121).

96. Rumi, *Divān* 797; trans. Chittick, *Sufi Path of Love*, 142. Cf. *Divān* 3050 (Arberry 2:140 [#394]).

97. Rumi, *Divān* 1135; trans. Chittick, *Sufi Path of Love*, 329.

98. Rumi, *Divān* 1713; trans. Schimmel, *Triumphal Sun*, 78.

99. Rumi, *Divān* 294; Arberry 1:32 (#33). Cf. *Masnavi* I.17, II.3139–3144 (Nicholson 1:5, 384).

100. Rumi, *Divān* 1022; trans. Arberry 1:111 (#130).

101. Rumi, *Divān* 250; trans. Arberry 1:30 (#31).

102. Rumi, *Divān* 110; trans. Arberry 1:17 (#13).

103. Nicholson, *Tales of Mystic Meaning* (London, 1931), quoted in Lewis, 287.

104. Rumi, *Masnavi* I.135–137; trans. Mojaddedi, 12.

105. Rumi, *Masnavi* I.1–18; trans. Mojaddedi, 4–5.

106. Rumi, *Divān* 612; trans. Barks, *Essential*, 146.

107. Rumi, *Masnavi* I.247–323 (parrot and greengrocer), II.1131–1177 (falcon and owl); II.3436 ff. (mouse and camel), VI. 2632 ff. (mouse and frog).

108. Rumi, *Masnavi* V.1333–1429. Given Victorian mores, Nicholson (3:82–87) felt he had to render the sexually explicit sections not in English, but in Latin!

109. Rumi, *Masnavi* V.2497; trans. Schimmel, *Mystical Dimensions*, 319–320.

110. Rumi, *Masnavi* IV.158–214, II.3506–3572; Nicholson, 2:281–284, 1:403–407.

111. Rumi, *Masnavi* III.4233–4236; trans. Nicholson, 2:237, modified in light of Lewis, 395.

112. Rumi, *Masnavi* VI.2652–2653; Nicholson, 3:404–405.

113. Rumi, *Masnavi* VI.2091–2095; trans. Nicholson, 3:374.

114. Rumi, *Masnavi* II.1351; trans. Chittick, *Sufi Path of Love*, 192.

115. Rumi, *Masnavi* III.2570–2599; Nicholson, 2:144–146. Cf. *Divān* 892 and 1892 (Arberry 1:100 [#115]; Arberry 2:21 [#226]). For his meditation on the Annunciation framed in the context of a discussion of *fanā'*, see Rumi, *Masnavi* III.3700–3776 (Nicholson, 2:207–211).

116. Rumi, *Masnavi* I.504; trans. Mojaddedi, 34.

117. Rumi, *Fihe mā Fih* (*What's In It Is In It*) 5; trans. A. J. Arberry, *Discourses of Rumi* (1961; reprint: Surrey: Curzon Press, 1993), 33.

118. Rumi, *Masnavi* IV.790; Nicholson, 2:315.

119. Rumi, *Masnavi* VI.2248; trans. Nicholson, 3:383.

120. Rumi, *Masnavi* VI.1528; trans. Nicholson, 3:343.

121. Rumi, *Masnavi* VI.4916; trans. Nicholson, 3:529.

122. Rumi, *Masnavi* I.3086; trans. Lewis, 406.

123. Rumi, *Masnavi* II.2123–2124; trans. Nicholson, 2:118. Cf. Barks, *Soul,* 47, whose translation misconstrues the context of Rumi's ecumenism.

124. Rumi, *Fihe mā Fih* 6; trans. Arberry, *Discourses,* 36.

125. Rumi, *Masnavi* VI.699; trans. Nicholson 3:296.

126. Rumi, *Divān* 364, 376, 381; Arberry 1:40 (#43); 1:40 (#44); 1:41 (#45). On this signature and Rumi's broader "poetics of silence," see Fatemeh Keshavarz, *Reading Mystical Lyric: The Case of Jalāl al-Dīn Rumi* (Columbia: University of South Carolina Press, 1998).

127. Rumi, *Divān* 2117; trans. Arberry 2:52 (#266). Cf. *Divān* 45, 100, 213, 221, 631 (Arberry, 1:12 [#6]; 1:16 [#12]; 1:26 [#26]; 1:27 [#27]; 1:70 [#80]).

CHAPTER 9

1. Merton, preface, *Mystics and Zen Masters* (New York: Farrar, Straus, and Giroux, 1967), viii.

2. D. T. Suzuki, *An Introduction to Zen Buddhism* (New York: Grove Press, 1964), 8, 11. This passage struck Merton, who quotes it in *Mystics and Zen Masters,* 301 n. 8.

3. D. T. Suzuki, *Essays in Zen Buddhism* (London: Rider, 1949), 1:270. On Suzuki's terminology of mysticism as reverse Orientalism, see the analyses of Bernard Faure, *Chan Insights and Oversights: An Epistemological Critique of the Chan Tradition* (Princeton: Princeton University Press, 1993), 60–67.

4. Heinrich Dumoulin, *A History of Zen Buddhism* (New York: Pantheon Books, 1963). The German original was published in 1959. Thirty years later, Dumoulin published a thoroughly revised and vastly improved edition, more than double the size of the original: *Zen Buddhism: A History,* 2 vol., trans. James W. Heisig and Paul Knitter (1988–1990; reprint: Bloomington, IN: World Wisdom, 2005).

5. Merton, *Mystics and Zen Masters,* 34–37. Merton was clearly discomfited by what he read of Dōgen. He read him *inaccurately* as being opposed to the Ch'an of Hui-Neng. He also read Dōgen *inaccurately* as representative of the so-called gradual-enlightenment Northern Ch'an of Shen Hsiu. Merton was unaware that the *Platform Sūtra of Hui-Neng* was, in fact, a propaganda piece posing as history.

6. On Suzuki's sectarian biases and its consequences for Western understandings of Zen, see Faure, *Chan Insights and Oversights,* especially 52–60.

7. Dōgen, *Bendōwa* ("Negotiating the Way"), answer 5; trans. *Heart,* 18.

8. The term "single practice" (*shugyō*) was applied also against the Pure Land sect, known for its stress on single-minded chanting of the name of Amitibha Buddha (*nembutsu*).

9. Dōgen, *Shōbōgenzō,* "Menju" ("Face-to-Face Transmission"); trans. Tanahashi, *MD,* 175.

10. Li Tsun-hsü, *T'ien-sheng kuang-teng lu* (*Record of the Extensive Transmission [of the Lamp] compiled during the T'ien-sheng era*). For an analysis, see Albert Welter, "Mahākāśyapa's Smile: Silent Transmission and the Kung-an (Kōan) Tradition," in *The Kōan: Texts and Contexts in Zen Buddhism,* ed. Steven Heine and Dale S. Wright (New York: Oxford University Press, 2000), 75–109.

11. For a historical critical study of Bodhidharma, see Jeffrey L. Broughton, *The Bodhidharma Anthology: The Earliest Records of Zen* (Berkeley: University of California Press, 1999). John R. McRae, *Seeing through Zen: Encounter, Transformation, and Genealogy in Chinese Chan Buddhism* (Berkeley: University of California Press, 2003), 24–28, has argued against any historical credibility to the hagiography that surrounds Bodhidharma legend.

12. The earliest surviving attribution of this teaching to Bodhidharma appears in the sayings of Ch'an master Huai (992–1046), *Tsu-t'ing shih-yüan*, compiled by Mu-an in 1108. See Welter, "Mahākāśyapa's Smile," 77–80.

13. That, at least, is the standard explanation. Taigen Daniel Leighton, in a note to me, pointed out that the more likely origin is that "the Ts'ao refers to Ts'ao-Chi, temple of the Sixth Ancestor. Because of the non-chronological order and the fact that Ts'ao-shan's lineage was not the long-lived branch of Tung-shan's lineage, the name must refer to the Sixth Ancestor and Tung-shan."

14. McRae, *Seeing through Zen*, especially 2–11. McRae argues for two humorous and telling "rules of Zen studies": (1) "It's not true, and therefore it's important" and (2) "Lineage assertions are as wrong as they are strong."

15. D. T. Suzuki has profoundly shaped how Westerners have understood the kōan genre. See his classic essay, "The Koan Exercise," in *Essays in Zen Buddhism (Second Series)* (1953; reprint: London: Rider, 1980), 18–226. For recent reassessments, see Steven Heine and Dale S. Wright, eds., *The Kōan: Texts and Contexts in Zen Buddhism* (New York: Oxford University Press, 2000), especially the opening essay, T. Griffith Foulk, "The Form and Function of Koan Literature: A Historical Overview," 15–45.

16. *Wu-men kuan (Gateless Gate)* case #37; trans. Katsuki Sekida, *Two Zen Classics: The Gateless Gate and The Blue Cliff Records* (Boston: Shambhala, 2005), 110. This appears also in Dōgen's own *Mana Shōbōgenzō*, case #119; trans. Tanahashi, *TDE*, 162.

17. *Wu-men kuan*, case #18 (Sekida, 71) and *Pi-yen lu (Blue Cliff Record)*, case # 12 (Sekida, 179). See also Dōgen, *Mana Shōbōgenzō*, case #172 (Tanahashi, *TDE*, 231).

18. *Wu-men kuan*, case #21 (Sekida, 77).

19. *Wu-men kuan*, case #14 (Sekida, 58–59); *Pi-yen lu*, case #63 (Sekida, 319). See also Dōgen, *Mana Shōbōgenzō*, case #181 (Tanahashi, *TDE*, 243).

20. *Chung-feng ho-shang, kuang-lu (Extensive Record of Master Chung-feng)*, quoted in Foulk, "Form and Function," 21.

21. *Wu-men kuan*, case #1 (Sekida, 28).

22. For issues in a historical-critical interpretation of Dōgen's biography, see Carl Bielefeldt, "Recarving the Dragon: History and Dogma in the Study of Dōgen," in *Dōgen Studies*, ed. William R. LaFleur, Koroda Institute Studies in East Asian Buddhism 2 (Honolulu: University of Hawaii Press, 1985), 21–53. For a comprehensive and magisterial study of Dōgen's life, see Steven Heine, *Did Dōgen Go to China? What He Wrote and When He Wrote It* (New York: Oxford University Press, 2006).

23. On this Tendai doctrine, see Jacqueline I. Stone, *Original Enlightenment and the Transformation of Medieval Japanese Buddhism* (Honolulu: University of Hawaii

Press, 1999); for a brief overview, see Stone, "Original Enlightenment (*Hongaku*)," in *Encyclopedia of Buddhism*, ed. Robert E. Buswell (New York: Thomson/Gale, 2002), 2:618–621.

24. *Kenzeiki* 17.16a; quoted in Masao Abe, *A Study of Dōgen: His Philosophy and Religion*, ed. Steven Heine (Albany, NY: SUNY, 1992), 19. See also Abe's discussion, 19–23.

25. Dōgen, *Bendōwa*; trans. Tanahashi, *MD*, 144.

26. Dōgen, *Hōkyō–ki* ("Memoirs of the Hōkyō Era"); trans. Tanahashi, *EU*, 3. These memoirs, a record of his conversations with Ju-ching, were traditionally believed to date from Dōgen's time in China and thus seemed to offer an unvarnished view of his early career. That interpretation has been strongly challenged, and some have questioned its authenticity altogether. The consensus now seems to be that it is authentic, but its current redaction dates from the very end of his life (late 1240s or 1250s), even if it draws on earlier notes. As such, later issues and conflicts are at play beneath its autobiographical surface. See Heine, *Did Dōgen Go to China?*, 36–38.

27. Dōgen, *Bendōwa*; trans. Tanahashi, *MD*, 144.

28. The issue was a technical one concerning the level of "precepts" that Dōgen had and had not received. On this, see Heine, *Did Dōgen Go to China?*, 102–117.

29. Dōgen, *Hōkyō–ki*; trans. Tanahashi, *EU*, 8.

30. Dōgen, *Hōkyō–ki*; trans. Tanahashi, *EU*, 8.

31. *Kenzeiki*. On this episode and the awakening catch-phrase, see Steven Heine, "Dōgen Casts Off 'What'?: An Analysis of *Shinjin Datsuraku*," *Journal of the International Association of Buddhist Studies* 9 (1986): 53–70. I have used Heine's translation except for the key phrase, translating *shinji datsuraku* as "dropping off body-mind" rather than "casting off body-mind." "Casting off" implies a more active process, whereas "dropping off" implies a natural letting go (the way trees drop their leaves). Heine discusses the strengths and weaknesses of these and other translations. I have followed here the recommendation of Taigen Daniel Leighton, one of Dōgen's recent translators.

32. Hee-Jin Kim, *Eihei Dogen: Mystical Realist*, 3rd ed. (Boston: Wisdom Publications, 2004), 33. For an analysis, see especially 100–106.

33. Dōgen, *Bendōwa*; trans. *Heart*, 9.

34. Dōgen, *Shōbōgenzō*, "Menju" ("Face-to-Face Transmission"); Tanahashi, *MD*, 175–176.

35. Dōgen, *Eihei kōroku* 1.48; trans. Leighton, 111.

36. Kim, *Eihei Dōgen*, 38, voices the traditional view when he speaks of the *Fukanzazengi* as a "manifesto of Dōgen's 'new' Buddhism vis-à-vis the established Buddhism of Japan." This interpretation has been dismantled by Carl Bielefeldt in his *Dōgen's Manuals of Zen Meditation* (Berkeley: University of California Press, 1988). He carefully compares and analyzes the 1233 autograph version of the *Fukanzazengi* (discovered in the 1920s), its better-known and later Vulgate version, and its Chinese source. (More on this later.)

37. Dōgen, *Bendōwa*; trans. Tanahashi, *MD*, 144. *Bendōwa*, which is dated 1231, is typically listed as the first essay in the 95-fascicle *Shōbōgenzō*. This inclusion was not

Dōgen's; it only appeared in a 1684 edition of the *Shōbōgenzō*. Its question-and-answer format uses a different literary genre from the typical essay in the *Shōbōgenzō*. See Heine, *Did Dōgen Go to China?*, 122–125, 128–132.

38. Abe, *Study of Dōgen*, 18.

39. Heine, *Did Dōgen Go to China?*, 150–152, notes that 63 fascicles of the 75-fascicle *Shōbōgenzō* were composed between 1240 and 1244.

40. On the complex questions surrounding competing recensions of the *Shōbōgenzō*, see Heine, *Did Dōgen Go to China?*, 51–87. For a listing of the contents of the 75- and 12-fascicle editions, see Heine, *Did Dōgen Go to China?*, 242–248; Kim, *Eihei Dōgen*, 247–250.

41. On its discovery, see Steven Heine, *Dōgen and the Kōan Tradition: A Tale of Two Shōbōgenzō Texts*, SUNY Series in Philosophy and Psychotherapy (Albany, NY: SUNY, 1994), esp. 9–10. Heine shows how its discovery and its role in Dōgen's other works revolutionizes our understanding of the wider kōan tradition. I touch on this below.

42. Dōgen, *Eihei kōroku* 1.34; trans. Leighton, 103.

43. Steven Heine, "The *Eihei kōroku*: The Record of Dōgen's Later Period at Eihei-ji Temple," in Steven Heine and Dale S. Wright, *The Zen Canon: Understanding the Classic Texts* (New York: Oxford University Press, 2004), 245–274.

44. Dōgen, "Death Poem"; trans. Heine, *Did Dōgen Go to China?*, 229. Dōgen says here he is fifty-four. Japanese number their age differently than Westerners: a person is said to be one year old at birth (Tanahashi, *EU*, xiii).

45. I follow Tanahashi's translation of the title *Fukanzazengi*. Other renderings capture other nuances: "Principles of Seated Meditation" (Bielefeldt), "Universal Promotion of the Principles of Zazen" (Waddell and Abe), and "General Advice on the Principles of Zazen" (Kim).

46. Dōgen's source is the *Tso-ch'an i* by Ch'ang-lu Tsung-tse, and appeared in a Ch'an monastic code, the *Ch'an-yüan ch'ing-kuei*. For a valuable analysis, see Bielefeldt, *Dōgen's Manuals*, esp. 109–132. Bielefeldt has a translation of Dōgen's early autograph version and his later Vulgate version as well as Tsung-tse's text in parallel, allowing one to see Dōgen's subtle and often artful revisions; see 174–187.

47. Dōgen, *Fukanzazengi*; *Heart*, 2–3.

48. Dōgen, *Fukanzazengi*; trans. Tanahashi, *EU*, 33.

49. Dōgen, *Fukanzazengi*; trans. *Heart*, 4. This is repeated word for word in *Shōbōgenzō* "Zazenji" ("Principles of Zazen," *Heart*, 110). This terminology is drawn from a famous dialogue between a monk and the Ch'an master Yüeh-shan Wei-yen (751–834) recorded in the *Ching-te ch'uan teng lu*. Dōgen comments on the episode in *Shōbōgenzō* "Zazenshin" ("Admonitions for Zazen").

50. T. P. Kasulis, *Zen Action, Zen Person* (Honolulu: University of Hawai'i Press, 1981) 75, 73. This psychological interpretation is a popular one. Bielefeldt, in *Dōgen's Manuals*, especially 146–160, has highlighted obscurities and ambiguities in the text and the traditions behind it, and suggests that, contrary to orthodox Sōtō interpretation, "nonthinking," in Dōgen's time, could have involved some kōan study.

51. Dōgen, *Bendōwa*; trans. *Heart*, 11.

52. Dōgen, *Bendōwa*; trans. *Heart*, 15.

53. Dōgen, *Hōkyōki*; trans. Tanahashi, *EU*, 9. Dōgen often had a reformer's single-minded zeal, and his nonsectarian rhetoric could mask what became sectarian results. Dōgen also may well have put his own reformist cast and accent on many things he attributes to Ju-ching. This is a complex issue in current Dōgen research and is an important overarching theme in Heine's recent study, *Did Dōgen Go to China?*

54. Dōgen, *Eihei kōroku* 3.207; trans. Leighton, 219.

55. Dōgen, *Fukanzazengi*; trans. *Heart*, 3.

56. Dōgen, *Fukanzazengi*; trans. Tanahashi, *EU*, 32.

57. Dōgen, *Shōbōgenzō* "Zazenshin"; trans. Bielefeldt, *Dōgen's Manuals*, 197.

58. Dōgen, *Shōbōgenzō* "Zazenshin"; trans. Bielefeldt, *Dōgen's Manuals*, 197.

59. Dōgen, *Fukanzazengi*; trans. *Heart*, 4.

60. Dōgen, *Bendōwa*; trans. *Heart*, 19.

61. Dōgen, *Fukanzazengi*; trans. *Heart*, 3.

62. Dōgen, *Fukanzazengi*; trans. *Heart*, 4.

63. Dōgen, *Bendōwa*; trans. *Heart*, 13–14.

64. Dōgen, *Shōbōgenzō* "Kokyō"; trans. Kōsen Nishiyama and John Stevens, *Shōbōgenzō* (Tokyo: Kawata Press, 1975–1983), 3:45.

65. Dōgen, *Bendōwa*; trans. *Heart*, 8.

66. Abe, *Study of Dōgen*, 26.

67. Dōgen, *Bendōwa*; trans. *Heart*, 19.

68. Tanahashi uses it as the title for a collection of his translations of Dōgen's works.

69. Ta-hui's criticism was directed against Dōgen's Ts'ao-tung predecessor, Hongzhi Zhengjue (d. 1157), onetime abbot of Mt. T'ien-tung. For selections of his teaching, see Taigen Daniel Leighton and Yi Wu, trans. and eds., *Cultivating the Empty Field: The Silent Illumination of Zen Master Hongzhi*, rev. ed. (Charles E. Tuttle, 2000).

70. The classic version of the story is found in *Ching-te ch'uan teng lu*. I have drawn here from the translation in Bielefeldt, *Dōgen's Manuals*, 141.

71. Dōgen, *Mana Shōbōgenzō*, case #8; Tanahashi, *TDE*, 11–12.

72. Dōgen, *Shōbōgenzō* "Kokyō"; trans. Bielefeldt, *Dōgen's Manuals*, 143.

73. Dōgen, *Shōbōgenzō* "Kokyō"; trans. Nishiyama and Steven, *Shōbōgenzō*, 3:59.

74. The story of Hsiang-yen Chih-hsien's stone-striking-bamboo appears as case #17 in Dōgen, *Mana Shōbōgenzō*. Dōgen comments on it in *Shōbōgenzō* "Gyōji 1" ("Continuous Practice"), "Menjū,", and *Bendōwa*; there is also a poetic commentary in *Eihei kōroku* 9.62 (Leighton, 578). The story of Ling-yün Chih-ch'in's peach blossom appears as case #155 in *Mana Shōbōgenzō*; Dōgen comments on it in *Bendōwa* and *Shōbōgenzō* "Keiseisanshoku", "Udonge"; see *Eihei Kōroku* 9.72 (Leighton, 585).

75. Dōgen, *Shōbōgenzō Zuimonki*; trans. Tanahashi, *EU*, 56.

76. Dōgen, *Shōbōgenzō* "Gyōji 1"; trans. Tanahashi, *EU*, 127. The reference to "everyday tea and rice" refers to a kōan about T'ou-tzu Ta-t'ung (819–914), which Dōgen discusses more fully in *Shōbōgenzō* "Kajō" ("Everyday Activity") (Tanahashi,

MD, 124–128). For the kōan itself, see Dōgen, *Mana Shōbōgenzō*, case #143 (Tanahashi, *TDE*, 194).

77. Kim, *Eihei Dōgen*, 247.

78. Dōgen, *Shōbōgenzō* "Genjōkōan"; trans. *Heart*, 41.

79. Dōgen, *Shōbōgenzō* "Genjōkōan"; trans. *Heart*, 41–42.

80. On this dharmic dynamism, see Hee-Jin Kim, " 'The Reason of Words and Letters': Dōgen and Kōan Language," in LaFleur, *Dōgen Studies*, 59.

81. Dōgen, *Bendōwa*; trans. *Heart*, 13–14.

82. E.g., Waddell and Abe, *Heart*, 39–40.

83. Dōgen explores the question of the heightened psychic powers of those who have experienced realization (and the renunciation of those powers) in *Shōbōgenzō* "Tashintū" ("Reading Others' Minds"). For a translation and commentary, see Carl Bielefeldt, "Reading Others' Minds," in *Buddhism in Practice*, ed. Donald S. Lopez, Jr. (Princeton: Princeton University Press, 1995), 69–79. In *Shōbōgenzō* "Yuibutsu Yobutsu" ("Only Buddha and Buddha"), Dōgen plays on the metaphor of traces in a more literal way. Buddhism is typically called a "pathway" and being a Buddhist one follows the "footsteps" or "traces" of the Buddha. Dōgen plays on this and notes that just as a bird's path leaves no trace, so the Buddha's leaves no trace "when you are not a buddha." For a translation, see Tanahashi, *MD*, 161–167.

84. Dōgen, *Shōbōgenzō* "Genjōkōan"; trans. *Heart*, 40.

85. *Nirvāṇa Sūtra* 27, quoted in Dōgen, *Shōbōgenzō* "Busshō"; trans. *Heart*, 60.

86. Abe, *Study of Dōgen*, 38–40.

87. Dōgen, *Eihei kōroku* 3.194; trans. Leighton, 210–211. Dōgen expands on this theme of the Buddha-nature of insentient beings in *Shōbōgenzō* "Mujō Seppō" ("Insentient Beings Speak Dharma") (Tanahashi, *EU*, 185–195).

88. Dōgen, *Shōbōgenzō* "Busshō" (*Heart*, 63), refers to as "the Senika heresy"; cf. *Bendōwa* (*Heart*, 21). *Nirvāṇa Sūtra* 39 claims the heresy occurred within Buddha's life.

89. Dōgen, *Shōbōgenzō* "Busshō"; trans. *Heart*, 64–65.

90. Dōgen, *Shōbōgenzō* "Busshō"; trans. *Heart*, 67.

91. Dōgen, *Shōbōgenzō* "Busshō"; trans. *Heart*, 65. Dōgen attributes the words here to Buddha himself, but they are actually drawn from Po-chang's paraphrase of a sūtra, apparently the *Nirvāṇa Sūtra*. See Waddell and Abe, *Heart*, 65, n. 23.

92. Dōgen, *Shōbōgenzō* "Busshō"; trans. *Heart*, 65–66.

93. Dōgen, *Shōbōgenzō* "Busshō"; trans. *Heart*, 77.

94. Dōgen, *Shōbōgenzō* "Busshō"; trans. *Heart*, 76–77.

95. Abe, *Study of Dōgen*, 58.

96. Dōgen, *Shōbōgenzō* "Genjōkōan"; trans. *Heart*, 42.

97. Dōgen, *Shōbōgenzō* "Genjōkōan"; trans. *Heart*, 43.

98. Dōgen, *Shōbōgenzō* "Menju"; trans. Tanahashi, *MD*, 175–183.

99. Dōgen, *Shōbōgenzō* "Busso"; trans. Tanahashi, *MD*, 184–185.

100. Dōgen, *Shōbōgenzō* "Bukkyō." For a discussion, see Kim, *Eihei Dōgen*, 53–54; Heine, *Did Dōgen Go to China?*, 205–209. Cf. *Hōkyōki* (Tanahashi, *EU*, 4–5).

101. Taigen Dan Leighton, "The *Lotus Sūtra* as a Source for Dōgen's Discourse Style," in *Discourse and Ideology in Medieval Japanese Buddhism*, ed. Richard K. Payne and Taigen Dan Leighton (New York: Routledge, 2006), 195–217.

102. Dōgen, *Shōbōgenzō* "Sansui-kyō"; quoted in Hee-Jin Kim, " 'Reason of Words and Letters,' " 56–57. For the full text, see Tanahashi, *MD*, 97–107.

103. This point is evident in the full text of the kōan. Readers tend to be familiar only with the abbreviated version as passed on in the *Gateless Gate*. In the full version, Chao-chou first answers "yes" to the question about a dog having Buddha-nature. The monk then counters: "If so, how does [Buddha-nature] get into its skin bag?" See Dōgen, *Mana Shōbōgenzō* case #114 (Tanahashi, *TDE*, 154–155); also Dōgen's commentary in, *Shōbōgenzō* "Busshō" (*Heart*, 91–94).

104. Ta-hui and his later Korean disciple Chinul outlined ten types of wrong answers that came from those who tried to solve the kōan. See Heine, *Dōgen and the Kōan Tradition*, 234.

105. Ta-hui, quoted in Heine, *Dōgen and the Kōan Tradition*, 233–234.

106. Heine, *Dōgen and the Kōan Tradition*, 234, compares Ta-hui's approach to the one-word approach advocated by the anonymous writer of *The Cloud of Unknowing*. As we have seen, Cassian is the earliest exponent in the Christian mystical tradition.

107. Dōgen, *Shōbōgenzō* "Kattō"; trans. Heine, *Dōgen and the Kōan Tradition*, 244.

108. Dōgen, *Shōbōgenzō* "Kattō"; trans. Tanahashi, *MD*, 171, 172, 173. Cf. "Gabyō" ("Painting of a Rice-Cake") (Tanahashi, *MD*, 130, 131, 132).

109. Dōgen, *Shōbōgenzō* "Ikka Myōju"; trans. *Heart*, 32–33.

110. The severity of Hsuan-sha's response likely comes from his disciple's dismissive repetition. Loori, in his modern commentary on Dōgen's kōan collection, puts it this way: "Following after another's words and mimicking others' actions is the practice of monkeys and parrots. As a Zen practitioner you should be able to show some fresh provisions of your own" (Tanahashi, *TDE*, 21).

111. Dōgen, *Shōbōgenzō* "Ikka Myōju"; trans. *Heart*, 33–34.

112. Dōgen, *Shōbōgenzō* "Ikka Myōju"; trans. *Heart*, 34.

113. *Lotus Sūtra*, chap. 8 ("The 500 Disciples Chapter"); see Burton Watson, *The Lotus Sutra* (New York: Columbia University Press, 1993), 150–151.

114. Dōgen, *Shōbōgenzō* "Ikka Myōju"; trans. *Heart*, 36.

115. Dōgen, *Shōbōgenzō* "Ikka Myōju"; trans. *Heart*, 37.

116. Heine, *Dōgen and the Kōan Tradition*, 231–242. See also Heine, "Does the Koan Have Buddha-Nature? The Zen Koan as Religious Symbol," *Journal of the American Academy of Religion* 58 (1990): 357–387.

117. Dōgen, *Shōbōgenzō* "Busshō"; *Heart*, 91–94.

118. Heine, *Did Dōgen Go to China?*, x.

CHAPTER 10

1. For a survey and analysis of the last 100 years of the scholarly study of mysticism, see McGinn, "Theoretical Foundations: The Modern Study of Mysticism,"

Foundations of Mysticism, 263–343. For a follow-up and update, see his "Quo Vadis? Reflections on the Current Study of Mysticism," *Christian Spirituality Bulletin* (Spring 1998) 13–21.

2. Underhill, *Mysticism*, 76.

3. Thomas Cleary, *Rational Zen: The Mind of Dōgen Zenji*, reprinted in *Classics of Buddhism and Zen*, vol. 3 (Boston: Shambhala, 2001), esp. 364 ff.

4. For an argument that mysticism is ultimately a misguided category, see Hans H. Penner, "The Mystical Illusion," in Katz, *Mysticism and Religious Traditions*, 89–116. Penner is attuned especially to Hindu traditions and argues that the Western category of "mysticism" or even "mystical element" distorts the context of Hindu practices and thought.

5. T. S. Eliot, "Burnt Norton" V, ll. 150–153, and "East Cooker" V, ll. 178–180, *Four Quartets* (New York: Harcourt Brace Jovanovich, 1971), 19, 30–31.

6. For a discussion of this, see Carl A. Keller, "Mystical Literature," in *Mysticism and Philosophical Analysis*, ed. Steven Katz (New York: Oxford University Press, 1979), 75–100.

7. Steven Katz, "Mysticism and the Interpretation of Sacred Scripture," in Katz, *Mysticism and Sacred Scriptures*, 7.

8. On Origen, see Joseph W. Trigg, *Origen*, Early Church Fathers (New York: Routledge, 1998), and Henri Crouzel, *Origen*, trans. A. S. Worrall (Edinburgh: T & T Clark, 1998).

9. On the Zohar, see Moshe Idel, "The Zohar as Exegesis," 87–100, and Michael Fishbane, "The Book of Zohar and Exegetical Spirituality," 101–117, in Katz, *Mysticism and Sacred Scriptures*.

10. See William C. Chittick, *The Sufi Path of Knowledge: Ibn al-'Arabi's Metaphysics of Imagination* (Albany, NY: SUNY, 1989).

11. Bonaventure, *Hexaem.* 1.37 (Qrc 5:335); trans. Hayes, 52.

12. Simon Tugwell, review of Bernard McGinn's *Foundations of Mysticism*, in *Journal of Theological Studies* 44 (1993): 685–687. Tugwell regards McGinn's project of writing a history of mysticism as flawed in its very conception, wondering whether it is "a history of anything at all."

13. Michael Sells notes this when speaking about Origen in "From a History of Mysticism to a Theology of Mysticism," *Journal of Religion* 73 (1993): 391.

14. On the convergence of postmodern theorists and mysticism, see Amy Hollywood, *Sensible Ecstasy: Mysticism, Sexual Difference, and the Demands of History*, Religion and Postmodernism Series (Chicago: University of Chicago Press, 2002).

15. E.g., Don Cupitt, *Mysticism After Modernity*, Religion and Modernity (Oxford: Blackwell, 1998).

16. Sells, *Mystical Languages of Unsaying*, 3.

17. Robert Gimello, "Mysticism in Its Contexts," in Katz, *Mysticism and Religious Traditions*, 86.

18. MacRae, *Seeing through Zen*, 74–100; also MacRae, "The Antecedents of Encounter Dialogue in Chinese Ch'an Buddhism," in Heine, *The Kōan*, 46–74.

19. On this, see Outram Evennett, *The Spirit of the Counter-Reformation*, ed. John Bossy (Notre Dame: University of Notre Dame Press, 1968), 45–46. On the broader context, see John O'Malley, *The First Jesuits* (Cambridge, MA: Harvard University Press, 1993).

20. Augustine, *De doctrina christiana* IV.xii.27–xiii.29.79; trans. R. P. H. Green, *Saint Augustine: On Christian Teaching*, Oxford World's Classics (New York: Oxford University Press, 1997), 117–119.

21. *Verbum seniorum* 10.114 (PL 73:932); trans. Benedicta Ward, *The Desert Fathers: Sayings of the Early Christian Monks* (London: Penguin Books, 2003), 116.

22. Evagrius Ponticus, *Praktikos* 91 and 100 (SC 171:692, 710); trans. Sinkewicz, 112, 113.

23. Evagrius Ponticus, *De oratione* 60 (PG 79:1180); trans. Sinkewicz, 199.

24. Gerson, *De Mystica Theologica* I.2.5 (Combes, 10); trans. McGuire, 267.

25. Dante, *Paradiso*, Cantos 31–32. For the Italian text with a parallel translation, see Allen Mandelbaum, trans., *Paradiso* (New York: Bantam, 1986).

26. Dōgen, *Shōbōgenzō* "Genjōkōan" (trans. *Heart*, 43); "Gyōji 1" (trans. Tanahashi, *EU*, 127).

27. D.T. Suzuki, *Mysticism Buddhist and Christian*, Routledge Classics (1957; reprint: New York: Routledge, 2002); Rudolf Otto, *Mysticism East and West: A Comparative Analysis of the Nature of Mysticism*, trans. Bertha L. Bracey and Richenda Payne (New York: Macmillan, 1969).

28. Robert K.C. Forman, *Meister Eckhart: The Mystic as Theologian: An Experiment in Methodology* (Rockport, MA: Element, 1991), reads Eckhart as focused on mystical experiences and even of plotting steps in a mystical journey. Forman's "pure consciousness" thesis (see below) leads him to turn Eckhart's ontological language into experiential language. Such an experientialist reading of Eckhart, as I noted in chapter 6, does not hold up well to critical scrutiny.

29. Eckhart, *Predigt* 102, 103 (DW 4:412–413, 488); trans. Walshe, 1:16–17, 45.

30. Pseudo-Dionysius speaks repeatedly of this three-fold dynamic of purgation (*katharsis*), illumination (*photismos*), and perfection (*teleiosis*) or union (*henosis*): *De ecclesiastica hierarchia* 5.I.3, 5.I.7 (PG 3:504, 508; Rorem, CWS, 235, 238); *De caelesti hierarchia* 3.2, 7.2–3, 10.1 (PG 3:165, 208, 272; Rorem, CWS, 154, 162–164, 173). However, Pseudo-Dionysius does not see this in some individualist fashion, but as exemplary of a much wider ecclesial, angelic, and cosmic process.

31. E.g., in the Abhidharma literature; for an overview, see Sakurabe Hajime, "Abhidharma," in *Buddhist Spirituality I: Indian, Southeast Asian, Tibetan, Early Chinese*, ed. Takeuchi Yoshinori (New York: Crossroad, 1993), 67–78.

32. See Idel and McGinn, *Mystical Union*; also Bernard McGinn, "Mystical Union in Judaism, Christianity, and Islam," in *Encyclopedia of Religion*, ed. Lindsay Jones, 2nd ed. (Detroit: Macmillan Reference USA/Thomson Gale, 2005), 9:6334–6341.

33. Underhill, *Mysticism*, 72.

34. McGinn, "Comment," in Idel and McGinn, *Mystical Union*, 183, notes its absence in medieval authors and the great sixteenth-century Spanish mystics. One of

the earliest uses is found in the seventeenth-century theorist Maximilian Sandaeus, *Pro theologia mystica clavis* (Cologne, 1640), 365–366.

35. Gerson, *De mystica theologica* 1.28.4–7 (Combes, 72); trans. my own.

36. Evagrius Ponticus, *Epistula ad Melaniam* 27; trans. Casiday, 69.

37. McGinn, "Mystical Union in Judaism, Christianity, and Islam," 9:6334.

38. Augustine's famous accounts of his contemplative ascents appear in *Confessions* 7.10.16, 7.17.23, 7.20.26, 9.10.23–26. There are long-standing (and sometimes misguided) disputes on Augustine as a mystic. For a fine contemporary study, see John Peter Kenney, *The Mysticism of Saint Augustine: Rereading the Confessions* (New York: Routledge, 2005).

39. Augustine, *De trinitate* 15.14–15.26. Cf. *De civitate Dei* 22.29; *Ep.* 147.22.51; *De Genesi ad litteram* 12.28.56.

40. Cassian, *Collationes* 10.7.2 (SC 54:81); trans. Ramsey, ACW 57: 375–376.

41. Aldous Huxley, *The Perennial Philosophy* (New York: Harper & Row, 1940); Rudolph Otto, *Mysticism East and West*, trans. Bertha Bracey and Richenda Paye (New York: Macmillan, 1960); Joseph Maréchal, *Studies in the Psychology of the Mystics*, trans. Algar Thorold (London: Burns, Oakes & Washbourne, 1927); William Johnston, *The Still Point* (New York: Harper & Row, 1970); Mircea Eliade, *The Sacred and the Profane*, trans. Willard R. Trask (New York: Harcourt Brace Jovanovich, 1959); and Ninian Smart, "Interpretation and Mystical Experience, *Religious Studies* 1 (1965): 75–87. Robert F. C. Forman, "Introduction: Mysticism, Constructivism, and Forgetting," in *The Problem of Pure Consciousness: Mysticism and Philosophy* (New York: Oxford University Press, 1990), 3–4, has suggested referring to this position as the "perennialist philosophy school."

42. W. T. Stace, *Mysticism and Philosophy* (London: Macmillan, 1961), 34–35.

43. Stace, *Mysticism and Philosophy*, 31.

44. Stace, *Mysticism and Philosophy*, 94.

45. On Stace's mishandling of texts, see Katz, "Language, Epistemology, and Mysticism," in Katz, *Mysticism and Philosophical Analysis*, 46–47, 52–53.

46. Stace, *Mysticism and Philosophy*, 94–96, treating texts from Jan van Ruusbroec.

47. Stace, *The Teachings of the Mystics* (New York: New American Library, 1960), 23.

48. Stace, *Mysticism and Philosophy*, 103; see also *Teachings of the Mystics*, 24.

49. Stace, *Mysticism and Philosophy*, 103.

50. Stace, *Teachings of the Mystics*, 24.

51. Katz, "Language, Epistemology, and Mysticism," in Katz, *Mysticism and Philosophical Analysis*, 26.

52. Katz, "Language, Epistemology, and Mysticism," 26.

53. Katz, "Language, Epistemology, and Mysticism," 27; also Katz, "The Conservative Character of Mystical Experience," in Katz, *Mysticism and Religious Traditions*, 5.

54. Katz, "Language, Epistemology, and Mysticism," 62.

55. Katz, "Mystical Speech and Mystical Meaning," in Katz, *Mysticism and Language*, 5.

56. Katz, "Mystical Speech and Mystical Meaning," 5.

57. Eckhart, *Predigt* 16b (DW 1:274); trans. *Teacher*, 278.

58. The two volumes edited by Forman are: *The Problem of Pure Consciousness* (1990) and *The Innate Capacity: Mysticism, Psychology, and Philosophy* (New York: Oxford University Press, 1998). He sets out his own position in more detail in *Mysticism, Mind, Consciousness* (Albany, NY: SUNY, 1999).

59. Forman, "Introduction: Mysticism, Constructivism, and Forgetting," in *Problem of Pure Consciousness*, 7–8.

60. Forman notes his debts to his transcendental meditation teachers in *Mysticism, Mind, Consciousness*, x, and cites his own and other transcendental meditators' experiences in "Introduction: Mysticism, Constructivism, and Forgetting," 27–28. He appeals to the *Upanishads*, Eckhart, and Dōgen, in *Mysticism, Mind, Consciousness*, 11–17. I noted earlier my difficulties with his experientialist reading of Eckhart. I do not think he really engages Dōgen as a thinker, though he claims evidence for his reading of things by appealing to a contemporary Zen master, John Daido Loori (21–24).

61. Forman, "Mysticism, Constructivism, and Forgetting," 7.

62. Amy M. Hollywood, *The Soul as Virgin Wife: Mechthild of Magdeberg, Marguerite Porete, and Meister Eckhart*, Studies in Spirituality and Theology (Notre Dame: University of Notre Dame Press, 1995).

63. Evagrius Ponticus, *De oratione* 3 (PG 79:1168); trans. Sinkewicz, 193.

64. McGinn, *Foundations of Mysticism*, xvii.

65. Friedrich von Hügel, *The Mystical Element of Religion: As Studied by Catherine of Genoa and Her Friends*, ed. Michael Downey, Milestones in the Study of Mysticism and Spirituality (2nd ed., 1923; reprint: New York: Herder & Herder, 1999).

66. McGinn, *Foundations of Mysticism*, xv–xvi.

67. Louis Bouyer, "Mysticism: An Essay on the History of the Word," in *Understanding Mysticism*, ed. Richard Woods (Garden City, NY: Doubleday Image, 1980), 45. The English version is abbreviated. For the French original, see Bouyer, "*Mystique*: Essai sur l'histoire d'un mot," *Supplement de la Vie spirituelle* 9 (May 1949): 3–23.

68. Origen, *Commentary on the Gospel of John* 1.88–89, 13.264–265 (SC 120:104, 172). See also Clement of Alexandria, *Paedagogus* 1.7.59; *Stromateis* 6.15.127.

69. On mystagogy, see William Harmless, *Augustine and the Catechumenate* (Collegeville, MN: Liturgical Press [A Pueblo Book], 1995), 69–74, 300–339.

70. Bouyer, "Mysticism: History of the Word," 47–50, surveys the key patristic texts.

71. Pseudo-Dionysius, *Mystica theologia* 1.1, 1.3 (PG 3:998, 1001; Rorem, 135, 137); *De divinis nominibus* 2.9 (PG 3:648; Rorem, 65). For commentary, see Bouyer, "Mysticism: History of the Word," 51–53; McGinn, *Foundations of Mysticism*, 157–182.

72. Lorenzo Valla, *Opera*; quoted in Certeau, *Mystic Fable*, 75.

73. Certeau, *Mystic Fable*, 94.

74. Certeau, "Mystique," in *Encyclopaedia universalis*, rev. ed. (Paris: Encyclopaedia universalis France, 1990), 15:1032. The translation here is my own. For a complete English version, see Michel de Certeau, "Mysticism," *Diacritics* 22 (1992): 11–25.

75. Certeau, *Mystic Fable*, 94–112.

76. On the history of Western Orientalism and its applying the terminology of mysticism to Ch'an Buddhism, see Faure, *Chan Insights and Oversights*, 18–51. Ernst, *Shambhala Guide*, 1–18, offers a similar critical study of the biases of Western Orientalism and its uses of mysticism vis-à-vis the Sufis.

77. Charlotte Dormandy, "The Flowering of the Romantic Spirit," in *Spirituality and the Secular Quest*, ed. Peter H. Van Ness, World Spirituality 22 (New York: Crossroad Herder, 1996), 157–184.

78. On Rahner's mystical theology and theology of mysticism, see Philip Endean, *Karl Rahner and Ignatian Spirituality*, Oxford Theological Monographs (New York: Oxford University Press, 2001). For an introduction with texts and commentary, see Harvey D. Egan, *Karl Rahner: The Mystic of Everyday Life*, Crossroad Spiritual Legacy Series (New York: Crossroad, 1998).

79. Karl Rahner, "Teresa of Avila: Doctor of the Church," in *The Great Church Year: The Best of Karl Rahner's Homilies, Sermons, and Meditations*, ed. Albert Raffelt, trans. Harvey Egan (New York: Crossroad, 1994), 362–363.

80. Karl Rahner, *Hearer of the Word: Laying the Foundation for a Philosophy of Religion*, trans. Joseph Donceel (New York: Continuum, 1994).

81. Karl Rahner, "Experience of Transcendence from the Standpoint of Christian Dogmatics," in *Theological Investigations*, vol. 18, *God and Revelation*, trans. Edward Quinn (New York: Crossroad, 1983), 174–176.

Select Bibliography

CHAPTER I

Jean Gerson: Texts and Studies

For Gerson's original Latin and French texts, see P. Glorieux, *Jean Gerson: Oeuvres complètes*, 10 vols. (Paris: Desclée, 1960–1970). For a critical edition of his *De mystica theologia*, see André Combes, ed., *Ioannis Carlerii de Gerson: De Mystica Theologia* (Lugano, Switzerland: Thesarus Mundi, 1958). For a partial translation, see Brian Patrick McGuire, ed., *Jean Gerson: Early Works*, CWS (New York: Paulist Press, 1998). For a study of Gerson's life, world, and thought, see Brian Patrick McGuire, *Jean Gerson and the Last Medieval Reformation* (University Park, PA: Pennsylvania State University Press, 2005). For an analysis of Gerson's mystical theology, see Steven Ozment, *Homo Spiritualis: A Comparative Study of the Anthropology of Johannes Tauler, Jean Gerson, and Martin Luther (1509–16) In the Context of Their Theological Thought*, Studies in Medieval and Reformation Thought (Leiden: Brill, 1969). See also:

Brown, D. Catherine. *Pastor and Laity in the Theology of Jean Gerson.* Cambridge: Cambridge University Press, 1987.
Combes, André. *Jean Gerson: Commentateur dionysien.* Paris: J. Vrin, 1940.
———. *Le théologie mystique de Gerson, profil de son évolution.* 2 vols. Rome: Desclée, 1963–1964.
Oakley, Francis. *The Western Church in the Later Middle Ages.* Ithaca, NY: Cornell University Press, 1979.
Posthumus Meyjes, G. H. M. *Jean Gerson, Apostle of Unity: His Church Politics and Ecclesiology.* Trans. J. C. Grayson. Studies in the History of Christian Thought 94. Leiden: Brill, 1999.

Swanson, R. N. *Universities, Academics, and the Great Schism*. Cambridge Studies
   in Medieval Life and Thought. 3rd ser., vol. 12. Cambridge: Cambridge University
   Press, 1979.

William James: Texts and Studies

The place to start is, of course, with William James's *The Varieties of Religious Experience: A Study in Human Nature, Being the Gifford Lectures on Natural Religion delivered
at Edinburgh in 1901–1902*. There are numerous reprints, but I recommend the 1985
critical edition found in the comprehensive collection of James's writings: *The Works of
William James*, 17 vols., ed. Frederick H. Burkhardt, Fredson Bowers, and Ignas K.
Skrupskelis (Cambridge, MA: Harvard University Press, 1975–1988). For an introduction to James, see Gerald E. Myers, *William James: His Life and Thought* (New Haven:
Yale University Press, 1986); see also the valuable essays in Ruth Anna Putnam, ed.,
The Cambridge Companion to William James (Cambridge: Cambridge University Press,
1997). Other important studies include:

Barnard, G. William. *Exploring Unseen Worlds: William James and the Philosophy of
   Mysticism*. Albany, NY: SUNY, 1997.
Capps, Donald, and Janet L. Jacobs, eds. *The Struggle for Life: A Companion to William
   James's The Varieties of Religious Experience*. Society for the Scientific Study of
   Religion Monograph Series, no. 9. Princeton: Princeton Theological Seminary,
   1995.
Lambert, David C. *William James and the Metaphysics of Experience*. Cambridge:
   Cambridge University Press, 1999.
Proudfoot, William, ed., *William James and a Science of Religions: Reexperiencing
   The Varieties of Religious Experience*. Columbia Series in Science and Religion.
   New York: Columbia University Press, 2004.
Ramsey, Bennett. *Submitting to Freedom: The Religious Vision of William James*. New
   York: Oxford University Press, 1993.
Simon, Linda. *Genuine Reality: A Life of William James*. New York: Harcourt Brace,
   1998.
Suckiel, Ellen Kappy. *Heaven's Champion: William James's Philosophy of Religion*. Notre
   Dame: University of Notre Dame Press, 1995.

CHAPTER 2

Thomas Merton: Texts

Merton was an extraordinarily prolific writer. The book that catapulted him to fame
was his autobiography, *The Seven Storey Mountain*, 50th anniversary ed. (New York:
Harcourt Brace, 1998). While Merton later rejected its romanticized vision of monasticism, it still may be the best place to start. Merton's best work on mystical spirituality
is *New Seeds of Contemplation* (New York: New Directions, 1962). The journal was a
genre Merton excelled in. His two best are *Conjectures of a Guilty Bystander* (Garden
City, NY: Doubleday, 1966) and the posthumously published *Asian Journal of Thomas*

Merton, ed. Naomi Stone, Patrick Hart, and James Laughlin (New York: New Directions, 1973). See also the excellent anthology by Lawrence S. Cunningham, ed., *Thomas Merton, Spiritual Master: The Essential Writings* (New York: Paulist Press, 1992). This provides not only selections from *The Seven Storey Mountain, New Seeds*, and *Conjectures*, but also important and hard-to-find essays such as "Day of a Stranger" and "Rain and the Rhinoceros." In the 1990s, Merton's private journals were finally permitted to be published and are available as a seven-volume set. For a selection, see Patrick Hart and Jonathan Montaldo, eds., *The Intimate Merton: His Life from His Journals* (San Francisco: HarperSanFrancisco, 1999). Other important works include:

Merton, Thomas. *The Cold War Letters.* Ed. Christine M. Bochen and William H.
      Shannon. Maryknoll, NY: Orbis Books, 2006.
————. *Contemplation in a World of Action.* Ed. Robert Coles. 1971. Reprint: Notre
      Dame: University of Notre Dame Press, 1998.
————. *Contemplative Prayer.* New York: Doubleday / Image, 1972.
————. *The Inner Experience: Notes on Contemplation.* Ed. William H. Shannon. San
      Francisco: HarperSanFrancisco, 2003.
————. *Mystics and Zen Masters.* New York: Farrar, Straus, and Giroux, 1967.
————. *The Sign of Jonas.* New York: Harcourt, Brace, 1953.
————. *Thoughts in Solitude.* New York: Farrar, Straus, Giroux, 1976.
————. *Zen and the Birds of Appetite.* New York: New Directions, 1968.
————, ed. *The Way of Chuang Tzu.* New York: New Directions, 1965.
————, ed. *Wisdom of the Desert.* New York: New Directions, 1960.

Thomas Merton: Studies

The most thorough biography of Merton is Michael Mott's *The Seven Mountains of Thomas Merton* (Boston: Houghton Mifflin, 1986). An especially valuable resource is *The Thomas Merton Encyclopedia*, ed. William H. Shannon, Christine M. Bochen, and Patrick F. O'Connell (Maryknoll, NY: Orbis Books, 2002). See also the *Merton Annual: Studies in Culture, Spirituality and Social Concerns*, published since 1987 and currently edited by George A. Kilcourse, Jr. and Victor A. Kramer. Other valuable studies include:

Baker, Rob and Gray Henry, eds. *Merton and Sufism: The Untold Story: A Complete
      Compendium.* Lexington, KY: Fons Vitae, 1999.
Carr, Anne E. *A Search for Wisdom and Spirit: Thomas Merton's Theology of the Self.*
      Notre Dame: Notre Dame University Press, 1988.
Cunningham, Lawrence S. *Thomas Merton and the Monastic Vision.* Library of
      Religious Biography. Grand Rapids, MI: William B. Eerdmans, 1999.
Finley, James. *Merton's Palace of Nowhere.* 1978. Reprint: Notre Dame: Ave Maria
      Press, 2003.
Hart, Patrick, ed. *Thomas Merton, Monk: A Monastic Tribute.* CS 52. Kalamazoo, MI:
      Cistercian Publications, 1983.
————, ed. *The Monastic Journey of Thomas Merton.* CS 133. Kalamazoo, MI: Cistercian
      Publications, 1977.

King, Thomas M. *Merton: Mystic at the Center of America.* Way of the Christian Mystics 14. Collegeville, MN: Liturgical Press [A Michael Glazier Book], 1992.

King, Robert H. *Thomas Merton and Thich Nhat Hanh: Engaged Spirituality in an Age of Globalization.* New York: Continuum, 2001.

Montaldo, Jonathan, ed. *Merton and Hesychasm.* Lexington, KY: Fons Vitae, 2002.

Rice, Edward. *The Man in the Sycamore Tree: The Good Times and Hard Life of Thomas Merton.* San Diego: Harcourt Brace Jovanovich, 1985.

Shannon, William H. *Silent Lamp: The Thomas Merton Story.* New York: Crossroad, 1992.

———. *Thomas Merton's Dark Path.* rev. ed. New York: Farrar, Straus, Giroux, 1987.

CHAPTER 3

Bernard of Clairvaux: Texts and Translations

A critical edition of the Latin text of Bernard's writings is the eight-volume *Sancti Bernardi Opera*, ed. J. Leclerq, C. H. Talbot, and H. Rochais (Rome, 1957–1977). For a selection of Bernard's mystical texts, see G. R. Evans, *Bernard of Clairvaux: Selected Works*, Classics of Western Spirituality (New York: Paulist Press, 1987). Cistercian Publications has been steadily translating Bernard's complete works, as well as those of his Cistercian friends and followers. See especially:

Stiegman, Emero, trans. *Bernard of Clairvaux: On Loving God; An Analytical Commentary.* CF 13B. Kalamazoo, MI: Cistercian Publications, 1996.

Walsh, Kilian, and Irene Edmonds, trans. *Bernard of Clairvaux: On the Song of Songs.* 4 vols. CF 4, 7, 31, and 40. Kalamazoo, MI: Cistercian Publications, 1971–1980.

Bernard of Clairvaux: Studies

For an introduction to Bernard's life, world, and thought, see G. R. Evans, *Bernard of Clairvaux*, Great Medieval Thinkers series (New York: Oxford University Press, 2000). An excellent study of Bernard's mysticism is Bernard McGinn's *The Growth of Mysticism: Gregory the Great Through the 12th Century* (New York: Crossroad, 1994), 158–224. A classic study, dated but still valuable, is Étienne Gilson's *The Mystical Theology of St. Bernard*, trans. A. H. C. Downs, CS 120 (1940; reprint: Kalamazoo, MI: Cistercian Publications, 1992). For a survey of the wider historical context, see Colin Morris, *The Papal Monarchy: The Western Church from 1050 to 1250*, Oxford History of the Christian Church (New York: Oxford University Press, 1991). See also:

Berman, Constance Hoffman. *The Cistercian Evolution: The Invention of a Religious Order in Twelfth-Century Europe.* Philadelphia: University of Pennsylvania Press, 2000.

Bernard de Clairvaux: Histoire, mentalités, spiritualité. Colloque de Lyon-Cîteaux-Dijon. SC 380. Paris: Éditions du Cerf, 1992.

Bredero, Adriaan H. *Bernard of Clairvaux: Between Cult and History.* Grand Rapids: Wm. B. Eerdmans, 1996. A critical revisionist study of the biographical sources.

Bynum, Caroline Walker. *Jesus as Mother: Studies in the Spirituality of the High Middle Ages*. Berkeley: University of California, 1982. Valuable essays on Cistercian spirituality.

Casey, Michael. *Athirst for God: Spiritual Desire in Bernard of Clairvaux's Sermons on the Song of Songs*. CS 77. Kalamazoo, MI: Cistercian Publications, 1988.

———. "Bernard's Biblical Mysticism." *Studies in Spirituality* 4 (1994): 12–30.

Kinder, Terryl N. *Cistercian Europe: Architecture of Contemplation*. CS 191. Kalamazoo, MI: Cistercian Publications, 2001.

Lekai, Louis J. *The Cistercians: Ideals and Reality*. Kent, OH: Kent State University Press, 1977.

Leclerq, Jean. *Bernard of Clairvaux and the Cistercian Spirit*. Trans. Claire Lavoie. CS 16. Kalamazoo, MI: Cistercian Publications, 1976.

———. *The Love of Learning and the Desire for God: A Study of Monastic Culture*. 3rd ed. Trans. Catharine Mirsrahi. New York: Fordham University Press, 1982.

———. *A Second Look at Bernard of Clairvaux*. Trans. Marie-Bernard Saïd. CS 105. Kalamazoo, MI: Cistercian Publications, 1990.

———. "General Introduction to the Works of Saint Bernard," *Cistercian Studies Quarterly* 40 (2005): 3–25, 243–252, 365–394.

Pennington, M. Basil, ed. *Saint Bernard of Clairvaux: Studies Commemorating the Eighth Centenary of His Canonization*. CS 28. Kalamazoo, MI: Cistercian Publications, 1977.

Sommerfeldt, John R. *The Spiritual Teachings of Bernard of Clairvaux*. CS 125. Kalamazoo, MI: Cistercian Publications, 1991. Part anthology, part commentary.

———, ed. *Bernardus Magister: Papers Presented at the Nonacentenary Celebration of the Birth of Saint Bernard of Clairvaux*. Kalamazoo, MI: Cistercian Publications, 1992.

CHAPTER 4

Hildegard of Bingen: Texts and Translations

Critical editions of Hildegard's Latin texts are steadily being edited and published in the *Corpus Christianorum Continuatio Medievalis* (CCCM). For the Latin text of Hildegard's *Scivias*, see *Hildegardis Bingenis Scivias*, ed. Adelgundis Führkotter and Angela Carlevaris, CCCM 43–43A (Turnhout: Brepols, 1978); for an English translation, see Columba Hart and Jane Bishop, trans., *Hildegard of Bingen: Scivias*, CWS (New York: Paulist Press, 1990). For a selection of her letters, see Joseph L. Baird, ed., *The Personal Correspondence of Hildegard of Bingen* (New York: Oxford University Press, 2006). See also:

Atherton, Mark, trans. *Hildegard of Bingen: Selected Writings*. Penguin Classics. London: Penguin, 2001.

Baird, Joseph L., and Radd K. Ehrman, trans. *The Letters of Hildegard of Bingen*. 3 vols. New York: Oxford University Press, 1994–2004.

Dronke, Peter, ed. *Nine Medieval Latin Plays*. Cambridge Medieval Classics 1. Cambridge: Cambridge University Press, 1994. Contains Hildegard's *Ordo Virtutum*.

Hozeski, Bruce W., trans. *Hildegard of Bingen: The Book of the Rewards of Life (Liber Vitae Meritorum)*. New York: Oxford University Press, 1997.

Silvas, Anna, ed. *Jutta and Hildegard: The Biographical Sources*. Brepols Medieval Women Series. University Park: Pennsylvania State University Press, 1998.

Hildegard of Bingen: Discography

In Hildegard's case, it is essential not only to read her writings but also to listen to her music. The early music group Sequentia has steadily recorded all her major works. For a selections from her music, see Sequentia (director: Barbara Thornton), *Hildegard von Bingen: Canticles of Ecstasy* (Deutsche Harmonia mundi, 1994); see also Sequentia's performance of Hildegard's *Ordo Virtutum* (Deutsche Harmonia mundi, 1998). For Hildegard's song texts in Latin and English, see Barbara Newman, ed., *Saint Hildegard of Bingen: Symphonia; A Critical Edition of the Symphonia armonie celestium revelationum*, 2nd ed. (Ithaca, NY: Cornell University Press, 1998).

Hildegard of Bingen: Studies

For a survey of Hildegard's wide-ranging talents and interests, see Barbara Newman, ed., *Voice of the Living Light: Hildegard of Bingen and Her World* (Berkeley: University of California, 1998). Also valuable is Heinrich Schipperges, *The World of Hildegard of Bingen: Her Life, Times, and Visions*, trans. John Cumming (Collegeville, MN: Liturgical Press, 1999); this has color plates from Hildegard's manuscripts. See also:

Beer, Frances. *Women and Mystical Experience in the Middle Ages*. Rochester, NY: Boydell Press, 1992.

Bent, Ian D., and Marianne Pfau. "Hildegard of Bingen." In *The New Grove Dictionary of Music and Musicians*, 2nd ed., ed. Stanley Sadie and John Tyrell, 11:493–499. New York: Macmillan, 2001.

Burnett, Charles and Peter Dronke, eds. *Hildegard of Bingen: The Context of Her Thought and Art*. Warburg Colloquia. London: University of London, 1998.

Davidson, Audrey Ekdahl, ed. *The Ordo Virtutum of Hildegard of Bingen: Critical Studies*. Early Drama, Art, and Music Monograph Series 18. Kalamazoo, MI: Medieval Institute Publications, 1992.

Dronke, Peter. *Women Writers of the Middle Ages*. Cambridge: Cambridge University Press, 1984.

Flanagan, Sabina. *Hildegard of Bingen, 1098–1179: A Visionary Life*. 2nd ed. New York: Routledge, 1988.

Haverkamp, Alfred. "Tenxwind von Andernach und Hildegard von Bingen: Zwei 'Weltanschauungen,' in der Mitte des 12. Jahrhunderts." In *Institutionem, Kultur und Gesellschaft im Mittelater: Festschriften für Josef Fleckenstein*, ed. L. Fenske, W. Rösener, and T. Zotz, 515–548. Sigmaringen: J. Thorbecke, 1984.

———, ed. *Hildegard von Bingen in ihrem wissenschaftlicher Kongreß zum 900 jährigen Jubiläum, 13.–19. September 1998, Bigne am Rhein*. Mainz: Verlag Philipp von Zabern, 2000.

Hollywood, Amy. "Ca. 1147: Hildegard of Bingen Writes to Bernard of Clairvaux." In *A New History of German Literature*, ed. David E. Wellbery. Cambridge, MA: Harvard University Press, 2004. 39–44.

Kazarow, Patricia A. "Text and Context in Hildegard of Bingen's *Ordo Virtutum*." In *Maps of Flesh and Light: The Religious Experience of Medieval Women Mystics*, ed. Ulrike Wiethaus. Syracuse, NY: Syracuse University Press, 1993. 127–151.

King-Lenzmeier, Anne H. *Hildegard of Bingen: An Integrated Vision*. Collegeville, MN: Liturgical Press, 2001.

Mooney, Catherine M., ed. *Gendered Voices: Medieval Saints and Their Interpreters*. Philadelphia: University of Pennsylvania Press, 1999.

Newman, Barbara. *Sister of Wisdom: St. Hildegard's Theology of the Feminine*. Berkeley: University of California Press, 1987.

CHAPTER 5

Bonaventure: Texts and Translations

For Bonaventure's Latin text, see *Doctoris Seraphici S. Bonaventurae opera omnia*, 10 vols. (Quaracchi: Collegium S. Bonaventurae, 1882–1902). *The Mind's Journey into God* (*Itinerarium Mentis in Deum*) is found in 5:295–313. The standard translation is by Ewert Cousins, *Bonaventure: The Soul's Journey into God, The Tree of Life, The Life of St. Francis*, CWS (New York: Paulist Press, 1978). Also useful is the edition by Philotheus Boehner and Zachary Hayes, eds., *Itinerarium Mentis in Deum*, rev. ed., WSB 2 (St. Bonaventure, NY: Franciscan Institute Publications, 2002), which has the Latin text and an English translation on facing pages. Bonaventure's vast corpus of theological writings is slowly being translated (or retranslated) in George Marcil and Zachary Hayes, eds., *Works of Saint Bonaventure* (St. Bonaventure, NY: Franciscan Institute, 1978–). Older but still useful is *The Works of Bonaventure*, trans. José de Vinck, 5 vols. (Patterson, NJ: St. Anthony Guild Press, 1960–1970). This offers the only complete translation of Bonaventure's *Collations on the Six Days* (*Collationes in Hexaemeron*).

Bonaventure: Studies

For an introduction to Bonaventure's theology, one that carefully balances precision, lucidity, and brevity, see Zachary Hayes, "Bonaventure: Mystery of the Triune God," in *The History of Franciscan Theology*, ed. Kenan Osborne (St. Bonaventure, NY: Franciscan Institute, 1994), 39–126. Also helpful is Christopher M. Cullen, *Bonaventure*, Great Medieval Thinkers (New York: Oxford University Press, 2006). See also:

Anderson, C. Colt. *A Call to Piety: St. Bonaventure's Collations on the Six Days*. Studies in Franciscanism. Quincy, IL: Franciscan Press, 2002.

Blanco, Francisco de Asis Chavero, ed. *Bonaventuriana: Miscellanea in onore di Jacques Guy Bougerol*. 2 vols. Rome: Edizioni Antonianum, 1988.

Brooke, Rosalind B. *The Image of St. Francis: Responses to Sainthood in the Thirteenth Century*. Cambridge: Cambridge University Press, 2006.

Burr, David. *The Spiritual Franciscans: From Protest to Persecution in the Century after Saint Francis*. University Park: Pennsylvania State University Press, 2003.

Carpenter, Charles. *Theology as the Road to Holiness in St. Bonaventure*. Theological Inquiries. New York: Paulist Press, 1999.

Cousins, Ewert H. "Bonaventure's Mysticism of Language." In *Mysticism and Language*, ed. Steven T. Katz. New York: Oxford University Press, 1992. 236–258.

———. "Francis of Assisi: Christian Mysticism at the Crossroads." In *Mysticism and Religious Traditions*, ed. Steven T. Katz. New York: Oxford University Press, 1983. 163–190.

Delio, Ilia. *Crucified Love: Bonaventure's Mysticism of the Crucified Christ*. Quincy, IL: Franciscan Press, 1998.

Gilson, Étienne. *The Philosophy of St. Bonaventure*. Trans. Illtyd Trethowan and Frank J. Sheed. Paterson, NJ: St. Anthony Guild Press, 1965.

Hayes, Zachary. *The Hidden Center: Spirituality and Speculative Christology in St. Bonaventure*. Bonaventure, NY: Franciscan Institute, 1992.

Johnson, Timothy. *Iste Pauper Clamavit: Saint Bonaventure's Mendicant Theology of Prayer*. Europäische Hochschulschriften, Theology (ser. 23), vol. 390. Frankfurt am Main: Peter Lang, 1990.

LaNave, Gregory. *Through Holiness to Wisdom: The Nature of Theology According to St. Bonaventure*. Rome: Istituto Storico dei Cappuccini, 2005.

Lambert, M. D. *Franciscan Poverty: The Doctrine of Absolute Poverty of Christ and the Apostles in the Franciscan Order, 1210–1323*. London: Society for the Promotion of Christian Knowledge, 1961.

Lawrence, C. H. *The Friars: The Impact of the Early Mendicant Movement on Western Society*. London and New York: Longman, 1994.

McGinn, Bernard. *The Flowering of Mysticism: Men and Women in the New Mysticism, 1200–1350*. Vol. 3 of *The Presence of God*. New York: Crossroad, 1998.

Moorman, John. *History of the Franciscan Order: From Its Origins to the Year 1517*. 1965. Reprint: Chicago: Franciscan Herald Press, 1988.

Ratzinger, Joseph. *The Theology of History in St. Bonaventure*. Trans. Zachary Hayes. Chicago: Franciscan Herald Press, 1981.

Tavard, George H. *Transciency and Permanence: The Nature of Theology According to Bonaventure*. St. Bonaventure, NY: The Franciscan Institute, 1954.

Turner, Denys. "Hierarchy Interiorised: Bonaventure's *Itinerarium Mentis in Deum*." In *The Darkness of God: Negativity in Christian Mysticism*, 102–134. Cambridge: Cambridge University Press, 1995.

Zinn, Grover A. "Book and Word: The Victorine Background of Bonaventure's Use of Symbols." In *San Bonaventura, 1274–1974*, ed. Jacques Guy Bougerol, 5 vols. Rome / Grottaferrata: Collegio S. Bonaventura, 1974. 2:151–164.

Augustine of Hippo: Studies

The finest biography of Augustine is that of Peter Brown, *Augustine of Hippo: A Biography*, rev. ed. (Berkeley: University of California Press, 2000). For valuable studies of his works and theology, see especially Allan D. Fitzgerald, ed., *Augustine Through the Ages: An Encyclopedia* (Grand Rapids: Eerdmans, 1999). The debates on Augustine as a mystic are complex. For an excellent study, see John Peter Kenney, *The Mysticism of Saint Augustine: Rereading the Confessions* (New York: Routledge, 2005). This will set the parameters for future discussions. See also Frederick Van Fleteren, ed., *Augustine: Mystic and Mystagogue*, Collectanea Augustiniana (New York: Peter Lang, 1994), especially Gerald Bonner's essay, "Augustine and Mysticism," 113–57.

Pseudo-Dionysius: Texts and Studies

For the Greek text of Pseudo-Dionysius's works, see J. P. Migne, *Patrologia Cursus Completus, Series Graeca* (Paris: 1857), vol. 3. For a translation, see Colm Luibheid, trans., *Pseudo-Dionysius: The Complete Works*, CWS (New York: Paulist Press, 1987). For an introduction to Pseudo-Dionysius as a thinker, see Andrew Louth, *Denys the Areopagite*, Outstanding Christian Thinkers (Harrisburg, PA: Morehouse Publishing, 1989). For a commentary, see Paul Rorem, *Pseudo-Dionysius: A Commentary on the Texts and An Introduction to Their Influence* (New York: Oxford University Press, 1993).

CHAPTER 6

Meister Eckhart: Texts and Translations

For Eckhart's complete works, see Josef Quint and Georg Steer, eds., *Meister Eckhart: Die deutschen und lateinischen Werke herausgegeben im Auftrag der deutschen Forschungsgemeinschaft* (Stuttgart: W. Kohlhammer, 1958–); there are five volumes of Latin works and five volumes of Middle High German works (several more fascicles are forthcoming). For a translation of Eckhart's major works, see the two volumes in Classics of Western Spirituality: *Meister Eckhart: The Essential Sermons, Commentaries, Treatises, and Defense*, trans. Edmund Colledge and Bernard McGinn (New York: Paulist Press, 1981), and *Meister Eckhart: Teacher and Preacher*, trans. Bernard McGinn and Frank Tobin (New York: Paulist Press, 1986). Also dependable are the following:

Davies, Oliver, ed. *Meister Eckhart: Selected Writings*. Penguin Classics. London: Penguin Books, 1994.
Walshe, Maurice O'C. *Meister Eckhart: Sermons and Treatises*. 3 vols. Rockport, MA: Element, 1990.

Meister Eckhart: Studies

For a magisterial study of Eckhart, see Bernard McGinn, *The Mystical Theology of Meister Eckhart: The Man from Whom God Hid Nothing*, Edward Cadbury Lectures (New York: Herder / Crossroad, 2001). There are wide-ranging approaches and sometimes conflicting interpretations of Eckhart as a mystic and theologian. See also:

Caputo, John. "Fundamental Themes in Meister Eckhart's Mysticism." *Thomist* 42 (1978): 197–225.

Davies, Oliver. *God Within: The Mystical Tradition of Northern Europe*. 1988. Reprint: Hyde Park, NY: New City Press, 2006.

———. *Meister Eckhart: Mystical Theologian*. London: SPCK, 1991.

———. "Why Were Meister Eckhart's Propositions Condemned?" *New Blackfriars* 71 (1990): 433–445.

Dierkens, Alain and Benoit Beyer de Ryke, eds. *Maître Eckhart et Jan van Ruusbroec: Etudes sur la mystique 'rhéno-flamande'*. Problemes d'histoire des religions. Editions de l'université de Bruxelles, 2004.

Hollywood, Amy M. *The Soul as Virgin Wife: Mechthild of Magdeburg, Marguerite Porete, and Meister Eckhart*. Studies in Spirituality and Theology. Notre Dame: University of Notre Dame Press, 2001.

Kelley, C. F. *Meister Eckhart on Divine Knowledge*. New Haven: Yale University Press, 1977.

Kertz, Karl. "Meister Eckhart's Teaching on the Birth of the Divine Word in the Soul." *Traditio* 15 (1959): 327–363.

Kieckhefer, Richard. "Meister Eckhart's Conception of Union with God." *Harvard Theological Review* 71 (1978): 203–225.

Lerner, Robert. *The Heresy of the Free Spirit in the Later Middle Ages*. 2nd ed. Notre Dame: University of Notre Dame Press, 1997.

———. "New Evidence for the Condemnation of Meister Eckhart." *Speculum* 72 (1997): 347–366.

Libera, Alain de. *Eckhart, Suso, Tauler ou la divinisation de l'homme*. Paris: Bayard Édition, 1996.

———. "L'Un ou la Trinité." *Revue des sciences religieuses* 70 (1996): 31–47.

Milem, Bruce. *The Unspoken Word: Negative Theology in Meister Eckhart's German Sermons*. Washington, DC: Catholic University of America Press, 2002.

McGinn, Bernard. *The Harvest of Mysticism in Medieval Germany*, 94–194. Vol. 4 of *Presence of God: A History of Western Christian Mysticism*. New York: Herder & Herder, 2005.

———. "Eckhart's Condemnation Reconsidered." *Thomist* 44 (1980): 390–414.

———. "The God Beyond God: Theology and Mysticism in the Thought of Meister Eckhart." *Journal of Religion* 61 (1981): 1–19.

———. "Meister Eckhart on God as Absolute Unity." In *Neoplatonism and Christian Thought*, ed. Dominic O'Meara. Albany, NY: SUNY, 1982. 128–139.

McGinn, Bernard, ed. *Meister Eckhart and the Beguine Mystics: Hadewijch of Brabant, Mechtild of Magdeburg, and Marguerite Porete*. New York: Continuum, 1994.

Mjojsisch, Burkhard. *Meister Eckhart: Analogy, Univocity, and Unity*. Trans. Orrin F. Summerell. Amsterdam: B. R. Grüner, 2001.

Ruh, Kurt. *Meister Eckhart: Theologe, Prediger, Mystiker*. Munich: Verlag C. H. Beck, 1985.

Steer, Georg, and Loris Sturlese, eds. *Lectura Eckhardi: Predigten Meister Eckharts von Fachgelehrten gelesen und gedeutet*. 2 vols. Stuttgart: Verlag W. Kohlhammer, 1998, 2003.

Stirnimann, Hienrich, and Ruedi Imbach, eds. *Eckhardus Theutonicus, homo doctus et sanctus: Nachweise und Berichte zum Prozeß gegen Meister Eckhart.* Freiburger Zeitschrift für Philosophie und Theologie 11. Freiburg, Schweiz: Universitätverlag Freiburg, 1992.

Tobin, Frank. *Meister Eckhart: Thought and Language.* Philadelphia: University of Pennsylvania, 1986.

Woods, Richard. *Eckhart's Way.* Way of the Christian Mystics. Collegeville, MN: Liturgical Press, 1990.

CHAPTER 7

Evagrius Ponticus: Texts and Translations

Critical editions of Evagrius's works are gradually being published by the Sources chrétiennes (SC). These include the Greek text with a parallel French translation and a commentary. The place to start is with Evagrius's *The Monk* (*Praktikos*): Antoine Guillaumont and Claire Guillaumont, eds., *Évagre le Pontique: Traité pratique ou le Moine,* SC 170–171 (Paris: Éditions du Cerf, 1971). Others Sources chrétiennes volumes are listed below. Several of Evagrius's major works have still not yet received a critical edition, but can be found in the *Patrologia Graeca* under the name of Nilus of Ancyra: *Chapters on Prayer* (*De oratione,* PG 79:1165–1200) and *On the Eight Spirits of Evil* (*De octo spiritibus malitiae,* PG 79:1145–1164). A fairly complete translation of Evagrius's surviving Greek works is now available in Robert Sinkewicz, ed., *Evagrius of Pontus: The Greek Ascetic Corpus,* Oxford Early Christian Studies (London and New York: Oxford University Press, 2003). Other key works, including his *Letter to Melania* and *Letter on the Faith,* are now available in the anthology by A. M. Casiday, *Evagrius Ponticus,* Early Church Fathers (New York: Routledge, 2006). One brief but important work is Evagrius's *Reflections* (*Skemmata*); for a translation and detailed commentary, see William Harmless and Raymond R. Fitzgerald, " 'The Sapphire Light of the Mind': The *Skemmata* of Evagrius Ponticus," *Theological Studies* 62 (2001): 498–529. See also:

Bamberger, John Eudes, trans. *Evagrius Ponticus: The Praktikos; Chapters on Prayer.* CS 4. Kalamazoo, MI: Cistercian Publications, 1971.

Bunge, Gabriel, ed. *Evagrios Pontikos: Briefe aus der Wüste.* Sophia 24. Trier: Paulinus-Verlag, 1985.

Driscoll, Jeremy, trans. *Evagrius Ponticus: Ad Monachos.* ACW 59. Mahwah, NJ: Paulist Press, 2003.

Frankenberg, Wilhelm, ed. *Euagrios Ponticus,* Abhandlungen der königlichen Gesellschaft der Wissenschaften zu Göttingen; Philol. His. Klasse, Neue Folge, 13.2. Berlin, 1912. This contains Evagrius's texts, such as his *Letter to Melania* and other letters, preserved only in Syriac.

Géhin, Paul, ed. *Évagre le Pontique: Scholies aux Proverbes.* SC 340. Paris: Éditions du Cerf, 1987.

———. *Évagre le Pontique: Scholies à l'Ecclésiaste.* SC 397. Paris: Éditions du Cerf, 1993.

Géhin, Paul, Claire Guillaumont, and Antoine Guillaumont, eds. *Évagre le Pontique:
Sur les pensées*. SC 438. Paris: Éditions du Cerf, 1998.

Guillaumont, Antoine, ed. *Évagre le Pontique: Le gnostique ou a celui qui est devenu digne
de la science*. SC 356. Paris: Éditions du Cerf, 1989.

———, ed. *Les six centuries des "Kephalaia gnostica" d'Évagre le Pontique: Édition critique de la version syriaque commune et édition d'une nouvelle version syriaque*. PO
28, fasc. 2. Paris: Firmin Didot, 1958.

Parmentier, Martin. "Evagrius of Pontus and the 'Letter to Melania.' " *Bijdragen:
Tijdschrift voor filosofie en theologie* 46 (1985): 2–38. Reprinted in *Forms of Devotion:
Conversion, Worship, Spirituality, and Asceticism*, ed. Everett Ferguson. New York:
Garland, 1999. 272–309.

Evagrius Ponticus: Studies

For a survey of Evagrius's life and theology, as well as an overview of the world of early
Egyptian monasticism, see William Harmless, *Desert Christians: An Introduction to the
Literature of Early Monasticism* (New York: Oxford University Press, 2004). See also
Antoine Guillaumont and Claire Guillaumont, introduction, *Évagre le Pontique: Traité
pratique ou le Moine*, SC 170:21–125. An excellent recent study of Evagrius's spirituality
is Luke Dysinger, *Psalmody and Prayer in the Writings of Evagrius Ponticus*, Oxford
Theological Monographs (Oxford: Oxford University Press, 2005). See also:

Balthasar, Hans Urs von. "Metaphysik und Mystik des Evagrius Ponticus." *Zeitschrift
für Aszeze und Mystik* 14 (1939): 31–47.

Brakke, David. *Demons and the Making of the Monk: Spiritual Combat in Early
Christianity*. Cambridge, MA: Harvard University Press, 2006.

Bunge, Gabriel. *Akedia: Die geistliche Lehre des Evagrios Pontikos vom Überdruß*.
Cologne: Luthe-Druck, 1989.

———. "Evagre le Pontique et les deux Macaires." *Irénikon* 56 (1983): 215–227, 323–
360.

———. *Geistliche Vatershaft. Christliche Gnosis bei Evagrios Pontikos*. Studia Patristica et
Liturgica 23. Regensburg: 1988.

———. " 'Priez sans cesse': Aux origines de la prière hésychaste." *Studia Monastica* 30
(1988): 7–16.

———. "The 'Spiritual Prayer': On the Trinitarian Mysticism of Evagrius of Pontus."
Monastic Studies 17 (1987): 191–208.

Driscoll, Jeremy. *Steps to Spiritual Perfection: Studies on Spiritual Progress in Evagrius
Ponticus*. Mahwah, NJ: Newman Press/Paulist Press, 2005. This reprints a
number of his valuable studies.

———. "*Apatheia* and Purity of Heart in Evagrius Ponticus." In *Purity of Heart in
Early Ascetic and Monastic Literature: Essays in Honor of Juana Rausch, O.S.B.*, ed.
Harriet Luckman and Linda Kulzer. Collegeville, MN: Liturgical Press, 1999.
141–159.

Dysinger, Luke. "The *Logoi* of Providence and Judgment in the Exegetical Writings of
Evagrius Ponticus." *Studia Patristica* 37 (2001): 462–471.

Elm, Susanna. "Evagrius Ponticus' *Sententiae ad Virginem.*" *Dumbarton Oaks Papers* 45 (1991): 97–120.

Guillaumont, Antoine. *Aux origines du monachisme chrétien: pour une phénoménologie du monachisme.* Spiritualité orientale 30. Bégrolles-en-Mauges: Abbaye de Bellefontaine, 1979.

———. *Études sur la spiritualité de l'Orient chrétien.* Spiritualité orientale 66. Bégrolles-en-Mauges: Abbaye de Bellefontaine, 1996.

———. *Les Kephalaia gnostica d'Évagre le Pontique et l'histoire de l'origénisme chez les grecs et chez les syriens.* Patristica Sorbonensia 5. Paris: Éditions du Seuil, 1962.

Harmless, William. "'Salt for the Impure, Light for the Pure': Reflections on the Pedagogy of Evagrius Ponticus." *Studia Patristica* 37 (2001): 514–526.

Hausherr, Irénée. *Les leçons d'un contemplative: Le* Traité de l'oraison *d'Évagre le Pontique.* Paris: Beauchesne, 1960.

———. "L'origine de la théorie orientale des huit péchés capitaux." *Orientalia Christiana Analecta* 30 (1933): 164–175.

Refoulé, François. "La mystique d'Évagre et l'Origénisme," *Vie spirituelle supplemente* 64 (1963): 453–472.

———. "Rêves et vie spirituelle d'après Évagre le Pontique," *Vie spirituelle supplemente* 56 (1961): 470–516.

Spidlik, Tomás. *The Spirituality of the Christian East: A Systematic Handbook.* Trans. Anthony P. Gythiel. CS 79. Kalamazoo, MI: Cistercian Publications, 1986.

———. *Prayer. The Spirituality of the Christian East.* Vol. 2. Trans. Anthony P. Gythiel. CS 206. Kalamazoo, MI: Cistercian Publications, 2005.

Stewart, Columba. "Evagrius on Prayer and Anger." In *Religions of Late Antiquity in Practice,* ed. Richard Valantasis. Princeton: Princeton University Press, 2000. 65–81.

———. "Imageless Prayer and the Theological Vision of Evagrius Ponticus." *Journal of Early Christian Studies* 9 (2001): 173–204.

Young, Robin Darling. "Evagrius the Iconographer: Monastic Pedagogy in the *Gnostikos.*" *Journal of Early Christian Studies* 9 (2001): 53–72.

CHAPTER 8

Rumi: Texts and Translations

For critical editions of Rumi's works, see M. Estelami, ed, *Masnavi,* 7 vols. (Tehran, 1999) and Badī al-Zamān Furūzānfar, *Kullīyāt-i Shams,* 8 vols. (Tehran, 1957–1966). For a good selection of Rumi's *ghazals* from the *Divan-e Shams,* see A. J. Arberry, trans. *Mystical Poems of Rūmī, First Selection, Poems 1–200* (Chicago: University of Chicago Press, 1968) and *Mystical Poems of Rūmī: Second Selection, Poems 201–400* (Chicago: University of Chicago Press, 1991). For a recent, partial translation of the *Masnavi,* see Jawid Mojaddedi, trans., *Rumi: The Masnavi: Book 1,* Oxford World's Classic (New York: Oxford University Press, 2005); for an older, complete translation, see Reynold A. Nicholson, *The Mathnawī of Jalālu'ddin Rūmī,* 3 vols. (1926; reprint: Warminster, Wiltshire: Aris & Phillips, 1990). For a remarkable rendering of Rumi in contemporary American free verse, see Coleman Barks, trans., *The Essential Rumi,* 2nd ed. (San

Francisco: HarperSanFrancisco, 2004), and *The Soul of Rumi: A New Collection of Ecstatic Poems* (San Francisco: HarperSanFrancisco, 2001); note that Barks sometimes abbreviates things and glosses over the traditional themes and over technical theological terminology in an effort to make Rumi accessible to a modern audience. See also:

Aflākī, Shams al-Dīn Ahman-e. *The Feats of the Knowers of God (Manāqeb al-'arefīn)*, trans. John O'Kane. Islamic History and Civilization: Studies and Texts, vol. 43. Leiden: Brill, 2002.

Arberry, A. J. *Discourses of Rumi [Fihe mā Fih]*. 1961. Reprint: Surrey: Curzon Press, 1993.

Barks, Coleman, and John Moyne, trans. *The Drowned Book: Ecstatic and Earthy Reflections of Bahauddin, The Father of Rumi [Ma'āref]*. New York: Harper Collins, 2004.

Chittick, William C., ed. *Me and Rumi: The Autobiography of Shams-i Tabrizi [Maqālāt]*. Louisville, KY: Fons Vitae, 2004.

Rumi: Studies

The finest survey of Rumi in English is by Franklin Lewis, *Rumi: Past and Present, East and West* (Oxford: OneWorld, 2000). This is virtually a Rumi encyclopedia. Lewis has remarkable mastery of the sources and carefully roots Rumi in his Sunni Islamic, Hanafi, and Sufi traditions. Lewis also analyzes the contemporary Rumi craze and alerts readers to its biases and deficiencies. For a fuller analysis of Rumi as a thinker and a poet, see especially Annemarie Schimmel, *The Triumphal Sun: A Study of the Works of Jalāloddin Rumi*, Persian Studies 8 (Albany, NY: SUNY, 1993). See also:

Banani, Amin, Richard Hovannisian, and Georges Sabagh, eds. *Poetry and Mysticism in Islam: The Heritage of Rumi*. Cambridge: Cambridge University Press, 1994.

Bürgel, Johann Christoph. "Ecstasy and Order: Two Structural Principles in the Ghazal Poetry of Jalāl al-Dīn Rumi." In *The Legacy of Medieval Persian Sufism*, ed. Leonard Lewisohn. Oxford: Oneworld, 2000. 61–74.

Chittick, William C. *The Sufi Path of Love: The Spiritual Teachings of Rumi*. Albany, NY: SUNY, 1983. This is both a study and a thematic anthology.

———. "Rūmī and the Mawlawiyyah." In *Islamic Spirituality II: Manifestations*, ed. Seyyed Nasr Hossein. World Spirituality 20. New York: Crossroad, 1991. 105–126.

Keshavarz, Fatemeh, *Reading Mystical Lyric: The Case of Jalāl al-Dīn Rumi*. Columbia: University of South Carolina Press, 1998.

Renard, John. *All the King's Falcons: Rumi on Prophets and Revelations*. Albany, NY: SUNY, 1994.

Schimmel, Annemarie. *Rumi's World: The Life and Works of Rumi*. Boston: Shambhala, 2001. (Previously published in 1996 under the title *I Am Wind, You Are Fire*).

Sufism: Texts and Studies

For a good compilation of classical Sufi texts prior to Rumi, see Michael A. Sells, ed. and trans., *Early Islamic Mysticism: Sufi, Qur'an, Mi'raj, Poetic and Theological Writings*, CWS (New York: Paulist Press, 1996), and John Renard, ed. and trans., *Knowledge of*

God in Classical Sufism: Foundations of Islamic Mystical Theology, CWS (New York: Paulist Press, 2004). For a valuable introduction to Sufism, see Carl W. Ernst, *The Shambhala Guide to Sufism* (Boston: Shambhala, 1997); and Annemarie Schimmel, *Mystical Dimensions of Islam* (Chapel Hill: University of North Carolina Press, 1975). See also:

Abrahamov, Binyamin. *Divine Love in Islamic Mysticism: The Teachings of al-Ghazali and al-Dabbagh*. New York: Routledge, 2002.

Chittick, William C. *Sufism: A Short Introduction*. Oxford: One World, 2000.

———. *The Sufi Path of Knowledge: Ibn al-'Arabi's Metaphysics of Imagination*. Albany, NY: SUNY, 1989.

Ernst, Carl W. *Words of Ecstasy in Sufism*. Albany, NY: SUNY, 1985.

Hossein, Seyyed Nasr, ed. *Islamic Spirituality I: Foundations*. World Spirituality 19. New York: Crossroad, 1987.

———. *Islamic Spirituality II: Manifestations*. World Spirituality 20. New York: Crossroad, 1991.

Lewisohn, Leonard, and David Morgan, eds. *The Heritage of Sufism*. 3 vols. Oxford: One World, 1992–2000.

Massignon, Louis. *Hallaj: Mystic and Martyr*. Trans., ed., and abridged Herbert Mason. Princeton: Princeton University Press, 1994.

Moosa, Ebrahim. *Ghazali and the Poetics of Imagination*. Chapel Hill, NC: University of North Carolina, 2005.

Renard, John. *Seven Doors to Islam: Spirituality and the Religious Life of Muslims*. Berkeley: University of California Press, 1996.

Schimmel, Annemarie. *As Through a Veil: Mystical Poetry in Islam*. New York: Columbia University Press, 1982.

Sells, Michael. "Bewildered Tongue: The Semantics of Mystical Union in Islam." In *Mystical Union in Judaism, Christianity, and Islam: An Ecumenical Dialogue*, ed. Moshe Idel and Bernard McGinn. 1989. Reprint: New York: Continuum, 1999. 87–124.

CHAPTER 9

Dōgen: Texts and Translations

For a critical edition of Dogen's works, see Kagamishima Genryū, et al., *Dōgen zenji zenshū*, 7 vols. (Tokyo: Shunjūsha, 1988–1993). For a valuable selection of Dogen's writings, see Kazuaki Tanahashi's two anthologies: *Enlightenment Unfolds: The Essential Teachings of Zen Master Dōgen* (Boston: Shambhala, 1999); and *Moon in a Dewdrop: Writings of Zen Master Dōgen* (San Francisco: North Point Press, 1985). Given the difficulty of Dōgen's *Shōbōgenzō*, the best place to start is the carefully selected translations of Norman Waddell and Masao Abe, eds., *The Heart of Dogen's Shobogenzo* (New York: SUNY, 2002). Dōgen's other major work has been translated into English only recently: see Taigen Daniel Leighton and Shohaku Okumura, *Dogen's Extensive Record: A Translation of Eihei Koroku* (Boston: Wisdom Publications, 2004). Other key texts include:

Bielefeldt, Carl. "Reading Others' Minds." In *Buddhism in Practice*, ed. Donald S. Lopez, Jr. Princeton: Princeton University Press, 1995. 69–79.

Leighton, Taigen Daniel and Shohaku Okamura, trans. *Dogen's Pure Standards for the Zen Community: A Translation of Eihei Shingi*. Albany, NY: SUNY, 1996.

Masunaga, Reihō, trans. *A Primer of Sōtō Zen: A Translation of Dōgen's Shōbōgenzō Zuimonki*. Honolulu: East-West Center Press, 1971.

Tanahashi, Kazuaki and John Daido Loori, trans. *The True Dharma Eye: Zen Master Dōgen's Three Hundred Kōans*. With commentary and verse by John Daido Loori. Boston: Shambhala, 2005.

Dōgen: Studies

For an excellent historical-critical study of Dōgen's life and writings, see Steven Heine, *Did Dōgen Go to China? What He Wrote and When He Wrote It* (New York: Oxford University Press, 2006). For a survey of Dogen's mystical thought, see the newly revised work of Hee-Jin Kim, *Eihei Dogen: Mystical Realist*, 3rd ed. (Boston: Wisdom Publications, 2004). A more philosophical approach is the important study by the Japanese philosopher Masao Abe, *A Study of Dogen: His Philosophy and Religion*, ed. Steven Heine (Albany, NY: SUNY, 1992). See also:

Bielefeldt, Carl, *Dōgen's Manuals of Zen Buddhism*. Berkeley: University of California Press, 1988. This offers a superb study of Dōgen's *Fukanzazengi*.

Bodiford, William M. *Sōtō Zen in Medieval Japan*. Kuroda Institute Studies in East Asian Buddhism 8. Honolulu: University of Hawaii Press, 1993.

Heine, Steven. *Dōgen and the Kōan Tradition: A Tale of Two Shōbōgenzō Texts*. SUNY Series in Philosophy and Psychotherapy. Albany, NY: SUNY, 1994.

———. "An Analysis of Dōgen's *Eihei Goroku*: Distillation or Distortion?" In *Zen Classics: Formative Texts in the History of Zen Buddhism*, ed. Steven Heine and Dale S. Wright. New York: Oxford University Press, 2006. 113–136.

———. "The *Eihei kōroku*: The Record of Dōgen's Later Period at Eihei-ji Temple." In *The Zen Canon: Understanding the Classic Texts*, ed. Steven Heine and Dale S. Wright. New York: Oxford University Press, 2004. 245–274.

———. "Empty-Handed, but Not Empty-Headed: Dōgen's *kōan* Strategies." In *Discourse and Ideology in Medieval Japanese Buddhism*, ed. Richard K. Payne and Taigen Dan Leighton. New York: Routledge, 2006. 218–239.

Karulis, T. P. *Zen Action, Zen Person*. Honolulu: University of Hawaii Press, 1981.

Kim, Hee-Jin. *Dōgen on Meditation and Thinking: A Reflection on His View of Zen*. Albany, NY: SUNY, 2006.

Kodera, Takashi James. *Dōgen's Formative Years in China: An Historical Study and Annotated Translation of the 'Hōkyōki'*. Boulder: Prajña Press, 1980.

LaFleur, William R., ed. *Dōgen Studies*. Koroda Institute Studies in East Asian Buddhism 2. Honolulu: University of Hawaii Press, 1985. Includes excellent essays by Abe, Bielefeldt, Kim, and Karulis.

Leighton, Taigen Dan. "The *Lotus Sūtra* as a Source for Dōgen's Discourse Style." In *Discourse and Ideology in Medieval Japanese Buddhism*, ed. Richard K. Payne and Taigen Dan Leighton. New York: Routledge, 2006. 195–217.

Zen Buddhism: Texts and Studies

For a survey of the history of Zen, see Heinrich Dumoulin, *Zen Buddhism: A History*, 2 vols. trans. James W. Heisig and Paul Knitter (1988–1990; reprint: Bloomington, IN: World Wisdom, 2005). Recently Dumoulin has been criticized for being insufficiently critical in his use of sources; still, his narrative offers much of value in introducing newcomers to leading figures, schools, and developments. Kōans are, of course, the most famous form of Zen literature. The best contemporary introduction to them is Steven Heine, *Opening a Mountain: Kōans of the Zen Masters* (New York: Oxford University Press, 2002), which offers not only a translation, but also a helpful historical-critical commentary that puts these mind-teasing stories back into their literary and historical context. This equips one to appreciate the fine essays in Steven Heine and Dale S. Wright, eds., *The Kōan: Texts and Context in Zen Buddhism* (New York: Oxford University Press, 2000). For other important studies of Zen and its history, see also:

Broughton, Jeffrey L. ed. *The Bodhidharma Anthology: The Earliest Records of Zen.* Berkeley: University of California Press, 1999.

Buswell, Robert E. ed. *Encyclopedia of Buddhism.* 2 vols. New York: Thomson / Gale, 2002.

Faure, Bernard. *Chan Insights and Oversights: An Epistemological Critique of the Chan Tradition.* Princeton: Princeton University Press, 1993.

———. *The Rhetoric of Immediacy: A Cultural Critique of Chan/Zen Buddhism.* Princeton: Princeton University Press, 1994.

———, ed., *Chan Buddhism in Ritual Context.* London: Routledge Curzon, 2003.

Heine, Steven and Dale S. Wright, eds. *The Zen Canon: Understanding the Classic Texts.* New York: Oxford University Press, 2004.

———, eds. *Zen Classics: Formative Texts in the History of Zen Buddhism.* New York: Oxford University Press, 2006.

Kapleau, Philip. *The Three Pillars of Zen: Teaching, Practice, and Enlightenment.* Rev. expanded ed. New York: Doubleday Anchor, 1989.

McRae, John R. *Seeing Through Zen: Encounter, Transformation, and Genealogy in Chinese Chan Buddhism.* Berkeley: University of California Press, 2003.

———. *The Northern School and the Formation of Early Ch'an Buddhism.* Kuroda Institute Studies in East Asian Buddhism 3. Honolulu: University of Hawaii Press, 1986.

Sekida, Katsuki, trans. *Two Zen Classics: The Gateless Gate and The Blue Cliff Records.* Boston: Shambhala, 2005.

Stone, Jacqueline I. *Original Enlightenment and the Transformation of Medieval Japanese Buddhism.* Honolulu: University of Hawaii Press, 1999.

Williams, Duncan Ryken. *The Other Side of Zen: A Social History of Soto Zen Buddhism in Tokugawa Japan.* Princeton: Princeton University Press, 2005.

Williams, J. P. *Denying Divinity: Apophasis in the Patristic Christian and Sōtō Zen Buddhist Traditions.* New York: Oxford University Press, 2001.

Yampolsky, Philip, ed. and trans. *Platform Sutra of the 6th Patriarch: The Text of the Tun-Huang Manuscript.* Records of Civilization, Sources and Studies 76. 6th ed. New York: Columbia University Press, 1978.

CHAPTER 10

Christian Mysticism: Texts and Anthologies

The most important collection of mystical texts in English is the 100 + volume, *Classics of Western Spirituality* (New York: Paulist Press, 1978–). Each volume offers complete or near complete works by individual authors (or important movements) in the Christian, Jewish, and Islamic traditions. Many readers find it helpful to start with a one-volume collection of sources. Here are some of the best anthologies:

Dupré Louis, and James A. Wiseman, eds. *Light from Light: An Anthology of Christian Mysticism.* 2nd ed. New York: Paulist Press, 2001.

Egan, Harvey. *An Anthology of Christian Mysticism.* 2nd ed. Collegeville, MN: Liturgical Press/Pueblo, 1991.

Madigan, Shawn, and Benedicta Ward, eds. *Mystics, Visionaries, and Prophets: A Historical Anthology of Women's Spiritual Writings.* Minneapolis: Fortress Press, 1998.

McGinn, Bernard, ed. *The Essential Writings of Christian Mysticism.* New York: The Modern Library, 2006.

Tyson, John R., ed. *Invitation to Christian Spirituality: An Ecumenical Anthology.* New York: Oxford University Press, 1999.

Christian Mysticism: Historical Surveys

The most thorough and up-to-date survey of the Western mystical tradition is the massive, multivolume, but still incomplete history by Bernard McGinn, *The Presence of God: A History of Western Christian Mysticism* (New York: Crossroad, 1991–). Volume 1, *The Foundations of Mysticism: Origins to the Fifth Century* (1991) covers both the Greek and Hebrew roots of Christian mysticism and surveys early Christian mysticism through Pseudo-Dionysius; volume 2, *The Growth of Mysticism: Gregory the Great through the 12th Century* (1996) focuses on the early Middle Ages and includes in-depth studies of leading figures such as Gregory the Great and Bernard of Clairvaux; volume 3, *The Flowering of Mysticism: Men and Women in the New Mysticism, 1200–1350* (1998) focuses on the Franciscans and Beguines; volume 4, *The Harvest of Mysticism in Medieval Germany*, focuses on Meister Eckhart, Johannes Tauler, and Heinrich Suso, as well as their Dominican predecessors, Albert the Great and Thomas Aquinas. The most important reference work on Christian mysticism is the seventeen-volume *Dictionnaire de Spiritualité: Ascetique et mystique, doctrine et histoire*, ed. Marcel Viller, F.

Callavera and J. de Guibert (Paris: Beauchesne, 1932–1991). This massive study—some sixty years in the making—examines every dimension of Christian spirituality, with articles on all major figures, movements, and themes. Each article is done by a leading specialist, and many of them have been written since the 1970s, so the scholarship is generally up to date. See also:

Bouyer, Louis, ed. *A History of Christian Spirituality*. 3 vols. New York: Seabury, 1962–1964.

Certeau, Michel de. *The Mystic Fable*. Vol. 1. *The Sixteenth and Seventeenth Centuries*. Trans. Michael B. Smith. Religion and Postmodernism Series. Chicago: University of Chicago Press, 1992.

Dupré, Louis, and Don E. Saliers, eds. *Christian Spirituality III: Post-Reformation and Modern*. New York: Crossroad / Herder & Herder, 1991.

Egan, Harvey. *Christian Mysticism: The Future of a Tradition*. New York: Pueblo, 1986.

Fanning, Steven. *Mystics of the Christian Tradition*. New York: Routledge, 2001.

Jones, Cheslyn Jones, Geoffrey Wainwright, and Edward Yarnold, eds. *The Study of Spirituality*. New York: Oxford University Press, 1986.

McGinn, Bernard, and John Meyendorff, eds. *Christian Spirituality I: Origins to the Twelfth Century*. New York: Crossroad / Herder & Herder, 1985.

Raitt, Jill, ed. *Christian Spirituality II: High Middle Ages and Reformation*. New York: Crossroad/Herder & Herder, 1987.

Mysticism: Classic Studies

In chapter 1, we examined William James and his influential classic, *The Varieties of Religious Experience*. There are other classic studies, which, while sometimes deficient in terms of the historical scholarship on which they depend and in terms of aspects of their theoretical apparatus, still have much of value. For a survey and analysis of the last 100 years of the scholarly study of mysticism, see Bernard McGinn, "Theoretical Foundations: The Modern Study of Mysticism," in *Foundations of Mysticism*, 263–343. Here are a handful of classic studies:

Butler, Cuthbert. *Western Mysticism: The Teachings of Saints Augustine, Gregory and Bernard on Contemplation and The Contemplative Life: Neglected Chapters in the History of Religion*. New York: Dutton, 1923.

Maréchal, Joseph. *Studies in the Psychology of the Mystics [Études sur le psychologie des mystiques*, 2 vols., 1926, 1937]. Trans. Algar Thorold. London: Burns, Oakes & Washbourne, 1927.

Otto, Rudolf. *The Idea of the Holy: An Inquiry Into the Non-Rational Factor in the Idea of the Divine and Its Relation to the Rational [Das Heilige*, 1917]. Trans. John W. Harvey. New York: Oxford University Press, 1958.

Scholem, Gershom. *Major Trends in Jewish Mysticism*. New York: Schocken, 1961.

Stolz, Anselm. *The Doctrine of Spiritual Perfection [Theologie der Mystik*, 1936]. Trans. Aidan Williams. Milestones in the Study of Mysticism and Spirituality. 1938. Reprint: New York: Herder & Herder, 2001.

Underhill, Evelyn. *Mysticism: A Study in the Nature and Development of Man's Spiritual Consciousness.* 1901. Reprint: Oxford: OneWorld, 1999.

———. *The Essentials of Mysticism and Other Essays.* New York: Dutton. 1920.

von Hügel, Friedrich. *The Mystical Element of Religion: As Studied by Catherine of Genoa and Her Friends.* Ed. Michael Downey. Milestones in the Study of Mysticism and Spirituality. 2nd ed., 1923. Reprint: New York: Herder & Herder, 1999.

Zaehner, R. C. *Concordant Discord: The Interdependence of Faiths, Being the Gifford Lectures on Natural Religion Delivered at St. Andrews, 1967–1969.* Oxford: Clarendon Press, 1970.

———. *Mysticism Sacred and Profane.* Oxford: Clarendon Press, 1957.

Mysticism: Theoretical Issues, Disputed Questions, and Special Topics

The broader theoretical literature on mysticism is vast. What follow is a modest selection of works on a variety of topics. A good entry point into this sometimes complex literature is via the essay collections edited by Steven Katz; each volume offers contributions by major scholars on specific topics, and the perspectives address questions of mysticism across the breadth of the world's religions: *Mysticism and Philosophical Analysis* (New York: Oxford University Press, 1979); *Mysticism and Language* (New York: Oxford University Press, 1992), *Mysticism and Religious Traditions* (New York: Oxford University Press, 1983), and *Mysticism and Sacred Scriptures* (New York: Oxford University Press, 2000). Another important area of research has been on mystical apophaticism; on this, see especially Michael Anthony Sells, *Mystical Languages of Unsaying* (Chicago: University of Chicago Press, 1994). Some of the most creative reflection in recent decades has focused on asceticism, for example: Gavin Flood, *The Ascetic Self: Subjectivity, Memory, and Tradition* (Cambridge: Cambridge University Press, 2004). Other helpful works are:

Davies, Oliver, and Denys Turner, eds. *Silence and the Word: Negative Theology and Incarnation.* New York: Cambridge University Press, 2002.

Forman, Robert K. C. *Mysticism, Mind, Consciousness.* Albany, NY: SUNY, 1999.

———, ed. *The Innate Capacity: Mysticism, Psychology, Philosophy.* New York: Oxford University Press, 1998.

Hägg, Henry Fiska. *Clement of Alexandria and the Beginnings of Christian Apophaticism.* Oxford Early Christian Studies. New York: Oxford University Press, 2006.

Hollywood, Amy. *Sensible Ecstasy: Mysticism, Sexual Difference, and the Demands of History.* Religion and Postmodernism Series. Chicago: University of Chicago Press, 2002.

Idel, Moshe, and Bernard McGinn, eds. *Mystical Union in Judaism, Christianity, and Islam: An Ecumenical Dialogue.* 1989. Reprint: New York: Continuum, 1999.

Jantzen, Grace. *Power, Gender, and Christian Mysticism.* Cambridge: Cambridge University Press, 1995.

Kessler, Michael, and Christian Sheppard, eds. *Mystics: Presence and Aporia.* Chicago: University of Chicago Press, 2003.

Marshall, Paul. *Mystical Encounters with the Natural World: Experiences and Explanations.* Oxford: Oxford University Press, 2005.

McIntosh, Mark A. *Mystical Theology: The Integrity of Spirituality and Theology.* Challenges in Contemporary Theology. Malden, MA: Blackwell, 1998.

Russell, Norman. *The Doctrine of Deification in the Greek Patristic Tradition.* Oxford Early Christian Studies. New York: Oxford University Press, 2004.

Sheldrake, Philip. *Spirituality and History: Questions of Interpretation and Method,* 2nd ed. Maryknoll, NY: Orbis Books, 1998.

————. *Spirituality and Theology: Christian Living and the Doctrine of God.* Maryknoll, NY: Orbis Books, 1999.

Turner, Denys. *The Darkness of God: Negativity in Christian Mysticism.* Cambridge: Cambridge University Press, 1995.

Wimbush, Vincent L., and Richard Valantasis, *Asceticism.* New York: Oxford University Press, 1998.

Index

CPSIA information can be obtained
at www.ICGtesting.com
Printed in the USA
BVHW060021281122
652732BV00002B/3